RESEARCH METHODS IN LIBRARIANSHIP

Techniques and Interpretation

LIBRARY AND INFORMATION SCIENCE

CONSULTING EDITORS: *Harold Borko and G. Edward Evans*
GRADUATE SCHOOL OF LIBRARY SCIENCE
UNIVERSITY OF CALIFORNIA, LOS ANGELES

A complete list of titles in this series is available from the Publisher upon request.

RESEARCH METHODS IN LIBRARIANSHIP

Techniques and Interpretation

CHARLES H. BUSHA

STEPHEN P. HARTER

ACADEMIC PRESS, INC.
Harcourt Brace Jovanovich, Publishers
San Diego New York Boston
London Sydney Tokyo Toronto

ACADEMIC PRESS, INC.
1250 Sixth Avenue, San Diego, California 92101

United Kingdom Edition published by
ACADEMIC PRESS, INC. (LONDON) LTD.
24/28 Oval Road, London NW1 7DX

Library of Congress Cataloging in Publication Data

Busha, Charles H.
  Research methods in librarianship.

  (Library and information science)
  Includes bibliographical references and index.
  1. Library science––Research––Handbooks, manuals,
etc. I. Harter, Stephen P. , joint author. II. Title.
Z669.7.B87   020'.7'2   79–8864
ISBN 0–12–147550–6

Contents

Preface   *xi*

PART I
SCIENCE AND LIBRARIANSHIP

CHAPTER 1
Research and Scientific Method   **3**

Introduction   3
Basic Concepts of Research   7
Components of Scientific Method   15
Explanation of a General Model for
  Scientific Inquiry   19
Finding a Research Topic   21
Ethical Considerations in Research   25
Evaluation of Completed Research   27
Conclusions   29
References   30
Selected Bibliography   30

PART II
METHODS OF RESEARCH

CHAPTER 2
Experimental Research in Librarianship:
Introduction to Experimentation   **35**

Basic Concepts   35
The Four-Cell Experimental Design   38
Using a Table of Random Numbers   40
Evaluation of an Experiment   42
Ex Post Facto Study   43
Examples of Experimentation and
  Quasi-Experimentation in Library Research   44

Summary   50
References   51

CHAPTER 3
Survey Research in Librarianship   **53**

Introduction   53
Principles of Survey Research   54
Populations   56
Planning the Survey   57
Some Survey Guidelines   58
Selection of Samples   59
Questionnaires   61
What Will You Ask?   64
Types of Questions   66
Unstructured and Structured Questions   70
Cautions Concerning Questions and Questionnaires   71
Scaling Fixed Responses   74
Semantic Differential Scale   76
Interviews   77
Review of Completed Survey Research   79
Summary   87
References   88
Selected Bibliography   89

CHAPTER 4
Historical Research in Librarianship   **91**

Introduction   91
Meaning and Value of History   92
Library History   92
Present Status of Library History   96
Obtaining Historical Evidence   98
An Example of the Search for Evidence   102
Evaluation of Sources and Evidence   106
Preparing Historical Narratives   110
Some Representative Historical Studies   111
Summary   113
References   115
Selected Bibliography   117

CHAPTER 5
Operations Research in Librarianship:
Quantitative Approaches to the Analysis of Management Problems **121**

Introduction   121
Models   123

Systems Analysis   124
Computer System Simulation Models   125
Concept of the Mathematical Model   126
Exponential Growth as an
   Illustrative Mathematical Model   128
Other Applications of Exponential
   Growth to Librarianship   131
Queuing Theory as a Second Illustrative Model   132
Applications of Queuing Theory to Librarianship   134
Single Server Queue: Mathematical Models and
   Predictive Formulae   135
Testing the Fit of the Model   138
Selected Examples of Operations Research   138
Conclusions   140
Appendix: Problems for Solution   141
References   143

CHAPTER 6
Additional Research Methods in Librarianship   145

Introduction   145
Observation and Description   147
The Case Study Method   151
Library User Studies   154
Evaluation Research   160
Library Surveys   164
Community Surveys   167
Comparative Librarianship   169
Content Analysis   171
Delphi Method   176
Documentary Research   178
Summary   180
References   181
Selected Bibliography   186

PART III
DESCRIPTIVE STATISTICS

CHAPTER 7
Measurement and Statistical Methods: An Introduction   191

Analysis of Quantified Data   191
Applications of Statistical Methodology
   to Librarianship   192
Statistical Symbols   194

Measurement and Scaling 195
Summary of Remaining Statistical Chapters 198
Appendix: Problems for Solution 198
References 199

CHAPTER 8
Graphical Representation of Data **201**

Introduction 201
Frequency Distributions 201
Graphs 206
Smoothing Frequency Polygons 207
Cumulative Frequency Distributions 209
Bivariate Graphs 212
Pie Chart 214
Appendix: Problems for Solution 216

CHAPTER 9
Central Tendency and Variability **219**

Introduction 219
Central Tendency 219
Variability 232
Mean Deviation 235
Appendix: Problems for Solution 240

CHAPTER 10
The Normal Distribution **249**

Introduction 249
Areas under the Normal Curve 249
The Distribution of Sample Means 256
The t-Distribution 261
Estimating the Value of a Proportion 263
Appendix: Problems for Solution 264
References 266

PART IV
INFERENTIAL STATISTICS

CHAPTER 11
Linear Regression and Correlation **269**

Introduction to Regression and Correlation 269
Advanced Topics 278

Appendix: Problems for Solution   290
References   294

CHAPTER 12
Statistical Significance and Hypothesis Testing   **297**

Introduction   297
The Chi-Square Test   300
The Sign Test   309
Some Parametric Tests   311
Summary   316
Appendix: Problems for Solution   317
References   324

PART V
AIDS TO RESEARCH

CHAPTER 13
The Computer and Calculator as Aids to Research   **327**

Introduction   327
Computer System Hardware   328
Computer Software   330
Statistical Package for the Social Sciences (SPSS)   331
Preprogrammed Electronic Calculators   334
Conclusions   340
References   341

CHAPTER 14
Writing the Research Proposal   **343**

Introduction   343
Planning an Investigation   343
Value of Research Proposals   345
Generalizable Components of Proposals   346
Inadequacies of Proposals   349
Costs and Budgetary Considerations   351
Sources of Information for Literature Searches   359
Summary   367
References   368
Selected Bibliography   369

CHAPTER 15
Writing the Research Report   371

Introduction   371
Selecting Report Vehicles and Audiences   372
Organization of Reports   376
Additional Suggestions for Reports   380
Grammar, Punctuation, and Word Usage   383
Preparation of Manuscripts   387
Summary   388
References   389
Selected Bibliography   390

APPENDICES

APPENDIX A
One-Thousand Random Digits   395

APPENDIX B
Statistical Symbols Used in the Text   397

APPENDIX C
Cumulative Normal Frequency Distribution   399

APPENDIX D
Percentage Points of the *t*-Distribution   401

APPENDIX E
Percentage Points of the χ^2 Distribution   403

Index   *405*

Preface

This book is an introductory account of the rationale and methods for research in library and information science. Our goal is to provide practical and theoretical insights, as well as to discuss technical skills needed to plan research projects and to collect and analyze research data effectively. The work is directed toward several audiences and is designed to be used in various ways, including the following: (*a*) as a textbook treating scientific methods of investigation to be used by beginning students in the field of librarianship; (*b*) as a supplementary sourcebook in advanced library science courses; and (*c*) as a handbook for practicing professionals or other consumers of research who need a manual for the conduct of their independent investigations or a guide to the evaluation of completed research pertaining to all types of libraries.

Our focus in this work is upon methods of inquiry in librarianship, including design, measurement, and analysis. In addition, we intended to provide a work that could give readers better understandings of the past, present, and future roles of research in library and information science. We hope that this book will make a contribution to the establishment of systematic inquiry as a fundamental facet of the study of library science and of the practice of librarianship, thereby helping to align the field with more established disciplines and professions.

Our hope is that readers will be able to become more competent in both intellectual and technical aspects of research methodology through the careful study of the contents of this book. The illustrative problems and examples offered throughout the text have been selected for their relevance to librarianship and for their potential usefulness as models or strategies from which ideas for new empirical studies can be gleaned. An understanding of these problems and examples ought to aid students and other readers to grasp not only the fundamental concepts of scientific inquiry, but many principles of librarianship as well. We intend this guide to research to be useful to practicing professionals at all levels and in all types of libraries—academic, public, school, and special. Thus, the book's focus is not upon the esoteric problems encountered by research specialists in very large libraries or by theorists in information science.

Inevitably, not all librarians conduct or care to conduct research; however, each of us, as a professional person, has a responsibility to consume the products of systematic studies in our field. Thus, one of the benefits to be derived from the careful study of this book is a greater capacity to make competent evaluations of reports of completed research.

When used as a textbook, this work can be completed by students in a one-semester research methods course. Library educators can use the book in a sequential manner, or they can approach it selectively by incorporating the study of statistical methods (Chapters 7–12) with the remaining material. Both approaches have been used successfully by the authors.

Although many methods treated herein are accompanied by specific examples, the applicability of research methods to potential topics in librarianship is by no means limited to these examples. Readers are encouraged, therefore, to employ their imagination with respect to the use of described techniques. We should also note that although statistical analysis of quantified data is discussed in various chapters, a mathematical background is neither expected nor required of users of this book.

A note regarding terminology is also in order. We believe that the principles and concerns of modern librarianship encompass many aspects of the communication process, including concepts of traditional librarianship as well as those of information science and media services. Thus, rather than repeating the words "library science," "information scientists," "media services," "learning resources centers," and so on, we most often refer simply to libraries, librarians, and librarianship, trusting that our usage of these terms in their generic contexts will be understood by readers.

Research methods in librarianship borrow from and are intertwined with those of other professions and disciplines. For a fuller understanding of any one of the investigative techniques discussed in this text, readers are encouraged to pursue information in the literature of education, psychology, sociology, statistics, information science, operations research, or any of a dozen other fields. For the purpose of directing readers to additional and in many cases more technical information, lengthy bibliographies have been appended to many chapters.

We believe that this product of our long and persistent labors can assist real and potential research scholars to see themselves in perspective—that is, in relation to their formative and summative roles in the context of the goals and objectives of libraries and librarianship. Our hope is that this book will help to build a firmer foundation upon which needed skills and understandings can be developed for the conduct and evaluation of scientific inquiry in librarianship. If our work is successful in this respect, our goals will have been achieved.

PART I

Science and Librarianship

CHAPTER 1

Research and Scientific Method

INTRODUCTION

Human beings appear to stand alone among the earth's creatures in their desire to better understand their existence and the world about them. This want or need can be partially satisfied by knowledge gained as a result of everyday occurrences, including trial and error; the formulation of generalizations based upon first-hand experience; and the use of logical reasoning. A more efficient and effective approach to expand knowledge, however, is the conduct of special, planned, and structured investigations—a process known as _research_. In its largest context research is a "systematic quest for knowledge,"[1] but scientifically conducted research is much more exacting than this brief definition might imply. Scientists specify their research objectives; offer explanations of investigative problems; relate research questions or hypotheses to appropriate theories; and select methods whereby phenomena can be observed, measured, and interpreted in relation to key hypotheses.[1] Scholars who undertake disciplined inquiry also define their terms, pose questions or propositions that incorporate the terms in an explanatory fashion, and test them with productive analytical schemes.

In the scientific community, research is undertaken to attack problems of significance or to increase theoretical knowledge, both purposes of which may be accomplished when hypotheses are subjected to systematic, empirical tests. A great deal of research has been conducted by academic institutions. Indeed, research has long been considered an important function of universities, together with teaching and community service. Following the model of the great German universities and beginning in the United States with the establishment of Johns Hopkins University in 1876, the higher education community produces a large proportion of the research conducted today in the nation. Academic curricula in the twentieth century have been greatly expanded by the growth of scientific knowledge. The research library in the United States had its origins in

3

the institutionalization of research that began in the 1850s and was greatly strengthened in the last decade of the nineteenth century. Thus, librarianship has been intimately involved with the increasing impact of scientific research on many areas of knowledge, including library and information science itself.

Librarianship in the United States has traditionally been a problem-oriented field. Librarians have tended to focus more attention on practical problems in the "real world" than they have on theoretical issues. This focus continues to be reflected in the contemporary body of inquiry of the field. For example, current publications in the area of information storage and retrieval are largely concerned with examinations of existing information systems rather than theoretical or philosophical questions. However, a primary objective of research—including inquiry in librarianship—is the development of a general and systematic set of theories from which hypotheses can be generated and tested. But if the levels of explanation for library phenomena are based solely upon the collective experience and know-how of practicing professionals, then information generated in this manner will not provide verified data to allow reliable conclusions or predictions. *Science* may be viewed as "the systematic, objective, deliberate, and controlled search for insights and accurate knowledge about a realm of phenomena" as well as "a verified and valid body of knowledge."[2] The term *scientist* was first used in the English language circa 1840 to designate a person who acquired empirical truths as opposed to an intellectual who produced new knowledge by nonempirical means.[3] Contrary to popular misconceptions, science is not concerned merely with the development of orderly sets of data, the establishment of facts and figures, or the utilization of "common sense." Above all, science is a process for gaining an awareness and understanding that is useful in the formulation of explanations about phenomena. Science should not be confused with attempts to merely determine unalterable statements of fact. The term *scientific method* serves as a descriptor for an investigative approach in which the objective of the inquirer is to achieve precise and reliable knowledge. This is not to imply that only one research methodology is appropriate, however; rather, the term *scientific method* is used to characterize many effective techniques of inquiry.

If librarianship is to merit the coveted designation "science," a significant number of scholars and research workers must regularly apply scientific method to analyze relationships among the problems which librarians are obligated to explore and which they are qualified to solve. Moreover, the study of library science can attain recognition as a true science only when a general body of theory is developed. Once relatively substantial and adequate bodies of theory are available, tentative explanations can be made of phenomena relating to libraries and to their communication and information problems. Substantive research questions can then be systematically generated and tested. Thus, the major thesis of this book is that scientific method *can be used* effectively in the study of library and information science, allowing the derivation of systematized knowledge from observation, experimentation, and other productive research methods.

To produce new knowledge, scientists think and work in special ways, using exacting methods to describe and explain phenomena. In *The Principles of Scientific Thinking,* Romano Harré noted that if science is conceived as the investigation of the way things and materials behave and the exploration of their nature, it "will be a dialogue in which the ascription of powers prompts the investigation of nature, and the analysis of nature leads to the discovery of new kinds of things and materials to which powers are again ascribed, restarting the cycle."[4] The work of scientists is important if the overall knowledge of any subject field is to be expanded. Although not all inquiries undertaken by research workers result in immediate and penetrating scientific discovery, scientists build upon the completed work of other investigators. The cumulative effect of this gradual progression of discovery leads to an increasing verification of truth and the reduction of error in many subject areas. Thus, science is self-correcting; through its methods spurious information is identified and subsequently replaced by more accurate knowledge.

In the early 1930s, when perceptive librarians began to display serious interest in the conduct of scientific inquiry, Charles C. Williamson wrote: "To my mind the real reason that there is so little scientific study of the problems of library service is that practically no librarians have been trained in scientific methods."[5] At the same time, Arnold K. Borden also made the following observation: "From the point of view of history as well as from that of contemporary conditions, the library needs to be studied in the light of sociology, economics, and other branches of human knowledge."[6] The starting point in library science inquiry was with pure description—that is, inquiries designed to explain *what* and *what happens*. Librarians eventually realized the usefulness of research that progressed beyond the mere elucidation of events and processes. Increasingly, they are also learning that scientific method can be applied effectively in librarianship to investigate theoretical issues and practical problems that are unique to libraries and other information centers.

With reference to science and librarianship, Herbert Goldhor wrote:

> It is assumed that librarianship is at least in part more than an art, or a skill, or a field of practice in which all that we know or do is either because of agreed-upon conventions, generalizations from experience, philosophical assumptions, or administrative judgments.[7]

Indeed, librarians must put more faith in the application of scientific method to study the issues and problems of librarianship. Although the field is not likely to become an exact or demonstrative science in the foreseeable future, librarians, like other behavioral and social scientists, can be optimistic about the field's potential to evolve into an empirical science in which broad principles can be generalized from particular instances.

Nevertheless, the generation of a body of truly scientific knowledge about library and information science and librarianship's subsequent attainment of full, widespread professional and scholarly recognition hinge upon the following future accomplishments: the development of a solid structure of theoretical and practical knowledge, the willingness of librarians to question assumptions and to test hypotheses, and the continuous conduct of rigorous and meaningful research by a larger and more highly qualified group of persons within the profession. Placing more dependence on scientific method will increase the store of librarianship's scientific knowledge. And, as Horst Kunze has written: "Learning to master, theoretically and in practical application, the ground rules of research creates the best foundation for continuing growth in a profession."[8] Among additional benefits that can be expected to accrue are (a) the improvement of practices in local library operations, (b) a greater capability to evaluate published research in librarianship, and (c) an awareness of the research process in which many clientele of special and academic libraries are engaged. This latter benefit cannot fail to improve library informational and reference practices, because it must lead to an increased awareness of the special needs of the research scholar.

Scientific research in librarianship is a careful process by which librarians can acquire more accurate knowledge and understanding of libraries and librarianship. Library science research is a cognitive endeavor concerned in a large measure with the study of library methods for the acquisition, cataloging, storage, and dissemination of books and other media of communication. By and large, research in the area of information science is broader in scope than inquiry in traditional librarianship; its focus is upon the study of techniques whereby information is created, used, and communicated, as well as upon the discovery of quicker and more efficient methods to present the right recorded facts and figures to persons who need them, once the information has been stored.[9]

Knowledge about numerous facets of library and information science can be obtained by asking questions, thinking of possible answers, and testing the possibilities by means of careful inquiry. In order to study phenomena relating to libraries, information, or communication, some method must be devised to measure them (or some part of them) or to otherwise perceive them with the senses and, perhaps, with the aid of special instruments. By asking questions about pertinent phenomena and then rigorously testing the answers, librarians and information scientists are more likely to produce *scientific knowledge*. This is not to imply that all library and information science knowledge generated as a result of research will be absolute or scientific; only those concepts, issues, and questions within the field that are amenable to testing can be included within the realm of science.

Unfortunately, a large proportion of librarianship's research has been uneven in quality and demonstratively weak methodologically; therefore, too much of it has only approximated scientific inquiry. Some investigators within the field have apparently been reluctant to use the key instrumentation of science—*experimental research*. However, the hue and cry for more meaningful research on the part of perceptive librarians and scholars appears to be gradually weakening librarianship's general resistance to scientific inquiry concerning libraries and librarianship. Serious investigators now regard the scientific approach to research as an ideal— something to which librarianship not only aspires but which it can actually realize through persistent, diligent, and rigorous inquiry. Furthermore, the complexity of modern science and the accelerated rate of technological development have altered traditional relationships among libraries and a significant number of their clientele. Many contemporary library decisions now have important scientific and technological components, even though these might not always be perceived clearly by persons who are making the decisions. If the administrative and operational judgments of modern librarians are to be sound, they must be based upon a greater understanding of the content, process, and consequences of science and scientific method.

BASIC CONCEPTS OF RESEARCH

Each discipline or field of knowledge uses a special terminology—the jargon peculiar to the field. Meanings for some of these terms may differ somewhat from those for the same words in the layperson's vocabulary. Numerous research concepts in this book are defined when they are first discussed in the various chapters; however, some basic terms must be briefly defined in the present chapter to provide readers with a general overview of the inquiry process.

First, the difference between two broad types of research should be noted. *Basic research* includes studies conducted to achieve a fuller understanding of a phenomenon without consideration of how findings will be applied. A study undertaken primarily to acquire knowledge for its own sake can be classified as basic research (also sometimes labeled *pure research* or *theoretical research*). Basic research is derived from fundamental, intellectual problems; it tends to be of an original and theoretical nature. On the other hand, *applied research* is pragmatic; its purposes are more specific and are generally aimed at solving practical problems or at the discovery of new knowledge that can be utilized immediately in actual "real world" situations. Of course, findings from basic research can be applied later to the solution of pragmatic problems, and data from applied studies might, in turn, be incorporated into the body of knowledge from which the theoretical problems of basic research are derived. In some situations, distinctions cannot easily be made between basic and applied research, especially in cases pertaining to subject areas that are in the process of theory building.

On the whole, completed studies in librarianship have been of an applied nature. Like any developing discipline, the study of library science is characterized by a weak body of theory and research findings that are often irreconcilable with previously acquired knowledge. Most contributions to the study of libraries have been concerned more with the collection of information that allows library phenomena to be identified and described, rather than for the purpose of explaining *why* and *how* library circumstances occur. An apparent distrust of theory on the part of many investigators in librarianship has contributed to a neglect of basic research in the field. One reason for this situation may be the inadequate attention that library schools have given to the need for instruction about research methods and theory. Whatever the cause, many scholars in librarianship have tended to rely upon basic knowledge gleaned from other disciplines (e.g., communication, sociology, psychology, and computer science). Thus, library and information science is ripe for the conduct of numerous kinds of basic inquiry.

Many special terms are employed by scientists to describe various characteristics of research studies. *Reliability* is used to characterize stable, consistent, and dependable research methods, instruments, data, or results. On the other hand, *validity* is the essential characteristic of these entities, procedures, or devices *actually* to measure the dimensions that they purport to measure. Scientists also use the terms *objectivity* and *subjectivity* to label research data, depending upon the degree to which observations are free of personal biases. Objectivity is the capacity of a research worker to see the empirical world as it actually exists (insofar as this is possible), relatively free of the distortions that are often caused by emotional feelings or personalized interpretations. On the other hand, subjectivity is a characteristic of research observations, data, or findings that primarily reflect personal and psychological factors.

The term *variable* is used by researchers to refer to an element, entity, or factor (quality or quantity) that is under study in an empirical investigation. At times, the values of variables change during the course of a research project. A major part of the research process consists of the measurement of changes or differences between or among the values of pertinent variables. Research factors that cannot be quantified are known as *qualitative variables*. For example, in a study concerned with government documents from countries of the Far East, the language in which a document is written might be a variable. Thus, such written languages as Chinese, Japanese, or Korean would be values of a qualitative variable—language. In another study, the gender of subjects (female or male) might be a qualitative variable of interest to investigators. Additional variables could include such factors as the occupation, religion, or political affiliation of subjects. Some factors in empirical investigations can be expressed numerically (quantified) and are known as *quantitative variables*. Examples of quantitative variables are such characteristics of research subjects as age, income, intelligence quotient, reading speed, number of books read in a given period, number of children, height, weight, or time required to complete a task or react to a stimulus. Investigators often attempt to determine how qualitative and quantitative characteristics of research subjects or objects affect variation in a phenomenon being studied. For example, variations in the utilization of libraries by people have been found to be affected by such factors as education, age, intelligence, social class, occupation, location of the library, and quality or size of the collection.

Research variables may also be classified according to their relationships in a given study. A *dependent variable* is a factor whose changes or different states are explained or predicted in the course of an empirical investigation. In research that is concerned with cause-and-effect relationships (i.e., experimental research), the effect variable (observed and measured after some factor has been manipulated by the investigator) is known as the *dependent variable*. For example, suppose an investigator is attempting to determine the impact of a film which is highly favorable to labor unions on a group of library administrators. A pretest could be administered to the group prior to the showing of the film to measure the subjects' "before" attitude scores toward labor unions; a posttest could then be conducted after the film was shown to the group. The dependent variable in this study would be the "after" attitude scores of the librarians. Thus, the dependent variable may be a consequence of the action.

An *independent variable* is a factor that is manipulated by researchers; its effect on the dependent variable is observed during the course of an investigation. Independent variables are sometimes also referred to as *predictor, experimental,* or *causal variables.* For example, an investigator might attempt to identify relationships between the ages and job mobility of librarians. In this type of study, age would be an independent variable, and the degrees of job mobility would comprise the dependent variable. Thus, the independent variable (age) may be an antecedent of the action (mobility). When a variable of an empirical study has not been precisely identified but its effect is assumed, the term *intervening variable* is sometimes used in reference to the unknown element.

In scientific inquiry, the *hypothesis* is a tentative, declarative statement about the relation between two or more variables which can be observed empirically. As a vitally important intellectual instrument of research, the hypothesis is a scientific guess about the relationship among variables related to a practical or theoretical problem. Hypotheses can be derived from intuition or theories, and from relevant facts produced during the course of previous observation, research, or experience. Hypotheses offer explanations for certain phenomena and serve as guides to the collection and analysis of research data. Implicit in the process of hypothesis formulation is the notion that statements of the relationship between or among variables must be tested. The essential function of the hypothesis in scientific inquiry is to guide the collection of research data and the subsequent discovery of new knowledge.

Intuition comes into play when investigators obtain immediate, clarifying insights or illuminating ideas relating to a question or problem of significance. Although ideas gained through such mental processes do not always prove to be fruitful, research often entails making decisions that are based upon the personal judgments and ideas of investigators. As opposed to sudden insights that result from intuition, however, reason also comes into play in research. *Reason* is a mental process based upon clear and logical thinking. Investigators employ reason as they interpret and associate research data with relevant theoretical schemes. Two broad reasoning processes, deduction and induction, can be used by investigators when inquiries are conducted and data are analyzed. *Deduction* refers to logical inference, in which conclusions follow necessarily from premises and in which reason progresses from general principles and established "truths" to particular instances. Thus, investigators rely upon deduction when they reason from the general to the specific. On the other hand, *induction* is a form of inference whereby generalizations for a whole class are made as a result of evidence obtained from limited particulars— that is, observations from a few members of the class. Reasoning on the basis of induction relies upon rather confined extrapolations from specific observations to more general statements.

Another term often used in the research process is *assumption,* a word which designates a proposition that is taken for granted at face value, rather than put forward as an assertion to be tested. Assumptions upon which research is based should be explicitly identified by investigators. Scientists often place emphasis upon the uncovering and rigorous examination of assumptions about various phenomena under investigation. Listed below are several declarative statements which would be functioning as assumptions in studies in which these statements are accepted as being true for the purpose of the inquiry. In other studies, these statements might function as hypotheses.

1. When audiovisual materials are incorporated into the collections of libraries, persons who are not attracted to print media are enticed to make more use of libraries.
2. For the purpose of developing collections of materials, most librarians recognize the value of selection policies that have been clearly formulated into written statements.
3. Users prefer to find library materials on the same subjects shelved together so that these materials can be easily examined, rather than having to locate whatever is needed through the exclusive use of subject bibliographies or catalogs.
4. Books are sources of information, comfort, and pleasure for everybody.
5. Reference personnel are more qualified than other librarians to select and organize informational materials in libraries.
6. Regardless of the subject area of knowledge, books are consulted more often for information than any other medium within the available array of materials in libraries.
7. Reference librarians are better bibliographic experts than other library employees.
8. The faculty of a university is more competent than library selectors to choose library materials in support of research and instruction in a given subject area.

The means, techniques, and frames of reference by which researchers approach and carry out inquiry are known as *methodology.* Thus, methodology could be viewed as the essence of scientific investigation. Various research methodologies are discussed at length in subsequent chapters of this book, and readers should be aware that no single method is appropriate for all types of investigations.

One of the most widely used methods of science is *observation,* the direct surveillance and recording of dimensions of a phenomenon that is to be measured or evaluated. This close perception of a phenomenon facilitates a detailed and exact explanation of how the phenomenon behaves under known conditions. An example of observation is watching students use the library card catalog to determine the effectiveness of their search habits. The locales in which scientists make observations can be classified into three broad categories: (*a*) natural settings; (*b*) field studies; and (*c*) laboratories. When sight, sound, smell, or touch are inadequate as observational techniques for data gathering, human perception is often augmented—even replaced—by data obtained with the aid of special devices. *Instruments* are devices that facilitate the assignment of measurement symbols which cannot be obtained through human perceptual organs alone. For example, in an attempt to determine the chemical composition of a sheet of paper, an observer without instruments would, perhaps, be able to note only the paper's color, texture, or odor. With appropriate instruments, however, the paper's chemical composition could be measured precisely by a qualified chemist.

Data collection usually involves measuring some research phenomenon, whether it is a process, an object, or a human subject's behavior. The objects of measurement will differ, of course, from one research project to another, depending upon the purpose of the inquiry and the availability of suitable instruments. Although many persons tend to associate the term *instrument* with some kind of device used primarily in the physical sciences (e.g., thermometers, barometers, Geiger counters, electron microscopes, or even yardsticks and rulers), the instruments used by behavioral and social scientists include such tools as questionnaires, written or oral tests, checklists, attitude scales, and other similar indexes.

When investigators attempt to characterize the status of a phenomenon by assigning numbers or other symbols to certain dimensions of it, *measurement* is used. Measurement can be employed only when the dimensions to be described, ranked, or assigned a scale number are clearly defined, differ with respect to measures, are common to a group or class of things, and produce highly similar data among many impartial observers. Typically, the utilization of measurement techniques will produce indicators of the scale position, rank, or classification of certain dimensions of phenomena that are being examined. For example, measurement may reveal that a reference book is 12 inches high and 9 inches wide, that a library school student ranks sixth on a civil service test for librarians, that the distance between the central metropolitan library and its closest branch is 1.2 miles, or that library technician "A" requires 3 more minutes to perform a bibliographic search than library technician "B."

When correctly applied, measurement often strengthens the rigor and enhances the exactness of a research project.

Another important facet of scientific method is *experimentation,* a controlled problem-solving technique used either to confirm or disprove research propositions. As the most rigorous method of science, experimentation entails the observation of events under known conditions so that the relationships between phenomena (i.e., between independent and dependent variables) can be accurately measured while other variables are held constant. In experimental studies, the researcher attempts to control all pertinent factors except the manipulated variable. Experimenters are often concerned with *causality,* the concept that two or more observed entities are associated in a cause-and-effect relationship. A major notion associated with causality is that a precise set of conditions will invariably produce similar or identical effects. Hypotheses which propose causal relationships will state that the presence or action of variable X is a determining factor in relation to some aspect of variable Y. Experimental research and related concepts are discussed more thoroughly in Chapter 2.

Yet another method or device often used by scientists is the *model,* a verbal, mathematical, or graphical construct representing a phenomenon. The model serves as an aid in making observations and explanations of phenomena. Models can assist investigators in relating more accurately to reality; they also aid scientists to describe, predict, test, or understand complex systems or events. Thus, models often provide a framework for the conduct of research. Models might consist of actual objects or abstract forms, such as sketches, mathematical formulas, or diagrams. In addition to tradition and to the application of practices derived from previous library experience, current library performance is based largely upon imitations of models of library service, such as library demonstration projects. Many of these models, traditions, and practices are in need of empirical verification. Although models often serve as useful research tools, these devices are sometimes misused in the conduct of inquiry. When models have not been properly validated, their employment as a knowledge source might be unwarranted. In addition, unless care is taken, models often invite overgeneralizations.

A collection of assumptions, definitions, and propositions which explains a group of observed facts or phenomena in a field or discipline is known as *theory.* Ideally, the elements of a theory are logically interrelated, involving both inductive and deductive reasoning processes. Although insight and intuition can be used in the development of a body of theoretical knowledge, scientific theories are based primarily upon partially verified data, or those that are subject to verification. From a body of theory, various hypotheses can be deduced, based upon expected relationships between particular variables. Conrad H. Rawski has pointed out that the target of inquiry "is scientific theory, i.e., theory that supports explanations of facts and their patterns by means of a deductive system, and thus allows us to address meaningfully the realities, both actual and possible, of the librarian's world."[10] Because theory encompasses knowledge about broad principles and methods as opposed to specific practices, it can be characterized as "pure" rather than "applied."

Complete bodies of theory do not exist in many areas of the social and behavioral sciences, and most of librarianship's theories are presently in a state of early formulation. Because some research efforts in the field have been relatively unproductive and because others have been associated with irrelevant questions and issues, the present body of theoretical library science knowledge contains some ill-defined concepts, inferences, plausible explanations, and general orientations toward selected subject areas in the field. In addition, library science theoretical knowledge is encumbered with various generally accepted, but largely unverified, propositions that serve as unique and often isolated explanations for complex library and information phenomena. In a discussion about librarianship as a profession, Pierce Butler noted: "The modern libary . . . has come into existence, spontaneously and almost inadvertently, by a cumulation of immediate empirical procedures, without anyone planning or foreseeing very far ahead. . . . Theory followed practice instead of leading it."[11] Thus, librarianship's theories are particularly vulnerable to change and modification; they represent a fertile area of inquiry for contemporary researchers who are ambitious enough to conduct empirical tests.

Operationally, theory can be used to improve performances of practicing professionals because it should incorporate the basic principles of librarianship. Theory can also improve librarianship's contribution to society because it allows scholars and practicing professionals to conceptualize the role of libraries in human information and communication systems. Furthermore, the ability of library schools to impart library science knowledge can be stimulated by theory. It is apparent, however, that some instruction offered by library schools has not suggested bases for innovation because too much attention has been devoted to the transmission of information about established library techniques, methods, and policies. In addition, some of this imparted information has not been derived from theories in which library experience was distilled. No doubt, vestiges of this type of instruction still persist in some library schools. In any event, the slowness to recognize the value of sound principles of inquiry within librarianship is undoubtedly associated with the field's weak theoretical base.

Of more importance to the future research scholar, however, is the fact that theory can help to discourage the conduct of irrelevant or inconsequential research studies. When an investigator is cognizant of the theoretical implications of a study, more pertinent and potentially significant research questions are likely to be posed. Questions and hypotheses that are amenable to scientific inquiry are more likely to be investigated when hypothetical implications of a research issue have been thoroughly reviewed. In addition, questions that prompt inquiry are more likely to be stated in a form that includes the pertinent variables and their relationships. On the basis of appropriate theory, investigators are inclined to pose exacting hypotheses at a level of abstraction permitted by the theory. Scientists who are able to form theories (i.e., to speculate and to conjecture) can often suggest hypotheses that would not occur to persons who have not formed mental "floor plans." Thus, theory can serve as a guide to the form, range, and clarity of hypothesis formulation. The utilization of theoretical knowledge results in additional research benefits, including an aid to the identification of the specific area to be investigated, the selection of productive methods of inquiry, the identification of data that should be sought, and how the data ought to be evaluated.

With reference to theory and the interpretation of research findings, scholars who fail to place their inquiries within a theoretical framework have not always been able to discern whether conclusions clash with, or contribute to, theory. Thus, theoretical knowledge often provides scholars with standards for weighing the validity of their research findings. Successful research workers have used theoretical knowledge as a guide to subsequent, follow-up studies; thereby, the continuity of research efforts in some areas of librarianship has been enhanced. Alert investigators have also used negative or contradictory findings to develop new theories—and innovative investigations.

COMPONENTS OF SCIENTIFIC METHOD

Because of the interdisciplinary nature of librarianship and the broad scope of the profession's concerns, numerous library science topics are appropriate for exploration; many research methods may also be suitable, depending upon the particular problem under study. After deciding exactly what will be investigated in a particular study, the research worker must then structure hypotheses (or exploratory questions); select a method to test or answer them; develop an appropriate design to collect the necessary data; and plan techniques whereby research data can be analyzed and conclusions can be drawn, based upon the data. The investigator may conduct an experiment and thereby take advantage of a controlled situation in which conditions are devised to test specific hypotheses. Unobtrusive and/or participant observation in a library might be used to study the roles played by librarians and clients of libraries in actual service settings. A survey among librarians or library users might be conducted by means of interviews or mail questionnaires. A past event might be examined in a historical context as primary and secondary documents are analyzed. Many additional kinds of studies may be proposed and later conducted within the field. In some situations, researchers might even replicate an earlier study to verify previous findings or to determine the effects of some new development on a problem that has already been explored.

Investigators without research plans could be compared with carpenters without blueprints. Just as builders without plans are not likely to produce the most functional, well-constructed, or aesthetically pleasing buildings, research workers without adequately conceptualized and well-planned studies may fail to recognize the full potentials of research projects and may run the risk of producing meaningless findings. The investigator who does not carefully consider the problems and methods of an investigative situation is not likely to develop appropriate hypotheses, effective data-gathering techniques, or productive analytical schemes. Persons who carry out ill-planned studies will have difficulty interpreting collected data. Such persons are likely to find themselves in a position similar to that of a forgetful host who is faced with invited guests at the door for whom refreshments and entertainment have not yet been planned—so many people (or so many data, as the case may be) and no clear conception of what to do with them. Some graduate students have found themselves in this predicament, especially those beginners who approached inquiries with the idea of conducting research *about* a topic, rather than having developed plans and proposals that clearly outline the purpose, scope, and techniques of anticipated studies, including the formulation of specific hypotheses to be tested.

Good research questions force research workers to think carefully about the kinds of information needed and the most appropriate and expeditious methods to obtain it. In addition to the need for careful considerations of the scientific problem and method of the study, investigators will have to answer certain questions about the research project early in the planning stage. Among the most important of these are the following: How much time and money will be required by the research project?; What potential does the planned study have to improve existing practices in the field or to contribute to the body of library science theory?; How much success and what degree of accuracy can be achieved with available resources and methods?

A successful investigation cannot be planned and conducted in a vacuum. The knowledge and research expertise that an investigator brings to the anticipated study is the product of a number of factors, including the following: all the significant practical experience, all the formal education, all the reading and study, and all the thought and consideration that the researcher has accomplished or undergone prior to the conceptualization of the idea for a systematic inquiry. The degree of preparation among investigators can be measured, in part, by their abilities to recognize a significant problem, to utilize research methods effectively, to pursue scientific exercises to successful completion, and to communicate research intentions and activities in narrative reports such as proposals. Closely related to these considerations is another important criterion that should be recognized: *awareness of the theoretical framework that encompasses the research problem.* Sound theoretical knowledge about the problem area from which the research task originated is necessary to the conduct of meaningful inquiry, no matter what the subject of the project may be.

A thorough familiarity with current literature relevant to facets of a problem to be investigated will help research workers compile a list of important issues, theories, or questions that can then be categorized, ranked, and utilized according to their value in the frame of reference of a particular inquiry. When researchers prepare to conduct a study, they realize the value of consultations with qualified subject experts. Students who plan to undertake research are advised to discuss their ideas and problems with faculty advisors, with other professors who are familiar with and interested in the topic of concern, and with their own peers in the academic community. Investigators—whether they are students or seasoned research scholars—need to achieve competence in, and confidence with, the general subject area of the problem that is to be carefully examined.

The recognition of a problem or topic for exploration is often a byproduct of careful and extensive reading of appropriate research reports, articles, or other literature. Through the devotion of study and attention to a particular subject, writers of research proposals can gain insights into the best procedures to solve or clarify problems associated with an investigative task. Competency with the methodological techniques to be employed in an inquiry can often be obtained through the successful completion of a well-directed, graduate-level research methods course; through independent study and preparation; or through an apprenticeship with an experienced research scholar. Without knowledge of scientific method, an uninitiated investigator will be ill-prepared to identify, explain, propose, plan, or conduct a valuable research project.

Let us be more specific in regard to the components of scientific method. Figure 1.1 illustrates a general model for the conduct of a scientific inquiry. The model may be misleading in the sense that it might imply that the steps indicated are discrete, are always followed in the order shown, and are all necessary to scientific research. All of these may be false in specific research projects; however, the model is useful when considered as a frame of reference. Thus, each of the components identified in Figure 1.1 is discussed individually and in some detail in the following sections of this chapter.

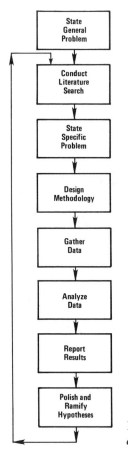

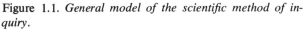

Figure 1.1. *General model of the scientific method of inquiry.*

EXPLANATION OF A GENERAL MODEL FOR SCIENTIFIC INQUIRY

STATE GENERAL PROBLEM

The problem under investigation may originate as a practical library matter or situation that is perplexing, as a result of intuition, or as an inference from previously derived theory. Whatever its origin, the problem has a context that needs to be understood before the research can properly proceed. The choice of a problem is important. Some problems are trivial; others are beyond the scope or talents of the investigator; still others are not amenable to research at all. Seasoned investigators (such as qualified academic advisors) can often be helpful in this initial stage of problem selection and formulation.

CONDUCT OF LITERATURE SEARCH

As part of the process of understanding the general problem and its context, the relevant professional and scholarly literature should be carefully reviewed and synthesized. Indeed, the selection of a specific area of exploration can often be the byproduct of extensive reading and study. In addition, through the devotion of attention and consideration to a subject, scholars often gain insights into the most suitable methods to define and attack a given research problem. In view of the importance of literature reviews to the completion of successful inquiries, perhaps this component of scientific research should be examined more thoroughly. A *literature search* (or literature review) is an attempt to identify, locate, and synthesize completed research reports, articles, books, and other materials about the specific problems of a research topic. The literature search and subsequent review can be of value to researchers by helping them to regard their studies as contributions to a larger topic of which the inquiry at hand is only a part—rather than as isolated or esoteric collections of facts.

Other benefits of literature reviews are that they: (*a*) help to narrow and to more clearly delineate the research problem, (*b*) reveal overlooked conclusions and facts that ought to be taken into consideration before a research project is actually initiated; (*c*) suggest new approaches to the planning of investigations; (*d*) uncover methodologies that were used successfully by other research workers; (*e*) help in the determination of the degree to which particular problems have already been investigated; and (*f*) assist investigators to develop firmer understandings of theoretical implications of proposed inquiries. The techniques used to accomplish a literature search are somewhat involved; numerous bibliographic and indexing tools can be consulted. Thus, this topic and many relevant citation sources are discussed in considerable detail in Chapter 14, "Writing the Research Proposal."

STATE SPECIFIC PROBLEM

At this state of the research process, the specific problem to be focused upon is identified. The relationship of the question under investigation to the general problem area is also taken into careful consideration, and limitations of the study are identified. Pertinent independent and dependent variables are recognized. Assumptions that underlie the research problem—but that will not be tested—are also explicitly described, and relevant terms are defined. Thus, in this stage of the inquiry, the specific problem area under investigation is clearly and precisely outlined, in as much detail as possible.

DESIGN OF METHODOLOGY

The next stage of the research process involves the design of procedures and methods by means of which the identified problem will be studied. For example, the following questions are among those that should now be posed and answered: What is the population under investigation? How will a sample be drawn from the population, and how large should the sample be? Where and when will the study be conducted? What are operational definitions of the variables relevant to the research problem? How will the needed research data be collected and analyzed? (Data analysis often involves the utilization of statistical techniques, many of which are discussed in Chapters 7–12.)

In the conduct of inquiry in librarianship, many methods can be employed. For example, *experiments* may be designed that take advantage of controlled conditions which allow tests of specific propositions. On the other hand, investigators can rely exclusively upon the *direct observation* of certain library operations (e.g., case studies of the roles of librarians and library users in actual service settings). Moreover, *historical research* can be used to examine past events by means of analyses of available information contained in pertinent records and evidence. In addition to these types of projects, other inquiries might be undertaken. Specific characteristics of many modes of research are examined more closely in subsequent chapters of this text.

DATA GATHERING AND ANALYSIS

In this stage of inquiry, research methodology is employed to gather needed data. When the data have been collected, they are then analyzed according to the methods specified. Although data gathering and data analysis are necessary elements of a research project, in a properly designed study these states of inquiry are essentially mechanical. The creative process is not particularly utilized in these stages but in the choice and statement of the research problem and in the design of a methodology to attack the problem.

REPORT RESULTS OF STUDY

Finally, results of the study are recorded and reported. In this way, findings are made available to a potentially wide audience of peers, who can learn from, and build upon, the completed research project. A more detailed examination of the research report and its value in the conduct of a scientific inquiry is provided in Chapter 15, "Writing the Research Report."

FINDING A RESEARCH TOPIC

In the scientific community, research is not used as an attempt to prove preconceived conclusions, to confirm biases, to praise admirers, or to condemn adversaries. Scientists have a responsibility to search for real solutions to both practical and theoretical problems. Productive research is the product of tests of propositions or searches for answers to exploratory questions; however, these activities cannot be accomplished unless a need for specific information has been recognized and pertinent phenomena have been pinpointed that can be observed, interpreted, and evaluated. Thus, the selection of a topic for a disciplined inquiry is a key element of the research process. As an aid to the inexperienced student of research, some suggested general topics and subject areas for inquiries in library and information science are listed in Table 1.1.

Although experienced research workers within librarianship are aware of numerous problems and subjects that require either original or replicated exploration, research novices are often stymied in their efforts to focus upon a significant question. Finding a topic and the posing of a germane research question represent the important, initial steps in the conduct of an organized, disciplined search for truth. We use the term *finding* here rather than *choosing* because the process is more analogous to the search for a specific bibliographic citation for a book rather than the choice of one from a list of several recommended titles.

Table 1.1. *Some Suggested Broad Areas and Subareas for Research*

Library use and nonuse
  Who uses the library?
  Among the population of possible users, who does not use the library?
  What kinds of uses are made of the library and by whom?
Catalog use
  Who uses the library card catalog?
  What kind of searches are made and what is their frequency?
  What kinds of searching errors are made?
  What type of library catalog is optimal?
  How adequate are subject headings?
Communication media
  What medium is most appropriate for a given communication task?
  Which medium delivers particular kinds of information most effectively?
Reference service
  What are criteria for evaluations of reference service?
  What are behaviors in a reference search (i.e., the librarians' and the clientele's)?
  What are standards of reference service?
  How important is nonverbal communication to the reference task?
  Who are the library clientele that benefit most and least from available reference services?
Serial publications
  What are criteria for evaluations of both individual serials and collections of these publications?
  When should serials be retired (placed into storage areas)?
  When should subscriptions be canceled?
Library collections
  What are quantitative measures of the quality of collections (sizes, growth rate, expenditures, etc.)?
  What are appropriate qualitative measures?
Benefits derived from library use
  How do various measures of library activity relate to benefits–costs?
  What kinds of factual information can be provided to justify the library's existence?
Circulation studies
  What kinds of materials circulate in libraries?
  How does circulation relate to benefits?
  What should be the criteria for weeding a collection?
  What criteria can be used as guides to determine when materials should be retired to remote storage?
  Why does a book circulate?
Availability of materials
  How can the need for duplicate copies of library materials be predicted?
  Who uses interlibrary loan? How effective is this service?
  What is the effect of different loan periods on the availability of materials?
  To what extent do censorship and related repressions affect the availability of certain materials?
  Do cooperative projects among libraries increase the availability of materials?
Catalog record
  What information should be included in the catalog record of a book or other medium of communication (especially in modern, computerized catalogs)?

Table 1.1 (*Continued*)

What bibliographic characteristics of library materials do users tend to remember?

What should be included in the records of a particular, specialized library, such as a school media center?

What catalog record is required so that patrons can most effectively utilize library collections?

Discrimination in sex or race

Does racial or sex discrimination exist in a given locality or profession (e.g., librarianship)?

How can such discrimination be measured?

What effects does discrimination have in the library?

Fines for overdue materials

How effective are library fines as deterrents to overdues?

Are there alternatives to fines?

What is the purpose of fines—punishment, deterrent, source of library revenue, etc.?

Usefulness of abstracting and indexing tools

To what extent do library clientele use abstracting and indexing tools?

To what extent are clientele pleased with available tools?

Are abstracting and indexing tools worth the price that libraries must pay for them?

How much repetition or overlap exists among the coverage of these tools?

Abstracts/titles

How much information do abstracts or titles convey to readers?

Who reads abstracts?

Do readers make relevance judgments on titles?

How accurate are relevance judgments based solely on abstracts or titles?

Browsing in the library

How important is browsing to library clientele?

How does browsing function?

Could browsing be eliminated in particular instances?

What is the effect of closed stacks on the research process?

Microforms

How can user acceptance and utilization of various microforms be increased?

What are the unique problems of microform usage in libraries?

How can microform collections and services be evaluated?

Selection of materials by patrons

Why do children select a given book or other medium of expression?

Why do adults select certain kinds of library materials?

Can certain characteristics of a medium of communication be identified, such as color, cover design, etc., that influence the selection of a given book or other piece of library material?

What are the implications of these selection characteristics?

Automatic indexing or abstracting

What are formal criteria for abstracting or indexing a document?

Can a computer be programmed to recognize "significant" words or phrases in the full texts of documents? How?

The type and specific nature of a selected research project depends upon several factors. For example, when research is to be performed under the auspices of an institution, sponsor, or funding agency, a specific program of inquiry might have already been earmarked. In such situations the investigator may not be free to select a unique research problem. In other instances, the choice of a problem or topic may depend upon the interests and capabilities of research workers, as well as the time available to conduct the inquiry. The first-hand familiarity with—or frequent observation of—a library phenomenon will sometimes cause perceptive librarians to raise questions that can be refined into research hypotheses. Many librarians question theoretical concepts related to routine library procedures or practices without realizing that, in so doing, a form of research hypothesis is actually posed. Therefore, from a very practical standpoint, the most productive avenues to a research topic might be questions which originate from day-to-day library activities and routines. Some librarians are inspired to conduct a disciplined study after reading a provocative article in a journal, a scholarly treatise, or a magazine of professional news and discussion. The reading of current library and information science literature can certainly stimulate curious readers to thought, and the output may be a significant research question. Furthermore, some investigators in the field have relied upon their accumulated past experience or professional education within librarianship for sources of new research opportunities. The satisfaction of one's intellectual curiosity is another important source of ideas for disciplined inquiry. Serendipity and accidental discovery can also be the point of origin for new research possibilities. For example, investigators working diligently with a library experiment (guided by a particular problem and goal) might accidentally encounter an unexplained phenomenon that should be examined apart from that of the ongoing project. Furthermore, informal conversations with professional associates, as well as formal papers and lectures presented at conferences, might also stimulate curiosity about a problem that is in need of either original or replicated study.

Another productive area for research ideas or topics is the body of reports, dissertations, and theses produced at library schools as a result of systematic inquiry in fulfillment of advanced degree requirements. Writers of research reports frequently make suggestions for further related inquiries. By following these leads, eager but inexperienced researchers may be able to contribute to the continuity of inquiry. Of course, the success of this approach depends upon the degree of knowledge, expertise, and interest that research workers bring to the recommended investigative tasks. Whatever the source of suggestions for research, the investigator must, above all, possess the ability and background knowledge necessary to cope successfully with a selected research task.

Articles devoted to problems in library science and papers that contain state-of-the art reviews of various areas within the field are sometimes useful to students who need ideas about new research possibilities.

ETHICAL CONSIDERATIONS IN RESEARCH

With regard to inquiry in its broadest context, researchers in librarianship generally expect the products of their efforts to benefit the clientele of libraries, to enhance the professional development and welfare of librarians, or to lead to the improvement of libraries. Moreover, serious investigators usually anticipate that their work will help accomplish one or more of the following objectives: (a) contribute to the development of library and information science theories; (b) stimulate rational decision-making; or (c) advance constructive change within librarianship. The overall purpose of the conduct of inquiry is not to expose the personal weaknesses of individual librarians or library users, to engage in vindictive "axe grinding" activities, or to suppress human freedoms. In essence, research goals and practices of librarians ought to be guided by a sense of social and professional responsibility. Furthermore, professional ethical standards should be heeded during all phases of the research process. Practitioners of science cannot afford to ignore ethical rules and social standards which should govern the actual conduct of inquiry and guide the selection of research priorities, the context in which research is undertaken, and the application of results.

Persons who conduct research ought to commit themselves to the maintenance of conditions under which careful, unbiased studies can be accomplished without adverse interference from public or private interests. Within this framework, freedom of thought, inquiry, and expression is a democratic essential that legitimate scientists recognize and exercise. At the same time, special ethical considerations arise in the conduct of inquiry with regard to humans as participants or subjects. A major problem faced by many research workers in the social sciences is that of obtaining an optimal amount of information about people and their behavior—within a humane and ethical (moral) framework.

Because many studies and evaluations in the field of library science focus upon the observation of human behavior, investigators must devote careful attention to the selection and utilization of nonoffensive research methods and to the establishment and preservation of trusting relationships with participating subjects. In some investigative situations, a certain degree of *temporary* deception might be necessary to disguise the true nature of a sensitive study (i.e., until the project has been completed). But researchers in this situation, as in all other similar cases, have a responsibility as scientists to respect the dignity of participating subjects and to refrain from creating unnecessary anxiety or discomfort. Although the protection of individual privacy should be a general area of concern in all the sciences, apparently the issue has not been as pertinent in library science research in the past as it has been in social and psychological inquiry. Nonetheless, all studies should be disciplined by careful attention to the preservation of personal privacy. On the other hand, this consideration ought not to be so stringent that effective and nonoffensive methods are automatically ruled out when they are based upon the discreet observation of private behavior.

Whatever techniques may be employed in a project, attention must always be given to the selection of methods that will effectively prevent unnecessary invasions of personal privacy but which will permit the collection of useful research data without adversely manipulating subjects or exposing their personal weaknesses. Special precautions must be taken in sensitive areas of inquiry so that all personal data are treated with scrupulous care. Furthermore, the utilization of such information must be handled judiciously. Because scholars are obligated to make their work available for scrutiny by the larger scientific community, broad target populations must be identified; however, the identity of specific persons within populations or samples of subjects must not be reported when studies have been completed. Persons who agree to participate as research subjects should also be assured that their identities will *always* remain anonymous and that any information provided to investigators will be kept confidential; this assurance must then be operationalized (transformed into a reality).

Ethical Guidelines

The following general principles are widely accepted in the scientific community as fundamentals of the inquiry process and are presented as ethical bench marks.

1. Maintain high standards of work directed toward the constant improvement of the quality of research.
2. Strive to preserve open channels of communication among research workers, scholars, practicing professionals, and other persons or groups who might benefit from or apply research results.
3. In planning, conducting, and reporting studies, do not misrepresent

the investigative competencies and abilities of research workers or associates.

4. Protect human subjects by taking all possible measures to respect privacy and the confidentiality of personalized research data.
5. Unless subjects have been fully informed of psychological or other risks involved in a given project and have consented to serve as research subjects in full realization of the possibility of stress or discomfort, do not utilize techniques that pose threats to subjects' well-being.
6. Let the study's nature and purpose determine the degree of candor to be displayed regarding the exact purpose of a study; as a general rule, however, follow the principle of full disclosure of intent to subjects.
7. Report procedures and findings as accurately as possible.
8. Give credit to persons whose earlier research was especially useful in the conduct of another project.
9. Give credit to research associates who provided direct assistance.
10. Acknowledge the aid of persons who served as consultants or helped to plan, conduct, or report research activities.
11. When applicable, acknowledge sources of financial grants and other forms of direct or indirect aid.
12. Always resist the temptation to accept premature explanations; have the patience to wait for more verified data related to an observed but heretofore inadequately explained phenomenon.
13. Always place a high value on intellectual honesty.

Although ethics in inquiry is a most important topic, space does not permit a more detailed discussion here. The general phenomenon of professional ethics and their application to librarianship were the subjects of a doctoral dissertation written in 1976 by Johan Bekker.[12] Furthermore, a group of thoughtful and distinguished scientists, philosophers, and jurists has recorded informative deliberations about the subject in *The Ethics of Teaching and Scientific Research,*[13] a book edited by Sidney Hook and others.

EVALUATION OF COMPLETED RESEARCH

Not all librarians are qualified to conduct research, as judged by their training and experience. Others are simply not interested in undertaking scientific investigations, even though they might be qualified. But all competent professionals in the field should know enough about research meth-

Table 1.2. *Evaluation of Research: Some Questions*

What are the conclusions of the research? Does the study answer the research question posed?

Is the methodology adequate for the research problem under investigation?

Have assumptions been explicitly identified and are they reasonable and acceptable?

Are the instruments or indexes used by the investigator adequate reflections of the conceptual variables of the study?

If a test or experiment was conducted as a part of the research, are the results sufficiently conclusive so that the hypotheses can be accepted as tentative, theoretical knowledge or put to practical use?

Can conclusions of the study be generalized to a larger population?

Are the conclusions linked to other assertions so that findings can be incorporated into existing theory?

What was the hypothesis or the research question?

Was the hypothesis of social or theoretical significance and was the problem stated so that it can be solved?

What were the independent and dependent variables of the research?

Did investigators appear to be aware of any intervening variables, and, if so, how did the researchers account for them?

What are the theoretical implications of the research? Did the researcher appear to be aware of them?

Were graphical or tabular formats appropriately used to display pertinent data?

If sampling procedures were used, were they adequately explained in the research report?

If the investigator claimed to have selected a random sample, was it actually chosen so that each member of the population had an equal chance of being selected?

Was the methodology explained in an understandable manner so that it can be easily replicated?

What techniques (statistical or others) were used to analyze quantitative or qualitative data? Were these techniques appropriate for the investigation?

Did the investigator conduct a literature search prior to the project's initiation? If so, was the study then related to past, similar investigations?

Did the investigator make recommendations for future study?

Was the research report written in a factual, straightforward, honest, and lucid manner, and was it free of incorrect grammar, spelling errors, and emotionally laden words and phrases?

---

odology to judge the scientific merits of reported studies in library and information science journals and other literature. Therefore, readers may benefit from a list of the most commonly-used criteria for the evaluation of completed research projects. In Table 1.2, various evaluation guidelines are listed in random order.

Perhaps an awareness of these evaluative criteria will help instill among librarians a career-long desire to understand both basic and problem-solving inquiry. Through an understanding of evaluative criteria for completed research, librarians can better comprehend how empirical investigations provide information for the immediacies of operational and managerial decisions, as well as generate other knowledge required for progress in the field.

CONCLUSIONS

Carefully conducted research can facilitate the quest for solutions to practical and theoretical problems in our technological age characterized by rapid change. Progress in many areas of library and information science has been impeded because of both the inadequate amount and deficiencies of completed inquiries. To ensure that libraries remain viable social institutions in any locale and in whatever setting they might be found and that library collections and programs of service are relevant to the information and communication needs of clientele, librarians must continue to explore new approaches and methods that are applicable to the roles of libraries. These new approaches will require imagination and originality, as well as sound decisions rooted in objectively collected and carefully analyzed data. Although some progress has been made in the area of library science research, it is apparent that librarianship has not achieved the coveted status of a scholarly or scientific discipline. To realize this sought-after intellectual and professional maturity, astute and knowledgeable application of scientific method to the procurement of new library science knowledge is required.

No longer can librarians afford to question whether scientific method is applicable to the study of library phenomena. Because it is highly unlikely that persons from other disciplines or professions will undertake many of the needed empirical investigations in librarianship, answers to urgent questions must originate from "within ranks." Certainly, the status of librarianship as a viable profession and the position of library science as a meaningful and worthwhile field of study hinge upon the question of whether practicing professionals and scholars in the field can develop a structure of theoretical and practical knowledge; generate hypotheses relevant to pertinent theories; and plan, conduct, and evaluate both basic and applied research in a scientific manner. The promise of the future is bright for library and information science researchers; advances made thus far in the field appear to be only the beginning. Research in librarianship is a relatively new and still fragmented field of endeavor. Thus, knowledge already produced as a result of systematic inquiry is small, indeed, in view of the important work that remains to be accomplished.

REFERENCES

1. Charles H. Busha, "Research Methods," *Encyclopedia of Library and Information Science, 25*(1978):254.
2. John T. Zadrozny, *Dictionary of Social Science*. Washington, D.C.: Public Affairs Press, 1959, p. 259.
3. Sydney Ross, " 'Scientists': The Story of a Word," *Annals of Science, 18*(1962):65.
4. Romano Harré, *The Principles of Scientific Thinking*. Chicago, Ill.: University of Chicago Press, 1970, p. 314.
5. Charles C. Williamson, "The Place of Research in Library Service," *Library Quarterly, 1*(January 1931):10.
6. Arnold K. Borden, "The Sociological Beginnings of the Library Movement," *Library Quarterly, 1*(July 1931):282.
7. Herbert Goldhor, *An Introduction to Scientific Research in Librarianship*. Washington, D.C.: U.S. Department of Health, Education, and Welfare, Bureau of Research, 1969, p. 30.
8. Horst Kunze, "On the Professional Image and the Education of the Librarian," in Conrad H. Rawski, ed. *Toward a Theory of Librarianship: Papers Presented in Honor of Jesse Hauk Shera*. Metuchen, N.J.: Scarecrow Press, 1973, p. 520.
9. Joseph Becker, *The First Book of Information Science*. Washington, D.C.: United States Atomic Energy Commission, Office of Information Services, 1973, p. 17.
10. Conrad H. Rawski, "Introduction," in Conrad H. Rawski, ed., *Toward a Theory of Librarianship: Papers Presented in Honor of Jesse Hauk Shera*, Metuchen, N.J.: Scarecrow Press, 1973, p. 43.
11. Pierce Butler, "Librarianship as a Profession," *Library Quarterly, 21*(October 1951):236.
12. Johan Bekker, *Professional Ethics and Its Application to Librarianship* (unpublished doctoral dissertation, Case Western Reserve University, 1976).
13. Sidney Hook *et al.,* eds., *The Ethics of Teaching and Scientific Research*. Buffalo, N.Y.: Prometheus, 1977.

SELECTED BIBLIOGRAPHY

SOURCES OF ADDITIONAL INFORMATION

Bernal, John D. *Science in History*. Cambridge, Mass.: M.I.T. Press, 1971.

Boldrini, Marcello. *Scientific Truth and Statistical Method,* translated by Ruth Kendall. New York: Hafner, 1972.

Braithwaite, Richard B. *Scientific Explanation: A Study of the Function of Theory, Probability and Law in Science*. New York and London: Cambridge University Press, 1968.

Buchanan, Scott M. *Truth in the Sciences*. Charlottesville: University Press of Virginia, 1972.

Bunge, Mario A. *Method, Model, and Matter*. Boston, Mass.: Reidel, 1973.

Davies, John T. *The Scientific Approach*. 2nd ed. New York: Academic Press, 1973.

Dellow, E. L. *Methods of Science: An Introduction to Measuring and Testing for Laymen and Students*. New York: Universe Books, 1970.

Descartes, René. *Discourses on Method, Optics, Geometry, and Meterology,* translated by Paul J. Olscamp. Indianapolis, Ind.: Bobbs-Merrill, 1965.

Dockx, Stanislas I., and Bernays, P., ed. *Information and Prediction in Science.* New York: Academic Press, 1965.

Dubin, Robert. *Theory Building.* New York: Free Press, 1969.

Fischer, Robert B. *Science, Man and Society.* 2nd ed. Philadelphia, Pa.: Saunders, 1975.

Freeman, Howard E. *Social Research and Social Policy.* Englewood Cliffs, N.J.: Prentice-Hall, 1970.

Galtung, Johan. *Theory and Methods of Social Research.* New York: Columbia University Press, 1967.

Hardyck, Curtis D. *Understanding Research in the Social Sciences: A Practical Guide to Understanding Social and Behavioral Research.* Philadelphia: Saunders, 1975.

Harris, Errol E. *Hypothesis and Perception: The Roots of Scientific Method.* New York: Humanities Press, 1970.

Humphreys, Willard C. *Anomalies and Scientific Theories.* San Francisco, Calif.: Freeman, Cooper, 1968.

Ingle, Dwight J. *Is It Really So? A Guide to Clear Thinking.* Philadelphia, Pa.: Westminister Press, 1976.

Jeffreys, Sir Harold. *Scientific Inference.* 3rd ed. New York and London: Cambridge University Press, 1973.

Lastrucci, Carlo L. *The Scientific Approach: Basic Principles of the Scientific Method.* Cambridge, Mass.: Schenkman, 1967.

Mach, Ernst. *Knowledge and Error: Sketches on the Psychology of Enquiry,* translated by Erwin N. Hiebert. Boston, Mass.: Reidel, 1975.

Meyers, Lawrence S., and Grossen, Neal E. *Behavioral Research: Theory, Procedure, and Design.* San Francisco, Calif.: W. H. Freeman, 1974.

Nagel, Ernest, *et al. Observation and Theory in Science.* With an introduction by Stephen F. Barker. Baltimore, Md.: Johns Hopkins Press, 1971.

Popper, Karl R. *The Logic of Scientific Discovery.* New York: Basic Books, 1961.

Schlegel, Richard. *Inquiry into Science: Its Domain and Limits.* Garden City, N.Y.: Doubleday, 1972.

Turbayne, Colin M. *The Myth of Metaphor.* Rev. ed. Columbia, S.C.: University of South Carolina Press, 1970.

PART II

Methods of Research

CHAPTER 2

Experimental Research in Librarianship:
Introduction to Experimentation

BASIC CONCEPTS

An *experiment* can be defined as a research situation in which investigators specify exactly, or *control,* the conditions that will prevail in the investigation. The values of one or more independent variables are then manipulated and the effect of the manipulation on the values of the dependent variables with respect to one or more *experimental groups* is observed. The effects of other factors that might possibly be relevant to the research problem (i.e., affect the values of the dependent variable) are minimized through careful experimental design. In this way, conceptual requirements of the research hypothesis are met by controlled experimental conditions.

In librarianship, experiments can be used to test new techniques for developing, maintaining, and utilizing library collections, to identify ill-defined or previously unobserved library or informational phenomena, and to explore conditions under which certain phenomena in library and information science occur.

A *subject* of an experiment is the basic unit on which an experiment is performed. In agricultural experimentation, subjects might be plants of certain types or perhaps plots of planted ground. In drug research, subjects might be white rats or guinea pigs. In library science, information science, and other social science research, subjects are frequently persons—for example, patrons, librarians or students.

In addition to subjects, a true experimental design involves a *control group* on which experiments are not performed. The purpose of the control group is to serve as a comparison. Treatments are applied to the experimental group but not to the control group, and the results are observed.

The fact that humans are frequently the subjects of social science experimentation implies a basic difficulty in applying the experimental ap-

35

proach to social science research in general and librarianship in particular. Humans cannot be manipulated as easily as white rats, for excellent moral, ethical, and legal reasons. Hence many research problems in the social sciences are not particularly amenable to the experimental approach.

A *treatment* is the condition that is applied to an experimental group of subjects. In agricultural research, a treatment may be the application of fertilizer to growing plants or the regulation of the amount of moisture which the plants receive. In medical research, the administering of drugs to patients (subjects) or the use of a surgical technique are examples of treatments. In librarianship, a treatment that is being tested might be a system of indexing, a mode of instruction, a type of catalog organization, or a method of book selection, among others.

Control is central to experimental research and is the feature that distinguishes experimental from other research methods, such as those in survey and historical research. The experimental method uses a control-group and one or more experimental groups. These groups of subjects are deliberately designed to be equivalent in all important respects in order to control the effects of the many variables that might interfere with the test of hypothesis. These effects can thus be predicted to be similar for the control and experimental groups. The effect on the dependent variable of varying the values of one or more independent variables (the treatment) can then be observed in the experimental group. Complete equivalence between experimental and control groups can seldom be obtained in research in the social sciences, however, because with human subjects there are always numerous environmental and heriditary factors that cannot normally be known. Thus, at best, equivalence can only be an approximate concept.

Consider the following hypothesis: that high school students who study a unit of instruction in library skills in conjunction with coursework in other subjects such as history or English literature (i.e., in an integrated approach) learn library skills more effectively than high school students who study an equivalent unit independently of other school subjects. To test this hypothesis, there are certain variables that need to be controlled. The two groups of students should be roughly equivalent in levels of motivation, intelligence, socioeconomic status, age, and perhaps other qualities as well. It is easy to see why this is so; any one of these variables might have a differential effect on otherwise equivalent students. For example, if the students of Group A manifest more collective intelligence than Group B, then that factor itself may cause students in Group A to learn library skills more effectively than those in Group B. But by designing an experiment so the two groups are roughly equivalent in intelligence, this variable is controlled, and thus the effect should be the same for both groups.

Because of the careful control that is exercised in its use, the experimental method is the most appropriate technique to test hypotheses which involve *causal* relationships. Theoretically, at least, by controlling all independent variables except a treatment variable, the differential effect on the dependent variable in the experimental and control groups can be said to have been caused by the independent variable.

It is sometimes useful to distinguish between *field experiments* and *laboratory experiments,* although the distinction between the two is often largely a matter of degree.[1] In a field experiment, the investigator operates in the real world—in a naturalistic setting. In contrast, laboratory experiments are normally conducted apart from real-world activities, although the investigator makes every attempt to simulate these activities—to artificially create a real-world environment. Without this attempt it would be impossible to justify generalization of the results of laboratory experiments to the real world. Both laboratory and field experiments control the conditions under which each develops, but it is usually possible to exert more control in a laboratory experiment than in a field experiment. This fact leads directly to characteristic strengths and weaknesses of the two approaches. Because of the increased control exerted, laboratory experiments often have more precise and replicable results than field experiments. On the other hand, the artificiality of the experimental conditions implies a certain difficulty in extrapolating the results of laboratory experiments to the real world.

Experimental research differs from other research methods principally in the fact that the independent variable, or treatment, is *introduced* into an experimental situation by the investigator. Measurement of the values of the dependent variables is, therefore, done at least twice, prior to as well as following the introduction of the independent variable (the *pretest* and *posttest,* respectively). In this way the effect of the treatment on the dependent variable can be observed.

Theoretically, an ideal experiment may be defined as one in which all factors that might affect the outcome of the experiment (the dependent variable) are controlled by the experimentor. As we have observed, this ideal situation can be approximated in the natural sciences; however, it is extremely difficult even to approximate in the social sciences, because of the complexity of the subject matter. Not only is the identification of all possible variables impossible, but even if it were not, the problem of how to control them would remain. The concept of *randomization* is employed as an attempt to overcome these difficulties. In essence, randomization involves the random assignment of subjects from the target population to treatment groups. Randomization protects against implicit or subconscious experimentor bias which might have a systematic effect on the results of the experiment. Although randomization will not eliminate the effect of uncontrolled variables, it should "average out" their effects. By assigning subjects to experimental and control groups at random, the experimenter reduces the possibility that the results will be due to conditions other than those associated with the manipulation of the independent variables.

Moreover, without random assignment of subjects to treatments, little statistical analysis of the ensuing results is possible. Random assignment is a *requirement* of statistical tests of the significance of experimental results. Statistical analysis of results will be valid only if this underlying assumption is correct.[2]

The extent to which an experiment accomplishes its goal is sometimes referred to as its *internal validity*. In other words, the investigator must pose and answer the following question: Does the experiment adequately test the treatment of interest or is it methodologically unsound? Internal validity implies freedom from bias and assurance that the observed effect on the dependent variable is actually due to the independent variable (the treatment). Thus, the internal validity of an experiment involves the concepts of randomization and control. The concept of *reproducibility* is closely related to internal validity. Ideally, experimental design should be reproducible whether it is prepared for application in the field or in the laboratory.

THE FOUR-CELL EXPERIMENTAL DESIGN

The simplest true experimental design is the classical pretest–posttest–control group experimental design—the so-called four-cell design. This design is illustrated in Figure 2.1. In the four-cell experimental design, there is one independent variable—the treatment—and one dependent variable. Subjects are assigned randomly to the control group and the experimental group. The dependent variable is then measured for both groups. This is sometimes called the *pretest*. After the pretest the treatment is introduced to the subjects in the experimental group only. The dependent variable is then measured again for both groups; this is the *posttest*.

The final step in designing an experiment involves an explicit and precise statement of the hypothesis to be tested. The general theoretical or research problem is often "fuzzy," or ill-defined. This problem needs to be refined and restated in terms of a specific hypothesis to be tested. For

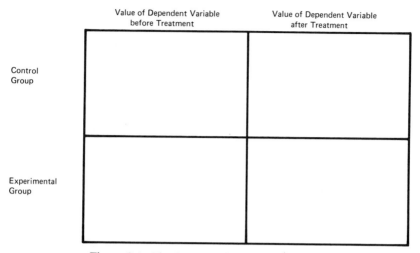

Figure 2.1. *The four-cell experimental design.*

example, part of the general problem area involved with the phenomenon of browsing can perhaps be stated as the fuzzy hypothesis: "Library patrons tend to select books that can be reached easily." This somewhat unclear hypothesis might be refined still further as: "Shelf height is a major determining factor (or *cause*) of book use."

In this last statement, the independent and dependent variables are clearly identified, but operational definitions of these variables remain to be constructed. A commonly selected surrogate of book use is circulation, an operational definition of the dependent variable. "Shelf height" might be operationalized simply as "number of inches from floor level." A particular library or group of libraries would also have to be identified as would the definition of "patron."

Once the hypothesis to be tested has been clearly stated and independent and dependent variables have been given operational definitions, subjects must be randomly assigned to control and to experimental groups. In this case, our subjects are books.

The treatment in our browsing example might be "placed on a good (or, by hypothesis, active) shelf" as opposed to a bad (inactive) shelf. Good and bad could be given explicit operational definitions in terms of the independent variable, "inches from the floor." Thus, for example, all shelves which are between 50 and 72 inches from the floor might be operationally defined as good shelves (reasonably within eye level), with all other shelves being bad shelves.

The pretest in our example would be "circulation before being placed on a good shelf''; the posttest would be ''circulation after being placed on a good shelf.''

There are many possible embellishments to the four-cell experimental design that are beyond the scope of this text. There may be more than one treatment, for example, and therefore more than one experimental group. Thus, in our example, each distinct shelf height might be regarded as a different treatment. In another variation, the value of the dependent variable might be measured more than once following the application of the treatment. *Factorial designs* involve two or more independent variables. Both the independent and the interactive effects of these variables on the dependent variable are studied. Research workers who contemplate the design of an experiment should consider consulting an expert in the use of experimental design or one or more additional treatments of the subject (e.g., references 1–6).

USING A TABLE OF RANDOM NUMBERS

Tables of random numbers, or digits, are frequently used to facilitate the selection of random samples and to assign subjects randomly to treatments as part of an experimental design. Appendix A, containing 1000 random digits, is such a table. There are many correct ways to use Appendix A; in general, a safe rule to follow is to devise a method for stripping numbers from the table which guarantees that each member of the population should have an equal chance of being selected.[7] We suppose that it is possible to assign a unique number to each member of the population. For purposes of discussion, let us assume that there are 800 members of a population in which we are interested and that we have assigned the numbers 1–800 to population members. We now discuss how a table of random numbers can be used to draw a random sample from this population.

One method would be to select a three-digit number at random from the table; suppose that this is 846.* Because this number is too large to refer to a member of our population, we ignore it. Examine the three-digit number immediately *below* the first selected number in the table; suppose this is 026. Population member 26 then becomes the first member of the sample selected. Proceed to examine the three-digit number immediately below 026; suppose this is 660. Population member 660 then becomes the second member of the sample. This procedure is repeated until enough members

---

* Appendix A contains random digits arranged in groups of four. To select a three-digit number, simply ignore the first (or last) digit in each group.

of the population for the sample we wish to draw have been selected. If a number is selected which had been chosen previously, it is ignored. This procedure ensures each member of the population an equal opportunity of being selected.

Example 1

A list of local business has been compiled (the population) and we wish to select a random sample to survey with respect to local library capabilities. Suppose that 214 such businesses have been identified, and the investigator wishes to select a random sample of 40 concerns from this population. Explain how the table of random numbers could be used to draw the sample.

Answer

Number the members of the population from 1 to 214. The method previously described can then be used to select the sample. Simply follow the procedure, examining one three-digit number at a time, discarding 000, all numbers larger than 214, and numbers referring to population members already selected. When 40 numbers have been chosen, the sample selection is completed.

Example 2

Use a table of random numbers to select a random sample of names from the white pages of a telephone directory.

Answer

The numbering of each individual in the directory, as in Example 1, is clearly not feasible. However, sample selection can be accomplished easily in a two-step process. For each name to be selected, use the table of random numbers to choose a *page* in the directory, and then use the table a second time to select a name from that page. Note that this procedure could be applied equally well to the selection of a sample of serials or new book acquisitions from printed lists.

Example 3

In an experiment designed to test the efficacy of three different overdue policies (the treatments), an experimentor wishes to assign each member of a population of library patrons randomly to one of the three treatments. How might this be facilitated with a table of random numbers?

Answer

Use the table to create a list of treatment assignment numbers by select-ing one-digit numbers, one by one, from the table. If the digit selected is 1, 2, or 3, assign the patron to treatment group number 1; if 4, 5, or 6, to treatment group two; and if 7, 8, or 9, to treatment group three. If the digit selected is 0, ignore the digit and choose another.

In all of these examples, simple random samples were drawn, or as-signments made. Another type of random sample is discussed in Chapter 3—the stratified sample. A table of random numbers should also be used in conjunction with the act of drawing samples of this type.

EVALUATION OF AN EXPERIMENT

Once an investigator has conducted an experiment, the results of the experiment—the experimental data—must be evaluated. Evaluation in-volves a number of concepts, including hypothesis testing, experimental error, sensitivity, internal validity, and external validity.

The evaluation of an experiment involves a test of a *null hypothesis,* a statement that no significant difference exists between the control and experimental groups. In other words, the null hypothesis asserts that within specified limits of credibility, the control and experimental groups are essentially equivalent. Two groups of subjects will rarely perform identically; some variation will probably occur under any circumstances. The investigator, however, must determine whether differences between the performances of the control and experimental groups are statistically significant. A test of a null hypothesis is an attempt to disprove the asser-tion of "no difference"; to show that the experimental group has in fact been affected by the treatment in such a way as to significantly change the value of the dependent variable. The concept of hypothesis testing is treated more fully in Chapter 12. An appropriate procedure to test the significance of a treatment using the four-cell experimental design may be the *t*-test, which is applied to the differences between pretest and posttest scores for the control and experimental groups. The chi-square test may also be appropriate. *Analysis of variance* is required for more complex designs.

The *sensitivity* of an experiment is its ability to detect relatively small effects. One way to increase the sensitivity of an experiment is to increase the number of subjects; this decreases the chance for random error (or *experimental error*) to affect the results in a significant way. This option always adds to the expense of conducting the experiment, however. Another way to reduce experimental error is to exert additional control over the experiment, to ensure that the control and experimental groups are composed of similar subjects. This is sometimes done by *matching* subjects on the basis of as many variables as possible. Another measure of an experiment's adequacy is its internal validity. Are variables sufficiently controlled? Has randomization been employed throughout?

A final crucial consideration in the evaluation of an experiment lies with its *external validity*. Can the results of the experiment be generalized? If so, what is the population to which it can be generalized? External validity is associated with questions concerning the extent to which a sample is representative of the target population. Can the results of an experiment be generalized to the real world? It is normally easier to justify such generalization for field experiments than for laboratory experiments because of the artificiality of the latter. Overall, experimental findings are evaluated in terms of the reliability of the data, the scientific importance of the results, and the extent to which the data can be generalized.

EX POST FACTO STUDY

The Latin ex post facto means literally, after the fact, or retrospectively. Although an ex post facto study is not really an experimental design, such a study sometimes is confused with the experimental method, and is frequently discussed with it. What is lacking in the ex post facto study is control. Rather than introducing an independent variable and controlling other variables, the ex post facto study seeks to analyze what has already happened in an effort to isolate the cause of the events. Mouly asserts that

> This is experimentation in reverse . . . the obvious weakness of such an "experiment" is that we have no control over the situations that have already occurred and we can never be sure of how many other circumstances might have been involved. [8]

Ex post facto study is a type of *quasi-experimental* design.

Consider the hypothesis that academic courses in research methods affect graduate library science students in such a way as to cause them to be better librarians than librarians who did not complete such a course. An ex post facto analysis of graduated librarians with respect to an operational definition of success in librarianship (such as salary or job title) might well reveal that a strong relationship does indeed exist between completing a course in research methods and professional success in librarianship. But is the observed relationship causal in nature? Does the course cause the success?

Some thought will reveal another plausible set of hypotheses which would equally well explain the hypothetical relationship. Research methods in librarianship is an elective course in many library schools. It might be that only the more serious, motivated, or intelligent students tend to elect such a course. But such students might also be expected to enjoy a higher degree of success in their chosen profession because of these personal characteristics. Thus, the act of *self-selection* could reflect a causal factor which explains both the completion of research methods courses and success in librarianship. Presumably there are other possible explanations as well.

The original hypothesis could be tested, albeit with some difficulty and over a period of years, by the experimental method. Such an approach might involve the random division of a group of equivalent students into two groups, a control group—students not permitted to take research methods—and an experimental group—students who are required to take research methods. The effect of the course on graduated students could then be observed over the students' careers. Relative success or failure in librarianship, however the definition is operationally defined, could then be said to have been caused by the treatment, in this case completing or not taking the course in research methods. Obviously, this research question is not well suited to analysis by the experimental method.

EXAMPLES OF EXPERIMENTATION AND QUASI-EXPERIMENTATION IN LIBRARY RESEARCH

In this section we discuss in some detail several experiments that have been conducted in various areas of librarianship. These examples pertain to research problems in information science, academic and public libraries, and school media centers. The purpose of examining these examples is to indicate the variety of research problems that are suited to an experimental approach and that have actually been conducted in the field. The first example is of an ex post facto study conducted by G. Edward Evans.[9]

BOOK SELECTION AND USAGE IN ACADEMIC LIBRARIES

Three common methods of selecting library materials are examined in this study, with particular attention given to the subsequent *usage* of materials that were selected by each of the three methods. The methods studied were: (*a*) faculty selection, (*b*) librarian selection, and (*c*) blanket-order approval selection.

Selection method is the independent variable in this research. The assumption underlying the research is that the purpose of a library is to develop the most useful collection possible, where useful is defined in terms of the patrons' use of library materials in the particular library in question. If it could be established that the three selection methods listed above were not equivalent insofar as subsequent patron use of materials is concerned, this information might then prove very useful in future decision making.

The working hypothesis of the study was that the group of book selectors having the greatest contact with library patrons would select materials circulating most frequently. Specifically, Evans hypothesized that in order of success in selection, the selector groups would be: librarians, faculty, jobbers. In particular, if the traditional assumption is valid that a book selector have a good knowledge of the clientele for whom he or she is selecting, then "an approval plan, unless there is a vigorous review procedure, [might be expected to] bring into the library system a high percentage of marginal (nonused) items" [p. 298].[9] Stated as a null hypothesis, the major hypothesis of the study was that there is no statistically significant difference between the success of selector groups in anticipating patron use of selected materials; that is, that these groups are equivalent in this respect.

The dependent variable, use of materials, was operationally defined in terms of circulation. Two assumptions were explicitly stated, that "recorded use is a relatively objective measure of library effectiveness," and "unrecorded use is roughly proportional to recorded use."

Because of the particular nature of this research problem, a true experiment could not be performed. For this research problem, it is impossible to assign subjects (selected materials) randomly to selection groups. The only way in which the hypothesis can be tested is through an after-the-fact, or ex post facto, analysis. Four academic institutions having the necessary records were selected. Some control was exercised over possible independent variables that might affect the outcome; the libraries shared the following characteristics: (*a*) they were American institutions of higher education; (*b*) they were 4-year institutions having graduate programs including at least one Ph.D. program; (*c*) they were located in the central third of the United States; (*d*) they had used at least two of the three methods of collection development; (*e*) they had the necessary acquisition records and were willing to allow the investigator access to these records.

A random sample of at least 500 titles was drawn for each method of selection employed at each library. A total of 6891 titles was included in the study. Each title was examined to see whether it had circulated within the first 12 months following the initial date of availability. Thus, the titles were identified as either circulating or noncirculating. The chi-square test was then used to analyze the data (see Chapter 12).

The data were found to support the hypothesis; that is, librarians did select a significantly higher percentage of circulated titles than either faculty or jobbers. Details of the study are clearly presented in the paper, to which readers are referred for further information. The author also made a number of useful suggestions for additional related studies.

THE FORMAT OF LIBRARY CATALOGS

In a study conducted by James Krikelas,[10] the effectiveness of two approaches to catalog arrangement was studied. The controversy generated by the question of whether library catalogs ought to be divided or dictionary style is not new in librarianship, but little experimental evidence has been presented in support of either view. Krikelas' study was an attempt to assess objectively the effectiveness of the two methods experimentally.

A divided catalog was operationally defined as one in which subject entries are filed in one alphabetical sequence, whereas author and title entries are filed separately into a separate alphabetical sequence. In a dictionary catalog, all entries are filed into a single sequence.

The specific hypothesis tested was that subject searches would be more effective in a divided subject catalog than in a dictionary catalog. Stated as a null hypothesis, the hypothesis tested in the study was that no significant difference would exist between the effectiveness of subject searches in a divided subject catalog and a dictionary catalog. Two university catalogs were selected for the study: one in which the catalog was dictionary style and one in which the catalog was divided. The universities were similar in size, geographical location, and reputation.

A list of search problems was compiled by random sampling from the dictionary catalog and by sampling from Library of Congress subject headings. These were pretested to examine alternative methods of wording the questions.

Subjects were randomly selected from the undergraduate populations of the two universities. Subjects were matched in pairs according to previous library experience and class standing, with one member of each pair from each of the two universities. The searching results were then treated as having been generated by a single person. Subjects were given a number of searches to perform in the catalog of their university and for each, a "success ratio"—based on whether or not the exact subject heading requested had been found—was computed.

The *t*-test was used in an analysis of the experimental data (see Chapter 12). Differences between the two sets of data were found to be not significant, and therefore the null hypothesis could not be rejected. The author concluded that in this study there was no evidence that either method of catalog organization was superior to the other. A number of related results were also reported.

THE RELATIVE PERFORMANCE OF INDEXING SYSTEMS

Some of the earliest applications of experimental methodology to librarianship and information access were conducted over a period of years by Cyril Cleverdon and his colleagues at the College of Aeronautics in Cranfield, England. The general goal of the Cranfield Projects was to evaluate the relative performance of various indexing methods and systems. In the second Cranfield project (sometimes referred to as Cranfield II, the methodology of which is summarized here), the more specific goal was to evaluate the relative effect of various "recall devices" and "precision devices"—approaches to indexing designed to improve retrieval recall and precision, respectively.[11]

Many variables might affect the performance of an information retrieval system, including the following: the way in which the patron's information need is translated to the index language; the materials comprising the document collection; the identity of the individual who judges effectiveness and the method of so judging; the efficacy of the indexing classification system used; and the effectiveness of indexers.

The null hypothesis of Cranfield II was that the various index language devices tested performed equally well. To test the hypothesis, 221 real research questions were gathered and a test collection of 1400 research papers was established. The same documents and questions were used for each of the tested index language devices; thus, these variables were controlled in the Cranfield experiments. The relevance of each of the 1400 documents with respect to each of the 221 questions was established.* All indexing was carefully performed by staff members of the College of Aeronautics Library.

Thus, all variables that might conceivably affect performance were controlled except for the pertinent independent variable—index language de-

---

* In most cases, an initial assessment of relevance was not made by the author of the research question but by postgraduate students. It has been suggested that this procedure may have introduced a systematic bias into the judging process.[12,13]

vice. The dependent variable was performance. Operationally, performance was measured by *precision*—the proportion of retrieved documents that are relevant—and by *recall*—the proportion of relevant documents that are retrieved. A single performance measure, *normalized recall,* was also used. Each index language device (as well as many combinations of these) was used to index each of the documents in the collection. Therefore, for each device, the value of the dependent variable—the performance of the device for the 221 questions—could then be assessed. Rather than conducting a formal test of the null hypothesis, the investigators reported their results in the form of a ranked list of 33 indexing languages.

COLOR AS AN INSTRUCTIONAL VARIABLE

A study conducted by Francis M. Dwyer examined the effect of color as a variable in the design of instructional materials.[14] In his introduction to the research problem, Dwyer states that very little experimental evidence exists as to how the addition of color to visual illustrations affects student achievement, although some evidence does exist and is summarized in the initial paragraphs of the paper. Dwyer hypothesized that student achievement might increase following the introduction of color on the basis of various "realism theories"—theories which assume that learning will be more complete as the number of visual cues in the learning situation increases.

The instruction was a 2000-word unit describing the parts of the human heart and some of its internal processes. The specific null hypothesis tested in the study was that there were no significant differences in achievement among students receiving nine particular methods of instruction in this unit. These treatments consisted of a control group that was given an oral presentation of the unit without visuals, and eight treatment or experimental groups given the same oral presentation complemented by slides of the heart in the following treatments: (*a*) simple line illustrations (black and white), (*b*) simple line illustrations (colored), (*c*) detailed, shaded drawings (black and white), (*d*) detailed, shaded drawings (colored), (*e*) heart model photographs (black and white), (*f*) heart model photographs (colored), (*g*) realistic heart photographs (black and white), and (*h*) realistic heart photographs (colored).

An effort was made to control independent variables that might affect the results of the instruction. All drawings and photographs were the same size and presented in the same format. The same printed symbols (arrows, etc.) were used in all slides, and the use of audio signals on an instructional tape guaranteed that the oral presentations were identical and that the oral and visual instruction was presented simultaneously for each of the treatment groups.

Members of a psychology class at The Pennsylvania State University served as subjects. Subjects were randomly assigned to one of the nine treatment groups.

As a pretest, all subjects were given a mental ability examination. Following the instruction, four different criterial tests were conducted involving: drawing, identification, terminology, and comprehension. Test scores were then combined. The five scores were operational definitions of the effectiveness of the instruction, the dependent variable. Statistical analysis of the pretests showed that the nine student groups were, for the purposes of the experiment, equivalent in mental ability. Analysis of variance was used to test students' scores in the nine treatment groups. The author reported numerous results and concluded that color does in fact significantly affect instruction in a positive way, for several of the criterial tests.

THE EFFECT OF PRIME DISPLAY ON PUBLIC LIBRARY BOOK USE

In study conducted by Herbert Goldhor, an experiment was motivated by an hypothesis that adults borrow books from public libraries primarily as a result of browsing, and that whatever facilitates browsing will significantly increase book circulation.[15] A research project was designated that made use of both experimental and field methods. An approximation of the classical four-cell experiment was set up within two medium-sized Illinois public libraries. Public libraries in the cities of Champaign and Urbana were selected because of their comparable sizes and similar collections. A list of "good books," both fiction and nonfiction, compiled by the New Haven (Connecticut) Free Public Library was used for selecting 110 titles to serve as subjects in the study. Circulation records for these titles were maintained for a 6-month pretest period. After the pretest period, Champaign was designated as the experimental library, and the selected titles were placed in a "prime location." Urbana was designated as the control library, and the books there were left in their normal shelf positions. Library employees cooperated in the experiment by keeping circulation records for the selected books. Book cards were marked with a red stripe to indicate that they were subjects of the study. Circulation assistants put aside the designated books when they were spotted in the daily circulation files, and records were collected weekly by research assistants.

The independent variable considered in the study was the location of books—whether they remained in their normal stack locations or were placed in a "prime location," special-book display near the circulation desk. The dependent variable was book usage, as measured by circulation.

After the circulation data were compiled for the second 6-month period of the study, a chi-square test was conducted to determine whether there was a statistically significant difference between book circulation in the library where titles were placed in a display and in the library where they remained on the shelves. Book circulation in the experimental library was found to be larger, and the difference was statistically significant. Thus, Goldhor concluded that a positive relationship existed in the experimental study between browsing and the number of books circulated.

Looking at the hypotheses of this research in a theoretical context, the study is related to the idea that, by placing materials in a more accessible location where they are more likely to be noticed, librarians can exercise a positive influence on the reading habits of users. Thus, one might conclude that librarians concerned with increasing circulation of "good books" should increase the opportunities for patrons to browse among strategically placed book displays. Of course, "prime display" cannot be equated with "browsing"; indeed, browsing is a complex psychological concept which the idea of prime display only begins to explicate. We might also wish that instead of, or in addition to, "good books," Goldhor had used books of marginal value or worse. The results of such a study might have been even more illuminating (and sobering) than the results of the very useful study that was actually conducted.

SUMMARY

In experimental research, the investigator carefully controls the conditions of the experiment. In the simplest (four-cell) design, subjects who are equivalent in all important respects are assigned randomly to control and experimental groups. A pretest is administered to members of both groups. Members of the experimental group are given a treatment, the operational definition of the independent variable of interest, whereas members of the control group are not subjected to the treatment. In this way, the independent variable is manipulated, and the effect on the dependent variable can be observed on members of both the experimental and control groups. This effect is revealed in a posttest, again administered to members of both groups.

The careful control exercised in the experimental method makes it the most appropriate technique to test causal relationships. Because of ethical and practical reasons, however, the experimental method often cannot be used in situations involving humans. An ex post facto analysis may be required for research problems not suited for a true experimental design.

REFERENCES

1. Fred N. Kerlinger, *Foundations of Behavioral Research: Educational and Psychological Inquiry*. New York: Holt, Rinehart and Winston, 1964, pp. 379–386.
2. D. J. Finney, *The Theory of Experimental Design*. Chicago, Ill.: University of Chicago Press, 1960, pp. 7–11.
3. Leon Festinger, "Laboratory Experiments," in Leon Festinger and Daniel Katz, eds., *Research Methods in the Behavioral Sciences*. New York: Holt, Rinehart and Winston, 1966, pp. 136–172.
4. Paul D. Leedy, *Practical Research: Planning and Design*. New York: Macmillan, 1974, pp. 147–157.
5. Donald T. Campbell and Julian C. Stanley, *Experimental and Quasi-Experimental Designs for Research*. Chicago, Ill.: Rand McNally, 1963.
6. Herbert Goldhor, *An Introduction to Scientific Research in Librarianship*. Urbana: University of Illinois, Graduate School of Library Science, 1972, pp. 166–188.
7. Abraham Bookstein, "How to Sample Badly," *Library Quarterly, 44*(April 1974):124–132.
8. George J. Mouly, *The Science of Educational Research* 2nd ed. New York: Van Nostrand Reinhold, 1970, p. 340.
9. G. Edward Evans, "Book Selection and Book Collection Usage in Academic Libraries," *Library Quarterly, 40*(July 1970):297–308.
10. James Krikelas, "Subject Searches Using Two Catalogs: A Comparative Evaluation," *College and Research Libraries, 30*(November 1969):506–517.
11. Cyril Cleverdon, "The Cranfield Tests on Index Language Devices," *ASLIB Proceedings, 19*(June 1967):173–193.
12. Stephen P. Harter, "The Cranfield II Relevance Assessments: A Critical Evaluation," *Library Quarterly, 41*(July 1971):229–243.
13. Don R. Swanson, "Some Unexplained Aspects of the Cranfield Tests of Indexing Performance Factors," *Library Quarterly, 41*(July 1971):223–228.
14. Francis M. Dwyer, "Color as an Instructional Variable," *AV Communication Review, 19*(Winter 1971):399–416.
15. Herbert Goldhor, "The Effect of Prime Display Location on Public Library Circulation of Selected Adult Titles," *Library Quarterly, 42*(October 1972):371–389.

CHAPTER 3

Survey Research in Librarianship

INTRODUCTION

Because of the widespread use of survey research methods in many disciplines, several excellent treatises on the subject have been published. A number of these books are included in the bibliography provided at the end of this chapter; most of these works, however, are not written with the needs of librarians or library school students in mind. The present chapter is designed to provide an overview of some of the essentials of survey methods with an emphasis on their application to investigations in librarianship. The supplementary bibliography at the end of this chapter lists useful manuals, guides, and articles that contain information of a more technical nature about survey design and analysis.

Librarians have long conducted "surveys." Community surveys and library surveys are associated with attempts to gather information about many aspects of libraries in whatever setting these institutions might be located (e.g., in cities, schools, etc.). The *community survey* is conducted in an attempt to gather recorded and unrecorded data about the various social, political, and economic facets of the library's community so that more intelligent decisions can be made concerning the planning, development, and conduct of services. *Library surveys* are systematic, in-depth examinations of libraries, library systems, or networks of libraries. Typically, comparisons are made in these surveys among various libraries, or units thereof, and established professional standards. A number of publications in the literature of librarianship are concerned in whole or in part with the library survey, including the following: McDiarmid's *The Library Survey*, [1] Line's *Library Surveys: An Introduction to Their Use, Planning, Procedure and Presentation;* [2] *Proceedings* of the 1967 Conference on Library Surveys, held at Columbia University [3] Erickson's *College and University Library Surveys, 1938–1952;* [4] and Tauber's "Survey Method in Approaching Library Problems" in *Library Trends*. [5] Techniques for the conduct of traditional library and community surveys are discussed further in

Chapter 6 of this text. These techniques differ from the rigorous survey research methods developed by social scientists and opinion pollsters. An excellent, but brief treatment of the more exacting methods of survey research is provided by Goldhor in his *Introduction to Scientific Research in Librarianship.*[6]

[handwritten: links the real world w. theoretical ideas.]

PRINCIPLES OF SURVEY RESEARCH

[handwritten: based on observation or experiment not Theory]

Survey research is characterized by the selection of random samples from large and small populations to obtain empirical knowledge of a contemporary nature. This knowledge allows generalizations to be made about characteristics, opinions, beliefs, attitudes, and so on, of the entire population being studied. The methods of survey research allow investigators to gather information about target populations without undertaking a complete enumeration. In some inquiries, scholars in the field are unable to interview or to question an entire group of librarians, library users, or other subjects. Instead, they select a small proportion of the population (a *sample*) and then generalize their findings to the larger group. Thus, survey research techniques can save time and money, without sacrificing efficiency, accuracy, and information adequacy in the research process. Survey research methods are used to obtain three broad classes of data: (*a*) information about incidents and developments (data about events in a given period); (*b*) information about distributions and frequencies (data concerning the possessions or characteristics of each member of a subject group); and (*c*) information about generally known rules and statuses (data about institutional norms and conditions).

Field methods used to obtain survey research data generally consist of a combination of techniques such as mail questionnaires, interviews with respondents, and participant-observation. Because the purpose of most field studies is to obtain data that will allow accurate descriptions of situations or relationships between certain variables, informational adequacy and efficiency are usually major considerations in survey research. The specific techniques used in survey research will depend upon the desired level of informational adequacy (accuracy, precision, and completeness of data) and efficiency (cost per added input of information). Seasoned investigators are generally wary of placing too much faith in any one instrument or other technique; they tend to rely upon multiple data-gathering methods.

Within librarianship, survey research methods are the most suitable techniques presently available with which to discern:

1. Whether library users (or nonusers) are pleased with a library's collection or services

2. The amount of public information about a library's collection or services
3. The kinds of information needed by library users and nonusers, as well as the sources on which people most commonly rely (books, periodicals, newspapers, radio, television, etc.)
4. Attitudes and opinions of librarians about their profession (status, practices, standards, and policies)
5. What librarians think about their status within the profession (salary adequacy, perceived influence, sex discrimination in employment, etc.)
6. Attitudes of students toward library school curricula and education for librarianship in general
7. How well library schools have prepared former students to meet the demands of actual library employment
8. The degree to which trends, new developments, and innovations are anticipated, accepted, and utilized by librarians

These questions are only limited examples of some of the research tasks in the field of librarianship that can be effectively accomplished by means of survey research.

Many of the surveys conducted by librarians could be classed as *status surveys* because they merely assay conditions in a library, such as collection size, kinds of facilities and services available, amount of financial support, use and nonuse of the library, and the composition of the library's staff. Some of these surveys are routinely conducted by state and federal library agencies; local, regional, or national library associations; school districts; commercial surveying firms; and library consultants. In general, many of these surveys have been fact-gathering in nature; they were conducted to record the status quo rather than to determine relationships between variables or to test hypotheses.

Public opinion polls conducted by commercial polling agencies such as the American Institute of Public Opinion (Gallup Poll), the Roper Poll, and the Harris Poll are examples of the application of survey research techniques, as well as the use of data collected in surveys. These polls are based upon highly developed sampling procedures that allow the selection of small groups from the nation to determine public opinion about a variety of political, social, and economic issues. Samples selected by national pollsters are often comprised of only 1500 persons; however, the information gained in these rigorously conducted studies can be very accurate.

Pollsters realize that samples need not be very large. Using the laws of probability, research workers can often predict that a probable error of only three percentage points is possible with data obtained from a relatively small nationwide random sample. For example, on the eve of the

1976 presidential election, pollster Burns Roper predicted that presidential candidate Jimmy Carter would obtain 51% of the popular vote and that President Gerald Ford would receive 47% of the votes. The actual vote was 51% for Carter and 48% for Ford, the remaining 1% going to minor candidates. In the typical sample of a political poll, the laws of probability dictate that 95 times out of 100 the reported results will be within 2.5% of what would be found if the entire population were interviewed. (This topic is treated in detail in Chapter 10.) Like other survey research techniques, polling methods have their roots in scientific efforts to estimate agricultural crop production, economic statistics, and quantitative phases of social and health surveys.

Like opinion pollsters, scientists who conduct survey research rely heavily on *representative samples*—samples that are designed to correspond with (or to match) population characteristics that are deemed to be important for the purpose of the inquiry. When samples are taken so that all members of the target population have an equal chance of being chosen, the portions selected are known as *random samples*. These samples generally represent small fractions of their parent populations. Some researchers have mistakenly assumed that randomness can be ignored provided that a very large sample is utilized. But, contrary to intuition, samples need not be very large. The accuracy of survey data is not merely a function of sample size. A classic example of mistakenly assuming that accuracy of survey research data is highly dependent upon the selection of an extremely large sample is *The Literary Digest* poll of 1936. Conducted to determine whether Roosevelt or Landon would obtain the majority of the popular vote in that year's presidential election, the poll was based upon more than 2,225,000 ballots mailed to American citizens. As a result of the collected data, editors of *The Literary Digest* predicted a Landon victory. The magazine's prediction was found to be in error by 19 percentage points, however, when the actual popular votes were counted. After that polling fiasco, survey scientists began to look more critically at mail questionnaires and sampling techniques.

At this point, perhaps we should examine some of the fundamentals of survey research, an awareness of which will enable librarians to utilize survey techniques more effectively.

POPULATIONS

The concept of a population is fundamental to survey research. A *population* is any set of persons or objects that possesses at least one common characteristic. Various survey research projects within librarianship might define the following kinds of groups as populations:

1. All directors of libraries at state-supported colleges and universities
2. All books that circulated from the collection of the Chicago Public Library during December 1978
3. All graduates of American Library Association (ALA) accredited library science master's programs during calendar year 1978
4. All chief librarians of health-science libraries
5. All blacks employed in administrative positions in public libraries in South Carolina
6. All journals and periodicals published by the ALA
7. All female librarians employed in New York City
8. All articles based upon empirical investigations and published in library science professional journals in 1970
9. All heads of technical services departments in college libraries with collections of fewer than 500,000 volumes
10. All catalog cards prepared for materials added to the collection of the University of Virginia Library between January 1 and December 31, 1975
11. All requests for information received at the reference desk of a certain public library during a single day

This list of examples indicates that populations can be very large or very small, depending upon the size of the group of persons or objects about which the researcher plans to make inferences.

PLANNING THE SURVEY

After an anticipated survey's general purpose and scope have been determined by the investigator, the following types of decisions must also be made: (*a*) the specific research question or hypothesis to be answered or tested; (*b*) the nature and extent of the population to be surveyed, including the availability of lists or rosters that identify the entire subject group; (*c*) the type and size of the sample; (*d*) the nature of the questionnaire or interview schedule, including formats and logistical techniques for questionnaire pretesting and actual distribution; and (*e*) the identification of relevant independent and dependent variables. The more attention given to even the smallest detail of a survey research project, the smoother and more successful the entire study is likely to be. Careful planning is necessary for the conduct of a successful survey. After deciding that survey techniques will be employed in a study, investigators must then consider practical problems such as the following: (*a*) interviewing costs, including the training and supervision of interviewers, if necessary; (*b*) preparation of a questionnaire (survey instrument); (*c*) printing or duplication requirements and costs for stationary and supplies; (*d*) postage requirements for both the distribution and return of questionnaires; (*e*) services needed to accomplish tasks such as the scoring, verification, and coding of responses; (*f*) computer or data processing requirements for analyses of data; (*g*) techniques for recording, reporting, and transmitting the results of the study; and (*h*) amount of financial support required for the overall project.

SOME SURVEY GUIDELINES

Social scientist Daniel Katz has provided some useful guidelines relating to survey research, including the following which are paraphrased here: (*a*) assumptions of the survey should be outlined explicitly; (*b*) survey instruments should be structured around clearly stated hypotheses; (*c*) survey research methods appropriate to the research problem of the inquiry should be used; (*d*) the sample selected in a survey should be relevant to the inquiry; (*e*) questions posed should be related and dependent; and (*f*) respondents' frames of reference should be recognized.[7] In addition to Katz's recommendations, the following suggestions for the conduct of effective and meaningful surveys can also be listed:

1. Make a thorough literature search to determine what research has already been completed on the subject and to gain a better understanding of the many facets of the problem at hand.
2. Prepare a preliminary list of research questions out of which the hypothesis of the inquiry can be developed.
3. Design the survey sample so that it is random and representative.
4. When lists of population members are prepared, obtain accurate, complete, and adequate rosters and directories; update old lists and, if necessary, eliminate duplications of names.
5. Pretest the questionnaire or other instruments among respondents who are as similar to the target population as possible.
6. When the questionnaire is distributed, include a warm, friendly— but professional—cover letter so that respondents can be properly introduced to the survey's general purpose and sponsorship.
7. Maintain high professional and ethical standards; be prepared to point out the professional, social, and scientific value of the study to respondents.

8. Provide a stamped, self-addressed envelope for the return of the survey instrument.
9. Indicate a deadline or approximate date for the questionnaire's return, or specify a time period in which survey participants are expected to reply.
10. Prepare at least one follow-up letter as well as additional questionnaires to send to subjects who have not responded by the initial deadline.
11. Do not use tricky or biased questions.
12. Keep in mind that the purpose of questionnaires and interviews is to collect research data, rather than to instruct respondents or to disseminate propaganda to research subjects.

Although some of these suggestions are self-evident and need no further explanation, others warrant additional attention; thus, the latter category will be discussed in subsequent sections of this chapter.

SELECTION OF SAMPLES

Suppose that a nationwide survey is being planned to determine the attitudes of all librarians about federal aid to libraries. A random sample can be selected from the population of academic, public, school, and special librarians included in the nationwide subject group. Furthermore, to insure that the sample is representative of all librarians in the United States, the sample might be designed so that it is comprised of the same proportions of male and female, professional and nonprofessional, employed and unemployed librarians, etc., who are members of the population. Librarians from all regions of the country—Northeast, Southwest, etc.—could also be selected according to their geographic distribution in the population. For example, if 25% of all librarians in the United States were found to be in the South, then that proportion of southern librarians could be selected for the nationwide sample. Thus, a good sample resembles its parent population; it is also large enough to allow generalizations, within measurable limits of accuracy, to the subject group from which it was selected. The more *homogeneous,* or alike, a population is with respect to pertinent characteristics or variables, the smaller the sample can be. Conversely, the more *heterogeneous,* or unlike, a population is with respect to the characteristics under study, the larger the sample can be. The degree of similarity or dissimilarity within a population should also be considered when the nature of a sample is determined.

Several methods have been devised that allow researchers to choose segments that resemble the population from which samples were taken. *Randomization,* an inferential statistical technique, allows the selection of samples so that each individual has an equal chance of being selected. When investigators have a *frame,* or list, of the members of a *universe,* or population, and can accurately place individuals into homogeneous categories or *strata,* random samples may then be selected from each stratum. This refinement of the sampling technique is called *stratification;* it usually produces a more representative sample with less variation. Consequently, both variation within the sample and the sample size can be decreased. As an aid in deciding whether to stratify, the following guideline can often be used: If there is reason to believe that the responses of homogeneous subgroups within the population might be different, then it is desirable to stratify so that a determination can be made as to whether those respondents actually differ. If there is insufficient reason to believe that the responses of subject groups will differ, however, stratification according to a particular criterion or set of criteria is unnecessary. For example, stratification according to sex of respondents would not be pertinent when there is little or no indication in a particular study that differences between females and males exist.

When survey sampling procedures are being planned, a probability model should be constructed that will allow the establishment of a tolerable error, as well as the confidence limits of the data. (This procedure is discussed in Chapter 10.) Next, the population must be accurately identified, and a frame should be prepared from which a sample (or samples) can be selected. The frame might be based upon lists of such targeted respondents as library employees, registered borrowers, library benefactors, library board members, or students. Lists, rosters, or other devices can be employed to gain access to people. After the frame has been developed, sampling procedures must be determined. Techniques that will most appropriately allow the selection of a representative sample should be used. The next consideration relates to how the data will be analyzed, and includes such matters as statistical tests and methods for the calculation of the standard error (see Chapter 10). Sampling procedures used in survey research will depend upon such factors as the nature of the study, available financial support, time constraints, and the accessibility of respondents. Suppose that researchers want to select a proportional sample of public librarians from a single state and that they would like the sample to reflect the true distribution of librarians according to their location in communities, cities, and towns of various size. Also assume that the sample is to be comprised of 45 librarians, drawn from a population of 563. Realizing that the 45 librarians in the sample must be chosen from towns and cities categorized by size, the respondents must now be se-

Table 3.1. *Selection of a Stratified Sample of Respondents from a Population of 563 Public Librarians*

Size of city	Population	Number of librarians	Percent of total	Number in sample
Very small	500–24,999	225	40.0	18
Small	25,000–99,999	118	21.0	9
Medium	100,000–399,999	79	14.0	6
Large	400,000–1,200,000	68	12.0	5
Very large	above 1,200,000	73	13.0	6
Totals		563	100.0	44

lected based upon the representations of these research subjects in population strata.

The logical approach to this task is to first determine the percentages of librarians in each population category and then to compute the number of subjects needed in the sample according to calculated percentages. For example, if 225 of the 563 librarians are located in very small towns (i.e., towns with populations between 500 and 25,000), researchers would first compute the percentage in that stratum by dividing 563 into 225 (225/563 = .40). Having already determined that the sample will consist of only 45 librarians, they would then compute the number of respondents to be included in the sample from the "very small" stratum by determining the value of 40% of 45 (45 × .40 = 18). Following the same procedure, investigators would then select the number of sample respondents from the remaining population strata. Table 3.1 contains a display of this stratified sample, based upon a sample size of 45. Note that because of round-off error, the total sample size is 44 rather than 45.

QUESTIONNAIRES

Questionnaires are often used in surveys as the primary data-collection instruments. Care must be taken to develop the kinds of questions, or survey items, that will accurately measure what the investigator wants to know. The purpose of the research is to obtain valid and reliable information so that specific hypotheses can be tested or research questions answered. The investigator should conduct a thorough search and review of all literature related to the topic under study. An examination of the underlying theories, methods, and conclusions of related studies allows a better understanding of the research problem and contributes to the conduct of a better study.

Investigators should also consult with authorities in the topical area of the research so that first-hand, additional insights, suggestions, and information can be obtained from these experts. Many of the techniques for the development of questionnaires are also applicable to survey interviews. Although questionnaires are written instruments, interviews are verbal communications between respondents and an interviewer. Some of the unique characteristics of interviews will be discussed later in this chapter. As is the case with other research methods, the mail questionnaire has both advantages and disadvantages. Investigators should weigh all of these carefully before deciding that survey questionnaires are the appropriate tools for obtaining needed research data. Some of the characteristics of this fundamental tool of survey research are outlined in the following lists.

Advantages of the Questionnaire

1. Allows a wider range and distribution of the sample than the survey interview method
2. Provides greater access to more educated respondents and to persons in higher income brackets
3. Provides an opportunity for respondents to give frank, anonymous answers
4. Allows greater economy of effort (i.e., a single instrument, duplicated and distributed to numerous respondents, can produce a large amount of data)
5. Can be constructed so that quantitative data are relatively easy to collect and analyze
6. Can be designed to gather background information about respondents, as well as original hard-to-obtain data
7. Facilitates the collection of large amounts of data in a short period of time
8. Allows the collection, in exploratory studies, of insightful information about a relatively unexplored problem area or subject
9. Can be completed at the leisure of respondents—within time limits set by the surveyor—without imposing on research subjects
10. Through the preparation of a formal instrument, researchers are encouraged to define clearly the research problem, the implications of the problem, and the nature of the needed research data
11. In regard to ego-involving questions, can enhance the collection of objective data

12. Because of its fixed format, helps to eliminate variation in the questioning process

Disadvantages of the Questionnaire

1. Precludes personal contact with respondents, perhaps causing the investigator to gain insufficient knowledge about participants in a study
2. Does not allow respondents to qualify ambiguous questions
3. If the prepared instrument does not arouse respondent emotions (i.e., when the questionnaire is too impersonal), valid responses might not be elicited
4. Poorly worded or direct questions might arouse antagonism or inhibitions on the part of respondents
5. Difficulty in obtaining responses from a representative cross-section of the target population
6. Because opinionated respondents might be more likely than other subjects to complete and return it, use of a questionnaire might lead to nonresponse bias
7. Some potential respondents may be antagonistic toward mail surveys, regardless of the purpose or quality of the instrument distributed
8. Verification of the accuracy of questionnaire responses might sometimes be difficult, or even impossible
9. Uneducated subjects might not respond to a list of printed questions
10. Most questionnaires cannot be designed to uncover causes or reasons for respondents' attitudes, beliefs, or actions

A review of the literature of survey research in librarianship will reveal that frequently questionnaires distributed by persons within the field have not been properly conceptualized or effectively designed. Potential respondents are both discouraged by and unresponsive to ill-prepared questionnaires. To illustrate, a director of a large midwestern public library once revealed to a library science research seminar that 95% of all questionnaires received by his library were automatically discarded. Although such a policy is unfortunate and contrary to a spirit of cooperation in librarianship's research efforts, investigators who conduct survey research should be aware that busy librarians are reluctant to devote time to carelessly devised and poorly worded questionnaires. Undoubtedly, the indiscriminate distribution of badly prepared questionnaires has helped to create antagonism in some quarters toward survey instruments distributed through the mail. Thus, investigators have a professional responsibility

(*a*) to analyze carefully and understand their research problems; (*b*) to state their questions clearly; (*c*) to request only information that can be easily provided by respondents; and (*d*) to place emphasis upon brevity and economy of participant effort, consistent with an adequate treatment of the subject. Care should also be taken by the researcher to word all items in a mail questionnaire so that questions are conceptually valid, promote understanding and accuracy, and encourage respondents to participate in the research.

WHAT WILL YOU ASK?

Experienced investigators are well aware that one of their most difficult tasks is gathering necessary research data. The best approach to this task appears to be the identification of as many facets of the specific research problem as possible. The recognition of pertinent factors—including the independent and dependent variables—will enable a more systematic approach to the conduct of surveys. For example, suppose that a study is planned of all factors that governed employment of a group of beginning professional librarians within several large library systems during the past 5-year period. As investigators speculate about some of the significant factors of the study, the following factual-type questions might surface:

1. How many beginning librarians were employed by the systems during the 5-year period?
2. How many applicants were rejected?
3. What was the average age of these beginning librarians?
4. What was the typical salary at which they were employed? Highest? Lowest?
5. From what library schools were the new librarians graduated?
6. How many of the librarians had earned advanced academic or professional degrees in areas other than librarianship? What are these subject areas?

Although some answers to these questions can be easily obtained from personnel records, from employers, or from the new librarians themselves, other types of hard-to-get information might be needed. Additional questions such as the following might arise:

1. How did the newly employed librarians learn of the job vacancies?
2. What influence did geographic, political, economic, or cultural conditions of the area have on decisions of applicants to seek employment in the library systems?

3. How much prior knowledge did applicants have about various characteristics of the area and the library system?
4. Did prior knowledge about the area or its library systems have a bearing on decisions to submit job applications?
5. Were the librarians actually employed in positions in which they expressed primary interest?

Answers to most of the above questions could be provided only by the successful applicants themselves; more specific questions about each concept would have to be carefully structured so that the respondents could provide the necessary data. Further speculation about various facets of the problem might produce other questions, some of which could be even more difficult to answer:

1. What search and screening procedures were utilized by the library systems?
2. Did differences exist in the employment of these techniques among the various library units? If so, what were they?
3. What exceptions, if any, were made to established selection and evaluation criteria during the screening process?
4. For what reasons were unsuccessful applicants rejected?
5. What part, if any, did letters of reference have on decisions to employ or not to employ applicants?
6. How were applicants rated by former employers, faculty members, or other persons who submitted letters of reference in support of candidates' applications?
7. What role did face-to-face interviews play in the selection process?
8. What procedures were used to make final selections of employees?

All of these preliminary research questions would be refined, restated, and pretested. Although a few could be answered on the basis of recorded information in operating policies, staff manuals, and various administrative records of the library systems, much of the needed research data would be solicited from employers or from the beginning librarians themselves. In addition, further information might be needed from persons who wrote letters of reference. In the final analysis, this study appears to be a "natural" for the survey research approach. The preparation of questions to be submitted to all participants in the employment process, including the applicants themselves, would be very important in gaining the necessary facts, opinions, reactions, and interpretations.

In this hypothetical study of library employment factors, the dependent variable might be whether an applicant was selected or rejected. Independent variables could include factors such as (*a*) the nature of evaluations vis-à-vis letters of reference; (*b*) the academic performance of candidates; (*c*) the personalities, ages, and sexes of applicants; and (*d*) other real or assumed considerations associated with the selection or rejection of library employees. A carefully designed research plan incorporating questionnaires, interviews, and evaluations from available records would probably allow the investigator to reach valid conclusions about the significant factors that led to the employment of beginning librarians in the library systems. It should be apparent that an important determinant insofar as the success of this hypothetical research project is concerned is a questionnaire or interview schedule that would ferret out the essential data. A successful analysis of the collected data might prove beneficial not only to employers—that is, the library and personnel directors—but also to library schools and placement officials.

TYPES OF QUESTIONS

The preparation of an effective questionnaire entails writing questions or items that elicit required information. Several types of questions can be utilized, including factual, opinion and attitude, information, self-perception, and standards of action. *Factual questions* normally pertain to respondents' ages, education, library experience, memberships in professional organizations, or any other pertinent, personal data needed in the study. Often, factual questions are posed in survey research so that relationships between respondent characteristics (normally, the independent variables) and the object of the study (the dependent variable) can be determined. For example, in a study of factors associated with the unionization of library employees, librarians might be asked to list the length of their library experience so that comparisons may be made between library experience and attitudes about unionization. Thus, relationships between the independent variable and the dependent variable could be examined.

When the purpose of a survey is to obtain information about respondents' beliefs, feelings, values, and related concepts, *opinion and attitude questions* can be used. Such questions are valuable to obtain measures of the direction and intensity of research subjects' opinions about a topic or attitude object. An attitude has been defined as "a relatively enduring organization of interrelated beliefs that describe, evaluate, and advocate action with respect to an object or situation, with each belief having cognitive, affective, and behavioral components."[8] In the literature of survey research considerable attention has been devoted to relationships between respondents' attitudes and actions. Many behavioral scientists agree that, although personal verbal expression cannot always be used as an accurate predictor of subsequent action, attitudes entail respondent predispositions to react to attitude objects and to guide overt behavior. Robert Brannon and Howard Schuman conducted a field experiment to determine whether respondents' attitudes could be used to accurately predict the subsequent action of these research subjects.[9] Specifically, the investigators examined the relationship between survey participants' attitudes toward open housing and their willingness to sign a petition favoring either open housing or owner's rights. More than 600 randomly selected white adults from the Detroit metropolitan area were interviewed to determine their attitudes toward an open-housing law. Three months later, the same respondents were asked to sign either one of two petitions—one favoring open housing or the other favoring owner's rights. Respondents who signed the petitions were then asked whether their names could be used in public advertising concerning the issues. When all the survey research data were analyzed, a close, positive relationship was found between respondents' attitudes and actions. And another study conducted by Alan Weinstein provided useful insights into the relationship between behavior and action.[10] The research suggests that considerations of both the attitudes toward the issue and attitudes toward related action will allow more accurate predictions of the future behavior of respondents.

Attitudes appear to be the end products of the socialization process; they are one of the most readily available indicators of how a person reacts when confronted with attitude objects in various situations or when exposed to particular dispositional variables. The following are a few examples of questions designed to elicit opinions and attitudes.

1. Is the privacy of citizens unduly threatened by the expanding accumulation of personal data through government dossiers, credit-bureau files, and computerized information storage?
   a. yes
   b. no
   c. not sure
   d. no opinion
2. What are your feelings about a new proposal to increase the amount of academic credit required by this library school for the first professional degree in library science, so that the one-year master's program can be extended an additional year?
3. Librarians should carefully control the circulation of works containing radical and dangerous ideas.
   a. strongly agree

    b. agree

    c. undecided

    d. disagree

    e. strongly disagree

4. Explain why you believe that public libraries *should* or *should not* collect and preserve local underground newspapers and periodicals.

In some types of survey research, investigators might attempt to determine how respondents know about a given topic and how or when their research subjects gained certain knowledge. In these cases, surveyors might utilize *information questions,* of which the following are examples.

1. What do you like and dislike most about the library's reference services?
2. How and when did you learn about the library's new audiovisual media department?
3. Who is president of the American Library Association?
4. When was the Library Bill of Rights first adopted by the ALA Council?
5. Why was the Resolution on Challenged Materials adopted by the ALA Council?
6. When you consult the library's card catalog, exactly how do you use it?

Researchers sometime need information about the self-perceptions of respondents. *Self-perception questions* allow individual subjects to compare their ideas or actions with those of other persons. The following questionnaire items are examples of these kinds of questions.

1. How active are you in your state library association?
    a. very active
    b. active
    c. moderately active
    d. not active at all
2. If you were asked to evaluate your success as a library director insofar as obtaining the cooperation of your library staff, how would you rate your performance?
    a. very successful
    b. successful
    c. unsuccessful
    d. very unsuccessful
    e. uncertain

3. Compare your job performance in your present position with that of the position you held in the library last year.
4. What, in your opinion, was the most outstanding accomplishment of your first year as head of the library's public services department?

In some types of surveys, investigators might attempt to determine how respondents will act in certain circumstances or how subjects feel about a new development or forthcoming event. *Standards of action questions* could provide valuable information about future respondent behavior. Some of these types of questions follow.

1. If you could vote and a referendum to increase property taxes for the support of the public library were to be submitted to citizens for their approval or disapproval, what would you do?
    a. not vote at all
    b. vote for the increase
    c. vote against the increase
    d. vote for the increase and also try to persuade others to vote for it
    e. vote against the increase and also try to persuade others to vote against it
    f. undecided
2. Traditionally, interlibrary loan services of this library have been provided only to faculty members and graduate students. Recently, that policy was changed, and interlibrary loan services were extended to undergraduate students. Do you approve or disapprove of the change? Why?

At times, questions are used that allow respondents to answer inquiries in an indirect manner by imposing their personal feelings, attitudes, or beliefs on another person or group of persons. These *projective questions* sometimes can be useful in survey research, especially in inquiries that involve sensitive or controversial topics. Frequently, a two-step question is posed, the first of a projective nature and the second more personal or direct. Some examples of projective questions follow.

1. a. Approximately what percentage of your fellow students in the library school are satisfied with the academic instruction they receive here?
   b. We would also like to know how *you* feel; so, which one of the following terms most accurately reflects your personal evaluation of the library school's instruction?
      a. excellent

    b. good
    c. adequate
    d. barely adequate
    e. bad
    f. very bad
2. a. How do most of your library colleagues here at Smallwood University feel about working under the direction of a head librarian who is a woman?
   b. Do you feel that a female library director can manage a staff of men and women as well as a male director can?
    a. yes
    b. no
    c. not sure
    d. no opinion

UNSTRUCTURED AND STRUCTURED QUESTIONS

Questions can also be classified, on the basis of form and method of response, into two major categories: unstructured and structured. *Unstructured* questions allow respondents to reply freely without having to select one of several provided responses; thus, these questions could be described as "open ended." They can be useful in exploratory studies in which various dimensions and facets of a problem are examined, but in which hypotheses are not posed and tested. The free responses solicited by unstructured questions, however, tend to produce replies that are more difficult to analyze than those of their structured counterparts. *Structured questions* are characterized by a group of provided fixed responses; survey participants are allowed to choose among several answers designed to reflect various views, beliefs, or feelings. Thus, structured questions are closed because they do not elicit unpredictable responses. When numerical weights are assigned to fixed-alternative responses, the questionnaire is said to be *precoded*. The precoding of responses facilitates the analysis of survey data. Structured questions can also enhance reliability; if they are worded poorly, however, such items can force persons to select artificial responses. Another disadvantage of structured questions is that they can allow respondents to conceal ignorance, especially in cases where questionnaire items have not been carefully prepared. On the whole, investigators tend to prefer structured questions. But, sometimes unstructured questions are also used in a supplementary manner to obtain five response dimensions (*quintamensional responses*). For example, the typical approach employed by opinion pollsters incorporates the following combination of questions.

1. *Filter question*—determines whether a person is qualified to respond intelligently to a series of survey questions
2. *Open-ended question*—allows the respondent to freely discuss personal views or opinions
3. *Directional question*—reveals whether the respondent is favorably or unfavorably disposed toward the topic or object of the inquiry
4. *Intensity question*—allows respondents to show the depth of their feelings
5. *Why question*—designed to reveal reasons why respondents feel the way they do

Thus, assume that you are conducting a study to determine what a group of librarians thinks about *Library Journal,* a widely circulated professional journal of discussion, published by the R. R. Bowker Company. Using the quintamensional approach, the following questions might be posed.

1. How often do you read *Library Journal?*
2. What are your general views about *Library Journal?*
3. Everything considered, how would you rate *Library Journal?*
   a. an excellent periodical
   b. a good periodical
   c. a passable periodical
   d. not much of a periodical
4. How much do you feel that you really need *Library Journal?*
   a. not at all
   b. not much
   c. some
   d. very much
5. Why do you read *Library Journal?*

CAUTIONS CONCERNING QUESTIONS AND QUESTIONNAIRES

Experienced investigators are aware of numerous general misuses of questionnaires. Poorly worded questions in survey instruments have also been recognized by both the recipients of ill-prepared questionnaires and the critics of research in librarianship. The preparation of questionnaires is often the most critical—yet frequently the most underemphasized—part of research. Unfortunately, a widespread attitude among inexperienced survey research workers in the field has been the predisposition to compile a list of ill-prepared questions, to incorporate them into a hastily designed form, and to then label the resulting product a developed research instrument. But little valuable information is yielded when scant attention has been devoted to a critical appraisal of the research problem, to the exact nature of the needed survey data, or to the survey questionnaire itself. Therefore, some precautions concerning the preparation of questions and questionnaires will be outlined in this section for the benefit of inexperienced surveyors.

First, the objectives of the questionnaire and the nature of needed data must be precisely determined. The abilities and knowledge of respondents must also be considered. If the targeted survey participants do not possess the experience or knowledge to respond to questions, valid data will not be collected. Similarly, if research subjects are unwilling to provide the needed information, questionnaires will be of no value. Thus, the motivational and comprehension levels of the population to be surveyed should guide the content, degree of complexity, and length of the questionnaire. Questions used in a survey must also be applicable to all respondents, insofar as possible. All items should also be used to gather the specific research data desired. When unneeded or irrelevant questions are posed, some potential participants might become discouraged and fail to return the survey instrument.

Adept investigators carefully pare away excess verbiage in questions. The language used in all survey items should be concise and designed to elicit uniform data from the survey participants. A useful practice often followed in this respect is the shortening of questionnaire items by eliminating words without loss of meaning. The use of subjective and emotionally charged words in questions must also be avoided. Furthermore, the wording of questionnaire items must not be unfair or tricky. Another problem to be on guard against is unintentional bias. For example, leading questions can make one response more likely than another, no matter what the survey participant's feelings or opinions may actually be. Of course, serious investigators do not deliberately pose biased questions; however, bias has a way of creeping into questionnaires, even though the researcher may attempt to be objective. A subtle form of bias may be interjected into questions in which authority figures are cited. For example, an item such as "Do you agree with Senator Jones that the Library Finance Act should be amended to include libraries in state-supported colleges?" might attract more support than the direct question "Do you believe that the Library Finance Act should be amended . . . ?" Careful and repeated readings of all questionnaire items will often reveal problem words or phrases of potential difficulty to respondents. Moreover, pretests of survey instruments under realistic conditions can further aid in the identification of biased questions.

Ambiguous questions must also be avoided; a single item that actually addresses itself to more than one issue may elicit extremely confusing and unreliable data. Therefore, questionnaire items that convey double meanings or pose two questions at once ought to be restated or eliminated. For example, two issues are raised by the following poorly worded question: "Do you favor a decrease in property taxes at the local level for an increase in state aid to public libraries?" The first issue raised in this item is that of reducing local property taxes; the second pertains to state-aid to libraries as a means of effecting a local tax reduction. To eliminate this double-barreled approach, two or more items should be prepared to elicit the information that an ambiguous question is unlikely to obtain.

Other problems to avoid when survey items are written pertain to the selection of fixed-alternative responses for structured questions. First, research subjects may feel that a question has an expected or automatic answer. Therefore, questions should be worded so that respondents are at ease, whether their reply is "yes" or "no," "agree" or "disagree," "approve" or "disapprove," and so on. Still another problem to anticipate as questionnaires are prepared is that of positional or ordinal bias. Such bias is sometimes encountered when surveyors employ horizontal rating scales based upon a group of fixed responses such as "strongly agree, agree, disagree, strongly disagree." The order of these kinds of response alternatives should be reversed for randomly selected items in the questionnaire. The breaking up of response alternative patterns can discourage the tendency of some survey respondents to choose answers on the basis of position, whether the selected responses are located on the right, in the middle, or on the left of a continuum of provided replies.

Additional Suggestions for Questions and Questionnaires

Depending upon the nature and scope of the survey to be conducted, the following list of suggestions may also aid surveyors who wish to further improve the quality of their questionnaires.

1. Unless the nature of a survey definitely warrants their usage, avoid slang, jargon, and technical terms.
2. Whenever possible, develop consistent response methods.
3. Make questions as impersonal as possible.
4. Do not bias later responses by the wording used in earlier questions.
5. As an ordinary rule, sequence questions from the general to the specific.
6. If closed questions are employed, try to develop exhaustive and mutually exclusive response alternatives.

7. Insofar as possible, place questions with similar content together in the survey instrument.
8. Make the questions as easy to answer as possible.
9. When unique and unusual terms need to be defined in questionnaire items, use very clear definitions.
10. Use an attractive questionnaire format that conveys a professional image.

Should additional information be needed about the preparation of questions and questionnaires, readers are refered to the selected bibliography of sources about survey research methods at the end of this chapter.

SCALING FIXED RESPONSES

As noted previously, investigators often use scaled, fixed responses to measure the intensity of views held by people. Many structured questions are multiple-choice items, and respondents are asked to choose the "best" or "most appropriate" of several options. Numerical values assigned to precoded replies are based upon one or more of the following factors: (a) judgments of experts in the area of the inquiry; (b) established professional standards or principles for certain operations or behavior; or (c) prior research which has verified that a particular response has more positive, neutral, or negative content in relation to the topic under consideration. Precoding of scaled responses is undertaken carefully in survey research so that the validity and reliability of the data are enhanced. Many questions with fixed responses are similar to items in Likert-type scales; each has been assigned a numerical ranking based on a continuum that contains predetermined units of measurement. Likert-type scales are designed to show a differentiation among respondents who have a variety of opinions about an attitude object. Examples of these questions follow.

1. Should your library be damaged by a tornado and closed for a 2-week period, how much would you miss the library?
   a. a very great deal   (weight = 4)
   b. quite a lot   (weight = 3)
   c. not very much   (weight = 2)
   d. not at all   (weight = 1)
2. On the whole, how would you rate the quality of your library's book collection?
   a. very poor collection   (weight = 1)
   b. poor collection   (weight = 2)
   c. adequate collection   (weight = 3)

    d. good collection   (weight = 4)

    e. very good collection   (weight = 5)

Notice that the weight assigned to each of these responses hinges upon whether the reply is favorable or unfavorable to the pertinent concept (the attitude object). In both of the examples provided, choices that are most favorable to libraries are assigned the greatest weights, and the least favorable responses are assigned the lowest weights. The numerical values enclosed in parentheses in these examples should not be included on the survey instrument itself, because weights might influence respondents to choose replies that do not reflect their true feelings.

Scores for all questionnaire items with fixed and precoded responses are summed for each survey participant. Note that some respondents might obtain the same *summated* rating, or overall score, on a set of questionnaire items, even though they chose different fixed responses for various items. Participants who have generally selected the same responses to similar items, however, could be said to have related attitudes or opinions. Additional questions modeled after the Likert scale are provided below. The examples represent items that would be used in different scales. Furthermore, each item would be supplemented with additional, related questions.

1. What is your library's policy on unanswered requests for information when no further material is available on the pertinent subject in the library's collection?
   a. make no attempt to follow up and to obtain an answer (weight = 1)
   b. suggest resources of another library   (weight = 2)
   c. make an attempt to obtain the answer from other libraries (weight = 3)
2. A censorship controversy over a single book or magazine is not worth the adverse public relations that it could cause for the library.
   a. strongly disagree   (weight = 5)
   b. disagree   (weight = 4)
   c. undecided   (weight = 3)
   d. agree   (weight = 2)
   e. strongly agree   (weight = 1)
3. Does a person's prestige or status in your community affect the treatment that he/she receives at the public library?
   a. yes, a lot of difference   (weight = 4)
   b. yes, some difference   (weight = 3)
   c. no, very little   (weight = 2)
   d. no, none at all   (weight = 1)

Summated rating scales are constructed by first collecting a large number of statements relating to all facets of the subject under study (the attitude object). Both positive (favorable) and negative (unfavorable) statements are used. All the statements should be closely related to the attitude being measured; they should also be stated in a simple, straightforward manner so that the likelihood of ambiguity is eliminated. After the questions have been carefully edited, fixed-alternative responses are then assigned to each item. Responses might consist of words or phrases such as those provided in previous examples, or they could be similar to the following.

yes, certainly	poor	very adequate
yes, probably	fair	fairly adequate
undecided	not sure	adequate
no, probably not	good	inadequate
no, certainly not	very good	very inadequate

To conceal the exact intent of the survey research and the system of measurement devised for the scale, favorable responses to various concepts should be assigned high values in approximately one-half of the items and low values in the remainder. In addition, the location of items in the questionnaire itself should be based upon a random assignment.

Newly developed questionnaires ought to be pretested among respondents who are similar to the population that is targeted for the anticipated survey project. The number of respondents in the pretest should be between 80 and 100 for an effective analysis of questions. After the pretest, questionnaires are then scored according to the devised system. Items that do not discriminate between high- and low-scoring respondents should be eliminated from the survey instrument. Although some of the nondiscriminatory items might be recognized readily, others can be identified accurately by the use of statistical procedures such as the *t*-test or phi coefficient. The final survey instrument should include only those prepared items which the pretest showed to be highly discriminatory.

SEMANTIC DIFFERENTIAL SCALE

Another type of structured question is one that provides pairs of antonyms and synonyms, together with seven-step rating scales. The word pairs refer to an attitude object, and respondents are asked to check one of the positions on each continuum between the most positive and the most negative terms. This type of scale is often called a *semantic differential*. The following question (with sample responses) is an example of the use and scoring of the seven-step semantic differential rating scale.

Question: How would you rate the performance of the head of your department in the library during the past year?

				Evaluation of performance				
	(1)	(2)	(3)	(4)	(5)	(6)	(7)	
Bad	—	—	—	—	—	×	—	Good
Disorganized	—	—	—	×	—	—	—	Organized
Unfair	—	—	—	—	×	—	—	Fair
Uncertain	—	—	×	—	—	—	—	Resourceful
Erratic	—	—	—	×	—	—	—	Systematic
Preoccupied	—	—	—	—	—	×	—	Observant
Harsh	—	—	—	—	×	—	—	Gentle
Outspoken	—	—	×	—	—	—	—	Reserved
Withdrawn	—	—	—	—	—	×	—	Outgoing
Submissive	—	—	—	×	—	—	—	Dominant
Totals	0	0	6	12	10	18	0	

To obtain the respondent's overall rating of the performance of the department head, sum the total values of each column and divide by the number of continuum rows ($6 + 12 + 10 + 18 = \frac{46}{10} = 4.6$). Thus, the overall rating from this single instrument is 4.6, which falls on the low-positive side of the rating scale. The following questionnaire item is a variation of the semantic differential rating scale.

Question: How important are the following to you as a library school faculty member?

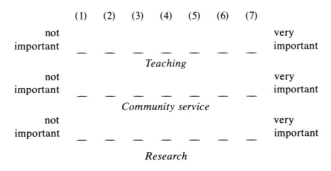

INTERVIEWS

In survey research, the search for new information is by no means limited to the use of questionnaires. As the purpose of surveys is to acquire current—rather than historical—information about such factors as the experiences and opinions of people, the interview also serves as a useful survey tool. Some investigators attest to the superiority of the interview technique over mail questionnaires, claiming that verbal communications with research subjects elicit significantly more complete answers to questions than a printed survey instrument. When researchers conduct interviews, they are attempting to gain information from persons who are able to provide research data. The information may be about the respondents themselves—their experiences, their opinions or attitudes, their reactions to trends and developments, their knowledge, etc. Verbal responses of the interviewee are often valuable, original evidence or research data. Skilled investigators can gain useful insights during interview situations, both from what is said and from what is not said. However, interviews can be very time-consuming and expensive. In addition, the investigator must arrange appointments and meet with the interviewee at the latter's convenience. When a large number of respondents are to be interviewed, the principal investigator must often train research assistants so that they are qualified for the task. These research assistants will also require supervision if the survey is to be conducted in a careful manner. Thus, one ought to cautiously weigh the advantages and disadvantages of mail questionnaires and interviews before deciding to use one or the other of these survey research techniques.

Although interviews are most successful when they are conducted in an informal, relaxed manner, the interviewer must be well prepared before the questioning process begins. Interviews are often unpredictable; thus, a researcher who is not prepared may run the risk of failing to collect necessary information. Skilled interviewers carefully plan their questions in advance. Although the researcher may not rely upon a visible questionnaire or checklist during the actual interview session, the interviewer should know exactly what questions are going to be asked, in what sequence the questions will be posed, and the method by which the data will be accurately recorded. All interviewers should be so familiar with their questions that interrogations can be conducted without constant referral to checklists of items. Well-planned interviews and carefully worded questions usually produce the most useful information, as well as supplementary, insightful observations and opinions from respondents. The following suggestions are offered for the conduct of succesful interviews.

1. Be thoroughly prepared in advance; know the topic and purpose of the survey so well that questions will elicit the desired research data.
2. Be friendly and courteous, and put the respondent at ease throughout the interview session.

3. Approach all respondents as individuals; assure them that their views are valuable and of significance to the survey being conducted.
4. Ask only one question at a time, making sure that each is concise and clear.
5. Do not attempt to put words into respondents' mouths; the purpose of the interview is to obtain the views of respondents rather than those of research workers who conduct interviews.
6. Do not react to respondents' replies by expressing approval, disapproval, surprise, or shock; always be appreciative of whatever information the respondent provides.
7. Do not directly dispute respondents, even though you may know or suspect that their replies are inaccurate.
8. Do not argue with respondents or condemn their views.
9. Be neutral in recording responses so that the collected data are accurate and objective.
10. Upon completion of interview sessions, express gratitude to the survey participants for their cooperation and assistance.

REVIEW OF COMPLETED
SURVEY RESEARCH

Apart from the conduct of library and community surveys and the utilization of status survey techniques, researchers in librarianship have employed survey research methods to test relationships between variables and to make generalizations about various library and information phenomena. Some survey research has been very effective. In the following sections of the chapter, a few successful projects that were based upon survey methods will be examined. Perhaps these examples will be useful in future research and help the reader gain a better understanding of how investigators have adapted survey methods to a variety of library-related topics and problems.

INFORMATION NEEDS OF RESEARCH ECONOMISTS

Utilizing survey research methods, Marilyn White studied the communication behavior of research economists in academic settings.[11] White attempted to specify the economists' behavior, as well as the channels they used to obtain information and the purpose for seeking data in three developmental stages of their research process: problem, methodology, and presentation. The investigator posed the hypothesis that academic economists change their communication behavior during the conduct of research projects. A self-administered questionnaire was distributed to 294 economists at 10 large universities. The survey instrument was devised to determine: (a) the ability of information systems to transmit various types of data, (b) the types of information needed to complete research tasks during several investigative stages, and (c) the degree to which subjects increase their knowledge as they carry out their research activities. Theoretical implications of the White study are that university librarians must take into account various information needs of research scholars. The focus of the study also implies that librarians ought to be more intimately involved in research activities in the academic community so that information needs of scholars can be anticipated and fulfilled. White identified seven information functions in each of the three research stages noted above, as well as the behavior patterns of research economists associated with each of the information functions. She concluded that information-gathering behavior of academic economists changes as they carry out inquiries. White also speculated that certain types of information—particularly that related to theoretical considerations—are more difficult for librarians to handle, and, as a result, the research economist is inclined to turn to other, more personal sources of knowledge.

LABOR UNIONS AND LIBRARIANS

Gail Schlachter's study of the attitudes of selected librarians toward unionism and professionalism was based upon a mail survey among a stratified random sample of 884 academic librarians.[12] The study was designed to determine: (a) whether professional library staff members are able to bargain successfully with employers, (b) whether labor unions are attracting librarians, and (c) whether the American Library Association can maintain its position as the dominant professional organization for librarians without becoming a "quasi union." The Schlachter survey challenged the traditional assumption that librarians are self-sacrificing, unaggressive, and indisposed to engage in labor union activities. The study concluded that librarians prefer to affiliate with a professional association turned part-labor-union (a collective bargaining organization), rather than with a traditional labor union.

PUBLISHERS AND DISCRIMINATION IN CHILDREN'S BOOKS

Paul Cornelius conducted an investigation of the problems and progress associated with interracial children's books.[13] The study utilized data that were collected earlier in a survey among 70 publishers of children's books. Surveyed publishers were members of the Childrens Book Council, all of whom had released trade books in the period 1962–1964. Cornelius' research was conducted to answer the following specific questions: (*a*) Why were racial minority groups inadequately represented in literature for children in the 1960s? and (*b*) What steps were being taken by publishers to redress racial imbalance in their books? Of the 70 publishers invited to participate in the survey, 63 responded. The publisher-respondents had released a total of 5206 children's books in the 4-year period covered by the survey; however, only 349 of these works (6.7%) included one or more black characters. Furthermore, only 44 of the 349 books were about blacks in contemporary society. This survey research and subsequent hearings in the U.S. House of Representatives served to create more interest in the topic of minority representation in works published for children. Presently, numerous interracial books—many by minority writers themselves—are available from most of the publishers who had reported no interracial titles in this study.

CITIZENS' ATTITUDES TOWARD A PUBLIC LIBRARY

In an attempt to determine the attitudes of California citizens about a public library and how their attitudes are related to actual use of the library, Charles W. Evans conducted a mail survey among registered voters in Oceanside.[14] The questionnaire-based study was undertaken to assess the role of the public library in meeting the informational, educational, recreational, and cultural needs of individual citizens and groups, as well as the responsibility of the library staff to determine both how the library can best serve its constituency and how it can attract nonusers. More than 500 usable questionnaires that contained a 16-statement, Likert-type attitude scale were returned by 367 library users and 153 nonusers. The dependent variable of the study was library usage—that is, whether respondents had or had not used the library; independent variables were respondents' educational levels, sex, duration of residence in the city, and attitudes toward the library. In a test of the hypothesis that a significant difference would be found between the attitudes of users and nonusers toward the library, Evans concluded that the opinions of nonusers about the library were less favorable than those of library users. On the other hand, serious dissatisfaction with the library was not found to be related to nonuse. But the investigator concluded that less favorable attitudes toward the library may discourage library usage.

QUALITY OF SCHOOL LIBRARY SERVICE

In her study of the relationship between school librarians' formal education and the quality of high-school library service in eight Illinois school libraries, Lucille Wert utilized survey research methods and other techniques.[15] The study centered around the question of whether a direct, positive relationship existed between the amount of formal education completed by librarians and the nature of the librarians' on-the-job performance. Librarians in four of the school libraries targeted for the research had obtained master's degrees in library science; the other four librarians had completed undergraduate minors, or less, in library science. The study made use of the following data-gathering techniques: questionnaires completed by students and teachers (evaluations of libraries and their services); interviews with librarians, school administrators, and teachers; observation of each library program; daily records of librarians' activities; and a checklist of reader services that were offered by libraries. Wert concluded from the data gathered by these methods that librarians with higher education attainment levels had developed more extensive reader services which were used more frequently by students and teachers than were library programs directed by less-educated librarians. Unfortunately, the sample of surveyed libraries in this inquiry was very small; therefore, conclusions of the study cannot be generalized to a larger group of school libraries.

USER FAILURE AT THE LIBRARY CARD CATALOG

A study of user failure at the library card catalog was conducted by Carol Seymour and J. L. Schofield to determine the extent of the problem and various reasons for failures.[16] Survey research methods were utilized to determine whether the card catalog was beneficial, in what respects it was not useful, and to suggest methods of improving catalog information services. Conducted by the Library Management Research Unit at Cambridge University in England, the study was accomplished in four libraries: Cambridge University Library, Leicester University Library, London University Institute of Education Library, and Bradford University Social Science Library. Catalog query slips were distributed in the catalog areas of these libraries, and library users were encouraged to complete the slips when a desired item could not be located in the catalog. The slips were designed to obtain information about the nature of the search (e.g., author, title, reader's status, etc.). Collected daily, the slips were checked to ascertain whether readers had made mistakes during catalog searches. Interviews with catalog users were also conducted daily during two periods of peak catalog usage to determine: (*a*) whether user searches had resulted in success or failure, and (*b*) to identify what steps users might take to obtain the sought-after library materials. The study proved to be beneficial; it allowed the systematic measurement of the usage of the public card catalog and patron success with the library's primary bibliographic tool.

ANALYSIS OF LIBRARY JOB TASKS

Survey research was also employed by Leslie Rothenberg and others in an attempt to develop a job-task index to measure the division of labor in health-science libraries.[17] This human resource utilization study was initiated jointly by the University of Texas Medical School and Case Western Reserve University. A total of 4727 institutions within the health sector were first identified and characterized by type, ownership, health involvement, and geographic location. In addition, staff levels and unfilled budgeted positions of the libraries were ascertained. A total of 14,938 professional and nonprofessional employees comprised the survey's universe. Investigators constructed a job-task index, based upon an abbreviated inventory of 27 library-related tasks. The index was combined with a scale designed to measure each respondent's involvement with the tasks. For example, a positive score on the scale indicated a greater involvement on the part of respondents with professional, rather than nonprofessional, job tasks. Four job-task groups were categorized with the index: (*a*) high professional; (*b*) low professional; (*c*) high nonprofessional; and (*d*) low nonprofessional. The degree of professionalism assigned to each job task on the index was determined by assessing the amount of formal education necessary for the adequate performance of specific duties. Theoretical implications of the research appeared to be that a system of job descriptions and career guidelines for all employment levels would facilitate measurement of librarians' performance in relation to education, experience, and related factors.

A mail questionnaire was distributed to a sample of 4000 professional and nonprofessional librarians selected from 116 libraries that employed five or more staff members. Responses of these librarians were then distributed over a nine-point professional–nonprofessional scale. This method revealed an overlap of duties performed by the two groups of librarians. Using the collected data, Rothenberg and her associates also recognized a general distinction between the jobs of professional and non-professional library employees; however, they concluded that many health-science librarians held positions that were inconsistent with their professional statuses, incomes, and ages. The survey also revealed that professionals in the health-science field often moved laterally into jobs similar to those they previously held, rather than upward into positions of greater responsibility. Because of the revealed misuse of human resources, the investigation underscored a general loss of professional talent, as well as a decrease in the status of health-science librarians.

Interlibrary Loan Networks among School Libraries

Ellen Altman's study of the feasibility of establishing interlibrary loan networks among secondary school libraries incorporated survey research techniques, among other methods.[18] As a basis for making predictions, a model interlibrary loan network was developed. The model allowed estimates to be made concerning title and volume increases that could be expected should New Jersey schools pool their book collections and form a network. Four hypotheses were tested: (a) the polling of books will increase net title resources by 700%; (b) the polling of collections will produce a net volume increase of 1200 items for the median library; (c) small school libraries can contribute to an interlibrary loan network because these libraries do not entirely duplicate library collections in larger schools; and (d) title diversity of a school library interlibrary loan network will exceed that of any single public library in the counties within the geographic area of the study. To test these hypotheses, a sample of 31 schools was selected from two New Jersey counties that approximated state averages in regard to size of library collection, books per student, and per-capita expenditure. Through interviews and questionnaires, teachers and librarians identified topics selected for student papers and independent study projects.

All 31 librarians and 60.4% of the teachers in the selected schools participated in the survey. As a basis for analysis, the 12 most popular study topics were chosen. The topics were assigned Dewey classification numbers so that library shelf-lists could be checked for book holdings in the pertinent subject areas. Based upon these data, a computer analysis projected the number of titles and volumes potentially available in various types and sizes of library pools. The study concluded that schools could increase title and volume diversity substantially by pooling library resources. The predicted net title and volume increases were corroborated by the collected data. Titles that were unique to one or two libraries figured largely in the collections; title diversity in three of the four school libraries exceeded that of any one public library in the two selected New Jersey counties. Altman concluded that the most effective school interlibrary loan network would be comprised of between 40 and 50 libraries.

CENSORSHIP ATTITUDES IN THE MIDWEST

Survey research methods were employed by Charles H. Busha in a study of the attitudes of midwestern public librarians toward intellectual freedom and censorship. [19] The research was based upon a mail questionnaire distributed under the title "Opinion Survey of Midwestern Public Librarians." The survey was conducted to determine (a) the relationship between librarians' attitudes toward intellectual freedom and censorship, and (b) the relationship between pro- and anticensorship attitudes and such librarian characteristics as age, education, position, state of employment, and size of the community of employment. In other words, the purpose of the survey was to obtain a measure of respondents' agreement with abstract concepts of intellectual freedom, as well as a measure of their agreement with these concepts when they were made "operative" through situational and other dispositional variables outlined in items of the questionnaire. Attitude scales were utilized by Busha to measure three dependent variables: the degree to which librarians approve of (a) intellectual freedom principles; (b) censorship practices; and (c) authoritarian ideas. Items of the three attitude scales were interspersed in one survey instrument to prevent respondents from recognizing the exact nature and purpose of the sensitive survey. A stratified random sample of 900 persons was selected from a population of 3153 librarians employed in Illinois, Indiana, Michigan, Ohio, and Wisconsin (east north–central states). All respondents were either library directors, assistant directors, heads of branches, heads of public service departments, or heads of subject, extension, or technical services departments. To obtain a more representative group of respondents, the investigator stratified the sample by state and city population-size categories. A total of 684 (or 76%) of the distributed questionnaires was returned by respondents; 624 of the completed instruments were usable.

Responses of librarians were quantified (scored) according to a prearranged scoring system. For example, responses to each item in the questionnaire had been assigned a weight based upon whether the statement was favorable or unfavorable to the attitude objects. A high overall score on certain questionnaire items indicated that respondents favored censorship. Scored responses were then converted into machine-readable form; correlational and analysis of variance methods were next used to test hypotheses statistically. These methods produced the following results: (a) significant and positive relationships existed between pro-censorship and pro-authoritarian attitudes; (b) positive relationships were found between independent variables (i.e., respondents' age, education, sex, etc.) and the attitudes of the subjects toward censorship and authoritarianism;

and (c) 14% of the librarians were very favorable to censorship, 22% were_ strongly opposed to censorship, and 64% were somewhat neutral, expressing neither approval nor disapproval of censorship practices.

Job Satisfaction among Librarians

American and Canadian participants in a motivational workshop completed a survey questionnaire which solicited information about the times that respondents felt "particularly good" or "particularly bad" about their library jobs and the reasons for such feelings.[20] The survey research was based upon Herzberg's "motivation-hygiene theory." It was part of an inquiry conducted by Kenneth Plate and Elizabeth Stone to study factors that affected librarians' job satisfaction. The investigators attempted to identify factors that produced job satisfaction and dissatisfaction, expecting work-process factors to be closely related to employee motivation. Results of the study indicated that motivators were the primary cause of job satisfaction; environmental factors were found to be the primary cause of job dissatisfaction. The study identified primary motivators, in the order of their significance, as achievement, recognition, the work itself, responsibility, advancement, and personal growth. Environmental ("hygiene") factors identified were institution policy, supervision, interpersonal relationships, working conditions, status, salary, and security.

Library Catalog Use at Yale

At Yale University, Ben-Ami Lipetz sought, by means of survey research, to determine the volume of library catalog use, the degree to which users achieved success at the catalog, and knowledge about needed improvements in the conventional card catalog.[21] The overall purpose of the study was to produce information to help librarians make decisions concerning the computerization of catalog data. For more than a year, Lipetz first observed traffic through the library's catalog area. Based upon these observations, an interview schedule was devised, and a traffic volume profile by hour of day, day of week, and time of year was then constructed. A questionnaire was also prepared to elicit the following needed data; (a) academic status of users (undergraduate or graduate student, faculty, etc.); (b) user's knowledge of the catalog; and (c) type and method of catalog search conducted during a 1-year period. Respondents were also interviewed to determine the degree of success that had been achieved. The data collected in this study of catalog use were analyzed with the aid of a computer as follows: (a) analysis of traffic at the catalog so that a pattern of demand on the facilities could be constructed, and (b) an analysis of the interview data to determine the objectives and degree of catalog search success. Although the study did not produce sufficient data to identify when a traditional card catalog should be computerized, it provided a vehicle to work toward that goal. The data support Lipetz's conclusion that knowledge of users' needs is valuable in developing an effective catalog (one that produces a high search success rate).

SELECTION OF POETRY IN ELEMENTARY SCHOOLS

Chow Loy Tom conducted a nationwide survey to determine how teachers choose poetry to read aloud to students.[22] A questionnaire was designed to elicit the following information: (a) titles of poems read in elementary school classes; (b) subjects of selected poems; (c) frequency of classroom use of poetry; and (d) professional preparation of teachers. A representative sample of 1040 teachers in elementary schools was selected from the states of Delaware, Vermont, West Virginia, and Arizona—these states represented four national geographical regions (Southeast, North Atlantic, Great Lakes, and Southwest). The sample was selected from a list of school districts and their fourth, fifth, and sixth grades in each state. Among the questionnaires returned, 582 were usable. The collected data revealed that 893 poems had been read by teachers to students; the most frequently used poem was "Paul Revere's Ride." The survey also produced the following disclosures: (a) teachers read a relatively small group of popular poems; (b) teachers depend primarily upon standard literature texts as sources of these poems; (c) the most frequently used poems were written prior to the twentieth century; and (d) many teachers were unfamiliar with modern poetry. The survey also revealed inadequate preparation on the part of many middle-grade teachers in oral poetry interpretation, selection of poetry, and poetry appreciation. An implication of this survey research project is that teachers and librarians should cooperate more in the selection and utilization of poetry collections developed for school libraries and media centers.

SUMMARY

Many of the so-called "library surveys" conducted in the field are status surveys, designed to describe the status quo—that is, existing library practices, circumstances, systems, services, institutions, etc. Although these types of studies can be useful as evaluative tools or vehicles for making improvements in libraries, they are not designed for testing hypotheses or for careful examination of relationships between variables. Survey research is characterized by the use of the following techniques of inquiry: (*a*) selection of representative, random samples of persons, objects, or other identifiable units from pertinent populations; (*b*) questioning and examining these samples through carefully planned interviews, questionnaires, attitude tests, or periods of observation to obtain information which can then shed light on research questions or be used to test hypotheses; and (*c*) analysis of data to show "how things happen" or how pertinent variables are related. Surveyors select samples in which characteristics of respondents or units are matched with populations. Samples of respondents are usually chosen in a manner that allows each member of the population an equal chance of being selected. Thus, samples are typically random and often very small segments of target populations. Even though samples are normally relatively small, precise techniques of selection and measurement allow the data to be extrapolated or generalized to a larger group.

Survey research has been used extensively in the social and behavioral sciences. Many studies in librarianship have also relied upon the survey approach. These surveys have allowed scholars to obtain contemporary data about the attitudes and opinions of librarians, the utilization of library services and collections, the roles of librarians in all types of libraries, and many other kinds of information relating to various facets of the profession. The primary components of survey research include such instruments and methods as questionnaires, interviews, tests, random and stratified samples, and a variety of statistical procedures to test hypotheses. Investigators must give careful attention to rigorous methods that have been developed to structure each component of the survey research process. Although the published literature of survey research is rather extensive, the selected bibliography for this chapter contains useful articles and books that could be valuable to librarians as they plan and conduct surveys.

REFERENCES

1. Errett W. McDiarmid, *The Library Survey: Problems and Methods*. Chicago, Ill.: American Library Association, 1940.
2. Maurice B. Line, *Library Surveys: An Introduction to Their Use, Planning, Procedure and Presentation*. New York: Archon Books, 1967.
3. *Proceedings* of the Conference on Library Surveys. New York: Columbia University Press, 1967.

4. Ernst W. Erickson, *College and University Library Surveys, 1938–1952* (unpublished doctoral dissertation, University of Illinois, 1958).
5. Maurice F. Tauber, "Survey Method in Approaching Library Problems," *Library Trends, 13*(July 1964):15–30.
6. Herbert Goldhor, *An Introduction to Scientific Research in Librarianship.* Champaign, Ill.: Illini Union Bookstore, 1969, pp. 116–140.
7. Daniel Katz, "The Functional Approach to the Study of Attitudes," *Public Opinion Quarterly, 24*(1960):167.
8. Milton Rokeach, "The Nature of Attitudes," in *International Encyclopedia of the Social Sciences.* Vol. 1. New York: Macmillan and the Free Press, 1968, p. 457.
9. Robert Brannon and Howard Schuman, "Attitude and Action: A Field Experiment Joined to a General Population Survey," *American Sociological Review, 38*(October 1973):625–636.
10. Alan G. Weinstein, "Predicting Behavior from Attitudes," *Public Opinion Quarterly, 36*(Fall 1972):355–360.
11. Marilyn D. White, "The Communications Behavior of Academic Economists in Research Phases," *Library Quarterly, 45*(October 1975): 337–354.
12. Gail Schlachter, "Quasi Unions and Organizational Hegemony Within the Library Field," *Library Quarterly, 43*(July 1973):185–197.
13. Paul Cornelius, "Interracial Children's Books: Problems and Progress," *Library Quarterly, 41*(April 1971):106–127.
14. Charles W. Evans, *The Attitudes of Adults Toward the Public Library, and Their Relationships to Library Use* (unpublished doctoral dissertation, University of California, Berkeley, 1969).
15. Lucille M. Wert, *Library Education and High School Library Services* (unpublished doctoral dissertation, University of Illinois, 1970).
16. Carol A. Seymour and Schofield, J. L., "Measuring Reader Failure at the Catalog," *Library Resources and Technical Services, 17*(Winter 1973):6–24.
17. Leslie B. Rothenberg, Lucianovich, Judith, Kronick, David A., and Rees, Alan M., "A Job-Task Index for Evaluating Professional Utilization in Libraries," *Library Quarterly, 41* (October 1971):320–328.
18. Ellen Altman, "Implications of Title Diversity and Collection Overlap for Interlibrary Loan Among Secondary Schools," *Library Quarterly, 42*(April 1972):177–194.
19. Charles H. Busha, *Freedom versus Suppression and Censorship.* Research Studies in Library Science, no. 8 (Littleton, Colorado: Libraries Unlimited, 1972).
20. Kenneth H. Plate, and Stone, Elizabeth W., "Factors Affecting Librarians' Job Satisfaction: A Report of Two Studies," *Library Quarterly, 42*(January 1972):129–138.
21. Ben-Ami Lipetz, "Catalog Use in a Large Research Library," *Library Quarterly, 42*(January 1972):129–138.
22. Chow Loy Tom, "Paul Revere Rides Ahead: Poems Teachers Read to Pupils in the Middle Grades," *Library Quarterly, 43*(January 1973):27–38.

SELECTED BIBLIOGRAPHY

Babbie, Earl R., *Survey Research Methods.* Belmont, Calif.: Wadsworth, 1973.
Backstrom, Charles H., and Hursh, Gerald D., *Survey Research.* Chicago, Ill.: Northwestern University Press, 1963.
Berdie, Douglas R., and Anderson, John F., *Questionnaires: Design and Use.* Metuchen, N.J.: Scarecrow Press, 1974.
Cannell, Charles, Lawson, Sally A., and Hausser, Doris L., *A Technique for Evaluating*

Interviewer Performance: A Manual for Coding and Analyzing Interviewer Behavior from Tape Recordings of Household Interviews. Ann Arbor: University of Michigan, Survey Research Center, 1975.

Cochran, William G., *Sampling Techniques.* 2nd ed. New York: Wiley, 1963.

Converse, Jean M., and Schuman, Howard, *Conversations at Random: Survey Research as Interviewers See It.* New York: Wiley, 1974.

Davis, James A., *Elementary Survey Analysis.* Englewood Cliffs, N.J.: Prentice-Hall, 1971.

Deming, W. Edward, *Some Theory of Sampling.* New York: Wiley, 1950.

Erdos, Paul L., *Professional Mail Surveys.* New York: McGraw-Hill, 1970.

Gallup, George H., *The Sophisticated Poll Watcher's Guide.* Princeton, N.J.: Princeton Opinion Press, 1972.

Glock, Charles Y., ed., *Survey Research in the Social Sciences.* New York: Russell Sage Foundation, 1967.

Gorden, Raymond L., *Interviewing: Strategy, Techniques, and Tactics.* Rev. ed. Homewood, Ill.: Dorsey Press, 1975.

Hyman, Herbert H., *Secondary Analysis of Sample Surveys: Principles, Procedures, and Potentialities.* New York: Wiley, 1972.

Kerlinger, Frederick N., *Foundations of Behavioral Research.* 2nd ed. New York: Holt, Rinehart and Winston, 1973.

Kish, Leslie, *Survey Sampling.* New York: Wiley, 1965.

Maranell, Gary M., ed., *Scaling: A Sourcebook for Behavioral Scientists.* Chicago, Ill.: Aldine, 1974.

Nemanich, Dorothy, and O'Rourke, Diane, *A Manual for the Coding of Survey Data.* Dubuque, Iowa.: Kendall/Hunt, 1975.

Parten, Mildred B., *Surveys, Polls, and Samples: Practical Procedures.* New York: Harper & Row, 1950.

Payne, Stanley L., *The Art of Asking Questions.* Princeton, N.J.: Princeton University Press, 1951.

Potter, Dale R. *et al., Questionnaires for Research: An Annotated Bibliography on Design, Construction, and Use.* Portland, Oregon: U.S. Department of Agriculture, Pacific Northwest Forest and Range Experiment Station, 1972 (USDA Forest Service Research Paper PNW-140).

Remmers, H. H., *Introduction to Opinion and Attitude Measurement.* New York: Harper & Row, 1954.

Richardson, Stephen A., Dorenwend, Barbara S., and Klein, David, *Interviewing: Its Form and Functions.* New York: Basic Books, 1965.

Rosenberg, Morris, *The Logic of Survey Analysis.* New York: Basic Books, 1968.

Ross, Robert, "Obtaining Original Evidence," in *Research: An Introduction.* New York: Harper & Row, 1974, pp. 57–80.

Sackman, Harold, *Delphi Critique: Expert Opinion, Forecasting, and Group Process.* Lexington, Mass.: Lexington Books, 1975.

Selltiz, Claire, *et al., Research Methods in Social Relations.* New York: Holt, Rinehart and Winston, 1959.

Stephen, Frederick F., and McCarthy, Philip J., *Sampling Opinions: An Analysis of Survey Procedure.* Westport, Conn.: Greenwood, 1974.

Stuart, Alan, *Basic Ideas of Scientific Sampling.* 2nd ed. New York: Hafner, 1976.

Sudman, Seymour, and Bradburn, Norman M., *Response Effects in Surveys; A Review and Synthesis.* Chicago, Ill.: Aldine, 1974.

Yates, Frank, *Sampling Methods for Censuses and Surveys.* 3rd ed. New York: Hafner, 1965.

CHAPTER 4

Historical Research in Librarianship

INTRODUCTION

Application of the scientific method to the conduct of inquiry is not limited to experimental and survey research. The scientific approach can also be used in historical inquiries. History is both a science and an art. Good historians make use of scientific methods when they collect, verify, and analyze information; the art of writing creative and interesting prose for historical narrative reports complements the scientific approach. The conduct of historical research entails the following steps: (*a*) the recognition of a historical problem or the identification of a need for certain historical knowledge; (*b*) the gathering of as much pertinent information about the problem or topic as possible; (*c*) if appropriate, the forming of hypotheses that tentatively explain relationships between historical factors (variables); (*d*) the rigorous collection and organization of evidence, and the verification of the authenticity and veracity of information and its sources; (*e*) the selection, organization, and analysis of the most pertinent collected evidence, and the drawing of conclusions; and (*f*) the recording of conclusions in a meaningful narrative. Historical research can be conducted most effectively with these procedures.

Some historians have argued that the discipline of history cannot be scientific because it lacks the means of achieving rigorous analytical precision and precise explanations. Rather than using the term *scientific* in reference to historical research in librarianship, for example, some historians in the field prefer to work toward *understanding* librarianship as it existed during a specified period of time, using all appropriate means to achieve that understanding. The approach that we shall take in this discussion of historical research, however, is aimed at making such inquiries more scientific. Robert F. Berkhofer, Jr., claims that the lack of the means for obtaining rigorous analytical precision and precise explanations in history does not prove that historians cannot be scientific, "only that it is very difficult for them to be so."[1]

Historical research can contribute to the body of knowledge about librarianship and it can also facilitate our understanding of when, how, and why past events occurred and the significance of these events to libraries as collectors, organizers, and disseminators of the products of humanity's intellects and emotions. In this chapter we shall explore the value of historical research in librarianship, the present status of library history, and some effective techniques that library historians can use in their attempts to give meaning to past phenomena.

MEANING AND VALUE OF HISTORY

The word *history* originated from the Latin term *historia,* which derived from the Greek. *Historia* was used to designate a learning by inquiry. This definition is not really relevant today; however, for the purpose of our discussion about historical inquiry, let us assume that this quest takes the form of research. The *Encyclopedia of the Social Sciences* notes that "the historical past exists only to the extent that there is an image of it—in other words, to the extent that it is recreated in the mind."[2] Although this statement is true, it represents a viewpoint that seems to omit *unrecorded* events. Other definitions of history included in standard reference works or offered by historians themselves mention past events and their relationship to the development of man, his society, and his institutions. J. H. Hexter has written: "In its broadest sense . . . 'history' means any patterned coherent account, intended to be true, or any past happenings involving human intention or doing or suffering."[3] According to B. A. Hinsdale, "history is the story of man living in social relations in the world, as traced in various records and memorials. More narrowly, it is the story of man living in the higher social relations that constitute the civil state or civilization."[4] Writing on the topic of historical research and library science, Felix Reichmann has underscored the scientific basis of history:

> The work of the historian is a complex intellectual activity. He collects his primary data with scientific care and precision. The vestiges of the past must be examined and authenticated, and classified by systematic methods and scrupulously weighed. All the techniques of modern science as far as applicable are put to the use of the historian.[5]

LIBRARY HISTORY

In *The Golden Chain; A Study in the History of Libraries,* Raymond Irwin has provided a broad and excellent definition of the scope of library history. Irwin wrote that when historians write about libraries, they are "concerned particularly with their purpose and their content, and with the social background which produced them; in consequence [they] become involved in the history not only of scholarship in its narrow sense, but of human civilization and culture and literacy."[6] Ronald Hagler, noting that so many topics and subjects are relevant to librarianship, would limit the scope of library history in terms of those persons who are best equipped to conduct historical research about various aspects of the field or of the potential whole.[7]

Now that we have examined a number of definitions for history and have read what some historians think about history in the field of librarianship, perhaps we should propose a definition of library history. *Library history* is the systematic recounting of past events pertaining to the establishment, maintenance, and utilization of systematically arranged collections of recorded information or knowledge. Carefully conducted library history relates the causes and results of events; it also often recognizes the social, economic, political, intellectual, and cultural environment in which these events occurred. Furthermore, library history is sometimes considered an exposition of past incidents and developments and their impact on later times. Circumstances and occurrences relating to libraries are detailed in narrations produced by the historians who write library history. These analyses are accomplished with careful attention to the significance of events—their common relations and their antecedents and consequences. Events are chosen and assembled in library history on the basis of their interest or relevance to librarianship. The term *library history* is commonly applied to an account of events that affected any library or group of libraries, as well as to the social and economic impacts of libraries on their communities. A biography of a prominent person who has in some way affected the development of libraries, library science, or librarianship is also considered to be library history.

The contents of the *Library Trends* issue entitled "American Library History: 1876–1976"[8] illustrate the diversity of historical topics within the profession. Articles are included about the distribution of libraries over the nation, research collection development, library statistics, library buildings, the library profession, library associations, publishing in the profession, librarians, "old" and "new" librarianship, the organization of library resources, and service aspects of librarianship—all are treated from a historical point of view. Because librarianship embraces a wide diversity of areas and practices, the breadth of historical studies in the field is extensive and apparently ever-expanding. In addition to the histories of various academic, public, and special libraries, historians have approached topics such as library equipment, facilities, and buildings;

education for librarianship; important concepts and ideas that have influenced library practices and the profession in general; and other library phenomena during particular times and in specific places.

In his treatise on library research, Herbert Goldhor recognized that history is more than the collection of sketches of information about isolated events. Goldhor wrote: "A concern for only specific facts constitutes antiquarianism and not history. The facts about specific events are building blocks for history, but they must be used to build something."[9] Michael Harris, a well-known library historian, has claimed that knowledge of past events might bring about "an end to the petty jealousies and antagonisms so rampant in modern librarianship. A clearer understanding of the historical definition of the function of libraries may well contribute to increased communication between libraries. . . ."[10] Although Harris' theory is interesting, it needs to be defended and verified. The reader might wonder if indeed this has ever happened, recalling, perhaps, instances in which a knowledge of history actually caused dissension and discord.

Pierce Butler wrote in *An Introduction to Library Science* that "librarianship, as we know it, can be fully appreciated only through an understanding of its historic origins."[11] The specific value of library history, according to Jesse Shera, is that it allows librarians to synthesize and to make generalizations from reconstructions of the past; this process of synthesis and generalization will not only recreate the past but can serve as an aid in understanding the present. According to Shera, librarians should possess a "clear historical consciousness" because they cannot function effectively (fulfill their social responsibility) when history is regarded merely as an esoteric aspect of knowledge.[12]

The number and quality of historical works in the field of library history have increased since Arnold K. Borden, in 1931, emphasized the sociological beginnings of the modern library movement.[13] Public libraries have been the subject of numerous historical inquiries. Among the better historical studies about public and other libraries are the following: Spencer's *The Chicago Public Library: Origins and Backgrounds,*[14] Shera's *Foundations of the Public Library,*[15] Whitehill's *Boston Public Library, A Centennial History,*[16] Williamson's *William Frederick Poole and the Modern Library Movement,*[17] Bobinski's *Carnegie Libraries, Their History and Impact on American Public Library Development,*[18] Kraus' *Book Collections of Five Colonial College Libraries: A Subject Analysis,*[19] and Collier's *A History of the American Public Library Movement Through 1880.*[20]

Librarians who have conducted historical studies have sometimes been interested in the general history of libraries or in library history in specific countries, states, or regions. Other librarian-historians have concentrated on broad periods of time or "ages"—ancient, medieval, or modern. A few history scholars have investigated aspects of large categories of librarianship, such as (*a*) libraries in the United States during the colonial period, (*b*) the period in which social libraries existed between 1731 and 1865, or (*c*) the nineteenth-century developmental period of the tax-supported public library in the United States. A number of historians have conducted inquiries into the histories of particular types of libraries such as academic, public, or special. The diversity of these studies in the field will be apparent from an examination of the bibliography of completed doctoral dissertations in Harris' *Guide to Research in American Library History*,[21] as well as from the list of additional studies provided at the end of this chapter. Indeed, the subject variety of library history is extensive; it includes various facets of the library's services, collection development, and leadership, as well as the history of education for librarianship, the acceptance and utilization of new communication media in libraries, and the growth of professional associations in the field of library science.

Unfortunately, a number of these studies appear to have been unique efforts; there is little evidence that some scholars have pursued their initial interest in historical inquiries beyond the writing of a single thesis, dissertation, or account of the founding and growth of a particular library. Howard W. Winger has written, in reference to this situation, "American library histories in large part are a collection of special studies carried out by too few students in pursuit of an academic goal, and left to hang on the vine."[22] Doctoral candidates enrolled in library schools have regularly produced historical dissertations pertaining to libraries, librarianship, and related subjects. Further interest in the historical approach as a means of closing gaps in background library science knowledge appears to have resulted from the increase in student enrollment in terminal degree library science programs in the 1960s and 1970s. A significant trend in this respect is the production of histories of various facets of the library's organization, administration, and services, rather than accounts of particular kinds of libraries or single institutions.

To study the scope and breadth of historical dissertations in library science, *Dissertation Abstracts* and Eyman's *Doctoral Dissertations in Library Science*[23] were examined. Research studies based primarily upon the historical method were identified and categorized. During the period 1930–1972, 472 doctoral dissertations were accepted by accredited library schools in the United States. Of these works, 150, or 32%, were of a historical nature. In addition, numerous other dissertations in the field were products of descriptive research techniques, possessing certain historical elements. Of the distinctly historical dissertations, 92, or 61%, were prepared for two library schools, the University of Chicago and the

University of Michigan. Between 1930 and 1972, each of these institutions accepted an equal number (46) of historical dissertations.

In view of the relatively large proportion of completed historical dissertations in the field, one might question whether an overemphasis has been placed on background or historical aspects of librarianship within the body of research completed by students in pursuit of terminal degrees in library science. Moreover, the greater proportion of these studies dealt with the history of books, printing, or publishing—topics that are not generally regarded as entirely within the scope of library science, being somewhat tangential to modern librarianship and the factors with which most librarians are professionally qualified to grapple. Some of these studies have dealt with the history of selected periodicals and newspapers. Many of the dissertations were based upon examinations of facets of book production and the book trade. Moreover, historical aspects of printing were of interest to some doctoral students. A bibliography of selected doctoral dissertations which fit squarely into the framework of library history is provided at the end of this chapter.

PRESENT STATUS OF LIBRARY HISTORY

In summarizing salient points made about historical research in librarianship by contributors to the "Research in Librarianship" issue of *Library Trends*, [24] Maurice Tauber noted that social, cultural, and other influences on library development have been recognized by librarians who have conducted the most successful historical studies. He wrote: "A good start has been made in the study of library history and bibliography, but the areas are wide open for research" [p. 107]. [24] Writing in 1957, Haynes McMullen recognized the need for additional "large synthesizing" investigations devoted to many historical periods and types of libraries. McMullen singled out the following subject areas that were in need of historical treatment: (*a*) public and social libraries other than those in New England and the Middle Atlantic States; (*b*) college libraries since 1776; (*c*) special and historical libraries; (*d*) periods of library growth such as the 1850s and the 1890s; and (*e*) library developments in the twentieth century. [25] Although 22 years have passed since McMullen outlined these research needs in the field of library history, this historian's observations are still valid, particularly in reference to twentieth-century library history.

The accelerated rate of change brought about by the impact of science and technology on librarianship has contributed to increased interest in recent past events. Since the latter part of the nineteenth century, each decade has witnessed the introduction of new communication media; innovations for acquiring, storing, organizing, and disseminating information; and political, social, and economic changes that have altered the contemporary roles, goals, objectives, and methods of operation of a significant number of institutions, including libraries. What historians once called the "past" is much closer chronologically today than it was when historical change was measured in terms of centuries or half-centuries.

Some library historians are now investigating events and developments in the recent past such as (a) the influence of legislators and of legislation such as Public Law 480, the Library Services and Construction Act, and the Higher Education Act; (b) library utilization of a variety of new communication media and technological innovations such as telefacsimile devices, television, microforms, data-processing equipment, computers, reprographic tools, and audiovisual materials; and (c) the impact of the Great Depression and World War II on libraries. Other subjects of contemporary historical studies have been: (a) library services to disadvantaged and culturally deprived citizens; (b) the roles of library associations and their impact on library development; (c) overseas library technical assistance; (d) the careers of black librarians; (e) women in positions of leadership in the profession; and (f) political leadership for library development.

Although historical inquiries have touched on many areas of knowledge within librarianship, there is still need for the replication of past studies. Replication was often discouraged in the past—particularly in advanced degree programs in the field of library science. But scholars now appear to be looking more favorably at the reexamination of topics or subjects that have already been investigated. This development is somewhat embryonic in application; however, old fears that a replicated study might be characterized as lacking originality have subsided somewhat. When studies are repeated, the reliability of previous research data can be tested. Increasingly, library historians are realizing that data and conclusions need to be verified and that new approaches to old topics can lead to (a) the application of different techniques of inquiry, (b) the new interpretation of old and new data, and (c) the generation of information that challenges, supports, or expands existing historical knowledge. Ronald Hagler has written:

> We need more than one major study by different people on many important topics. This is not because a first study is incomplete or poorly done (though this at present is often true) but because it is in the nature of history as a humanistic discipline to require many viewpoints, bred and nurtured of each other in some incestuous way, to eludicate a complex subject.[26]

Thus, replication is important; it can make historical knowledge more scientific—and thereby more certain.

The trend toward greater dependence on quantification, measurement, statistical analysis of research data, and hypothesis testing in research in librarianship is also affecting the writing of library history. Charles M. Dollar and Richard J. Jensen have written the *Historian's Guide to Statistics: Quantitative Analysis and Historical Research.* [27] This guide is a useful source of information for historians who attempt to increase the rigor and precision of their studies. Computers are being used increasingly in the analysis of some raw historical data. Thus, research workers are able to deal with larger information bases comprised of valuable social, political, and economic data. More hypotheses, or statements of the relationships between historical factors (qualitative and quantitative variables), can be generated and tested as data are subjected to speedier, more rigorous, and more accurate analysis. The testing of historical hypotheses contributes to the improved quality of library history. J. P. Wilkinson has outlined the importance of hypotheses in library history as follows:

> fact-finding alone is not research, nor is the simple descriptive narrative of those facts. To be regarded as research, the historical method *must* include a hypothesis. . . . Thus it is not possible to "establish the facts" alone; history inevitably involves the process of selection of fact, and it is at this level of selection that reasoning must enter. By what right, it has been asked, upon what premise and in the name of what principle, would the historian make his choice? Indeed, if history has a purpose at all (and to ask the question is, for the historian, to supply an affirmative answer), then that purpose must involve inductive inferences as a basis for selection. Such inferences, whether implicit or explicit, conscious or unconscious, are hypotheses, and thus the hypothesis and the research of which it is a part becomes an integral part of the purpose of history. Not only is history "researchable," but history is research, and the hypothesis is totally necessary to the historical method [p. 5]. [28]

Although Wilkinson is overstating his case somewhat and blurring the distinction between inferences and hypotheses, the point he is attempting to make should be quite clear: meaningful history relies heavily upon the testing of research hypotheses.

OBTAINING HISTORICAL EVIDENCE

Because most historians cannot carry out their studies by conducting experiments or by directly observing the event that is being investigated, they must rely upon the observations of others and the scraps of evidence which remain to be examined. Thus, in this section of the chapter, we will be concerned with the sources of historical evidence.

In the conduct of literature searches for background information, historians gather as much available evidence of a factual nature as possible before proposals are prepared and research is actually begun. Historians start by accumulating lists of sources of possible value, making use of their bibliographic expertise and all the investigative instincts they can muster. Published histories and chronological lists of events often serve as useful guides to the beginning historian, who should become familiar with methods and approaches that have already been used. Because most librarians are already familiar with techniques of bibliographical searches, as well as the great variety of bibliographic tools, guides, government documents, and other reference tools, they have overcome some of the primary obstacles that confront inexperienced historians in other fields. With their knowledge of the general content, organization, and services of libraries, librarians are also well prepared to ferret out many kinds of historical information. As a reminder and a guide for future historical studies, a bibliography that includes reference works useful to historians is provided at the end of this chapter. The bibliography may facilitate the conduct of literature searches; it might also be useful in helping the researcher to locate primary and secondary information.

Historians are concerned with *how past events actually occurred* rather than with how events should have happened. Historians did not make the past, but they can reconstruct parts of it in narrative form. The most valuable history is often based upon original documents and other remains that have been intelligently interpreted. Reliance upon these sources helps the historian to reconstruct certain past events. But before we enter into a discussion of the nature of historical evidence and how it can be located, perhaps we should briefly examine, as background information, some principles of historical research. First, we should be aware that a historian cannot produce a historical narrative that describes a past event 100% accurately. Good historians, however, attempt to make their histories as complete and accurate as possible.

Persons who conduct and report historical research should carefully document their sources and, if necessary, admit biases inherent in their approaches or work. Readers will then be able to identify ommisions and oversights and to evaluate the historian's conclusions. In addition, when historians reveal their "slants," the reader can be on guard against possible faulty interpretations and inaccurate conclusions. When judgments are made about the accuracy of documents, as well as the actions of persons involved in past events, the historian should outline criteria by which decisions were reached and then document available evidence. It has been said that simple people tend to look for simple solutions to complex problems. Perhaps we could extend this notion further: simple historians look for simple evidence and arrive at simplistic solutions. However, historical episodes result from a variety of precipitating, immediate, and underlying factors; most significant historical events are quite complex. Therefore, scholarly historians use the concept of *multiple causation* when they form hypotheses and collect evidence. The most useful history is free of simple and glib explanations for complex events of the past.

As an example of the failure to use the concept of multiple causation, suppose a historian is attempting to determine conditions that have favored the development of libraries over the world. Having recognized the relationship between the founding of libraries and the concentration of populations in urban centers and the development of public financial means to support cultural activities, an impatient historian might seize upon these causative factors alone and fail to recognize the significance of such additional circumstances as the following to the growth of libraries:

1. General recognition within societies of the value and necessity for collecting, preserving, and distributing knowledge
2. Attainment of periods of peace and political stability within a society
3. Availability of periods of leisure and the facility of people to enjoy them
4. Accumulation of vast, private fortunes which can lead to philanthropic gifts to educational and cultural institutions
5. Widespread recognition of the value of self-improvement and the placing of emphasis on a well-informed citizenry
6. Revival of learning which emphasizes the accumulation and utilization of collections of graphical materials
7. An atmosphere of permanence and stability for social institutions
8. Rise of creative literary activities that promote more writing and reading
9. Production of abundant supplies of paper, printing equipment, and other implements of communication
10. Interaction among different societies and cultures by means of commerce and travel
11. Desire of rulers and political leaders to compete with others in developing large depositories of recorded information
12. Development of educational institutions such as universities and public schools which depend upon repositories of knowledge
13. Rise of a nucleus of educated and civic-minded citizens

14. Accumulation of vast collections of public records and literary materials in a single language

Undoubtedly, additional causative factors could be added to this list; however, it should be evident that the development of libraries in various societies is the product of numerous contributing conditions and that historians should search for multiple causative variables.

A word of caution is in order, however, in relation to the topic of causative factors. Some historians have been *too* preoccupied with identifying causative factors so that explanations for *why* events happen could be made. Under such conditions, the investigator runs the risk of failing to provide adequate explanations of *what* happened. Thus, historians should refrain from collecting evidence that merely strengthens or corroborates their causal hypotheses, theses, mental sets, or predispositions. Intellectual dishonesty can produce a "history" that is more fiction than fact.

The examination of evidence from a singular point of view should also be avoided in historical inquiries. A careful historian will maintain an air of skepticism in both the collection of evidence and in the evaluation of documents. Skepticism helps the historian avoid the writing of dogmatic histories. Beginning historians in the area of librarianship should remember that their work will be judged by qualified scholars. These critics will be in a position to evaluate the essential worth and accuracy of completed research. Critical evaluations are likely to be comprised of an analysis of the sources of information, in terms of their worth to the subject under study, as well as the interpretation of the data.

Much of the evidence that leads to conclusions about past events must be obtained from *primary sources*—original materials such as official or personal documents which are records containing "first-hand" information. Primary sources of information contain eyewitness testimony which enhances the validity and value of history. In a discussion of the use of primary sources, J. Leonard Bates has noted that historians often classify their primary materials into two categories:

> "Primary: Manuscripts," broken down into subdivisions like the following: 1) personal papers; 2) archival records; 3) interviews; and 4) miscellaneous. Under the heading, "Primary: Printed," we would find, perhaps, 1) federal publications; 2) state publications; 3) autobiographies and memoirs; 4) collected speeches and letters; and 5) contemporary articles.[29]

Archives maintained by the federal and state governments and by educational, business, industrial, and private organizations contain a wealth of primary sources of historical information. Furthermore, private archives can be valuable as sources of personal papers. Oscar E. Anderson has pointed out that historians do not make as much use of federal archival materials as they should. He attributed neglect of archival records to: (*a*) "disenchantment with government that seems to run strong in the academic community," (*b*) "a widespread impression that the public records are not very valuable," and (*c*) "too many historians grow into academic maturity without learning its [archival record] richness and importance."[30] Philip C. Brooks' manual entitled *Research in Archives; The Use of Unpublished Primary Sources*[31] is an excellent guide for historians who plan to use archives and unpublished papers.

Secondary sources of information are records or accounts prepared by someone other than the person, or persons, who participated in or observed an event. Thus, secondary sources consist of testimony of individuals who were not eyewitnesses, but who prepared a record of an event, for one reason or another. In reference to secondary sources in library history, Haynes McMullen has written: "Some of the finest works in this field are good because of the way in which the authors set their libraries in the social or intellectual landscape of the time; the authors, of course, learned much of what they knew about that landscape by reading secondary works."[32] At this point a hypothetical example of a search for historical evidence might be helpful to illustrate the uses of, and differences between, primary and secondary sources of information.

AN EXAMPLE OF THE SEARCH
FOR EVIDENCE

Assume that you are writing a history of the administration of the Smallwood University Library. Your interest during one phase of the study pertains to changes in the library's administrative leadership. In the course of your investigation, you discover that in 1930 Arnold G. Ashley left his position as library director. Examinations of available university documents to determine the reason(s) for Mr. Ashley's departure produce only a brief mention of the event in the library's annual report to the university president. The report had been prepared by Dr. Samuel Munze, the acting director who replaced Mr. Ashley and who wrote that the former librarian had been named university archivist, would maintain an office in the library, and would no longer be the administrative head of the library.

You are puzzled about this event because, during the course of your general study of the library's administration, you found no mention of a university archivist, nor prior plans for the creation of that position at the university. Still unsatisfied, you continue your search and eventually locate an announcement of the event while reading microfilmed issues of *Spitfire,* the university's student newspaper. The article contains a glowing tribute to Mr. Ashley, the former library director, written both by Dr. Herman Stout, the university president, and Dr. George Crowell, the vice president for academic affairs. According to the newspaper account, Mr. Ashley was being "promoted to the important position of University Archivist."

As you continue your research, you learn from a present library staff member that the former head of the cataloging department of the library, Rose Murray, is still living in a nearby city and that she served under Mr. Ashley's direction prior to her retirement. Although she is quite elderly, Rose Murray agrees to participate in an in-depth, tape recorded "oral history" interview pertaining to her work in the library and other matters concerning Smallwood University more than 45 years ago. During the course of a long, taped interview, you ask Ms. Murray for her recollections about the library director's "promotion" to university archivist. According to your respondent, Mr. Ashley had been forced to step down from his position by President Stout, who had made the decision to remove the director after having received numerous complaints from faculty members, students, and the library committee about the "poorly operated library."

Continuing her version of the event, Ms. Murray stated that the now-deceased library director, Mr. Ashley, was a cousin of Christopher L. Rollins, who had been a member of the university's board of trustees during the library director's tenure. In the course of the interview, Ms. Murray notes that "rumors had abounded that the university's vice president for academic affairs wanted to replace Mr. Ashley with an old friend and that the decision to remove the library director had not been an easy one for officials of the university to make." In addition, your respondent stated: "President Stout hastily created a new position so that Mr. Ashley could be moved upstairs."

After the interview with Ms. Murray, you verify that Mr. Ashley had remained in his "upstairs" position until his retirement a little more than 2 years after he left the library directorship. You then obtain permission from university officials to examine a collection of old records maintained in the office of the present dean of academic affairs. The records pertain to academic matters extending over a period of 60 years. You conduct a thorough search of the documents, letters, memoranda, and other materials in hopes of locating a memorandum from the library committee about the library director; however, this search fails. Turning from these records, you examine old university bulletins in the "retired reference" collection of the library in search of the names of persons other than Mr.

Ashley who held the position of university archivist. After searching all pertinent bulletins, you conclude that apparently no replacement was ever made after Mr. Ashley retired as the archivist. The only person listed in that capacity was former library director Ashley, the subject of your inquiry.

Mr. Ashley was a member of a prominent family in the state; therefore, you wonder whether biographical sketches about him or a family genealogy have been published. You turn next to a bibliography of local family histories and discover a work entitled *Descendants of the Honorable Rupert P. Ashley*. A search through old biographical directories in the library's reference department allows you to verify that Mr. Ashley's father was Rupert Ashley, Jr. You then assume, for the time being, that you must have located the appropriate family genealogy, and you proceed to search for it. Checking the library's card catalog, you discover that the work is not owned by the Smallwood University Library; however, the inter-library loan librarian agrees to borrow the work from the state library's genealogy collection.

After a period of 1 week, the needed volume arrives. You immediately consult the book and verify that the librarian was indeed a cousin of Christopher L. Rollins. By examining a list of university trustees provided by a helpful reference librarian, you also verify that Mr. Rollins' name appeared on a 1930 roster of members of the Smallwood University board of trustees. Furthermore, you discover from a mimeographed list of papers contained in the library's manuscripts department that the trustee's papers were donated to the university by Mrs. Christopher L. Rollins. Although the collection of papers has not yet been classified or cataloged, you are given permission to use it by the head of the manuscripts department. You begin a careful examination of hundreds of documents in the "Rollins Papers" in search of evidence that will explain why Mr. Ashley left his administrative position. Finally, you discover a letter from the former library director to his cousin, the trustee. The letter is dated July 15, 1930. You verify that the handwritten letter was written by the librarian by comparing it with several memoranda penned that you had previously discovered and knew to be written by Mr. Ashley. In addition, the 1930 letter was written on university stationary with the subheading "Office of the Librarian."

Mr. Ashley's letter to Mr. Rollins contains a subjective explanation for the sudden change in the former director's status at the university. The librarian wrote that his health had steadily deteriorated during his last years as library director. According to Mr. Ashley, his authority had been "gradually usurped" by Dr. Munze, who had been the associate library director. Mr. Ashley explained that he was absent from work during several prolonged periods of illness and that the associate director took advantage of the situation by "taking over permanently." Mr. Ashley continued his letter by explaining that Dr. Crowell, the former academic vice president, and Dr. Munze had become close, personal friends while they were both members of the university's economics department. According to Mr. Ashley's letter, Dr. Crowell had "pushed" Dr. Munze on him despite the director's claim that the professor was not qualified to perform the duties of associate library director. Mr. Ashley stated in his letter that both Dr. Crowell and Dr. Munze had "plotted" to remove him from his directorship so that the associate director could become the head of the library.

Now, let us analyze and classify some of the kinds of sources you will use to draw conclusions about Mr. Ashley's sudden departure from the directorship. First, the library's annual report was an official document prepared for transmission to the university president by the acting library director. Although annual reports can at times be used as primary sources of information, you used the report as a secondary source; its brief note of the change in the library's administration was not written by the former director, but by an intermediary. Only cursory, inadequate information pertaining to your inquiry was provided by the annual report, although the document did provide a clue about the event. The news item about the event in *Spitfire* was also a secondary source for the same reason. The taped interview with the former head of the cataloging department, however, was a primary source; it reported an event by a person who was in a favorable position to know about reasons for staff changes. In fact, the recorded interview could further be used as an original source for other projects based upon oral history, particularly if it were made available for future and general use by other historians.

The official university bulletins, biographical directories, and the librarian's published family genealogy were also secondary sources. They aided you somewhat in your search for information; however, they did not provide original information. The librarian's personal letter to his cousin was an original source. The letter was handwritten by Mr. Ashley; it also contained a partial explanation of the event in question by a key participant. Therefore, the writer of the document provided his personalized first-hand account of the event. Although the contents of the letter were subjective, the information corroborated some of the verbal account given by Ms. Murray, the retired head of the cataloging department. By connecting all of these pieces of information and analyzing them carefully, you can arrive at an intelligent explanation for Mr. Ashley's removal from the directorship of the library. Perhaps further documents pertaining to the event could be found, should the search be continued during the course of your study of the library's administration.

This simplified, hypothetical explanation of a search for one facet of information to use in a larger historical inquiry illustrates that historians may use a variety of sources, some of which are more valuable than others. As demonstrated by this example, the historian's work is not unlike that of a detective who searches for and examines all relevant evidence before reaching conclusions. And, as is true with detectives, some historians do a more thorough job of ferreting out facts than others.

EVALUATION OF SOURCES AND EVIDENCE

The primary sources of information for historical research are *records*. The term *record* has many meanings. It can be applied to any writings, marks, tape recordings, photographs, films, or other traces useful as enduring testimony of an event. For example, a taped interview with a witness to an event is a record of a person's observations. A list of donors to a library building fund is a record. Printed copies of speeches delivered at library dedication ceremonies are records. City directories are records of the names of inhabitants of a community at a specific time. A diary is a record of selected actions, events, and thoughts in a person's daily life. The materials used for historical information include records such as annuals, archives, memorials, registers, oral traditions, pictures, and physical remains.

Now, let us briefly examine the characteristics of some of these kinds of records. The following list contains various types of materials used in historical research, together with brief definitions.

Annual. A record maintained on a yearly basis; usually records events chronologically without mention of their significance.

Archives. Public, official documents; term is also used to describe the depository in which documents are preserved, classified, and utilized.

Catalog. Complete list of articles (books, equipment, etc.), usually descriptive in nature and arranged according to a system.

Chronicle. Record of facts or events according to their occurence in time and without analysis or interpretation.

Deed. Official document that records the transfer of property from one person to another.

Legend. Story of extraordinary events passed from generation to generation; often has traditional or mythical origins and contains information that usually cannot be verified.

Manuscript. Document that has been handwritten or typed (including carbon copies of the same); included under the rubric of manuscripts are letters, telegrams, daybooks, receipts, personal accounts, inventories, minutes of meetings, contracts, tax records, legal certificates (birth, death, marriage, etc.), original copies of literary works, speeches, and many other documents which pertain to individual persons.

Memoir. Recollection or report of events based upon the writer's life, observations, or special information; when grouped, these records are termed *memoirs.*

Memorial. Something done, said, or constructed to keep a person or event in remembrance.

Muniment. Document providing evidence of title to property or claim to rights and privileges.

Register. Written record, usually official, maintained for future use; series of entries about events such as births or deaths.

Roll. List of names recorded for a particular purpose; used to check attendance (e.g., classroom) or to muster persons (military).

Schedule. Tabulated list of details or statements; often provides a record of recurring events, timetables, or plans for events according to prior arrangements.

Seasoned historians do not need to be reminded that documents and the contents of documents should be evaluated in terms of genuineness and reliability. However, mention should be made here—for the benefit of relatively inexperienced historians—of the evaluation of documents. All sources used to gain information in historical inquiries are appraised according to their worth in a particular study of an event or action. Information in documents can be classified into two categories: (*a*) consciously transmitted evidence (memoirs, diaries, chronicles, annuals, taped interviews, certain historical works of art, etc.); and (*b*) unconsciously transmitted evidence (business, commercial, or financial data; artifacts, buildings, etc.). Generally, unconsciously transmitted evidence is contained in records that were kept primarily for reference or other nonhistorical purposes. When evidence has been recorded with the intent of transmission, the recorder has an opportunity to select the information that is presented. Originators of such information can also analyze, interpret, or judge the information. When consciously transmitted records are used in historical inquiries, the historian often needs to be more concerned about the general qualifications and reliability of the recorder.

Historians also subject information sources to additional evaluations.

External criticism of records is concerned with the authenticity of each document used: whether it was actually written and distributed at the time and place listed on the document; whether it is true to the original if it is a copy; and other questions about the composition and production of the document. According to Arthur Bestor: "The historian must satisfy himself that he knows when, where, under what circumstances, and by whom the words were written or printed or incised upon a paper or the tablet that he holds in his hand."[33] Persons who are new to the field of history will rarely need to be concerned with external criticism; the documents which they usually consult have already been authenticated by scholars who have gone before them.

Internal criticism is a process used to judge the value of a document's *contents*. It is concerned with the question of whether the testimony contained in documents is factual. A useful guideline to the reliability of statements contained in documents is the prior knowledge about the subject of an inquiry that the historian brings to a selected area for investigation. If aspects of the information contained in a record are quite different from what the historian already knows or believes to be true, care is taken not to use the data until they have been verified in other sources. Steps should be taken to determine whether the information was recorded in good faith or with the intention of deliberately falsifying or distorting truth.

The beginning library historian might pose a question about the location of sources of information for historical research projects in librarianship. To answer this question, one would have to state that sources are as diversified as the topics of library historical research. In addition, it would be necessary to point out that the sources of information for one type of library, or for a particular subject, might be quite different from those for other kinds of libraries or topics. For example, documents for histories of public libraries can be very different in form, content, and location than those used in the history of a special library located in an industrial setting, medical college, or government agency. The time period covered by a study can also determine, to varying degrees, both the nature and the location of information sources.

Tax-supported libraries are public institutions. Thus, one might search through official documents in public archives for information about most municipal, county, state, and public school libraries. Enabling legislation upon which public and public school libraries were established can be found in (*a*) general laws relating to municipalities; (*b*) special legislation concerning cities and townships; (*c*) special legislation about a particular library; and (*d*) charters. Federal legislation, such as the Library Services Act and the Library Services and Construction Act (including all the related guidelines and reports of completed projects), contains information of value to some library historians. Local and county laws and city ordinances might also be consulted, depending upon the topic of the research. Library extension agencies, state libraries, and state departments of education sometimes maintain files of unpublished historical narratives pertaining to various public and school libraries. Some of these "histories" were written by amateur historians; however, the works might be used to determine facts of a general nature, such as the names of librarians and other staff members, board of trustee members, and basic facts and dates about library events. Annual reports of all types of libraries frequently contain data of value to library historians. Local published histories about communities and institutions should also be consulted for certain kinds of information. Public relations materials such as promotional pamphlets, brochures, and flyers might also be of value; however, the historian must exercise caution in using these materials because gaps might have existed between promises made in promotional literature and actual library services and conditions.

Many additional types of materials may be used in historical inquiries pertaining to libraries. News stories and feature articles in newspapers and periodicals could provide some useful data. Materials such as autobiographies, memoirs, biographies, and reminiscences of both librarians and library users could contain candid observations of benefit in historical inquiries. Written accounts of library-related events such as committee meetings, hearings, board deliberations, dedication ceremonies, unveilings, memorials, special library programs, and so on, could be useful, particularly if they were written by participants in these activities. Minutes of meetings are especially valuable in some inquiries. Letters of both an official or unofficial nature written by librarians, community leaders, legislators, consultants, and other persons who were in positions to observe library developments often provide factual, eyewitness accounts of library developments and events. Written reports of library surveys conducted by librarians or consultants often contain factual, background information about library collections, services, and facilities. Reports of community surveys are also useful sources of information about characteristics and needs of communities and users of libraries during particular periods of time. Legal instruments such as wills, contracts, and deeds sometimes contain data of value to library history. Printed or near-print bibliographies of library materials, including catalogs, reading lists, and special source lists, contain records of the holdings of libraries at particular times.

Remains of library buildings and library furnishings should not be overlooked as possible sources of information. Photographs of these remains can also be valuable, particularly if the relics that were photographed have been destroyed. Circulation records, registration forms, book cards, and related materials might also prove beneficial in some studies. Published and unpublished library histories for one library or for one facet of librarianship might throw additional light on another subject of historical inquiry. The success or failure of a search for information often depends on the imagination, determination, and perseverance of the historian. Library historical records have been located in such obscure places as the basements of courthouses; stored boxes containing old, unclassified correspondence in library closets; and even in scrapbooks kept in local history collections.

Thus far, we have discussed the collection of historical information and the evaluation of documents and their contents. We now turn to the final, yet major, step of the historical inquiry, the writing of the historical research report.

PREPARING HISTORICAL NARRATIVES

The preparation and presentation of facts and conclusions in a narrative report represent the third major step in the historical method. This step entails the actual production of what is popularly called "history." When preparing narrative reports, the history scholar is concerned with: (a) selection of the appropriate information to be used as evidence in the research project; (b) analysis of the collected information; and (c) organization, composition, and writing of the narrative report. Historians must place emphasis on the "bits" of evidence that appear to be the most significant and meaningful to their projects. This evidence must also be interpreted; readers of history are not usually interested in a catalog of mere facts. Data must be related and interpreted in light of the *purpose* of the historical study. In *The Conduct of Inquiry,* Abraham Kaplan wrote: "What a scientist provides is not an account free of *any* interpretation, but one free of arbitrary or projective interpretations."[34]

The historical narrative should be based upon critically evaluated evidence. Facts and interpretations are presented so that readers can evaluate conclusions in light of documented evidence. Historical evidence is blended into an account that accurately describes a past event. This process requires intelligence, imagination, discrimination, and sophistication. Lucid and unambiguous expression is a goal of good historians. The historical narrative should first be written in draft form, then carefully revised with emphasis on continuity, clarity of thought, and a flowing style. Beginning library historians are advised to write narrative reports as though their audience will be knowledgeable critics and scholars. Intellectual honesty ought to guide the preparation of historical narratives. According to Edward Holley: "The library historian, like historians generally, must always be willing to admit the tentativeness of his conclusions and equally willing to acknowledge that subsequent data may alter his conclusions either significantly or in some detail."[35]

When a historian's work is characterized by objective and valid explanations and interpretations, the truth of the history depends neither upon the person making the explanation nor upon the reader of the research report. Essentially, the truthfulness of the narrative is gauged by the degree to which the data and conclusions are tied to the evidence obtained and interpreted in an unbiased, objective manner. History should both satisfy the intellect and make the past interesting and comprehensible to present and future readers. Although some historical explanations can be semantically clear, at the same time they can also be inaccurate. For example, one might find that a historian has written a very clear explanation of events; however, the conclusions could be based on erroneous interpretations of how or why these events occurred. Such explanations are provided when historical inquiries have been incomplete, inconclusive, uncertain, or limited.

When the historian fails to take all pertinent factors into consideration, the history produced will be partial. Approximations rather than complete histories will be offered by historians who give explanations that deviate from those recorded by participants in the developments described. Explanations of historical events can also be inconclusive when relationships between events or actions and the ascribed motives of participants have not been firmly established. Uncertain historical explanations are based upon insufficient evidence, whereas limited histories are those that apply only to a particular or unique situation and cannot be generalized to similar situations.

SOME REPRESENTATIVE HISTORICAL STUDIES

Margaret Corwin's[36] study of the leadership roles of women in library associations during the last quarter of the nineteenth and the first quarter of the twentieth centuries is an example of historical research based upon hypotheses. The study is noteworthy because of the skillful manner in which prerecorded quantified data were used. The purpose of the research was to assess the degree of leadership provided by women in national, regional, state, and local library associations. The study was an extension of an earlier investigation of the feminization of American librarianship. Corwin's hypotheses were as follows: (*a*) offices of leadership held by librarians between 1876 and 1923 in national associations were not proportional to the male/female ratio of the profession; and (*b*) although women held leadership positions in local and state associations in proportion to their representation in the profession, they did not hold an equal proportion on the national level. To test these hypotheses, sexes of all persons who held leadership positions were ascertained. Sources for these data were official lists of national, state, local, and regional associations and commissions, together with various reports, publications, and correspondences.

In the study, the criteria used for the classification of persons in "positions of leadership" were whether individuals held the offices of association president or secretary for a period of at least six months. Sexes of subjects were determined by identifying given names from the compiled list of leaders. The dependent variable was the position held; the independent was sex. The following assumptions were made in the study: (*a*) "leadership" can be determined by the recognition that a librarian received from being elected to executive offices and to positions of responsibility; and (*b*) sexes of librarians can be deduced from given names or single initials included in lists of office holders of library associations.

Analysis of the data showed that within the 48-year period covered by the study, 31% of the national, associational leadership positions were held by women; 60% of the positions were held by women at the state level; and 68% were held by women at the local level. Thus, Corwin concluded that although males were in the minority in librarianship, they held more positions of national leadership than women. On the other hand, women held more leadership positions at the state and local levels. Corwin noted that women were overall actually more active than had been expected in view of the cultural and social climate that prevailed between 1876 and 1923.

In another project conducted by Paul Winckler,[37] the professional life of Charles C. Williamson was examined. Using historical methods in a biographical study, the investigator proceeded in his research with the hypothesis that Williamson's work led to the establishment of library education as a profession in the United States. Winckler's source materials consisted of documents given to him personally by Williamson, materials provided by Williamson's widow, information gleaned from a collection of Williamson's papers at Columbia University, records and files of various institutions and organizations where Williamson had studied and worked, and information about all aspects of Williamson's career obtained from interviews with the subject's colleagues. All source materials were subjected to both external and internal criticism prior to their use as evidence.

The hypothesis of Winckler's study was supported by the collected evidence. Furthermore, the investigator concluded that in addition to his subject's major role in establishing education for librarianship as a profession, other of Williamson's professional contributions were also noteworthy. Prior to the conduct of this study, the assumption was generally made within the field that Williamson's 1923 survey of library education, the report of which was entitled *Training for Library Service*,[38] represented the dawn of a new era in the professional education of librarians. Winckler's research demonstrates that this assumption was valid. The study's findings help to establish a well-earned place for C. C. Williamson among the founding fathers of modern librarianship.

In another study conducted by Leonaradas V. Gerulaitis,[39] the influence of humanism on printing and book production in Italy between 1469 and 1500 was investigated. Traditionally, humanism has been regarded as the most pervasive and influential movement of the Italian Renaissance. Using historical techniques, Gerulaitis questioned humanism's actual impact on Italian printing and reading. The research made use of the following methods: (*a*) an analysis of economic and social conditions as they existed in Italy during the pertinent period; (*b*) an examination of the early career of Aldus Manutius, a Venetian printer of the Italian Renaissance; and (*c*) an examination and analysis of Venetian incunabula contained in the catalog and collection of the British Museum.

The dependent variable of the study was the quality of books published between 1469 and 1500 in Italy in the following broad categories: university textbooks, professional literature, vernacular works, and books written by humanists. Independent variables were: (*a*) reading tastes of the public; (*b*) books chosen by printers for publication; and (*c*) the degree of ecclesiastical and civil censorship exercised. After examining all the available evidence, Gerulaitis concluded that humanism's impact on printing and publishing was minimal during the period investigated; thus he questioned the theory that humanism was the "very core of the Italian Renaissance."

SUMMARY

Historical inquiries have been conducted in many areas of librarianship. Much of this research has been undertaken by students in pursuit of advanced degrees in library science. Some doctoral dissertations have dwelt on antiquarian details of book, periodical, and newspaper printing and publishing; others have been histories of individual libraries. Still others were broader in scope and concerned with social or economic forces affecting libraries and librarianship. A number of nonlibrarians have also conducted valuable studies of a historical nature in the field. Today more attention is being devoted to the lives of librarians and other persons who have influenced libraries or librarianship.

Oral sources are increasingly being used in library historical studies. Based upon verbalized recollections of persons who participated in events that occurred in the immediate past, oral history consists of recorded interviews conducted with respondents who are able to provide eyewitness accounts of events. Transcriptions of these recorded interviews preserve information for future historians. Tape recorders are gaining more recognition as valuable tools for contemporary historical research. Library history is also increasingly dependent upon in-depth examinations of the backgrounds of libraries as social institutions and the growth of ideas and thought. Quantification and automation are playing greater roles in historical studies. Historical data are sometimes subjected to statistical and computer analysis; larger quantities of social and economic data are being incorporated into historical inquiries. Although the volume of such information is extensive for modern and contemporary historical inquiries, data are scarce for studies in ancient and medieval subject areas.

Information for historical inquiries is obtained from primary sources (eyewitness accounts) and secondary sources (records prepared by persons other than eyewitnesses). These sources contain historical evidence that was transmitted either consciously or unconsciously. Documents utilized in historical research are subjected to external and internal criticism. The writing of historical narratives represents the culminating stage of the research; narratives are based on a skillful analysis of collected evidence. This process requires intelligence and discrimination on the part of the historian. Hypotheses can be useful to historians as aids in the conduct of rigorous and productive inquiries. When they are used in historical studies, hypotheses are tested to determine actual relationships between relevant, past events and certain factors or variables.

The uninitiated research worker who plans to conduct a history study should first determine whether a reasonable amount of evidence about the selected topic is readily available, as well as how and where access to it can be gained. Good history cannot be written without adequate sources of information. Inexperienced historians should avoid selecting topics or problems that are too broad or complex. Beginning historians often pose research questions that require very extensive investigations. Some of the best and most useful histories have dealt with a single and sometimes even obscure event. The investigator should choose a subject area for investigation in which he or she feels most comfortable insofar as personal ability, background, experience, knowledge, and aptitude are concerned. Difficulties are likely to arise when historians have not acquired an in-depth knowledge about the targeted subject area. A thorough and accurate system of bibliographical control and note-taking procedures should be devised before a study is initiated. Moreover, literature searches are essential at an early stage of the investigative process.

Good historians realize that not all knowledge is absolute, nor is all knowledge scientific. Sound knowledge is obtained by posing hypotheses, reasoning out possible answers, and testing the answers. The scientific approach in historical inquiries produces knowledge that is more *certain*. The success or failure of historical inquiries will depend greatly upon the ability of the research worker to adequately conceptualize the purpose and problem of the research, to vigorously evaluate and categorize the collected evidence, and to analyze data intelligently in view of research objectives.

REFERENCES

1. Robert F. Berkhofer, Jr., *A Behavioral Approach to Historical Analysis*. New York: Free Press, 1969, p. 7.
2. Edwin R. A. Seligman, ed., *Encyclopedia of the Social Sciences*. New York: Macmillan, 1932, II–III:357.
3. J. H. Hexter, *The History Primer*. New York: Basic Books, 1971, p. 3.
4. B. A. Hinsdale, *How to Study and Teach History, with Particular Reference to the History of the United States*. New York: Appleton-Century-Crofts, 1894, p. 18.
5. Felix Reichmann, "Historical Research in Library Service," *Library Trends, 13*(July 1964):33.
6. Raymond Irwin, *The Golden Chain: A Study in the History of Libraries*. London: H. K. Lewis, 1958, pp. 3–4.
7. Ronald Hagler, "Needed Research in Library History," in Rolland E. Stevens, ed., "Historical and Bibliographical Methods in Library Research," *Research Methods in Librarianship*, monograph no. 10. Urbana: University of Illinois, Graduate School of Library Science, 1971, p. 133.
8. Howard Winger, ed., *American Library History: 1876–1976. Library Trends, 25*(July 1976).
9. Herbert Goldhor, *An Introduction to Scientific Research in Librarianship*. Champaign, Ill.: Illini Union Bookstore, 1969, p. 98.
10. Michael H. Harris, ed., *Reader in American Library History*. Washington, D.C.: NCR Microcard Editions, 1971, p. 1.
11. Pierce Butler, *An Introduction to Library Science*. Chicago, Ill.: University of Chicago Press, 1944, p. 81.
12. Jesse H. Shera, "On the Value of Library History," *Library Quarterly, 22*(July 1952):240–251.
13. Arnold K. Borden, "The Sociological Beginnings of the Library Movement," *Library Quarterly, 1*(July, 1931):278–282.

14. Gwladys Spencer, *The Chicago Public Library: Origins and Backgrounds*. Chicago, Ill.: University of Chicago Press, 1943.
15. Jesse H. Shera, *Foundations of the Public Library: Origins of the Public Library Movement in New England from 1629–1855*. Chicago, Ill.: University of Chicago Press, 1949.
16. Walter M. Whitehill, *Boston Public Library, A Centennial History*. Cambridge, Mass.: Harvard University Press, 1956.
17. William Williamson, *William Frederick Poole and the Modern Library Movement*. New York: Columbia University Press, 1963.
18. George S. Bobinski, *Carnegie Libraries, Their History and Impact on American Public Library Development*. Chicago: American Library Association, 1969.
19. Joe W. Kraus, *Book Collections of Five Colonial College Libraries: A Subject Analysis* (unpublished doctoral dissertation, University of Illinois, 1960)
20. Francis G. Collier, *A History of the American Public Library Movement Through 1880* (unpublished doctoral dissertation, Harvard University, 1951).
21. Michael H. Harris, *Guide to Research in American Library History*. 2nd ed. Metuchen, N.J.: Scarecrow Press, 1974.
22. Winger, *American Library History*, p. 3.
23. David H. Eyman, ed., *Doctoral Dissertations in Library Science: Titles Accepted by Accredited Library Schools, 1930–1972*. Ann Arbor, Mich.: Xerox University Microfilms, 1973.
24. Maurice F. Tauber, ed., *Research in Librarianship. Library Trends*, 6 (October 1957).
25. Haynes McMullen, "Research in Backgrounds in Librarianship," *Library Trends*, 6(October 1957):116–117.
26. Hagler, "Needed Research in Library History," p. 133.
27. Charles M. Dollar, and Jensen, Richard J., *Historian's Guide to Statistics: Quantitative Analysis and Historical Research*. New York: Holt, Rinehart and Winston, 1971.
28. J. P. Wilkinson, "To What Extent Is the Hypothesis Necessary to the Historical Method?," *Newsletter on Library Research*, No. 3 (September 1975):4–5 (mimeographed).
29. J. Leonard Bates, "The Importance of Using Primary Sources in Historical Research," in *Historical and Bibliographical Methods in Library Research*, p. 11.
30. Oscar E. Anderson, "The Use of Archives in Historical Research," in *Historical and Bibliographical Methods in Library Research*, pp. 43–45.
31. Philip C. Brooks, *Research in Archives; The Use of Unpublished Primary Sources*. Chicago: University of Chicago Press, 1969.
32. Haynes McMullen, "Primary Sources in Library Research," in *Historical and Bibliographical Methods in Library Research*, p. 24.
33. Arthur Bestor, "History as Verifiable Knowledge," in *Historical and Bibliographical Methods in Library Research*, p. 109.
34. Abraham Kaplan, *The Conduct of Inquiry: Methodology for Behavioral Science*. Scranton, Pa.: Chandler, 1964, p. 361.
35. Edward G. Holley, "Textual Criticism in Library History," in *Historical and Bibliographical Methods in Library Research*, p. 104.
36. Margaret A. Corwin, "An Investigation of Female Leadership in Regional, State, and Local Library Associations, 1876–1923," *Library Quarterly*, 44(February 1974):133–144.
37. Paul A. Winckler, *Charles Clarence Williamson, 1888–1965: His Professional Life and Work in Librarianship and Library Education in the United States* (unpublished doctoral dissertation, New York University, 1964).
38. Charles C. Williamson, *Training for Library Service*. New York: Carnegie Corporation, 1923.

39. Leonaradas V. Gerulaitis, *The Venetian Incunabula: Printers and Readers* (unpublished doctoral dissertation, University of Michigan, 1969).

SELECTED BIBLIOGRAPHY

INFORMATION SOURCES FOR HISTORICAL INQUIRIES

America: History and Life. A Guide to Periodical Literature. V. 1–, no. 1–. Santa Barbara, Calif.: Clio Press for the American Bibliographical Center, 1964–. Quarterly.

American Historical Association, *Guide to Historical Literature.* New York: Macmillan, 1961.

Ash, Lee, ed., *Subject Collections.* 5th ed. New York: Bowker, 1978.

Ballard, Martin, ed., *New Movements in the Study and Teaching of History.* Bloomington: Indiana University Press, 1970.

Billias, George, *Oral History in the U.S.: A Directory.* New York: Free Press, 1971.

Clark, G. Kitson, *Guide for Research Students Working on Historical Subjects.* 2nd ed. New York and London: Cambridge University Press, 1968.

Coulter, Edith M., and Gerstenfeld, Melanie, *Historical Bibliographies; A Systematic and Annotated Guide.* Berkeley: University of California Press, 1965.

Fang, Josephine R., and Songe, Alice H., *International Guide to Library, Archival, and Information Science Associations.* New York: Bowker, 1976.

Gottschalk, Louis R., *Understanding History: A Primer of Historical Method.* 2nd ed. New York: Knopf, 1969.

Harris, Michael H., and Davis, Donald G., Jr., *American Library History; A Bibliography.* Austin: University of Texas Press, 1978.

Harvard University. Henry Adams History Club. *A Selected Bibliography of History.* 4th ed. Cambridge: Harvard University, 1970.

Historical Abstracts. Bibliography of the World's Periodical Literature. Edited by Erich H. Boehm. v. 1–. March 1955 to the present. (Quarterly)

International Bibliography of Historical Sciences. Edited for the International Committee of Historical Sciences. New York: Oxford University Press, 1926–.

Johnson, Thomas H., *The Oxford Companion to American History.* New York: Oxford University Press, 1966.

Kaser, David, "Advances in American Library History," in Michael H. Harris, ed. *Advances in Librarianship,* vol. 8. New York: Academic Press, 1978, pp. 181–199.

Keeling, Denis F., ed., *British Library History, Bibliography, 1969–1972.* Compiled by R. J. Busby and others of the Library History Group of the Library Association. London: Library Association, 1975.

Kelly, Thomas, "Thoughts on the Writing of Library History," *Library History, 3*(Spring 1975):161–169.

Kent, Sherman, *Writing History.* New York: Appleton, 1941.

Kuehl, Warren F., *Dissertations in History; An Index to Dissertations Completed in History Departments of the U.S. and Canadian Universities, 1873–1960.* Lexington: University of Kentucky Press, 1965.

Langer, William L., *Encyclopedia of World History.* 5th ed. Boston: Houghton Mifflin, 1972.

Ladenson, Alex, ed., *American Library Laws.* 4th ed. Chicago, Ill.: American Library Association, 1974.

Lowitt, Richard, "Case Study in Biographical Research," *Journal of Library History,* 4(April 1969):123–133.

McCoy, Florence N., *Researching and Writing in History: A Practical Handbook for Students.* Berkeley: University of California Press, 1974.

McHenry, Robert, and Van Doren, Charles, *Webster's Guide to American History.* Springfield, Mass.: Merriam, 1971.

Metcalfe, Josephine, *A Chronology of Librarianship.* Metuchen, N.J.: Scarecrow Press, 1968.

Morris, Richard B., and Irwin, Graham W., *Harper Encyclopedia of the Modern World.* New York: Harper & Row, 1970.

Notable Names in American History: A Tabulated Register. Clifton, N.J.: James T. White, 1973.

Nugent, Walter T. K., *Creative History.* 2nd ed. New York: Lippincott, 1973.

Poulton, Helen J., and Howland, Marguerite S., *The Historian's Handbook: A Descriptive Guide to Reference Works.* Norman: University of Oklahoma Press, 1972.

Renier, G. J., *History, Its Purpose and Method.* Boston, Mass.: Beacon Press, 1950.

Shafer, Robert J., ed., *A Guide to Historical Method.* Rev. ed. Homewood, Ill.: Dorsey Press, 1974.

Shera, Jesse H., *Historians, Books and Libraries: A Survey of Historical Scholarship in Relation to Library Resources, Organization and Services.* Cleveland, Ohio: Western Reserve University Press, 1953.

Shorter, Edward, *The Historian and the Computer: A Practical Guide.* Englewood Cliffs, N.J.: Prentice-Hall, 1971.

Stephens, Lester D., *Historiography: A Bibliography.* Metuchen, N.J.: Scarecrow Press, 1975.

Stone, Elizabeth W., *American Library Development, 1600–1899.* New York: H. W. Wilson, 1977.

Thomison, Dennis, *A History of the American Library Association, 1876–1972.* Chicago, Ill.: American Library Association, 1978.

Thornton, John L., *Chronology of Librarianship: An Introduction to the Histories of Libraries.* London: Grafton & Company, 1941.

U.S. Bureau of the Census, *Historical Statistics of the United States, Colonial Times to 1957.* Washington, D.C.: U.S. Government Printing Office, 1960. Supplement to 1962, 1965.

U.S. Bureau of Education, *Public Libraries in the United States of America: Their History, Condition and Management.* Special Report, Part I. Washington, D.C.: U.S. Government Printing Office, 1876.

U.S. Library of Congress, *The National Union Catalog of Manuscript Collections, 1959–1961.* Ann Arbor, Mich.: Edwards, 1962. Washington, D.C.: Library of Congress, 1962. Annual.

U.S. National Historical Publications Commission, *The Territorial Papers of the United States.* Washington, D.C.: U.S. Government Printing Office, 1950–1970.

U.S. Office of Education, *Commissioner's Report, 1920.* Washington, D.C.: U.S. Government Printing Office, 1920.

Vincent, John M., *Aids to Historical Research.* Freeport, N.Y.: Books for Libraries Press, 1969 (Essay Index Reprint Series).

Winks, Robin W., ed., *Historian as Detective; Essays on Evidence.* New York: Harper & Row, 1969.

LIBRARY SCIENCE HISTORICAL DISSERTATIONS

Academic and Research Libraries

Bidlack, Russell E. "The University of Michigan General Library: A History of Its Beginnings, 1836–1852." University of Michigan, 1954.

Gorchels, Clarence. "A Land-Grant University Library: The History of the Library of Washington State University, 1892–1946." Columbia University, 1971.

McMullen, C. Haynes. "The Administration of the University of Chicago Libraries, 1892–1928." University of Chicago, 1949.

Maloney, Louis C. "A History of the University Library at the University of Texas, 1883–1934." Columbia University, 1970.

Peterson, Kenneth G. "The History of the University of California Library at Berkeley, 1900–1945." University of California, Berkeley, 1968.

Rouse, Roscoe, Jr. "A History of the Baylor University Library, 1845–1919." University of Michigan, 1962.

Slavens, Thomas P. "The Library of Union Theological Seminary in the City of New York, 1836 to the Present." University of Michigan, 1965.

Biographies

Grotzinger, Laurel A. "The Power and the Dignity: Librarianship and Katherine Sharp." University of Illinois, 1964.

Holley, Edward G. "Charles Evans: American Bibliographer." University of Illinois, 1961.

Lawson, Richard W. "Mary Josephine Booth: A Lifetime of Service, 1904–1945." Indiana University, 1975.

Waddell, John N. "The Career of Isadore G. Mudge: A Chapter in the History of Reference Librarianship." Columbia University, 1973.

Public Libraries

Anders, Mary E. "The Development of Public Library Service in the Southeastern States, 1895–1950." Columbia University, 1958.

Barr, Larry J. "The Indiana State Library, 1825–1925." Indiana University, 1976.

Bobinski, George S. "Andrew Carnegie's Role in American Public Library Development." University of Michigan, 1966.

Cao, Jerry F. "The Los Angeles Public Library: Origins and Development, 1872–1910." University of Southern California, 1977.

Dain, Phyllis. "The New York Public Library: A History of Its Founding and Early Years." Columbia University, 1966.

Goudeau, John M. "Early Libraries in Louisiana: A Study of the Creole Influence." Case Western Reserve University, 1965.

Kramp, Robert S. "The Great Depression: Its Impact on Forty-Six Large American Public Libraries; An Inquiry Based on a Content Analysis of Published Writings of Their Directors." University of Michigan, 1975.

McCauley, Elfrieda. "Mill-Girl Libraries in New England, 1820–1860." Columbia University, 1971.

Oehlerts, Donald E. "The Development of American Public Library Architecture from 1850–1940." Indiana University, 1975.

Spain, Frances L. "Libraries of South Carolina; Their Origins and Early History, 1700–1830." University of Chicago, 1944.

Vannorsdall, Mildred M. "The Development of Library Services at the State Level in Ohio, 1817–1896." University of Michigan, 1974.

Special Libraries

Dale, Doris C. "The Origins and Development of the United Nations Library." Columbia University, 1968.

Kruzas, Anthony T. "The Development of Special Libraries for Business and Industry." University of Michigan, 1960.

Mallison, David W. "Henry Lewis Bullen and the Typographic Library and Museum of the American Type Founders Company." Columbia University, 1976.

Paul, Gary N. "The Development of the Hoover Institution on War, Revolution and Peace Library, 1919–1944." University of California, Berkeley, 1974.

Stillman, Mary E. "The United States Air Force Library Service; Its History, Organization, and Administration." University of Illinois, 1966.

Library Services and Programs

Archer, Horace R. "Some Aspects of the Acquisition Program at the University of Chicago Library, 1892–1928." University of Chicago, 1954.

Carrier, Esther J. "Fiction in Public Libraries of the United States, 1876–1900." University of Michigan, 1960.

Clement, Evelyn G. "Audiovisual Concerns and Activities in the American Library Association, 1924–1975." Indiana University, 1975.

Hanson, Eugene R. "Cataloging and the American Library Association, 1876–1956." University of Pittsburgh, 1974.

Monroe, Margaret E. "Evolving Conception of Adult Education in Three Public Libraries." Columbia University, 1962.

Ranz, James. "The History of the Printed Book Catalog in the United States." University of Illinois, 1960.

Rothstein, Samuel. "The Development of Reference Service in American Research Libraries." University of Illinois, 1954.

Stanford, Edward B. "Library Extension under the W.P.A.: An Appraisal of an Experiment in Federal Aid." University of Chicago, 1942.

Contemporary History

Brewster, Frank M. "An Analysis of American Overseas Library Technical Assistance, 1940–1970." University of Pittsburgh, 1974.

Healey, James S. "The Emergence of National Political Leadership for Library Development: The Case of Representative John E. Fogarty." Columbia University, 1973.

McGowan, Frank M. "The Association of Research Libraries, 1932–1962." University of Pittsburgh, 1972.

Rhodes, Lelia G. "A Critical Analysis of the Career Backgrounds of Selected Black Female Librarians." Florida State University, 1975.

Suzuki, Yukihisa. "American Influence on the Development of Library Services in Japan, 1860–1941." University of Michigan, 1974.

Operations Research in Librarianship: Quantitative Approaches to the Analysis of Management Problems

INTRODUCTION *use of math models, it was designed to improve mgmt.*

Operations research (OR) is the application of scientific method to management *operations* in an effort to aid managerial decision-making. Techniques of operations research are concerned with the activities of organizations, or systems, and are designed to provide management with a quantitative basis for decision making. Thus, like the computer and techniques of statistical analysis, operations research can be a valuable management tool. Techniques of operations research have been applied to such diverse management problems as the makeup of investment portfolios, the allocation of scarce resources, traffic congestion and control, the disposition of military forces, design of telephone networks, determination of inventory policies, and strategies of game playing.

Operations research had its beginnings in military research in World War II, with the application of mathematical analysis to the treatment of such problems as weapons evaluation, assessment of bomb damage, and development of an optimal strategy to search for submarines. Science had been applied to the problems of war long before the 1940s, from the times of Archimedes and Leonardo da Vinci to the present. But the basic philosophical approach and body of analytical techniques uniquely defining operations research as it is conceived today can be traced to English and American research groups that supported the war effort. After the war, such organizations as the Rand Corporation refined and continued to apply the techniques of operations research to military problems. Meanwhile, other investigators entered industry and the business world where they began to utilize operations research in the analysis of different kinds of problems. Other practitioners joined the faculties of universities and established the seeds of formal academic programs in operations research. Today many universities and departments within academic institutions offer courses or programs in operations research.

Reflecting the increasing importance of operations research in the anal-

121

ysis of library phenomena, courses in this subject have been introduced into the curricula of several library schools, including those at the University of Chicago, State University of New York at Buffalo, and the University of Illinois. In some library schools, students are encouraged to elect courses in OR from other academic units of the university, especially business administration. This chapter presents a basic introduction to the general nature of OR and indicates a few of the applications of this approach to research in librarianship.

Operations research has been somewhat facetiously defined as "what operations researchers do." Although the circularity of this particular definition should be evident, it is difficult nevertheless to provide a definition of operations research that would satisfy all practitioners. In one of the earliest textbooks treating the subject, operations research is defined as "a scientific method of providing executive departments with a quantitative basis for decisions regarding the operations under their control."[1] Operations research is both a philosophical approach and a set of analytic tools arising from the application of scientific method to management problems. Philosophically, OR is in tune with the basic principles of scientific method:

> The approach of OR has much in common with the scientific method: it requires a precise, often abstract, formulation of the essential features of a problem, a willingness to undertake methodical investigation to produce the information needed for decision making, and the analytic ability to recognize the consequences of this information.[2]

Thus, an operations research approach involves three principal steps: (*a*) problem formulation; (*b*) design of methodology; and (*c*) data gathering and analysis. The problem formulation stage involves two properties which are characteristic of the OR approach. First, hypotheses are typically mathematical in nature, involving the statement of a *mathematical model*. Second, the problem statement usually involves an operational definition of the characteristics of a "best," or *optimal* solution to the management problem being studied. The methodology employed in an OR study is frequently experimental, or one that involves direct observation of the phenomena of interest. In the data analysis stage, relatively sophisticated mathematical or statistical concepts are often utilized.

Two related tools of modern management are *systems analysis* and *computer system simulation*. The lines of demarcation between operations research, system simulation, and systems analysis are by no means precise and clear; the terms are used virtually synonomously by some writers. Indeed, the three approaches have in common their application to management problems and their construction and use of *models* of "real-world" phenomona, or systems.

MODELS

In the sense in which the word is used here, the term *model* refers to a *representation* of a real-world phenomenon. For example, the child's toy plane or railroad is a rough model of operational planes and trains. Another type of model is a map, providing the configuration of cities, towns, rivers, and roads of a particular geographic locality. Some maps include the representation of certain geological features, whereas others do not. But even geological maps are only gross models of the actual terrain considered; at some level (e.g., at the level of individual rocks and trees) certain physical phenomona are ignored and are not represented as elements of the model.

Another example of a simple map model is the practice of many libraries of offering guidance to patrons in the form of a floor plan of the library, indicating the location of major sections of the collection, as well as information desks, rest rooms, staircases, and elevators. Again, although grossly accurate, such a model is obviously only somewhat representative of the actual library building.

These examples illustrate that models are usually not intended to be totally faithful representations of reality, although clearly they must in some sense "capture the essence" of the systems being modeled. For example, models often serve an instructional purpose; this purpose is obviously ill-served if the essential characteristics of the system are ignored or misrepresented. What is meant by "essential," however, is not so clear. We argue that the identification of such characteristics implies the assumption of a particular point of view. For example, from a library patron's perspective, it may be that a floor plan of a library building should indicate all *service* areas in which users may be expected to interface with the building and its contents. According to this viewpoint, stack areas would probably be broadly identified and the location of rest rooms and information desks would be provided. But from the perspective of a professional librarian a floor plan might emphasize quite different aspects of the library building and services. Designed for a librarian, one might expect *function* to dictate the features displayed. Details of the technical services, cataloging, binding, serial records, and other behind the scenes operations might be illustrated, as well as some (but probably not all) of the service areas displayed on the user-oriented floor plan. Thus, the same library might be modeled by two quite different floor plans. (It might legitimately be argued that librarians ought to look at their library as a patron does, that service rather than function should be the viewpoint underlying the creation of the model, even for librarians. This argument does not attack the function-oriented model per se; it attacks the assumptions underlying the model's creation.)

The previous example illustrates several characteristics of a model. The builder of a model usually has a purpose in mind, and that purpose defines a set of constraints governing the final properties of the model. A model is thus much more than a faithful reproduction or representation of "reality"; it is reality viewed in a special way. Models cannot be characterized as right or wrong or good or bad by themselves; they can only be judged in terms of the set of constraints assumed in their construction. The constraints themselves can of course be challenged on other grounds.

SYSTEMS ANALYSIS

The "systems approach" is both a philosophy and a body of analytical techniques by means of which an analyst attempts to consider all aspects of a system. In its most general sense, *system* refers to such diverse phenomena as the skeletal structure of an animal, a business enterprise, an electronic computer, ecological phenomena, and libraries.

We will not attempt to define system except in a very broad and general sense. In his excellent nontechnical book, *The Systems Approach,* C. West Churchman defines a system as "a set of parts coordinated to accomplish a set of goals."[3] Making his definition more precise, Churchman lists the five essential aspects of a system as:

1. The *objectives* of the system and the *performance measures* which surrogate the objectives
2. The *environment* of the system—the set of fixed constraints which limit the behavior of the system and are not under the direct control of the system's managers
3. The *resources* of the system—the money, personnel, and equipment available to the system
4. The *components* of the system—the operations and functions performed in each of its subsystems
5. The *management* of the system

Many papers and monographs have been written which explicate aspects of the systems approach in terms of libraries, media centers, and information centers (see, for example, F. W. Lancaster[4]). Among the first librarians to do so was Fremont Rider. Writing more than 30 years ago about past library practice, Rider communicated a need to apply a modern systems viewpoint (and more generally, principles of the scientific method) to the problems of librarianship:

> And the reason for our failure to integrate what were really facets of one single problem was that we were blinded by the *status quo.* We insisted on continuing to accept as library axioms, unalterable and unquestionable, cer-

tain assumptions which no longer had validity, such dicta, for instance, as: Libraries are collections of books; books are stored on shelves; library materials have to be cataloged; catalogs have to be made on cards; books must be arranged by their call numbers, etc., etc., etc.

It is not until we have looked behind, and beyond, every one of these—and many other—supposedly basic axioms of library method, and have seriously questioned their validity as axioms, that we begin to make any real progress.[5]

Fremont Rider also identified the "information explosion" as simple exponential growth, a mathematical model we shall examine more closely later in this chapter.

It is frequently the case that, in order to enhance his or her understanding of a system, an analyst will construct an abstract representation of the system, a model of the system. Of particular interest here are the models of operations research, which are analytical and mathematical in nature. But before proceeding to an examination of some of the models of operations research and their application to library management problems, we will briefly examine the concept of a simulation model.

COMPUTER SYSTEM
SIMULATION MODELS

It is possible to model very complex systems with a computer program. During the course of "running" such a simulation program, the parameters of the system can be varied and the effects of the variation on the performance measures of the system can be observed. Simulation programs often make use of *random number generators* to simulate probabilistic phenomona such as the results of tossing coins or rolling dice. In this way nondeterministic characteristics of a system can be modeled. Because this technique is based on notions of chance, it is often referred to as the *Monte Carlo* method.

In one of the first applications of Monte Carlo simulation to librarianship, the University of Lancaster Library built a simulation program to help solve the problem of determining an optimal loan policy in its library. The model considered such factors as the lengths of loan periods, the possibility of loan renewals, reservations, recalls, the existence of multiple copies of books, and the number and patterns of demands. Three separate performance measures were defined as operational surrogates of the library's general objective of providing patrons good access to materials. These were

1. *Immediate availability:* the probability that a request for a given book can be satisfied immediately

2. *Satisfaction level:* in a given time period, the probability that a random demand can be satisfied immediately
3. *Collection bias:* the proportion of the 10% most popular books which are absent from the shelves

A well-developed and efficient library should enjoy relatively high values of immediate availability and satisfaction level (ideally, 1.00) and a low collection bias (ideally, 0.00).

Based on the computer-produced values of these measures for various length loan periods and classes of books ("popular," "very popular," and "other") the University of Lancaster Library was able to select an optimal loan policy.[6]

CONCEPT OF THE MATHEMATICAL MODEL

Operations research makes particular use of the *mathematical model.* A mathematical model is in part a theory that is expressed in mathematical terms. But if the theory is to relate to the real world, then its abstract elements must also be identified with practical, physical objects. By definition, operations research is concerned with the decision-making process of managers in the real world; thus, as with other kinds of scientific research, there must be both a theoretical and a practical aspect to all operations research models.

Many of the earliest mathematical models developed by human beings have been applied to the solution of practical problems in mensuration. Figure 5.1 illustrates a problem involving the measurement of the distance between two trees, labeled A and B. Unfortunately, this distance cannot be measured directly, because a barrier (such as a large building) lies directly between the two trees. However, if a location C can be found such that the angle ACB is a right angle, and such that both AC and BC can be measured directly, the practical problem of measuring the distance AB can be solved by utilizing the mathematical theory of plane (or Euclidean) geometry.

If the abstract lines and points of Euclidean geometry are interpreted as locations A, B, and C, then a mathematical model of the problem is provided by the Pythagorean theorem: "the square of the hypotenuse of a right triangle is equal to the sum of the squares of the other two sides." This relationship is a deduction (or theorem) of Euclidean geometry. It is a true statement of our hypothetical practical problem, however, only if the assumptions underlying the theoretical system of Euclidean geometry are true in the physical situation depicted.

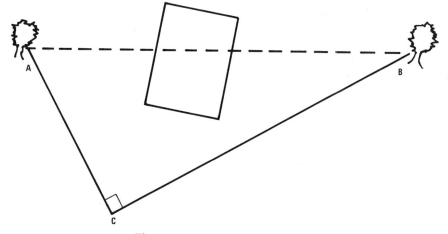

Figure 5.1. *A mensuration problem.*

The Pythagorean relationship can be expressed much more simply in the language of mathematics than it can be stated in the English language (or, indeed, in any natural language). If c, a, and b are the hypotenuse and legs of a right triangle respectively, then the Pythagorean relationship is given simply by the algebraic equation $c^2 = a^2 + b^2$. Identification of this theoretical result with our practical problem implies that

$$(AB)^2 = (AC)^2 + (BC)^2.$$

An additional characteristic of mathematical models can be illustrated by observing that knowledge of elementary algebra *alone* permits us to deduce a further result:

$$AB = \sqrt{(AC)^2 + (BC)^2}.$$

Thus, the distance between the two trees A and B can be found indirectly by measuring the distances AC and BC, by squaring these numbers and summing the squares, and finally, by extracting the square root of the sum. The point to be made is that once a relationship is expressed in mathematical terms, an entire system of theoretical mathematics (in this case, algebra) can be drawn upon to deduce new relationships. Clearly in this context mathematics is a powerful *tool*. It is this aspect of the mathematical model that sets it apart from other types of conceptual models such as those developed by the application of philosophical arguments or formal logical analysis. It is this characteristic of the mathematical model that makes it one of the most powerful analytical approaches to problem solving.

Perhaps a final statement should be added regarding the sense in which we use the term *mathematical model* to refer both to the mathematical theory and the interpretation of that theory in the real world. Some writers use the term *mathematical model* to refer to the theory only, and may largely ignore the important question of establishing a valid interpretation of the model (or demonstrating that the interpretation which they suggest is actually valid). It is possible (and, indeed, it sometimes happens) that a simple, elegant mathematical theory which is satisfying mathematically simply does not describe the real-world phenomenon in question. Such a theory may be a significant addition to already established abstract theory, but it would not necessarily contribute to the solution of real-world problems. An elegant mathematical theory is clearly of limited practical use if the assumptions that tie it to reality are not in fact valid.

EXPONENTIAL GROWTH AS AN ILLUSTRATIVE MATHEMATICAL MODEL

COMPOUND INTEREST

As we observed earlier, the fact that certain library phenomena could be described by the mathematical model of exponential growth has been known for more than 30 years. The exponential growth model is perhaps more commonly referred to by the layperson as the "compound interest" law. This model describes the growth of many natural as well as social organisms.

A fundamental characteristic of growth at compound interest is that the *increase* in size at any moment is proportional to the current size. Thus, if A dollars draw interest at the rate r (for example, $r = 4\%$, or .04) per year compounded annually, then the total amount of principal and interest A_1 at the end of 1 year is $A_1 = A(1 + r)$. Thus, if $r = .04$, $A_1 = 1.04A$. The number 1.04 is called the *constant of proportionality*.

At the end of 2 years, the total principal and interest amounts to $A_2 = (1 + r)[A(1 + r)] = A(1 + r)^2$ dollars. At the end of 3 years, a total of $A_3 = A(1 + r)^3$ dollars will have amassed. In general, at the end of n years, the total amount A_n of principal and interest accrued is given by

$$A_n = A(1 + r)^n. \tag{1}$$

Rate r is a *parameter* characteristic of a particular growth situation.

It is illustrative to compare growth at compound interest with that resulting from *simple interest*. For growth at simple interest, the interest is computed as a percentage of the principal, rather than as a percentage of

Table 5.1. *Growth of $100 at 6% Simple and Compound Interest over a 20-Year Period.*

n	Compound interest	Simple interest
0	$100.00	$100.00
1	106.00	106.00
2	112.36	112.00
3	119.10	118.00
4	126.25	124.00
5	133.82	130.00
6	141.85	136.00
7	150.36	142.00
8	159.38	148.00
9	168.95	154.00
10	179.08	160.00
11	189.83	166.00
12	201.22	172.00
13	213.29	178.00
14	226.09	184.00
15	239.66	190.00
16	254.04	196.00
17	269.28	202.00
18	285.43	208.00
19	302.56	214.00
20	320.71	220.00

the current size (principal plus interest) as with compound interest. Table 5.1 illustrates the growth of $100 invested at 6% annual simple interest and $100 invested at 6% interest compounded annually. The relative interest-earning power of compound interest over simple interest is immediately evident.

CONTINUOUS COMPOUNDING

A related mathematical growth model derives from compounding of interest *continuously* (as opposed to annually or monthly). It can be shown that with continuous compounding the total amount A_n of principal and accumulated interest after n periods of growth at a rate r per period is given by

$$A_n = Ae^{rn}, \tag{2}$$

where e is the transcendental number 2.71828 . . . , the base of natural logarithms. Table 5.2 provides values of e^x for various values of x and can be used to solve problems relating to continuous compound interest.

Example 1

The holdings of the Purdue University libraries are growing at "an amazingly steady" rate of about 6% per year.[7] If this rate of growth continues, by what factor will the size of the Purdue libraries have increased in a 30-year period?

Answer

From Equation (2), $A_n = Ae^{rn}$, where $r = .06$ and $n = 30$. Therefore, $A_{30} = Ae^{1.8}$. From Table 5.2, $e^{1.8} = 6.05$. Thus, if the observed rate of growth continues, the Purdue University Libraries will increase roughly by a factor of 6 in a 30-year period: $A_{30} = 6.050A$.

Example 2

A certain college library increased in size from 140,000 volumes in 1962 to 255,000 volumes in 1977. What is the rate of growth of the collection, compounded continuously, and when can the library be expected to reach the 1-million volume mark in holdings?

Answer

We are told that $n = 15$, $A_{15} = 255,000$, and $A = 140,000$. Substituting in Equation (2), we have $255,000 = 140,000e^{15r}$. Dividing both sides of

Table 5.2. *Values of e^x for $-3.0 \le x \le 3.0$.*

x	e^x	x	e^x	x	e^x
−2.9	.055	−.9	.407	1.1	3.004
−2.8	.061	−.8	.449	1.2	3.320
−2.7	.067	−.7	.497	1.3	3.669
−2.6	.074	−.6	.549	1.4	4.055
−2.5	.082	−.5	.607	1.5	4.482
−2.4	.091	−.4	.670	1.6	4.953
−2.3	.100	−.3	.741	1.7	5.474
−2.2	.111	−.2	.819	1.8	6.050
−2.1	.122	−.1	.905	1.9	6.686
−2.0	.135	−.0	1.000	2.0	7.389
−1.9	.150	.1	1.105	2.1	8.166
−1.8	.165	.2	1.221	2.2	9.025
−1.7	.183	.3	1.350	2.3	9.974
−1.6	.202	.4	1.492	2.4	11.023
−1.5	.223	.5	1.649	2.5	12.182
−1.4	.247	.6	1.822	2.6	13.463
−1.3	.273	.7	2.014	2.7	14.879
−1.2	.301	.8	2.226	2.8	16.444
−1.1	.333	.9	2.460	2.9	18.174
−1.0	.368	1.0	2.718	3.0	20.085

this equation by 140,000, we find that $e^{15r} = 1.82$. From Table 5.2, $e^{.6}$ is approximately equal to 1.82. Therefore, $15r = .60$ and $r = .04$.

At a 4% growth rate, we now wish to deduce when the library may be expected to reach the 1-million volume mark in holdings. Substituting the relevant numbers into Equation (2), we have

$$1,000,000 = 255,000e^{.04n}.$$

Then $e^{.04n} = 3.92$. From Table 5.2, $e^{1.4}$ is approximately equal to 3.92. Therefore $.04n = 1.4$ and $n = 35$ years. At a 4% growth rate, then, the library will reach 1 million volumes in holdings in approximately the year 2012.

Example 3

How many years will be required for a library that grows at a rate of 8% per year compounded continuously to double in size?

Answer

Substitution into Equation 2 yields

$$2A = Ae^{.08n}, \quad \text{or} \quad e^{.08n} = 2.$$

From Table 5.2, $e^{.7}$ is approximately equal to 2.0. Therefore, $.08n = .7$ and the doubling period is 8.75, or about 9 years.

A study by Steven Leach suggests that the exponential growth model does not describe the growth of large academic libraries as well as a model which reflects a "deceleration" in growth rate after a certain point.[8]

OTHER APPLICATIONS OF EXPONENTIAL GROWTH TO LIBRARIANSHIP

The model of simple exponential growth has been found to describe many other phenomena in librarianship in addition to the growth of library collections. For example, the number of both scientific journals and scientific abstracts published has been increasing exponentially at an annual rate of about 5%.[9] The often-used phrase "information explosion" can thus be given precise meaning as the exponential growth of the scientific journal literature.

From this, one might be tempted to ask if today's information explosion is really of greater urgency than it was some decades ago, because the rate of increase of literature has remained essentially constant and the same mathematical model has described the growth of the scientific literature for many decades. Not withstanding these facts, however, both the total volume and the annual production of scientific literature continue to increase yearly, and thus threaten our capacity to acquire, store, and access this national resource. These facts do imply a certain urgency to develop a set of solutions to the "information problem."

We conclude our discussion of exponential growth by observing that, as Derek Price points out in his book *Little Science, Big Science,*[9] it is logically impossible for uncontrolled exponential growth to continue indefinitely. Price suggests that the *logistic growth model* might well describe the future growth of science, and thus, the growth of scientific publication. For an intriguing discussion of this possibility, the reader is directed to Price's work.

QUEUING THEORY AS A SECOND ILLUSTRATIVE MODEL

SINGLE SERVER QUEUE

A mathematical theory of *waiting lines,* or *queuing,* has been under development and refinement since the early 1900s. Although the first applications of the theory were made to the design of service facilities in the telephone industry, the theory has since been found to apply to a myriad of real-world situations ranging from the design of transportation and production systems in industry to the determination of the number of check-out counters required in a supermarket. In addition to these applications to business and industry, there are many situations within a library that can properly be described by means of queuing theory.

A basic queuing model is applicable in a variety of situations characterized by congestion, which results because arrivals to a service facility (demands for the service) take place more rapidly than the service can be performed. A diagram of this situation in its simplest form is given in Figure 5.2, which depicts the arrival of individuals to a single service facility, or *channel*. Individuals are served on a first-come first-served

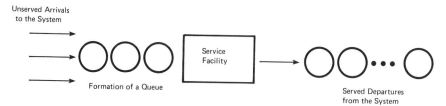

Figure 5.2. *The single service channel queuing model.*

basis. But because the rate of the service performed is not sufficient to meet the demand, a line, or queue, is occasionally formed behind the service facility. Eventually the service is performed for each person who then departs the system. Because only a single service channel is involved, this is the simplest formulation of the queuing situation. Clearly, however, the basic conceptual model depicted in Figure 5.2 can be generalized to include more than one service channel.

Now, obviously, we have already made a number of approximations to reality. In real-world situations, persons who arrive for service may find the length of the queue intolerable and refuse to queue up. Or, after having entered the line, individuals may become increasingly impatient and eventually decide to quit the line. These aberrant situations are referred to as *balking* and *reneging,* respectively, and are not explicitly treated in the simple queuing model.

The basic assumptions underlying the mathematical formulation of the single server queuing model are

1. Arrivals to the system are random (typically described by a Poisson distribution*) with a certain mean rate. This rate is denoted by the Greek letter λ (lambda).
2. Service times are of varying lengths (typically described by an exponential distribution) with the mean rate of service denoted by the Greek letter μ (mu). Quantities λ and μ are basic parameters of the queuing model.
3. No balking or reneging is considered in the model.

Now, let us apply this model to a library situation. Arrivals to a check-out desk in a library might occur at a mean rate of two individuals per minute ($\lambda = 2$), and be serviced at a mean rate of four individuals per minute ($\mu = 4$). Clearly, because *on the average* individuals are serviced faster than they arrive, the check-out desk will sometimes be idle. On the other hand, as arrivals are random, occurrences during some minutes may be as frequent as four or eight, whereas in other minutes no one may arrive. Occasionally, then, queues will build up. Some basic questions which will naturally arise from this formulation are, "How often will the service facility be idle?"; "What is the mean length of time required to receive service?"; and "How long, on the average, will the queue be?"

It is possible to answer these and other questions by the application of queuing theory to a particular situation. If the values of the parameters λ

---

* The Poisson and exponential distributions will be discussed more thoroughly later in the chapter.

and μ are known (i.e., have been estimated from library use data), it is possible to infer values for the following quantities, among others:

L = mean number of individuals in the system
L_q = mean length of the queue
T = mean waiting time in the system (including service time)
ρ = mean fraction of time the service facility is busy (ρ is the Greek letter, rho)
P_n = the probability that there are n individuals in the system

These values can be utilized by the management of the system to help determine an optimal configuration of service facilities. They provide the manager with information to be used in the decision-making process. We should be aware that the model and its implications do not and cannot tell the manager *what to do;* they merely provide quantitative bases on which more intelligent decision-making can be conducted. Superficially, an obvious solution to the problem of queue formation is simply to establish a sufficient number of service facilities so that a line will form only on rare occasions. (Thus, the provision of several hundred check-out counters in the typical supermarket would effectively eliminate the formation of lines except in most unusual circumstances.) Provision of such facilities is expensive, however. Clearly a trade-off exists between the costs incurred by the provision of extra service facilities and the cost incurred by user dissatisfaction. The manager can only weigh all available evidence and make a final determination based on that evidence.

APPLICATIONS OF QUEUING THEORY TO LIBRARIANSHIP

Philip Morse has described the basic elements of queuing theory and some of its applications to librarianship.[10] Obvious possible examples of queuing systems in libraries may be found at reference, reserve, and circulation desks. Also, as Morse points out, the library itself may be viewed as a queuing system. Users enter the library at a mean rate λ, remain for a period of time (i.e., are served), and leave at a mean rate μ. Here, however, there essentially exist an unlimited number of service channels and no queues ever form (unless there is a guard stationed at the exit).

Other examples of queuing systems within the library might involve the queue of books waiting to be catalogued, the queue of items waiting to be ordered, or the queue of serial publications waiting to be checked in. More complex queuing models exist in the library as well. For a discussion of some of these models and other applications of queuing theory to librarianship in general, the reader is referred to the excellent treatment of these subjects by Morse.[10]

SINGLE SERVER QUEUE: MATHEMATICAL MODELS AND PREDICTIVE FORMULAE

In this section we make explicit the mathematical formulation of a single server queuing system as an example of an operations research model and provide, without proof, predictive formulae for quantities of interest such as ρ, the percentage of time the service channel is utilized. We can begin by explicating in somewhat more detail the notion of a Poisson process, the usual model of "random arrivals." Essentially, a Poisson process results under the following conditions:

1. Events, in our case, arrivals, are as likely to occur in any one time interval as any other (the mathematical property of randomness).
2. The occurrence of one event has no effect on the occurrence of any other event (the mathematical property of independence).
3. The probability of two events occurring simultaneously in an arbitrarily small time interval is zero.

The mathematical formulation of a Poisson process is derived from these three assumptions and is expressed (without proof) by the formula

$$P(k) = \frac{e^{-\lambda}\lambda^k}{k!},$$

where $P(k)$ is the probability that k occurrences of the event will take place in one unit time and λ is the mean rate of arrival per unit time. The base of natural logarithms is e, and $k!$ is read k *factorial*.*

Values of e^{-x} for various values of x are provided in Table 5.2. Consulting Table 5.2, we have, for example, for $\lambda = 2$, $e^{-\lambda} = .135$. Then for a Poisson process with mean $\lambda = 2$, we obtain the following:

$$P(0) = \frac{(.135)(1)}{1} = .135\dagger$$

$$P(1) = \frac{(.135)(2)}{1} = .270$$

---

* $k!$ is defined as $1 \times 2 \times 3 \times \cdots \times k$. Thus, $3! = 6$, $4! = 24$, and so on. $0!$ is defined as being equal to 1.

† $\lambda^0 = 1$, for all nonzero values of λ.

$$P(2) = \frac{(.135)(4)}{2} = .270$$

$$P(3) = \frac{(.135)(8)}{6} = .180$$

$$P(4) = \frac{(.135)(16)}{24} = .090$$

$$P(5) = \frac{(.135)(32)}{120} = .036.$$

Thus, if the mean number of arrivals per minute is 2.0, then in 100 1-minute time intervals we can expect that in approximately 13 intervals there will be no arrivals, in 27 intervals there will be exactly one arrival, in 27 intervals there will be exactly two arrivals, and so on.

The *exponential distribution* is commonly found to describe the distribution of length of service times in queuing situations. The exponential distribution has the important property that it is "memoryless"—the liklihood that a service time will exceed a given length of time does not depend on the current length of service. Clearly, this assumption may not describe certain service situations, for example, the lengths of long-distance phone calls. Nevertheless, it does describe a wide variety of actual situations.

For an exponential distribution with a mean of μ, the probability that a service would exceed t units of time is given by the formula $P(t) = e^{-t/\mu}$. Suppose, for example, that the mean length of a service at a circulation desk in a library is known to be $\mu = 5$ minutes, and that the distribution of service times is exponential. Then the probability that a given service time will exceed 5 minutes is given by $P(5) = e^{-5/5} = e^{-1}$. Consulting Table 5.2, we find that $e^{-1.0} = .368$. Thus, in about 37 out of 100 cases, in excess of 5 minutes will be required to service a patron in this queuing situation. In a similar fashion, we can compute that

$$P(0) = 1$$
$$P(1) = .819$$
$$P(2) = .670$$
$$P(10) = .135.$$

Based on the assumption of Poisson arrivals and exponentially distributed service times, a number of properties of the basic queuing model can be inferred. The student is referred to any good text in operations research (for example, Hillier and Lieberman[11]) for proofs of the following results.

1. The proportion of time ρ that the service channel is busy is given by

$$\rho = \lambda / \mu$$

2. The mean length L_q of the queue is given by

$$L_q = \frac{\rho^2}{1 - \rho} = \frac{\lambda^2}{\mu(\mu - \lambda)}$$

3. The mean number L of individuals in the system (in the queue or being served) is given by

$$L = \frac{\rho}{1 - \rho} = \frac{\lambda}{\mu - \lambda}.$$

4. The mean waiting time T in the system (including service time) is given by

$$T = L/\lambda = 1/(\mu - \lambda).$$

5. The probability P_n that there are exactly n individuals in the system is given by

$$P_n = (1 - \rho)\rho^n.$$

The above formulas assume "steady state" conditions—that is, that sufficient time has elapsed since the initial state of the system so that the results are essentially independent of (not affected by) that state, whatever it may have been. The queue at a circulation desk, for example, is initially of length zero at the beginning of each day's work. This is the initial (daily) state of the circulation system.

We also observe that although there may be natural peaks in demands for service in a particular system, this does not mean that the Poisson distribution in particular or queuing theory in general cannot be utilized in a description of that system. It may be necessary to divide a day into distinct intervals, however, each characterized by its own Poisson distribution.

Example 4

Suppose that arrivals to a reserve reading desk are described by a Poisson distribution in which $\lambda = 6.0$ (that is, an average of 6.0 persons per minute arrive randomly and independently to the reserve desk). Further suppose that persons are served at the rate of eight per minute, and that the distribution of service times is exponential. Then the channel will be busy, on the average, about 75% of the time ($\rho = \lambda/\mu = .75$). Then L, the mean number of individuals in the system, is 3.0, the mean length of the queue L_q is 2.25, and T, the waiting time in the system, is approximately 30 seconds. Finally, the probability that there are exactly three individuals in the system is $(1 - .75)(.75^3)$, or about .11.

We have obtained what may be, to some readers, somewhat unexpected quantitative results—results that cannot be deduced without resorting to mathematics. The application of the mathematical theory of queue formation has enabled us to compute precise estimates for a number of quantities of interest. Neither intuition nor formal logical analysis permits this degree of precision. Thus, the mathematical deductions of queuing theory can be seen as a means of enhancing our natural intuition and logical comprehension of the queuing problem.

TESTING THE FIT OF THE MODEL

The previous section presented some of the basic theoretical results in one of the simplest queuing systems. Before this theory and its implications can indicate anything to us concerning a particular real-world system such as a library circulation desk, however, the basic assumptions underlying the model must be valid in that empirical system (as in any other operations research model). In particular, the queuing model previously described assumes that the distribution of arrivals to the system can be described by a Poisson distribution and that service times can be described by an exponential distribution. These assumptions must be verified by collecting and analyzing real-world data.

A crude but simple method that can be employed to test the hypothesis of Poisson arrivals is the computation of the mean and variance of a set of arrival data. (See Chapter 9 for discussion of mean and variance.) In a theoretical Poisson distribution, these two parameters are equal. Thus, empirical data generated by a Poisson process should reveal a mean and variance that are approximately equal. In a similar vein, one may make a quick check of empirical data to test the hypothesis that data are described by an exponential distribution by making use of the theoretical fact that the mean and standard deviation of an exponential distribution are equal. A more sophisticated and accurate method of testing the ''goodness of fit'' of empirical data to a theoretical model is the utilization of the chi-square test, which is discussed in some detail in Chapter 12.

SELECTED EXAMPLES OF OPERATIONS RESEARCH

Morse's Work at M.I.T.

How have the techniques of operations research (OR) been applied to library problems? Perhaps we should cite and very briefly describe some of the major achievements and landmarks in respect to operations research in librarianship.

One of the most thorough, early applications of the principles of operations research to librarianship can be found in Philip Morse's *Library Effectiveness*. [10] Morse, a member of the faculty at M.I.T., studied library operations as a class project in a graduate course in operations research, and his book evolved from that study. *Library Effectiveness* presents an initial discussion of considerations from probability theory. The book then provides a detailed discussion about applications of queuing theory and the theory of Markov chains to such problems as methods for satisfying circulation demand, for predicting future demand, for deciding when to retire a book or order multiple copies, as well as other problems. The text is not written on a particularly elementary level; some mathematical sophistication will be required to appreciate it fully.

LEIMKUHLER'S WORK AT PURDUE

Ferdinand Leimkuhler, another early investigator to apply operations research to library problems, is professor of industrial engineering at Purdue University. As was the case with Philip Morse, Leimkuhler's work was done with engineering classes using the library as a laboratory. Leimkuhler has published numerous research articles which describe mathematical models of library circulation, storage, shelving, and file organization, as well as pieces of more general interest. [7,12,13]

BUCKLAND'S WORK AT THE UNIVERSITY OF LANCASTER

Buckland's work has been referred to earlier in the context of a simulation model of the circulation process. That model was only one part of a comprehensive analysis of library operations conducted by the University of Lancaster Library. The University of Lancaster and its library were both established in the early 1960s, and librarians there began a research project to explore and to analyze in detail the processes underlying the provision of library services. The final report of the project was published in 1970 as *Systems Analysis of a University Library*. The spirit of systems analysis and operations research was well expressed in the introduction to the report where the development of an operations research model is discussed:

> The purpose of such a model or simulation is to form a suitable abstraction of reality, preserving the essential structure of the problems in such a way that analysis affords insight into both the original concrete situation and other similar situations. The manner in which these models and simulations are linked together will depend upon the particular management information which is required. [6]

The intense analysis of operations conducted by the University of Lancaster Library was one of the first large-scale operations research studies conducted by the staff members of a library. *Systems Analysis of a University Library* treats aspects of technical processing, strategies of purchasing and discarding, and loan and duplication policies, among other topics. It also includes an extensive bibliography of materials published prior to 1970 which treat aspects of the application of systems analysis, simulation modeling, and operations research to librarianship.

OTHER SELECTED PUBLICATIONS

The January 1972, issue of *Library Quarterly* contains the proceedings of the Thirty-Fifth Annual Conference of the Graduate Library School of the University of Chicago. This publication is notable because it combines in one volume several different applications of OR to librarianship described by a number of experts, including, among others, Morse, Leimkuhler, and Buckland. The issue also contains a selective bibliography of library OR prepared by Vladimir Slamecka.

Many of the applications of OR to librarianship are treated in one chapter of a volume produced by Professor Morris Hamburg *et al.* at the Wharton School, University of Pennsylvania.[14] This work is excellent for its presentation of the historical development of OR models to many problems of librarianship. The descriptions provided by Hamburg are (necessarily) quite terse, and students who have little knowledge or experience in relation to OR models will find parts of the text to be difficult reading.

CONCLUSIONS

Like statistical theory and the electronic computer, operations research is a research tool that is being increasingly applied to library problems. But OR is more than this; it is a philosophy, a state of mind as well. OR is sometimes erroneously viewed merely as a collection of analytical techniques. But the mathematical components of OR result essentially from the application of an intellectual framework, which can be characterized as scientific method, to the analysis of managerial problems. In a larger context, the basic philosophical approach of scientific method is much more significant than any of the individual mathematical models of operations research. It is true that, unlike some of the other applications of scientific method to the conduct of research, OR demands a certain mathematical sophistication, both in the formulation of a problem and in the ensuing analysis. This characteristic of OR should not be allowed to obscure the fact that in order for OR models to be meaningful to us about the real world, the *validity* of the models must be established. In this respect, the principles of scientific research must be rigorously applied to ensure that the assumptions underlying operations research models of library phenomena are indeed valid representations of reality.

APPENDIX: PROBLEMS FOR SOLUTION

1. Define a fourth operational performance measure for providing adequate access to library materials (i.e., a measure not utilized in the University of Lancaster simulation study). Discuss advantages and disadvantages of your defined measure.

2. What will $100 be worth at the end of a 20-year period if it is compounded at 6% continuous interest? Compare your answer with entries in Table 5.1 and comment on the comparison.

Answer

The answer is $332.00. Compounding continuously evidently increases, but not substantially, the interest earned by annual compounding.

3. According to the *Bowker Annual*, (twentieth edition), the aggregate number of volumes held by U.S. college and university libraries in Fall 1964 was 240,000,000, and this figure increased to 445,000,000 by Fall 1974. What was the rate of increase, compounded continuously, in volumes held during the 10-year period?

Answer

Approximately 6.5%.

4. A certain public library increased in size from 65,000 volumes in 1957 to about 220,000 volumes in 1970. (*a*) What is the growth rate of the collection, compounded continuously? (*b*) Assuming the same growth rate continues into the future, what will be the size of the library's holdings by 1996?

Answer

(*a*) Approximately 9.2%. (*b*) Approximately (11.02) (220,000) = 2,424,000 volumes.

5. From Example 3 in the text, one can see that the relationship between the number of years required for an organism to double, n, and the annual rate of growth compounded continuously, r, is given approximately by the formula $rn = .70$. (*a*) Explain the above assertion. (*b*) Use the formula to calculate the rate of growth for a library that doubles in size every 10 years; every 13 years. (*c*) Use the formula to find n (the doubling period) for an organism growing at a rate of growth of 4%, 5%, 6%.

Answer

(*b*) 7.0%; 5.4%; (*c*) 17.5 years; 14.0 years; 8.8 years.

6. Sketch a diagram of a model of a general queuing situation in which more than one service facility is involved.

7. Provide an example that was not discussed in the text of a service activity in which lines tend to form in libraries. Consider the basic assumptions underlying the queuing model with respect to this activity and formulate an hypothesis regarding the applicability of the assumptions to the activity selected. Explain how you would test your hypothesis.

8. Consider a Poisson process with mean $\lambda = 2$ describing the frequency of arrivals to a queuing system. Clearly there must be, in any given 1-minute interval, either zero arrivals, one arrival, two arrivals, and so on. There may, in fact, be 10 or 50 arrivals, but these are both unlikely (i.e., are relatively rare events). Thus, the sum of all the probabilities involved must sum to 1.0: $P_0 + P_1 + P_2 + P_3 + \cdots + P_n = 1$, or $\Sigma P_n = 1$. Use this fact to calculate the probability that six or more patrons will arrive in a given minute.

Answer

$$P_0 + P_1 + P_2 + P_3 + P_4 + P_5 = .981.$$

Therefore, $P_{n \geq 6}$ must be $1 - .981 = .019$.

9. Consider a single server queuing system in which arrivals are Poisson distributed with $\lambda = 18$ per hour and the service times are exponentially distributed with $\mu = 20$ services per hour. Compute ρ, L, L_q, T, and $P_{n \leq 4}$.

Answer

$$\rho = .9; \ L = 9; \ L_q = 8.1; \ T = 30 \text{ minutes}; \ P_{n \leq 4} = .40951.$$

10. Discuss a queuing situation for which $\lambda \geq \mu$. Couch your discussion in terms of the effect on the formulae given for L, T, and so on.

REFERENCES

1. Philip M. Morse and Kimball, G. E., *Methods of Operations Research*. Cambridge, Mass.: M.I.T. Press, 1951.
2. Abraham Bookstein, "Implications for Library Education," *Library Quarterly*, *42*(January 1972):140–151.
3. C. West Churchman, *The Systems Approach*. New York: Dell, 1968.
4. F. W. Lancaster, ed., *Systems Design and Analysis for Libraries, Library Trends*, *21*(April 1973).
5. Fremont Rider, *The Scholar and the Future of the Research Library*. New York: Hadham Press, 1944.
6. Michael K. Buckland, Hindle, A., Mackenzie, A. G., and Whitfield, Ronald M., *Systems Analysis of a University Library*, Final Report on a Research Project, University of Lancaster Occasional Papers, No. 4. University of Lancaster Library, 1970.
7. Ferdinand F. Leimkuhler, "Systems Analysis in University Libraries," *College and Research Libraries*, *27*(January 1966):15.
8. Steven Leach, "The Growth Rates of Major Academic Libraries: Rider and Purdue Reviewed," *College and Research Libraries, 37*(November 1976):531–542.
9. Derek J. deSolla Price, *Little Science, Big Science*. New York: Columbia University Press, 1965, p. 7.
10. Philip M. Morse, *Library Effectiveness: A Systems Approach*. Cambridge, Mass.: M.I.T. Press, 1968.
11. Frederick S. Hillier and Lieberman, Gerald J., *Introduction to Operations Research*. San Francisco: Holden-Day, 1967.
12. Ferdinand F. Leimkuhler, "A Literature Search and File Organization Model," *American Documentation, 19*(April 1968):131–136.
13. Ferdinand F. Leimkuhler, "Operations Research and Information Science— A Common Cause," *JASIS, 24*(January–February 1973):2–8.
14. Morris Hamburg, Clelland, Richard C., Bommer, Michael R. W., Ramist, Leonard E., and Whitfield, Ronald M., *Library Planning and Decision-Making Systems*. Cambridge: M.I.T. Press, 1974.

CHAPTER 6

Additional Research Methods in Librarianship

INTRODUCTION

The methodology of research includes all techniques employed by investigators to examine library and information phenomena. Thus, scholars and other research workers in the field have used a variety of proven methods; these investigators have rendered a multiform of knowledge on numerous levels of complexity and utility. In applying investigative talents to a wide range of library problems, some scholars have minimized chances of producing unreliable findings by using extreme care in selecting the most suitable data-collection methods. Generally, the type of information sought in a particular project has guided the application of appropriate research techniques. Previous chapters have been devoted primarily to specific research methods that rely chiefly upon indirect observation. For example, we have learned that investigators who conduct survey research usually depend upon the questioning of respondents and the recording of answers to ascertain how research subjects might act or think under certain circumstances, and historians acquire evidence indirectly by examining past records. Although many accomplished studies in the field could be classified under these types of methods or under some other technique based upon indirect observation, a number of additional approaches are also used to gather research information. Many of these portals to new knowledge have roots in methods based wholly or partly upon the *direct* observation and subsequent description of whatever was observed. Some scholars have applied the generic term *descriptive research* to many of these additional kinds of studies.

Empirical scientists in the modern world have traditionally relied upon carefully structured experiments. At times, scientists have conducted experimental studies in which phenomena were not directly observed in an actual (or "real") situation but in which prototypes of existing processes or events were closely examined. Nonetheless, some investigative tasks do not lend themselves readily to randomized experimental designs;

therefore, other methods of inquiry must be selected. For example, the following kinds of inquiries would not be particularly amenable to experimental designs because these studies would require either extensive direct observation or descriptive/historical methods.

1. An evaluation of the research and screening procedures used last year by a large research library to select new professional employees
2. A study of the impact of automation on a group of special libraries in the field of textiles over a 3-year period
3. A project designed to assess the effect of the attainment of faculty status among a group of academic librarians
4. An inquiry to determine factors related to the selection of library building consultants for a group of newly constructed metropolitan libraries in the South
5. An assessment of losses and thefts of college library books in a 5-year period
6. An examination of the administrative practices of a research library's serials department
7. An analysis of the role of state library consultants in the development of rural library programs during the early years of the Library Services Act
8. A study of the utilization of a computer-produced book catalog in a group of special libraries within the chemical industry
9. An evaluation of the use of student assistants in New York City school media centers
10. A project designed to trace the development of bookmobile library service in South Carolina between 1930 and 1960.

This list should demonstrate that experiments are not always appropriate in some settings or areas in which librarians seek new information. Therefore, in such situations, research workers can sometimes rely upon the direct inspection of "real-world" phenomena. Furthermore, several—often quite different—methods can be used to obtain optimal data in the course of conducting a single study. Sometimes, the use of multiple data-gathering techniques in a study enhances research precision. For example, two or more research processes can be used to compensate for inherent weaknesses of a primary data-gathering instrument, thereby producing supplementary research data that can be used to minimize error. Moreover, when research data are collected by means of several strategies, scientists can often be more certain and can draw more reliable conclusions. Even though several methods without definitude or distinction might be employed in a single inquiry, investigators may use the data obtained, provided that weaknesses are taken into consideration as the new information and its sources are evaluated and analyzed. Therefore, our concern in this chapter is with supplemental research techniques, many of which contain direct observational and/or descriptive elements.

OBSERVATION AND DESCRIPTION

Libraries are formal organizations that encompass a group of people, resources, services, facilities, and activities, all presumably directed toward common objectives. In addition to the research data-gathering methods outlined in previous chapters, origins of new research information about libraries as organizations and information systems include data obtained from the following sources: (*a*) institutional and agency records and collected statistics; (*b*) experiences of librarians as a result of "trial and error"; and (*c*) several observational and descriptive techniques, including the user study, evaluative study, library survey, community survey, content analysis, and comparative study, among others. To provide a logical discussion of these studies, methods associated with them will be approached separately in this chapter; however, the reader should be aware that differences are not always so clear-cut in actual research settings. In this approach to descriptive research, emphasis will be placed on several, well-defined observational strategies, some of which might be used to complement other useful research methods. Indeed, many descriptive procedures are based upon an amalgamation of methodological approaches.

Generalized procedures of scientific method provide leeway for the use of numerous research techniques, many of which cannot be classed as experimental, survey, or historical methods, but which are based upon direct observation and description of phenomena. The term *observation* is used to indicate that the object or subject of an investigation is being subjected to close—usually visual—surveillance and that the information obtained (i.e., the observations in the form of recorded data) will then be related to more general propositions or theories. Therefore, the term *observation* implies that some type of surveillance is undertaken for the purpose of satisfying an investigator's interest or curiosity about a distinct research task. Observation is widely recognized as a prime requisite of research in general and of descriptive research in particular. Although observation is a relatively primitive procedure, it is frequently very valuable in research and is often described aptly as a technique for securing "measurements" without the aid of instruments.

W. I. B. Beveridge points out in *The Art of Scientific Investigation* that ''observation involves noticing something and giving it significance by relating it to something else noticed or already known.''[1] Research subjects are commonly observed by scholars who intend to identify and delineate situations which the objects under observation ordinarily encounter and determine how these objects (or subjects) behave in the situations. When an investigator engages in the observed entity or activity, *participant observation* occurs. Investigators who use direct observation may employ either obtrusive or unobtrusive techniques. *Obtrusive observation* is forward and open; *unobtrusive observation,* however, is clandestine and discreet. Both methods can be employed by investigators without direct interaction with research subjects. For example, in a study of library services to migrant farm laborers, a research worker might observe the process as an outsider—watching but not participating in the service. On the other hand, the investigator might even pose as a migrant worker to gain a discreet position from which to examine the service from the recipient's viewpoint.

When research workers take special vantage positions to unobtrusively observe phenomena in a direct manner, *controlled observation* can be accomplished. For example, observers in a large university library might pose as students or other library users and station themselves in the reference department to discreetly observe activities of librarians and to record selected behavior of both the clientele and the reference personnel. · By observing the interactions of librarians with their clients in an actual service setting, samples of selected events can be procured. In turn, these observations may lead to valid conclusions about the observed phenomenon. The primary advantage of such observational strategies is the access they yield to a variety of perhaps unanticipated research data. However, clandestine observation does pose an ethical problem, and investigators must be sure that the privacy of research subjects is protected and the confidentiality of collected data is maintained.

In field studies, direct observation and the ensuing *description* of phenomena are used to better understand situations, processes, developments, events, or some other phenomenon. The act of describing also involves the preparation of factual reports about observed phenomena, including—insofar as possible—an account of relationships noticed among variables. Research data for many descriptive studies are comprised of newly generated information, rather than prerecorded data. In historical research projects, however, information contained in sources such as archives, journals, reference sources, government publications, or other media or agencies is often valuable. Studies in which a phenomenon will be characterized over a lengthy time period usually rely upon historical records or documents. In both descriptive and purely historical studies, however, investigators do not manipulate variables. Moreover, controlled conditions are not used to initiate the occurrence of a desired event. The direct observation of library phenomena—as distinguished from a contrived and controlled research situation—offers excellent opportunities for investigators to acquire new data. As events occur in natural settings, observational methods allow their documentation; thus, validity of the procured data can be very high. If research problems have been conceptualized clearly and productive investigative methods have been formulated so that observational data can be recorded systematically, validity and reliability checks might be made in the form of supplemental modes of inquiry. Under such conditions, direct observation becomes an effective and cogent research tool, and investigations can benefit from its high degree of reliability. Herbert Goldhor wrote that direct observation "is a good method by which to verify data secured by other methods, e.g., the interview; if those parts of the data which are verifiable turn out to be correct, one can have more confidence in the accuracy of the non-verifiable parts."[2]

In descriptive studies based upon direct observation, capable investigators are prudent to avoid the mere accumulation of facts. To be meaningful and fruitful, the observation undertaken in descriptive research must be followed by a synthesis, analysis, or interpretation of the collected data. Assume, for example, that an investigator will conduct a comparative study to determine how *planned* decentralization was accomplished in several academic libraries as opposed to *expedient* decentralization in a similar group of libraries. Research workers would probably interpret and compare data from the two groups in relation to factors such as user access to needed materials; supervision of staff and staff efficiency; problems related to the inefficiency of the duplication of library resources; faculty interest and input in library operations; sharing of materials; ordering, classifying, and cataloging materials; and many other pertinent variables. In descriptive studies, the process of observation normally takes precedence over that of evaluation. Moreover, generalizations are not made unless representative observations have been selected from samples of defined populations.

As noted in Chapter 4, historical studies assess past events—their incidences, distribution, and relationships. But, to determine *present* conditions (i.e., existing practices, procedures, activities, processes, etc.), investigators must seek contemporary data about ongoing phenomena. *Structured observation* can produce contemporary or current data about the actions of persons, or information about how phenomena occur in particular environments and under certain conditions. Structured observation is carefully planned; it commonly involves the deliberate, systematic viewing of critical aspects of an operational process or the behavior of particular groups of subjects. When the observer is well aware of the numerous activities and interactions pertaining to a phenomenon, structured observation can be most effective in gaining access to original information. For example, in examinations of the roles of groups such as boards of trustees, friends of the library, or library committees, investigators could carefully schedule and plan periods of direct observation of pertinent activities so that needed data about the functions and actions of group members might be obtained. Structured observation is also more conducive to examinations of hypotheses than unstructured observation, because the investigator is keenly aware of the kinds of data needed to test an unproven proposition and is in a favorable position to gather them. Interviews with subjects are sometimes conducted as concomitants to structured observational methods of descriptive studies.

Bias is a major problem related to observation and description. Thus, research workers must subdue their natural tendency to selectively view phenomena that tend to support personal conceptions, presumptions, and prejudices. When observations are not unduly distorted by biases and subjective interpretations, more objective and reliable data are collected. *Objectivity* has been defined as "the capacity of a scientific observer to see the empirical world as it 'actually' is and the resultant quality of the body of knowledge."[3] Therefore, objective research data are relatively free from personal bias and are not based upon value judgments. Objectivity is not so much a virtue of the data as it is an attitude of the investigator toward research evidence. In their attempts to eliminate biased distortions, scientists tend to explain phenomena more accurately, rather than to suppress information, criticize the object of the observation, or offer prejudicial explanations. For example, assume that a research worker has been engaged by a state library to examine and make a report on procedures whereby large municipal libraries submit their budgets to city officials. Although the investigator favors the practice of allowing the librarian to recommend a budget directly to the chief city administrators, data collected in the study support the tailoring of budgetary procedures to local practices of other public institutions, insofar as possible. Thus, in the collection, analysis, and reporting of the data, the research worker should objectively indicate the various advantages and disadvantages of different procedures for the submission of budgets, including the following practices: (*a*) the librarian's recommendation of the library budget directly to the chief administrator; (*b*) the adoption of the budget by the library board and the approval of tax monies only by the city council; (*c*) the submission of the budget by the library board to the city council through the chief city administrator; (*d*) the direct submission of the budget to the city council by the library board; and (*e*) other observed miscellaneous procedures. Thus, the investigator's report of budgetary procedures should reflect what was actually observed rather than what any one concerned individual, including the research worker, believes to be the best practice.

Recorded descriptions obtained as a result of inquiry are truly objective when they reflect *what* was observed, rather than *who* did the observing. But when investigators become personally and emotionally involved in an observed phenomenon, objective descriptions are difficult to obtain—if not impossible. Thus, observers who strive for objectivity will rely primarily upon physical inspection, rather than intuition or common sense. Many problems of bias can be reduced appreciably when investigators realize that the act of describing a phenomenon is not synonymous with theorizing or contriving appraisals and evaluations of it.

THE CASE STUDY METHOD

In numerous studies, comparisons are made among several entities or among many phenomena; however, some investigators are interested in a single research object and attempt to gather extensive data about it so that relationships among variables associated with the observed phenomenon can be identified. The *case study* is particularly appropriate for the latter type of inquiry; this approach allows a concentrated focus on a single phenomenon and the utilization of a wide array of data-gathering methods. The overall purpose of a case study is to obtain *comprehensive* information about the research object. Data-gathering methods used in case studies are based primarily upon direct observation; both participant and nonparticipant observation can be used. When necessary, these methods are supplemented by structured techniques such as interviews and questionnaires. In librarianship, the objects or subjects of a case study are typically one or more of the following entities: (*a*) organizations such as libraries, media centers, information centers, or library schools—or significant aspects of them; (*b*) librarians, library assistants, clerical workers in libraries, or groups of library users; or (*c*) programs or processes such as information systems and various library projects or techniques.

Case studies conducted in librarianship have focused on many groups of library clientele, including the following: persons in institutions (i.e., hospitals, correctional institutions, etc.); disadvantaged or culturally deprived citizens; children and high school students; college or university faculty members and students; professional workers such as doctors, lawyers, engineers, or professors; persons employed in business or industry; and other groups of library and information users and nonusers. Case studies allow close examinations of unique problems of individual groups or situations—something that many other methodologies do not readily permit. In view of concern about the social utility and responsibility of libraries as institutions, the case study approach to inquiry appears to be particularly appropriate in studying relationships between library services and a variety of social problems. Indeed, the case approach is particularly applicable in inquiries concerned with the role of libraries as social institutions—that is, their social control, performance, and impact on society in general and special groups in particular.

The primary advantage of case studies is the opportunity they afford for thorough and detailed examinations and analyses of a research problem so that findings can be applied directly to the object of an inquiry. On occasion, the case method has also been used in librarianship as an *exploratory study* (preliminary investigation), conducted to discover and describe what exists, rather than to measure relationships between variables. In some cases, these exploratory studies have been used to clarify vague concepts or to challenge assumptions so that more penetrating investigations could be undertaken in which hypotheses were tested. But case studies have disadvantages that should also be recognized; they tend to be time consuming and expensive. In addition, a single case study does not generally yield definitive results; therefore, collected data must be supplemented by information from other research modes, especially when research workers attempt to make generalizations about observed phenomena. When the objects of case studies are large groups of people or complex entities, several research workers might be needed to serve as observers. Because most observations generated by case studies result from nominal techniques of measurement and could be considered as "soft" rather than "hard" data, sophisticated statistical analysis of this collected information is difficult to accomplish, perhaps impossible in some instances. However, findings of case studies can be strengthened by utilizing whatever means of quantification are amenable in a given project. For example, even a simple record of the number of times an event occurs during a specified time period can sometimes be of value.

The following steps are generalizable procedures for the conduct of case studies:

1. The research object is explicitly identified and described at a level of explanation commensurate with whatever pertinent knowledge has already been produced about it.
2. Information about the research object and investigative task are then assembled and analyzed, and relevant terms and variables are defined and described.

3. The research question is stated or hypotheses are formulated—if appropriate—based upon available information and the body of theory related to the topic of the study (More often than not, case studies are based upon research questions rather than hypotheses; in any event, the research problem should be examined within the context of existing theoretical knowledge).
4. An entity (case) is chosen as the specific object to be studied with reference to the research problem.
5. The object of the study is then carefully observed, and, if necessary, causal factors associated with the observed phenomenon are identified.
6. If sufficient research data are collected, the hypothesis may be tested with some degree of certainty; however, investigators can be more certain when they select and examine similar cases (i.e., conduct follow-up case studies in the same problem area).

Should collected evidence fail to allow the hypothesis to be tested or to solve the research problem, propositions of the inquiry may need to be reformulated, or the examined phenomenon may need to be conceptually refined. An answer to the question of whether the collected data provided insights relating to the research question or whether they sustained the hypothesis might provoke adjunct studies that could lead to the identification of definite relationships between pertinent variables of the selected case.

Upon completion of some case studies, observers have elected to take an additional step—that is, to apply specific remedial procedures to the objects of research. When suggested operations or measures are applied, research workers normally follow through and attempt to observe whether these are effective. It should be apparent in the final analysis, however, that the case study method is a technique used to deal primarily with a variety of observational and descriptive tasks (in contrast to research methods designed to subject hypotheses to stringent tests). But this primary purpose does not necessarily preclude the testing of hypotheses in case studies, particularly in situations that allow collection of sufficient quantitative data. Descriptions obtained by conducting numerous, similar case studies of the observed phenomenon may be incorporated into the body of existing theory. In turn, these phenomena may also be associated with whatever theory is relevant to the specific topic of the inquiry.

The case study approach has been employed in librarianship by a number of investigators, including some doctoral students who have achieved varying degrees of success. One case study was conducted to determine the role of a large public library as an agency of social reform.[4] Other case studies have been directed toward the identification of library goals in terms of milieu requirements;[5] the effectiveness of the New York State Reference and Research Resources Program;[6] and the determination of whether four libraries in Kentucky had responded adequately to changes in the status of their parent institutions from that of state teachers' colleges to universities.[7] Venable Lawson employed the case study method to investigate reference services provided by two academic libraries.[8] The primary purposes of the inquiry were to determine the following: (*a*) whether reference services offered by the two institutions hinged upon objectives of the libraries and the academic institutions; (*b*) whether reference objectives were determined by the reference function itself, and (*c*) whether changes in services (i.e., extension, emphasis, curtailment or activities, etc.) were dictated by the objectives of reference services or by other identifiable factors. In this study, data were collected by means of the following methods: (*a*) an examination of library records and reports; (*b*) interviews conducted and questionnaires distributed among library directors and reference librarians; and (*c*) direct observation of reference services. The selected target libraries differed in size, resources, staff, and other pertinent factors. As a result of the case study, support of the institutions' instructional and research functions were revealed to be the primary objective of reference services in the two libraries. Reference services of both libraries were found to be similar; the amount of time devoted to these services by employees was also comparable. Direct reference assistance to undergraduate students was found to be largely instructional or directional in nature. Furthermore, more than half of the activities of reference librarians were devoted to efforts that were clearly not of a professional nature. On the basis of this study, it was learned that a reappraisal of reference service was needed to define its actual objectives and to more clearly understand the role of professional personnel providing such services.[8]

LIBRARY USER STUDIES

Among the questions that librarians have a distinct obligation to pose and attempt to answer are those relating to library effectiveness, including such factors as the choice and suitability of library materials; the nature of library collections in relation to needs of clientele; the use and nonuse of library materials and services; the degree of awareness about library collections and services among clientele or potential clientele of libraries; the efficiency with which information in libraries is stored, retrieved, and utilized; and user satisfaction or dissatisfaction with libraries. These are all closely related to the role of libraries as social, educational, or informational institutions—that is, to the nature and impact of libraries on their communities—whether the community is a university, industry, government agency, school, municipality, or some other entity. In other words, librarians should be concerned with the performance of their institutions as well as the influence that libraries and information centers exert on the lives of persons who can contribute to social, political, or economic change or stability. The librarian's interpretation of the utilization of recorded knowledge is based upon the moot question of whether libraries can stimulate or move people to thought, feeling, and action. The question of whether library clientele are *actually* induced to enter the arena of action, as a result of having made use of libraries, definitely falls within the scope of librarianship's research effort. Therefore, it is not surprising that many of the studies undertaken by librarians have contained heavy overtones of the descriptive sociological inquiry and, furthermore, that some investigations in the field have been directed toward socially significant problems. Among these are the following: cultural deprivation, illiteracy, censorship, adult education, rehabilitation of prisoners, and aging.

Studies in the field are often designed to identify and to analyze how various persons or groups use libraries. User studies are similar to audience research in the field of communication. The significance and value of knowing the communication needs and practices of library users and potential library users are being increasingly recognized as librarians find themselves in keen competition for financial resources that can be used to expand information services and resources—particularly new media of communication and innovations such as the electronic digital computer. In underscoring the need for libraries to obtain a better grasp of the process of human communication, Robert Taylor wrote: "The librarian must become a modern generalist, concerned and knowledgeable about print, sound, and image, about automation and computer technology, and about formal and informal communication systems."[9] Therefore, user studies are often instigated as attempts to understand, justify, explain, or expand library usage—and, consequently, to gain more knowledge about the process of communication insofar as libraries and their clientele are concerned.

Accounts about observed library usage are often incorporated into theories that attempt to clarify relationships between library clientele and the information resources, facilities, and services of libraries. Using close and systematic observations of communication and information-gathering habits of people, some librarians have attempted to predict future behavior of their clientele in regard to library usage. Furthermore, the findings of user studies have allowed modifications of clientele behavior with respect to the utilization of certain library resources and services. John Lubans has categorized major types of library use, including the following: browsing in the book stacks, locating useful information, borrowing books or other library materials, reading books or other printed materials in the library, seeking assistance from library staff members, and so on.[10] Lubans pointed out that most user studies attempt to relate demographic characteristics of populations to library use or nonuse. For example, investigators have commonly endeavored to establish relationships between the benefits of library usage and characteristics of users such as age, sex, income level, education level, ethnic origin, and occupation.[10] In many of these studies, qualitative and quantitative traits or characteristics of users have been dealt with as independent variables and have been associated with certain dependent variables—particularly with the degree of library use. The following kinds of questions reflect only a few of the areas that user studies have attempted to probe.

1. Why do people use or not use certain types of libraries?
2. What influences do libraries and librarians exert on reading habits and tastes of library clientele?
3. To what extent are clientele satisfied or dissatisfied with library materials, services, personnel, physical resources, etc.?
4. What groups borrow which kinds of library materials?
5. What groups use various kinds of library services?
6. What are significant factors related to use or nonuse of libraries by various individuals and groups?
7. What means are effective to stimulate the use of informational, recreational, and inspirational materials and the various services offered by libraries?
8. What communication media are consulted most frequently in libraries and for what purposes?
9. How do urban, suburban, and rural library use patterns differ?
10. Does exposure to certain mass media of communication (i.e., radio, television, newspapers, motion pictures, etc.) affect library usage?

Writing about research in the field of reading and communication, Alice Lohrer has recognized the need in librarianship for user studies:

> What people really want to read, to view or listen to may vary considerably from what they are able to secure in books or through the air or screen. How we can produce better what the consumer of media needs, how we get the product to the consumer in our bookstores, and how we can give better service to the patron in our libraries is of great significance. Knowledge of

what research tells us can help us to be more relevant in our programs of service and in producing better books and mass media.[11]

In a similar vein, Helen M. Focke wrote: "we do not know enough about our patrons, how their minds operate and what kinds of things they need and ask for, to do a really good job of serving them. We have not gathered objective data continually or been as research conscious as we should be."[12] Although much remains to be accomplished in examining the needs of library clientele, some research in this area has been undertaken. The range of theoretical and practical aspects of the library usage issue has required the employment of various techniques. Among others, these have included such methods as the following: analyses of circulation and reference statistics, interviews with users and nonusers of libraries, mail questionnaire surveys, direct observation, case studies of various programs and services, and various unobtrusive techniques (e.g., the study of wear of library materials). Perhaps a brief discussion of several reports of completed inquiries in this research area would be beneficial.

An early user study in the field was conducted in the late 1930s by Louis R. Wilson. The study was an attempt to investigate the distribution and status of libraries in the United States. A report of the study, *The Geography of Reading,* [13] was published by the American Library Association and the University of Chicago Press. Perhaps the most ambitious user study ever undertaken is the Public Library Inquiry, conducted in the late 1940s by the Social Science Research Council with a grant from the Carnegie Corporation of New York. Among the survey's purposes was an examination of the actual and potential role of public libraries in the United States. In addition, the Public Library Inquiry sought to determine the degree to which libraries were achieving their objectives. Based upon nationwide survey research, the study resulted in the publication of several book-length reports, including the following: *The Library's Public* by Bernard Berelson,[14] *The Public Library in the Political Process* by Oliver Garceau,[15] and *The Public Library in the United States* by Robert D. Leigh.[16] Recommendations that grew out of the Public Library Inquiry included the following: more emphasis on service to those who make the most use of libraries, an increase in the financial support of libraries to include federal funds, the establishment of larger units of public library service, and the development of better library collections with more emphasis upon materials containing quality information than upon popular and recreational works. Numerous additional user studies pertaining to public libraries have been conducted; however, few of them match the breadth of the Public Library Inquiry.

In 1963, findings of the "Access to Public Libraries" study were reported to the ALA Council. The study was conducted in order to examine the extent to which citizens had free and equal access to library services; to develop a framework for the improvement of library services; and to identify the accomplishments of some libraries with respect to free and equal access. As a result of the study, a need was recognized for further attention to library services for cultural and racial minorities, for the under-educated, and for persons who speak foreign languages.[17] A list of studies conducted in this area since 1970 is provided at the end of this chapter. The selected studies are examples of attempts to understand various uses made of libraries.

A survey was conducted at Purdue University among 6568 respondents to determine whether significant differences existed among uses made of the library by faculty members, graduate and undergraduate students, and other persons. Questionnaires were distributed to determine if these clientele were homogeneous with respect to primary and secondary reasons for using the academic library. Patterns of use were found to be of significant difference among the various categories of clientele.[18]

At Bell Laboratories' Library and Information Systems Center, a study was undertaken to evaluate the acceptability and use of microfiche and to measure the effects of microform formats on reading habits. Employees in a division of Bell Laboratories were selected as a test group for this user study. These subjects were issued microfiche rather than hard copies of technical reports during a 9-month period; questionnaires were then distributed to obtain user reactions. The investigator concluded that users were not adversely affected by microfiche formats of reports. Although microfiche reports were found to be generally acceptable, some users complained about an insufficient number of reading machines, as well as the poor quality of some of the machines and microfiche copies of reports.[19]

Government publications and their use by faculty members were examined in another user study at Case Western Reserve University, where documents were housed in a separate collection of the social sciences and humanities library. Data were collected by means of a questionnaire distributed to a sample comprising one-third of the social sciences and humanities faculty. The questionnaire elicited information about the extent and frequency of use of government documents and related bibliographical tools and the degree of user satisfaction with assistance provided by documents librarians. Response rate to the survey was 89%; 65% of the faculty members reported that they used government publications, regardless of where the documents were located within the library. A low correlation was found between use of the general library and that of the document collections. Three-fourths of the respondents reported having consulted documents in the past 10-year period after having found citations for them in professional journals. The majority of the respondents claimed that their use of the document collection was self-sufficient. Professors who needed help with documents indicated satisfaction with library assistance. Investigators concluded that neglect of government publications by some faculty members appeared to be associated with a lack of awareness of the library's resources.[20]

Another study was conducted by Cambridge University's Management Research Unit to develop techniques to measure the use and effectiveness of library services. The study was concerned with the failure of readers to locate needed materials in three academic libraries. Specifically, the following information was sought: (a) the proportion of books that readers failed to locate, and whether this proportion varied according to topics of materials and to types of users, (b) titles that were not usually available on bookshelves, and (c) causes of failures to locate books. Two data-collection techniques were employed: (a) records of failures to locate needed books were prepared by library clientele (including details such as the following: status of the user, subject area of the search, number of books located or not located, whether a substitute book was found, etc.); and (b) randomly selected readers were interviewed as they departed the library during certain periods of selected days. Although results differed somewhat among libraries, investigators concluded that the collected data allowed librarians to establish priorities, to pinpoint problem areas and procedures in need of change, and to reassess purchasing policies. This study was viewed by the investigators as an attempt to determine how librarians can better meet demands through an awareness of the information-seeking behavior and problems of readers.[21]

A final example of a user study was conducted at several colleges and universities in California, where investigators attempted to measure faculty awareness of various reference services offered by libraries. The purpose of the study was to determine whether libraries had successfully informed constituencies of the availability of library reference services. A checklist which included 13 selected reference services was distributed to a randomly selected sample of 1967 faculty members at six state-supported institutions (sample size was 30% of the total population). All services on the checklist were offered by the libraries on a regular basis, and respondents were asked whether the services were available in their academic libraries. The survey revealed that the typical faculty member was aware of less than half of the available services and that interlibrary loan was the most widely recognized service. On the whole, faculty members were least familiar with the reference service whereby libraries would provide tailored lists of information sources for specific courses.

Academic rank and years of employment were found to be positively related to higher degrees of service awareness among faculty members. As a result of this project, the investigator underscored the value of publicizing and promoting reference services so that more open channels of communication could be maintained between the faculty and librarians.[22]

EVALUATION RESEARCH

Studies conducted to obtain objective and systematic evidence of the success or failure of library projects and programs are often categorized as *evaluation research*. When a program is evaluated, its relative effectiveness in terms of standards, goals, and objectives is determined and described. Typically, evaluation research is an attempt to measure operations in terms of the goals of libraries or library projects or the end results sought. Librarians launch and carry out numerous routine and special projects designed to stimulate the use of services and to improve library operations. Considerable human and financial resources are utilized in these undertakings; thus, questions are often posed by trustees, library committee members, sponsors, or librarians themselves concerning the effectiveness of these efforts. Until recent decades, assessments of most library programs and projects were somewhat sporadic—if indeed they were even attempted for some projects. Although earlier evaluations were based primarily upon value judgments of sponsors or project coordinators, the current trend is toward more systematic accountability of library activities; thus, the success or failure of various programs is now measured. When financial support is provided for library demonstrations or for innovative projects of an experimental nature, the agencies or organizations providing grants often require thorough evaluations of supported activities. Like many other kinds of inquiries, evaluative research is conducted to describe phenomena, to reveal relationships between variables, and to identify cause-and-effect relationships whenever possible. Evaluative studies are not distinguished so much by their methods as they are by their purposes; thus, many research techniques are used to effectively evaluate library programs and projects.

Essentially, the process of conducting evaluation research can be divided into six broad steps as follows:

1. Determine what is to be evaluated and the reasons for the evaluation.
2. Establish the desired level of performance of the object of the evaluation with particular reference to existing standards, goals, and objectives.

3. Select appropriate investigative techniques, and, if necessary, prepare a suitable scale or instrument to measure levels of performance.
4. Measure or test subjects (objects) to determine actual level(s) of performance.
5. Compare the program's goals with its objectives (i.e., determine the extent to which goals were achieved).
6. Evaluate the project on the basis of analyzed data.

Some evaluative procedures are developed prior to the actual initiation of programs; they are then incorporated into the program's structure. Without a doubt, this approach to evaluation is the most efficient and effective. In other cases, evaluative procedures are developed after a program has been made operational or has even been completed. In the latter case, however, evaluators are somewhat disadvantaged because a project's completion precludes the manipulation of variables and comparisons between *before* and *after* conditions. When a program's objectives are unclear or "fuzzy," a meaningful evaluation is also impeded. For example, if the object of a summer reading program was to make young persons "more responsible citizens in a democratic society," the task of transforming this goal into measurable success indicators might be impossible. Of course, this problem is closely related to the need for establishing realistic program goals expressed in terms of measurable operational or behavioral objectives.

One method of evaluation is a simulation of the experimental technique; however, it by no means attains the level of precision normally expected when a true experiment is conducted. Using this technique, a test (experimental) group is randomly chosen from among persons who participated in or supposedly benefited from the program to be evaluated. A control group is then selected from among persons who are very similar to the experimental group, but who did not "benefit" from or participate in the program. A measurement index or test is then devised, pretested, and administered to both subject groups in an effort to determine whether they differ with respect to the dependent variable (normally the object or goal of the project). Because proper pretests and posttests are frequently lacking, this evaluative procedure is not highly reliable; however, in some cases it might render nominal indicators of project effectiveness. It should be apparent that the closer the design of evaluation research approximates that of a controlled experiment, the more revealing the evaluation is likely to be. At times, interviews or questionnaires are used among project beneficiaries to elicit personalized reactions or evaluations. A follow-up study conducted by a graduate library school to obtain evaluations by former students of their completed educational program is a type of evaluative project. These evaluations are also sometimes undertaken by library schools in attempts to measure the professional development of former students, as well as effects of professional education on job performances of graduates. Robert M. Ballard conducted a similar study at the University of Michigan, and the title of the dissertation based upon his inquiry clearly indicates the scope of the research: *A Follow-Up Study of the Academic Record and Career Experience of Students Enrolled for the A.M.L.S. Degree at the Department of Library Science, the University of Michigan, 1960–1961.* [23]

Meaningful research designed to produce evaluations of library programs will require more time and resources than the "off-hand" judgments of administrators and project coordinators which were typical in the past. Formal evaluations are often necessary to reveal whether a program is beneficial and worthy of continuation. When library projects or programs are complex, evaluation research often is the only means to arrive at intelligent conclusions about their effects and intrinsic values. Penland and Williams have outlined some criteria for evaluations of programs and services. [24] These criteria are grouped under broad categories of interpretation, including questions of whether the following were achieved: (*a*) the individual participant's objectives; (*b*) the organization's objectives; (*c*) the objectives for program design and communication; (*d*) community development and coordination; and (*e*) satisfactory organizational procedures and administration. The following publications by F. W. Lancaster are highly recommended to librarians who plan to conduct evaluation research: *The Measurement and Evaluation of Library Services* [25] and *Evaluation and Scientific Management of Libraries and Information Centers.* [26] In addition, Ellen Altman's *A Data Gathering and Instructional Manual for Performance Measures in Libraries* [27] and ALA's *Performance Measures for Public Libraries* [28] can be useful in certain types of evaluative studies.

Library science evaluation research has been used in several doctoral projects, including the following: an evaluation of information retrieval systems in terms of cost, [29] a study of the effectiveness of a public library's information service, [30] an investigation of library services designated for adults of low educational attainment, [31] an evaluation of the reactions of ethnic minority readers to indigenous ghetto literature, [32] and an investigation of regional resource centers in Pennsylvania in terms of their capability to provide social science periodicals. [33]

Another example of evaluation research in the field is a study conducted to determine the benefits and level of performance of the Faculty Document Delivery Service (FDDS), initiated in 1969 at the University of Colorado by the university's library. A provision of the service was the delivery of documents to the offices of faculty members. After FDDS had been in operation for an 18-month period, more than 33% of the faculty had requested the delivery of these library materials. In all, 3600 documents were provided to faculty members during the first year of the project's operation. To obtain users' evaluations of the service, a questionnaire was distributed to participants, and 55% of the faculty members responded. Among these, 68% rated FDDS as "excellent," and 28% rated it as "good." Many respondents noted that the delivery of documents had altered faculty library-use patterns and had saved time. Investigators concluded that: (a) FDDS was generally well received; (b) four-fifths of the requested items were delivered; (c) the service could be operated on a cost-effective basis; and (d) the service aided in ameliorating inconveniences sometimes encountered by users of a decentralized library collection.[34]

In another study, the utilization of facsimile communication for reference and interlibrary loan services was evaluated. A 3-month experimental demonstration was conducted by the South Carolina State Library in cooperation with the Charleston County Library and the Greenville County Library. The project was supported by funds made available by the Library Services and Construction Act. A triangular facsimile communication network among the state agency and the two participating libraries was established to determine whether the speed and accuracy of reference transactions could thereby be increased. Facsimile devices used in the project were both transmitters and receivers of materials in printed, typed, handwritten, photocopied, or graphical formats. A coupling device allowed the transmission of both requests and documents over ordinary telephone lines. Prior to the initiation of the project, the state agency devised an evaluation procedure, based upon the direct observation of operations and the completion of evaluation forms for each facsimile transaction. Investigators at the state agency and the participating public libraries measured the following factors: (a) quality of each facsimile copy (both transmitted requests and responses); (b) speed of each transmission; and (c) quality of the reference and interlibrary loan service in terms of accuracy and patron satisfaction. Investigators concluded that facsimile communication devices are simple and effective means to increase the speed and accuracy of reference and interlibrary loan transactions, and that excellent facsimile copies can be obtained of the following types of materials: printed matter with 8-point type or larger, typed materials, black and white photographs, newspaper clippings, first sheets of carbon copies, printed charts and graphs, printed materials in color with good contrast, handwritten materials in pen and ink or ballpoint, ink sketches, and mimeographed materials. Although the demonstration project was successful in improving the speed and quality of services, the volume of transactions was deemed to be insufficient to warrant continuation of the facsimile network on a cost-benefit basis.[35]

LIBRARY SURVEYS

In the decade of the 1930s, librarians became concerned that they were not "reaching" all potential users and that rental libraries, the radio, and motion pictures were making inroads on citizens' use of libraries. Apparently, this alleged competition—coupled with a pervasive desire to describe library phenomena—stimulated the development of studies designed to survey library conditions and services with an aim of improving their overall quality. Between 1930 and 1950, the *library survey* was among the most frequently used methods to observe, analyze, compare, and describe general conditions in and related to libraries. Many such efforts were status surveys, designed primarily to merely assay library conditions rather than to test hypotheses or to explore specific research questions thoroughly. In this respect, the traditional library survey differs considerably from the kind of survey research discussed in Chapter 3.

Results of two large library surveys were reported in 1936: Tommie Dora Barker's survey of libraries in the South[36] and the Wight and Carnovsky survey of library programs and services in New York's suburban Westchester County.[37] Another noteworthy study was William Haygood's survey of circulation and reference department clientele of the New York Public Library.[38] In 1939, Waples and Carnovsky reported the results of a survey of the libraries of New York State,[39] and Louis R. Wilson completed a survey of the University of Georgia Library.[40] Therefore, by 1940 the library survey had become an extremely popular technique for gathering contemporary data about the organization and composition of libraries and the status of library systems in various institutions, states, communities, and regions of the nation. From all apparent indications, the library survey was regarded as a kind of panacea to solve a multiform of library problems during the 1930s and 1940s. David Kaser has reflected upon uses of library surveys in the past and has noted that coming "at a time before there were either textbooks or an extensive open research literature, they pitted the wide proprietary knowledge borne of extensive experience—and after the sagacity and wisdom—of their authors against many of the peskiest problems of the profession."[41]

In 1940, the American Library Association responded to the need for a manual devoted to techniques of library surveys; thus, the organization published *The Library Survey*[42] by Errett W. McDiarmid. Also, Carleton B. Joeckel joined Leon Carnovsky in a survey of the Chicago Public

Library in 1940.[43] Furthermore, Louis R. Wilson continued to go about conducting library surveys—one for the University of Florida Libraries[44] and another for libraries in the Southeast as part of the Southeastern States Cooperative Survey, 1946–47.[45] In 1958, Ernst W. Erickson described college and university surveys conducted between 1938 and 1952 in a doctoral dissertation prepared at the University of Illinois.[46] In a similar vein, Peter Jonikas compiled a bibliography of public library surveys; it contains a listing of approximately 300 separate studies.[47] School libraries were also the objects of numerous surveys. Frances Henne estimated that between 1927 and 1947 surveys constituted almost 40% of all studies undertaken in the area of school library research.[48]

Therefore, it is apparent that the library survey has been one of the most frequently employed investigative methods in librarianship, even though its procedures are considered to be among the least exacting and reliable of all investigative techniques. Unfortunately, some library surveys have been rather nominal attempts to observe and describe existing library phenomena. Presumably, most of these studies were undertaken to obtain and analyze information that might allow more intelligent decisions about the development of library systems, collections, services, and other aspects of librarianship. In 1947, when the library survey was still the most popular kind of study in the field, Louis R. Wilson noted that surveys of academic libraries had helped to improve the communication of information about library support, stimulated library staffs, solved particular problems, and codified library policies.[49] In reference to the surveys of resources of libraries, however, Robert Downs wrote in 1957:

> the thoroughness, the amount of detail, the background of surveys, care in planning, form and arrangement of data, and other features differ considerably from one study to another. Because some have been sketchy, incomplete, and not well organized for use, doubts have been expressed as to the value of resources surveys.[50]

Other librarians have also questioned the degree of objectivity, reliability, and effectiveness inherent in the library survey approach. In addition, questions have arisen from time to time concerning the extent to which conclusions and findings of library surveys are actually utilized.

Three broad categories of information are normally gathered and reported in library surveys: (a) existing library conditions; (b) comparisons between present conditions and desired standards or goals; and (c) suggestions for the improvement of existing conditions. Thus, the data collected in most library surveys could be placed into the following subject categories: (a) the library environment, including factors such as facilities, buildings, organizational structure, location, space, resources, and so on; (b) the characteristics of library personnel, including features such as educational attainment, experience, sex, age, group memberships, and so on; (c) the nature of users and nonusers, including their age, socioeconomic backgrounds, sex, ethnic origins, communication patterns, recreational activities, reading habits, and so on; (d) the nature of certain library services (or the absence of services), including reference and interlibrary loan, audiovisual programs, bibliographic and directional assistance to clientele, programs for children and young people, bookmobile services, adult services, photocopying facilities, extension services, reserve book services, and so on; (e) nature and extent of library resources, including books, periodicals, pamphlets, documents, films, recordings, microforms, reproductions of paintings, and other collections of materials; and (f) degree to which innovations such as data processing and computerized information retrieval technologies have been applied to library operations. Data pertaining to these and other possible categories of information are obtained from numerous sources, including annual reports; government records; direct and indirect observation of services, resources, personnel, and facilities; and a variety of additional sources and methods. Maurice Tauber has noted that the methods of library surveys include all the major techniques of research as well as "documentary and statistical analysis, questionnaires, checklists, visits, interview, observation, and the compilation of specialized data for particular conditions."[51]

Typically, library surveys are conducted by persons other than staff members of the library being examined—that is, by outside consultants or agencies, as a general rule. However, sometimes a few of these studies are also undertaken by library staff members, who usually function as a team or self-study group. Therefore, *internal surveys* of libraries are self-studies conducted by the collective library staff or by a single designated member or committee from the staff. *External surveys* are accomplished by a person or persons from outside agencies, that is, state libraries, library associations, library consulting firms, library schools, etc. The advantages of both of these types of surveys have been described by Maurice F. Tauber.[52] Some noteworthy library surveys conducted since 1965 are listed at the end of this chapter.

In recent decades, use of the library survey technique in the field has appeared to be declining. Perhaps this method of gathering general information about libraries is being replaced by more exacting methods designed to solve specific library problems. Discussing the status of academic library surveys since the mid-1950s, David Kaser has speculated that "increasing professionalization" among resident staff members of libraries has reduced the former need to rely heavily upon outside help for the conduct of library-related studies.[53] Moreover, Kaser noted that the "democratization of knowledge" which results from the placing of more emphasis upon theory in the process of educating librarians may have enabled practicing professionals to find solutions to more of their own problems rather than to rely upon outside experts.

COMMUNITY SURVEYS

Closely related to the library survey is another descriptive approach— the *community survey*. Designed to allow careful inspections of the characteristics of communities and to relate the features to library goals and objectives, community surveys are attempts to obtain a detailed working knowledge of various pertinent dimensions, geographic areas, or "publics" served by libraries. Although these dimensions are in a constant state of fluctuation, they are all directly or indirectly related to such factors as local traditions and values, geographical conditions, the nature of the population, the political climate, economic development, human resources, and the unique features and problems of the community. A purely *descriptive community survey* is designed to characterize properties and conditions of a group of people living or working together in a district or within an institution. An *exploratory community survey* devotes attention to interrelationships between these characteristics and the use of various library resources, programs, and services. Some community surveys are attempts to accomplish both of these tasks.

Interest in studying relations between libraries and their communities was stimulated by such publications as Joseph Wheeler's *The Library and the Community* (1929),[54] Leon Carnovsky and Lowell Martin's *The Library and the Community* (1944),[55] ALA's *Studying the Community: A Basis for Planning Adult Education Services* (1960),[56] and Roland Warren's *Studying Your Community* (1952).[57]

Community surveys are often conducted by or for public libraries; however, they do not appear to be undertaken as frequently within the communities of other types of libraries. The techniques of the community survey are applicable to all types of libraries and information centers. The surveys can be conducted in academic, professional, industrial, business, and other communities served by libraries and information centers.

A variety of data-collection methods and information sources can be employed effectively in community surveys. We should point out that because the community survey is a type of nominal research which does not involve collecting data for use in testing hypotheses, this type of study deals with the identification and description of a variety of community features that have a real or assumed relationship to the utilization of library resources and services. The most effective surveys are often conducted as interdisciplinary studies, insofar as both the collection and analysis of data are concerned. Attempts to accurately assess environments of libraries typically focus on social, economic, and political institutions and services, as well as on actual or potential clientele of libraries.

Complete assessments of communities often consider the resources and information–communication needs of the following agencies, organizations, or entities: (*a*) educational institutions such as public and private schools, community or junior colleges, vocational and technical education centers, and formal and informal adult education programs; (*b*) recreational services and clubs such as parks, recreational departments, YMCAs, and YWCAs; (*c*) cultural groups such as arts councils and societies, little theatre groups, music clubs, crafts groups, and book clubs; (*d*) health facilities and services such as public health departments, community mental health centers, medical clinics, and hospitals; (*e*) community planning and development agencies such as city and county planning departments and United Way councils; (*f*) local governmental units such as the mayor's office, city manager, fiscal officers, and law-enforcement agencies; (*g*) citizens' groups such as the League of Women Voters, neighborhood development councils, and interracial groups; (*h*) individual persons such as community leaders or key resource people who possess a thorough knowledge of the service area to be surveyed, as well as selected representatives from various population groups; (*i*) business and labor organizations such as chambers of commerce, trade associations, and better business bureaus; (*j*) churches and other religious institutions and organizations; and (*k*) communication–information agencies such as newspapers, television, radio, motion picture theatres, bookstores, newsstands, information centers, and public relations representatives of various organizations.

Needed information about many community institutions can often be obtained from the institutions themselves. It is often supplemented with recorded data from local, state, and federal government documents; telephone directories; city, business, and industrial directories; annual reports, newspaper articles; published histories; and other relevant sources. Moreover, interviews and questionnaires can often be effective in collecting a considerable amount of contemporary information about the community and its citizens.

Surveys of communities can be used to conceptualize libraries as integral parts of their social, political, and economic milieus. An analysis of a library's community can identify groups of actual or potential users so that more meaningful and effective programs can be developed and the usage of library resources and services can be stimulated. Moreover, information collected in the course of these studies can be employed to develop appropriate library personnel, buildings, resources, and facilities. Surveys are often valuable means for collecting information to be used in planning new library buildings and expanding services and systems. In some instances, these surveys can indicate when certain services or programs should be discontinued or deemphasized in favor of others more suitable to an environment. In addition, an analysis of a community can aid librarians in determining the most suitable location for new branches within a city. Thus, the ultimate objective of most of these surveys is to secure an overview of the library's community so that library collections, facilities, and services can be tailored to the general needs of the entire service area, as well as to the unique requirements of special clientele within institutions.

COMPARATIVE LIBRARIANSHIP

For many years, comparative studies have been conducted by scholars in disciplines and professions such as economics, law, education, linguistics, and literature. Not until after World War II, however, did interest in international librarianship and comparative library science studies take root in the United States. Since that time, some insightful investigations of a comparative nature have been undertaken. These studies have encompassed comparisons of the practices and study of library science in nations and regions of the world; they have focused on such topics as education for librarianship, political control of libraries, library resources and services, publishing in relation to libraries, patterns of communication, cross-cultural influences in librarianship, and other related topics. Dorothy G. Collings has defined comparative librarianship as "the systematic analysis of library development, practices, or problems as they occur under different circumstances (most usually in different countries)—considered in the context of the relevant historical, geographic, political, economic, social, cultural, and other determinant background factors found in the situations under study."[58] J. Periam Danton, a pioneer in the area of comparative library science studies, has defined comparative librarianship as follows:

the analysis of libraries, library systems, some aspects of librarianship, or library problems in two or more national, cultural, or societal environments, in terms of sociopolitical, economic, cultural, ideological, and historical contexts. This analysis is for the purpose of understanding similarities and differences, and for determining explanations of the differences, with the ultimate aim of trying to arrive at valid generalizations and principles.[59]

According to Louis Shores, two research approaches can be taken in comparative librarianship—geographic comparisons and subject comparisons. Shores has also pointed out that, because quantitative comparisons are not likely to produce very reliable results, "the implication of this new research area . . . is to investigate parascientifically."[60] He also claimed that comparative librarianship can uncover "neglected approaches to important technical library problems" and, furthermore, that it can "suggest a new critical role for librarianship" [p. 206].[60] Sources of information for comparative studies in library science include the following: direct observation, historical records, statistical compilations, government documents, library science professional publications, and a variety of other recorded information that can be used to make qualitative and quantitative comparisons. Douglas J. Foskett has written that "comparative librarianship has been noted more for lack of a systematic approach than for its observance."[61] Foremost, comparative librarianship is a descriptive research approach; thus, several methods of investigation can be employed, including case studies, library surveys, survey research, and, in some instances historical studies of recent past developments. In 1974, Danton indicated that relatively few studies of a truly comparative nature had been undertaken in the field. In characterizing a genuine comparative study, Danton noted that it should be cross-societal, compare observed phenomena, explain differences, draw conclusions, and establish principles.[62]

In the mid 1960s interest in international and comparative librarianship at the University of Pittsburgh's Graduate School of Library and Information Sciences led to the establishment of an International Library Information Center. The purpose of the center is to support the study of international and comparative librarianship through the provision of information, training, and research opportunities. The International Library and Information Center also serves as a clearinghouse for data about libraries, documentation, and book production in the United States and in numerous foreign countries.[63]

Among the most useful publications containing information and guidelines for the conduct of comparative studies in the field are: John F. Harvey's *Comparative and International Library Science;*[64] J. Periam Danton's *Dimensions of Comparative Librarianship;*[65] Miles M. Jackson's *Comparative and International Librarianship;*[66] Simsova and MacKee's *A Handbook of Comparative Librarianship;*[67] and articles written by John F. Harvey,[68] Dorothy G. Collings,[69] and Douglas J. Foskett.[70] In addition, *Studies in Comparative Librarianship; Three Essays Presented for the Sevensma Prize, 1971,*[71] a publication of the Library Association (London), might be of value to librarians who plan to carry out comparative studies. A bibliography of noteworthy reports of completed studies in the area of comparative and international librarianship is provided at the end of the chapter.

CONTENT ANALYSIS

Many library science studies are focused on the *users* of various media of communication, including books, periodicals, newspapers, films, and government documents. Less frequently, inquiries in the field are concerned with the actual *content* of media. Among the useful methods in the field of communication that can be employed by librarians to investigate certain internal (content) features of media is *content analysis,* a procedure designed to facilitate the objective analysis of the appearance of words, phrases, concepts, themes, characters, or even sentences and paragraphs contained in printed or audiovisual materials. Bernard Berelson has described content analysis as "a research technique for the objective, systematic, and quantitative description of manifest content of communication."[72] Thus, this technique can be used to describe the contents of communication "messages"—that is, materials such as *novels* (i.e., the themes used—love, morality, idealism, power, outcast, career, etc.); *newspapers* (i.e., kinds of news—local, national, or foreign and editorials, sports, social items, art, entertainment, business, etc.); reference tools (i.e., treatment of professional groups such as medical doctors, lawyers, professors, psychologists, clergy, etc.); or a variety of additional media and descriptive tasks relating to their content. In an analysis of a communication's content, observed data are transformed into sets of symbols such as words, themes, motives, concepts, and so on. The appearance of such symbols in the material under analysis can then be quantified (measured); use of the obtained measurements will depend upon the purpose of the research and the study's expressed hypothesis. By breaking down the contents of materials into meaningful and pertinent units of information, librarians attempt to discern certain characteristics of messages. For example, the selection and analysis of information, situations, characters, or other elements in a communication can indicate pertinent features such as comprehensiveness of coverage or the intentions, biases, prejudices, and oversights of authors, publishers, creators, or other persons responsible for the content of materials.

In *Content Analysis of Communication,* Richard W. Budd and his coauthors wrote: "No content analysis is better than its categories, for a system or set of categories is, in essence, a conceptual scheme."[73] A *category* has been defined as "either the name given to any class of things, actions, or relationships which recur with sufficient (relative) uniformity and frequency as to render the class a useful subject of a prediction of the class itself."[74] Fred N. Kerlinger noted in *Foundations of Behavioral Research* that: (*a*) a category is a partition or subpartition set up according to some rule; (*b*) categories are established in regard to the purpose(s) of a unique investigative problem; and (*c*) categories are exhaustive and mutually exclusive.[75] The "things" placed into categories representing the contents of a document are called *units;* they are the individual observations or measurements which ordinarily comprise the dependent variable of a content analysis. For example, assume that an investigator is conducting a content analysis of several written policies of metropolitan public libraries regarding the selection of materials. The purpose of the study is to determine the extent of references in the selection policies to written statements of principles adopted by the American Library Association, such as the *Library Bill of Rights, Freedom to Read* statement, *Resolution on Challenged Materials,* and other related professional guidelines related to free access to library materials. Each reference to these adopted professional principles in the library selection policies could be counted and placed into a designated category representing one or another of the officially adopted policy statements; thus, references to these statements would comprise the counted units. The number of categories in any single content analysis depends, of course, upon the amplification of factors associated with the research problem to be solved.

Content analysis is aimed at exactness and the elimination of bias in the investigative process; its methods are employed to decrease the degree of subjectivity inherent in procedures designed to analyze or evaluate the contents of materials. Analyses of the contents of materials can be used to examine documents so as to make meanings or messages more explicit. Materials may be scrutinized to determine the relative importance or occurrence of textual or graphical elements under analysis. Literary and drama critics often evaluate media such as books, plays, and films; however, evaluations by these persons are not based upon rigorous quantifications of inherent elements of the object of evaluation. But the procedures used by investigators in a content analysis encompass a carefully prepared and reproducable plan for the collection and quantification of elements of communications. By determining the proportions of a message that fall into clearly defined, conceptually valid, and mutually exclusive categories, the research scholar attempts to increase unit frequency validity.

Although most library science inquiries based upon content analysis have been descriptive in nature, this technique can also be engaged to probe hypotheses pertaining to the contents of materials. For example, assume that a test will be made of the theory that themes of most contemporary best-selling novels are based primarily upon sex or violence. By clearly identifying activities that can be characterized as "sex" or "violence," and then by quantitatively analyzing the themes (content) of pertinent novels according to the established categories, the investigator could test the proposition. Furthermore, the hypothesis might be statistically tested, should the study be conducted rigorously. Hypothesis testing is especially facilitated when a comparison is sought in a study between or among elements of various documents.

Typically, the conduct of a content analysis is accomplished in the following general steps: (*a*) formulation of the research problem (For example, how was the appointment of Daniel Boorstin to the position of Librarian of Congress treated by such professional publications in the field as *Library Journal, American Libraries,* and *Wilson Library Bulletin;* how does the appointment relate to problems concerning the image of the "professional" librarian and to the theories of education for librarianship?); (*b*) definition and establishment of the hypothesis and the categories of analysis that will allow the hypothesis to be tested; (*c*) identification and selection of the materials to be analyzed (the target documents, messages, or media) and, if appropriate, selection of a sample of these; (*d*) analysis of relevant documents and the measurement of contents according to the predetermined and well-defined categories; (*e*) quantification and ordering of the categorized units; (*f*) analysis and comparison of attained data with respect to the independent variable(s); and (*g*) interpretation of the data insofar as the research question, hypothesis, or theory of the inquiry are concerned.

One problem that is often encountered by librarians in their attempts to analyze communication contents is the mass of cognate materials in many projects that can be subjected to examinations. Sampling procedures can sometimes be used to help solve this problem of having too many materials. Another useful method for reducing materials to a more manageable quantity is to limit the analysis to works published during a specific time period—for example, 6 months, 1 year, or 3 years, depending upon the latitude of an inquiry. Limitations can also be imposed by the selection of a particular media format for analysis (i.e., periodical articles about a topic rather than books and other publications relating to the same subject area). For example, an analysis of the writings of presidents of the American Library Association since 1940 to identify major professional interests of these leaders could be confined to the contents of the subjects' published speeches, rather than to all their journal articles. The selection of speeches as the object of a study might reduce the materials for analysis to a more manageable proportion. In addition, bibliographies that list the best, most significant, outstanding, or prize-winning publications can sometimes be used as selection guides for the research objects to be analyzed, thus limiting the range of pertinent items. The overall purpose of an inquiry and the research question itself must be carefully considered when limitations are placed on the range and quality of analyzed documents.

Techniques that can be reproduced by other investigators are employed in content analyses; thus, the procedures used should be explicitly identified and clearly elucidated in written reports of studies. These procedures should allow the classification of measurable data and the pursuit of concepts being investigated in terms of the frequency of their occurrence, as well as their interrelationships and meanings. No single model is applicable to all content analyses; each of these inquiries must be structured according to an analytical scheme directed toward the accomplishment of a specific research task. A unique feature of the content analysis approach is the investigator's reliance upon the quantifiable aspects of communications, rather than upon an expository treatment in the form of explanations.

Although content analysis has been employed in some inquiries in librarianship, an examination of various reports of relevant studies will reveal that this technique has not always been applied correctly. Unless categories of analysis are clearly and accurately defined and the classification and measurement of data are undertaken with objectivity, exactness, and rigor, a so-called content analysis can produce loosely knit or meaningless data. In a criticism of this technique as applied in librarianship, Jesse Shera has written:

> Though [content analysis] pretends to greater "objectivity" it is no less subjective than those forms of literary criticism against which it is supposed to be a "reaction." One does not achieve objectivity through the quantification of that which is itself subjective.[76]

The following types of content analysis projects are among studies completed by librarians: a comparison of the contents of best-selling novels with those that did not sell well, centering upon themes, readability, settings, and other elements in an attempt to identify the characteristics present in popular books and absent in works having less appeal;[77] a comparison of selected novels with the motion pictures based upon them;[78] an analysis of treatments given to the topic of blacks in the United States by four major adult encyclopedias;[79] a study of the roles of priests in contemporary British and American fiction;[80] an exploration of the contents of novels listed in supplements to the *Junior High School Library Catalog* in an attempt to characterize treatments given to the topic of adolescent culture;[81] an examination of the published writings of public library directors to determine the impact of the Great Depression on six metropolitan libraries;[82] a study of contemporary realistic fiction for children published since World War II;[83] and an analysis of information provided about educational filmstrips in selected periodicals.[84]

At this point, perhaps closer scrutiny of a completed study that employed the content analysis approach would be beneficial. One such study was completed by Joyce Haas.[85] Almost 2000 selected works of fiction included in New Jersey school libraries were examined in the analysis to determine the nature of the characters depicted, spoken communications, and settings in novels. Two primary questions were posed: (*a*) whether the contents of novels in school library collections supported a polarized society, and (*b*) whether the ethnic contents of fiction collections varied according to ethnic student enrollment of selected schools. The overall purpose of the research was to try to determine the degree to which fiction selected for school libraries prepared children for social change. The study's independent variable was the amount of ethnic enrollment in selected schools; the dependent variable was comprised of the ethnic characteristics of fiction in school library collections.

Haas accomplished the content analysis by first randomly selecting 30 New Jersey elementary school libraries from a list of the state's K–6 schools. The selected schools were then classified into five strata according to ethnic minority enrollment. Next, a sample of 1939 books was chosen from libraries in these schools and then analyzed by a group of 51 coders. The group of coders was comprised of persons of both sexes, of various ages, and of various ethnic-minority and ethnic-majority backgrounds. The established categories were used by coders to categorize the following facets of books: characters portrayed (e.g., ethnic group, sex, age, etc.); spoken communications included (e.g., ethnic group, sex, age, and responses); and characteristics of settings (e.g., story's time and place). After collecting and analyzing the data produced by coders, Haas concluded that contents of school fiction collections supported the ethnic polarization of American society and that factors related to patterns of national and regional book publication and distribution appeared to have precluded the development of less polarized library collections. This study relates to the following school library principles: (*a*) the library—like the classroom—should promote the socialization process of children, as well as their formation of value systems; (*b*) the materials in school libraries should prepare children for social change; and (*c*) library collections should be developed primarily with the needs of students in mind. The content analysis undertaken by Haas demonstrated that these tenents are sometimes difficult to achieve, especially when certain books are not available or are of such poor quality that they cannot be used in school library collections.

DELPHI METHOD

Comprised of a group of modified survey procedures, the *Delphi method* is designed for use in refining judgmental data collected from a panel of selected experts. The technique was developed in the early 1950s by the Rand Corporation to predict future developments related to national defense. Olaf Helmer, who was instrumental in helping to devise Delphi, characterized the method as "a carefully designed program of sequential individual interrogations (best conducted by questionnaires) interspersed with information and opinion feedback. . . ."[86] Delphi is a systematic approach to the generation of consensus opinions among a group of carefully selected and anonymous respondents. It is based upon the assumption that majority opinions will have greater credibility and authority than the surmise of only the most articulate spokespersons in a group of participating respondents. Panel participants are often selected because of their knowledge of the subject under investigation; however, the experts need not necessarily be members of the same discipline or possess similar backgrounds.

Most users of Delphi assume that the method prevents the opinions of experts from being contaminated by: (*a*) strong personalities of the dominant respondents, (*b*) the bandwagon effect, and (*c*) public opinion. The Delphi method is based upon a series of questionnaire interchanges often referred to as "rounds." Participants respond independently to one another's opinions about an assigned attitude object. Typically, consensus opinions are deemed by investigators to be those that fall within the interquartile range (e.g., between the first and third quartiles) of the original responses after they have been ranked repeatedly by all participants in the study. In the final statistical analysis of responses, opinions that fall outside the interquartile range (e.g., those that are ranked within the first and fourth quartiles) are considered to be aberrant. Four questionnaire interactions, or rounds, may be required to determine consensus opinions; however, three rounds usually suffice for this purpose.

Lending itself to a variety of judgmental tasks, Delphi has been in a process of evolution for almost two decades. That evolution has involved both Delphi's methodology and the range of problems to which it has been applied. Despite the rather widespread employment of the technique since information about it was declassified in the 1960s, the Delphi method does not have a sound theoretical base. Results of Delphi studies are often less than spectacular; however, some studies have yielded very useful data. The method does reduce communication barriers among participants and can be applied to problems that are not amenable to precise analytical techniques. Typically, such problems are "solved" using expert value judgments that were arrived at more or less intuitively. A variety of applications of Delphi are possible. For example, the method can be applied in the following areas: (*a*) in technological forecasting tasks; (*b*) in attempts to ascertain values and preferences; (*c*) in efforts to determine the quality of life or other conditions in future years; (*d*) in situations that can benefit from a stimulation of the decision-making process; and (*e*) in efforts to encourage the development of technical inventions ("inventive planning").

The Delphi method has been widely recognized as a means of supplementing information gleaned from past experiences, historical data, or other traditional data sources. One advantage of the technique is its applicability to the collection of information from respondents who possess widely differing views that appear to be irreconcilable. The method is also applicable to interrogations of persons who are widely dispersed geographically, and are thus unable to participate in a face-to-face "brainstorming" session or in other types of situations in which ideas are interchanged.

Steps of a Typical Delphi Study

Although the basic Delphi procedure has often been tailored to meet unique needs of a variety of disciplines and purposes, the following list is a somewhat typical series of steps utilized in Delphi studies.

Step 1: Select a panel of experts who are capable of providing insightful opinions concerning the pertinent topic. Explain the rationale of the study to the experts and request their anonymous participation as independent panel members.

Step 2: Ask each participant to compile a list of value judgments, predictions, or opinions about the assigned issue or topic. (In some cases, participants may be asked to respond to a list of statements preselected by the investigator.)

Step 3: Collect the initial responses and incorporate them into a questionnaire for use in a first-round interaction. Then, request that the same panel members rank the recorded statements according to independently perceived orders of priority or importance.

Step 4: Upon receipt of all first-round questionnaires from participants, analyze the data statistically (e.g., determine the median and interquartile range of responses). Subsequently, rearrange the statements according to the new, revised rankings; list them in another questionnaire to be used in the second round; and provide respondents with a statistical summary of the ranked statements.

Step 5: Submit the second-round instrument to the same panel members, asking them to reconsider their second responses, given the statistical summary of that round.

Step 6: Repeat Step 5 for the third-round questionnaire interaction. Respondents whose opinions still fall outside the interquartile range for the third round are asked to explain why their feelings did not change. At the conclusion of the third round (or, when consensus opinions have been obtained), the investigator prepares a final draft of the ranked statements, revealing how much opinion change has occurred. The consensus opinions are summarized, together with other pertinent comments elicited from participants.

A succinct and critical review of the use of the Delphi method in librarianship is contained in an article by Russell G. Fischer.[87] Sybilla A. Cook has also briefly described some library applications of the Delphi method in a popular article.[88] An explanation of the use of Delphi in Sweden to decrease uncertainty about future events relating to information and documentation is contained in an article by Ulf Wennerberg.[89] One of the most ambitious Delphi projects in librarianship was undertaken by the Library Research Unit at the University of California, Los Angeles. The study dealt with the future of library education in the United States and was the subject of a report written by Harold Borko.[90] Perhaps the most penetrating and definitive examination of the Delphi method to be published thus far is *The Delphi Method; Techniques and Applications,* a book of readings edited by Harold A. Linstone and Murray Turoff.[91]

DOCUMENTARY RESEARCH

For lack of a better phrase, the generic term *documentary research* is used here to refer to inquiries into the printed tools of librarianship—books, journals, and indexes. A sample of the broad research questions falling into this category include the following:

1. What are (or should be) the characteristics of a good index? Classification scheme? What kinds of indexes produce optimal retrieval results?

2. How can a computer be programmed to do automatic indexing? Automatic classification? Abstracting?
3. Will an analysis of citation patterns associated with journals in various subject literatures reveal anything useful about the importance of individual journals? Authors? The "hardness" of a subject field?
4. Are there optimal approaches to the design of subject heading lists or thesauri?
5. How does the depth of indexing affect retrieval effectiveness? The exhaustivity of indexing?
6. What effect does indexer/cataloger inconsistency have on subsequent retrieval? How prevelant is inter-indexer inconsistency?
7. How quickly do various classes of literature obsolesce, in the sense of "losing usefulness"? How fast are various subject classes of literature growing?
8. How productive are writers? Journals? What proportion of journals, ranked in order of usefulness, is required to satisfy a given percentage of potential information requests?

Studies designed to shed light on these and related questions frequently include an objective, quantitative analysis of words in the texts of documents, hence the term *documentary research*. In the paragraphs that follow, a few prototypical, substantive, and seminal studies in documentary research will be cited. Although we shall not attempt to provide a state-of-the-art summary of documentary research, a few examples of early studies in this area will be cited. Perhaps these will provide a flavor of the field.

Bibliometrics involves measurement of several interrelated aspects of writing and publication. "Bradford's law of scattering" relates the proportion of relevant papers in a field to the proportion of journals required to achieve this quantity, when the journals have been ranked according to productivity.[92,93] The productivity of scientists is the subject of treatment both by Derek Price[94] and Alfred Lotka.[95] George Zipf[96] looks at the productivity of words in text in much the same way as Bradford and Lotka. There have been several attempts to relate these bibliometric distributions, notably by Robert Fairthorne.[97]

In the second major thrust of bibliometrics, citation analysis is employed, often with the use of *Science Citation Index* and *Social Science Citation Index*. Many hundreds of studies have been performed using the techniques of citation analysis, all of which are based on the assumption that the act of citing an author is meaningful. For example, *bibliographic coupling* is rooted in the idea that two documents whose bibliographies share one or more citation are more likely to be related to each other than two documents which have no citations in common.[98] Research conducted to test this hypothesis would involve the careful counting of the number of citations common to pairs of documents in a test collection, followed by an independent evaluation of the "relatedness" of document pairs. Citation studies have been used to establish networks of scientific papers, to rank journals by importance, to generate additional documents relevant to a search question, and to evaluate a scientist's productivity.

Another body of documentary research deals with *automatic indexing, abstracting,* and *classification.* The broad task in this type of research is to define a formal process—a process which is in principle capable of being performed by a computer—to select keywords from the texts of documents likely to be useful as descriptors, to extract key sentences from the texts to serve as abstracts, or to assign documents to subject classes. As with bibliometric research, studies relating to this type of automatic language processing may be based on an experimental design and may borrow such techniques as decision theory from operations research. Sophisticated statistical techniques such as factor analysis may sometimes be utilized. But in the data-gathering and analysis stages of the research the approaches are characterized by a common need to analyze (count, tabulate, compare, associate) words in the text. For this reason, use of the computer is prevalent in this type of study. Seminal studies in automatic classification and automatic indexing were conducted by Harold Borko,[99] and by M. E. Maron and J. L. Kuhns,[100] respectively.

SUMMARY

Because all research techniques are means to ends rather than ends in themselves, competent investigators in librarianship have not revered a particular method as a sacred ritual. Indeed, reliable research evidence is not the baliwick of any single investigative technique or model. Most experienced investigators are aware that no research design is infallible, and, furthermore, that all methods of research are succeptible to methodological weaknesses under unfavorable or inappropriate circumstances. Thus, to examine libraries, information centers, facets of information technology, library materials, or even the behavior of librarians who work with or the people who use information systems, a number of efficacious methods can be used to expedite the collection, analysis, and verification of knowledge. In this chapter, our attention was directed toward techniques that can be used in lieu of, or as supplements to, other kinds of investigative methods, such as experimental, survey, historical, or operations research. Inquiries such as case studies, content analyses, user studies, evaluation research, library surveys, community surveys, comparative librarianship, the Delphi method, and documentary research can be effectively employed in many of the investigative settings in which librarians seek new knowledge.

REFERENCES

1. W. I. B. Beveridge, *The Art of Scientific Investigation*. London: Mercury Books, 1961, p. 105.
2. Herbert Goldhor, *An Introduction to Scientific Research in Librarianship*. Champaign, Ill.: Illini Union Bookstore, 1969, p. 132.
3. Julius Gould, and Kolb, William L., eds., *A Dictionary of the Social Sciences*. New York: Free Press, 1964, p. 621.
4. Rosemary R. Du Mont, *The Large Urban Public Library as an Agency of Social Reform, 1890–1915* (unpublished doctoral dissertation, University of Pittsburgh, 1975).
5. Henry C. Chang, *Library Goals as Responses to Structural Milieu Requirements: A Comparative Case Study* (unpublished doctoral dissertation, University of Minnesota, 1974).
6. Sylvia G. Faibisoff, *Descriptive Case Studies of Selected New York State Regional Interlibrary Lending Networks as an Approach to Measuring the Effectiveness of the New York State Reference and Research Resources Program (3R) in Meeting the Information Needs of the Serious Research User* (unpublished doctoral dissertation, Case Western Reserve University, 1975).
7. Janet S. Horton, *Library Response to Institutional Change: Case Studies of Four Former State Teachers Colleges in Kentucky* (unpublished doctoral dissertation, Indiana University, 1975).
8. Venable Lawson, *Reference Service in University Libraries, Two Case Studies* (unpublished doctoral dissertation, Columbia University, 1971).
9. Robert S. Taylor, *The Making of a Library: The Academic Library in Transition*. New York: Becker and Hayes, 1972, p. 9.
10. John Lubans, Jr., "Library User Studies," in *Encyclopedia of Library and Information Science*, 16(1975):147–160.
11. Alice Lohrer, *Research in the Fields of Reading and Communications, Library Trends*, 22(October 1973):77–78.
12. Helen M. Focke, "Library Users of Information and Their Needs," in *The Present Status and Future Prospects of Reference/Information Service*. Proceedings of the 1966 Conference held at Columbia University by the School of Library Service and the American Library Association, Reference Services Division. Chicago, Ill.: American Library Association, 1967, p. 32.
13. Louis R. Wilson, *The Geography of Reading: A Study of the Distribution and Status of Libraries in the United States*. Chicago, Ill.: American Library Association and the University of Chicago Press, 1938.
14. Bernard Berelson, *The Library's Public: A Report of the Public Library Inquiry*. New York: Columbia University Press, 1949.
15. Oliver Garceau, *The Public Library in the Political Process: Report of the Public Library Inquiry*. New York: Columbia University Press, 1949.

16. Robert D. Leigh, *The Public Library in the United States: General Report of the Public Library Inquiry*. New York: Columbia University Press, 1950.
17. "The Access to Public Libraries Study," *ALA Bulletin, 57*(September 1963):742–745.
18. Philip V. Rzasa, and Moriarty, John H., "The Types and Needs of Academic Library Users: A Case Study of 6,568 Responses," *College and Research Libraries, 31*(November 1970):403–409.
19. C. W. Christ, Jr., "Microfiche: A Study of User Attitudes and Reading Habits," *Journal of the American Society for Information Science, 23*(January 1972):30–35.
20. Dawn McCaghy, and Purcell, Gary R., "Faculty Use of Government Publications," *College and Research Libraries, 33*(January 1972):2–12.
21. John A. Urquhart, and Schofield, J. L., "Measuring Reader's Failure at the Shelf in Three University Libraries," *Journal of Documentation, 28*(September 1972):233–241.
22. Jerold Nelson, "Faculty Awareness and Attitudes Towards Academic Reference Services; A Measure of Communications," *College and Research Libraries, 34*(September 1973):268–275.
23. Robert M. Ballard, *A Follow-Up Study of the Academic Record and Career Experience of Students Enrolled for the A.M.L.S. Degree at the Department of Library Science, the University of Michigan, 1960–1961* (unpublished doctoral dissertation, University of Michigan, 1972).
24. Patrick R. Penland, and Williams, James G., *Community Psychology and Coordination*. New York: Marcel Dekker, 1974, pp. 153–161.
25. F. W. Lancaster, with M. J. Joncich, *The Measurement and Evaluation of Library Services*. Washington, D.C.: Information Resources Press, 1977.
26. F. W. Lancaster, and Cleverdon, C. W., eds., *Evaluation and Scientific Management of Libraries and Information Centers*. Bristol, Engl: NATO Advance Study Institute, 1975, p. 184.
27. Ellen Altman *et al.*, *A Data Gathering and Instructional Manual for Performance Measures in Libraries*. Chicago, Ill.: Celadon Press, 1976.
28. *Performance Measures for Public Libraries*. Chicago, Ill.: American Library Association, 1973.
29. Michael D. Cooper, *Evaluation of Information Retrieval Systems: A Simulation and Cost Approach* (unpublished doctoral dissertation, University of California, Berkeley, 1971).
30. Terence Crowley, *The Effectiveness of Information Service in Medium Size Public Libraries* (unpublished doctoral dissertation, Rutgers University, 1968).
31. Peter Hiatt, *Public Library Branch Services for Adults of Low Education* (unpublished doctoral dissertation, Rutgers University, 1963).
32. Laurence L. Sherrill, *The Affective Responses of Ethnic Minority Readers to Indigenous Ghetto Literature: A Measurement* (unpublished doctoral dissertation, University of Wisconsin, 1972).
33. Edward Wolf, *An Evaluation of the Capability of the Pennsylvania Regional Resources Centers to Provide for the Availability and Accessibility of Pennsylvania Social Sciences Periodicals* (unpublished doctoral dissertation, University of Pittsburgh, 1972).
34. Richard M. Dougherty, "The Evaluation of Campus Library Document Delivery Service," *College and Research Libraries, 34*(January 1972):29–39.
35. Charles H. Busha, and Landrum, John H., *Telefacsimile Communication with the Xerox-Magnavox Telecopier in Reference and Interlibrary Loans*. Columbia: South Carolina State Library Board, 1967, ERIC Document, ED 068 102.

36. Tommie Dora Barker, *Libraries of the South: A Report on Developments, 1930–1935*. Chicago, Ill.: American Library Association, 1936.

37. Edward A. Wight, and Carnovsky, Leon, *Library Service in a Suburban Area: A Survey and a Problem for Westchester County, New York*. Chicago, Ill.: American Library Association, 1936.

38. William C. Haygood, *Who Uses the Public Library: A Survey of the Patrons of the Circulation and Reference Departments of the New York Public Library*. Chicago, Ill.: University of Chicago Press, 1938.

39. Douglas Waples, and Carnovsky, Leon, *Libraries and Readers in the State of New York: The State's Administration of Public Library Services*. Chicago, Ill.: University of Chicago Press, 1939.

40. Louis R. Wilson, Branscomb, Harvie, Dunbar R. M., and Lyle, Guy R., *Report of a Survey of the University of Georgia Library*. Chicago, Ill.: American Library Association, 1939.

41. David Kaser, "A Century of Academic Librarianship, as Reflected in Its Literature," *College and Research Libraries, 37*(March 1976):112.

42. Errett W. McDiarmid, *The Library Survey: Problems and Methods*. Chicago, Ill.: American Library Association, 1940.

43. Carlton B. Joeckel, and Carnovsky, Leon, *Metropolitan Library in Action; A Survey of the Chicago Public Library*. Chicago, Ill.: University of Chicago Press, 1940.

44. Louis R. Wilson, Kuhlman, A. F., and Lyle, Guy R., *Report of a Survey of the University of Florida Library*. Chicago, Ill.: American Library Association, 1940.

45. Louis R. Wilson and Milczewski, Marion A., eds., *Libraries of the Southeast: A Report of the Southeastern States Cooperative Library Survey, 1946–47*. Chapel Hill: University of North Carolina Press, 1949.

46. Ernst W. Erickson, *College and University Library Surveys, 1938–1952* (unpublished doctoral dissertation, University of Illinois, 1958).

47. Peter Jonikas, *Bibliography of Public Library Surveys Contained in the Collection of the American Library Association*. Chicago, Ill.: American Library Association, 1958.

48. Frances Henne, "Libraries, School," in *Encyclopedia of Educational Research*. Rev. ed. New York: Macmillan, 1950, pp. 701–711.

49. Louis R. Wilson, "The University Library Survey: Its Results," *College and University Libraries, 8*(July 1947):368–375.

50. Robert B. Downs, "Research in Problems of Resources," *Library Trends, 6*(October 1957):154.

51. Maurice F. Tauber, "Survey Method in Approaching Library Problems," *Library Trends, 13*(July 1964):19.

52. Maurice F. Tauber, "Library Surveys," in *Encyclopedia of Library and Information Science, 16*(1975):74–90.

53. David Kaser, "A Century of Academic Librarianship, as Reflected in Its Literature," *College and Research Librarians, 37*(March 1976):125.

54. Joseph L. Wheeler, *The Library and the Community*. Chicago: American Library Association, 1929.

55. Leon Carnovsky, and Martin, Lowell, eds., *The Library and the Community*. Chicago: University of Chicago Press, 1944.

56. A.L.A. Library-Community Project Headquarters Staff, *Studying the Community: A Basis for Planning Adult Education Services*. Chicago, Ill.: American Library Association, 1960.

57. Roland Warren, *Studying Your Community*. New York: Russell Sage Foundation, 1955.

58. Dorothy G. Collings, "Comparative Librarianship," in *Encyclopedia of Library and Information Science, 5*(1971):492.

59. J. Periam Danton, *Dimensions of Comparative Librarianship.* Chicago, Ill.: American Library Association, 1973, p. 52.

60. Louis Shores, "Why Comparative Librarianship?," *Wilson Library Bulletin, 41*(October 1966):204–205.

61. D. J. Foskett, "Review of *The Dimensions of Comparative Librarianship* by J. Periam Danton," *Library Quarterly, 44*(July 1974):265.

62. J. Periam Danton, "Review of *Public Library Legislation: A Comparative Study* by Frank M. Gardner," *Library Quarterly, 44*(January 1974):73.

63. Richard Krzys, "International Library Information Center," in *Encyclopedia of Library and Information Science, 12*(1974):413–414.

64. John F. Harvey, ed., *Comparative and International Library Science.* Metuchen, N.J.: Scarecrow Press, 1977.

65. J. Periam Danton, *Dimensions of Comparative Librarianship.* Chicago, Ill.: American Library Association, 1973.

66. Miles M. Jackson, ed., *Comparative and International Librarianship; Essays on Themes and Problems.* Westport, Conn.: Greenwood Press, 1970.

67. S. Simsova and M. MacKee, *A Handbook of Comparative Librarianship.* London, Eng.: Clive Bingley, 1970.

68. John F. Harvey, "Toward a Definition of International and Comparative Library Science," *International Library Review, 5*(July 1973):289–319.

69. Dorothy G. Collings, "Comparative Librarianship," in *Encyclopedia of Library and Information Science, 5*(1971):492–502.

70. Douglas J. Foskett, "Comparative Librarianship," in R. L. Collison, ed., *Progress in Library Science.* London, Eng.: Butterworths, 1965, pp. 125–146.

71. Alfred D. Burnett, Gupta, R. K., and Simsova, S., *Studies in Comparative Librarianship; Three Essays Prepared for the Sevensma Prize, 1971.* London, Eng.: The Library Association, 1973.

72. Bernard Berelson, *Content Analysis in Communication Research.* New York: Free Press, 1952, p. 74.

73. Richard W. Budd, Thorp, Robert K., and Donohew, Lewis, *Content Analysis of Communication.* New York: Macmillan, 1967, p. 6.

74. Julius Gould and Kolb, William L., eds., *Dictionary of the Social Sciences.* New York: Free Press, 1964, p. 77.

75. Fred N. Kerlinger, *Foundations of Behavioral Research: Educational and Psychological Inquiry.* New York: Holt, Rinehart and Winston, 1967, p. 606.

76. Jesse H. Shera, *The Foundations of Education for Librarianship.* New York: Wiley, 1972, pp. 42–43.

77. John F. Harvey, *Content Characteristics of Best-Selling Novels* (unpublished doctoral dissertation, University of Chicago, 1949).

78. Lester E. Asheim, *From Book to Film, a Comparative Analysis of the Content of Selected Novels and the Motion Pictures Based upon Them* (unpublished doctoral dissertation, University of Chicago, 1949).

79. W. L. Hannah, *Comparison of the Negro in the United States in Four Major Adult Encyclopedias and Their Yearbooks* (unpublished master's thesis, Florida State University, 1959).

80. F. M. Crawley, *Priest in Contemporary British and American Fiction, 1940–1962* (unpublished master's thesis, Catholic University of America, 1963).

81. Marilyn Searson, *Adolescent Culture in Junior Novels: A Content Analysis of Selected Junior Novels Recommended in the 1972, 1973, and 1974 Supplements of the Junior High School Library Catalog* (unpublished doctoral dissertation, Florida State University, 1975).

82. Robert S. Kramp, *The Great Depression: Its Impact on Forty-Six Large American Public Libraries, an Inquiry Based on a Content Analysis of Published Writings of Their Directors* (unpublished doctoral dissertation, University of Michigan, 1975).

83. Tekla K. Bekkedal, *A Study of Contemporary Realistic Fiction for Children in the United States Since World War II* (unpublished doctoral dissertation, University of Illinois, 1975).

84. Dorothy M. Haith, *A Content Analysis of Information about Educational Filmstrips in Selected Periodicals* (unpublished doctoral dissertation, Indiana University, 1972).

85. Joyce Haas, *Ethnic Polarization and School Library Materials: A Content Analysis of 1939 Fiction Books from 30 New Jersey School Libraries* (unpublished doctoral dissertation, Rutgers University, 1971).

86. Olaf Helmer, and Rescher, Nicholas, "On Epistemology of Inexact Sciences," *Management Science, 6*(October 1959):47.

87. Russell G. Fischer, "The Delphi Method: A Description, Review and Criticism," *Journal of Academic Librarianship, 4*(May 1978):64–70.

88. Sybilla A. Cook, "The Delphi Connection: Public Library Know Thyself," *Wilson Library Bulletin, 52*(May 1978):703–706.

89. Ulf Wennerberg, "Using the Delphi Technique for Planning the Future of Libraries," *Unesco Bulletin for Libraries, 26*(September 1972):242–246.

90. Harold Borko, *A Study of the Needs for Research in Library and Information Science Education.* Washington, D.C.: U.S. Department of Health, Education and Welfare, Office of Education, Bureau of Research, 1970.

91. Harold A. Linstone, and Turoff, Murray, eds., *The Delphi Method: Techniques and Applications.* Reading, Mass.: Addison-Wesley, 1975.

92. S. C. Bradford. *Documentation.* London: Crosby Lockwood, 1948.

93. B. C. Brooks, "Bradford's Law and the Bibliography of Science," *Nature, 224*(December 6, 1969):953–956.

94. Derek J. de Solla Price, *Little Science, Big Science.* New Haven, Conn.: Yale University Press, 1963.

95. Alfred J. Lotka, "The Frequency Distribution of Scientific Productivity," *Journal of the Washington Academy of Science* (June 19, 1926):317–323.

96. George K. Zipf, *Human Behavior and the Principle of Least Effort.* New York: Hafner, 1972.

97. Robert A. Fairthorne, "Empirical Hyperbolic Distributions (Bradford-Zipf-Madelbrot) for Bibliometric Description and Prediction," *Journal of Documentation, 25*(December 1969):521–534.

98. M. M. Kessler, "Bibliographic Coupling between Scientific Papers," *American Documentation, 14*(January 1963):10–25.

99. Harold Borko, "The Construction of an Empirically Based Mathematically Derived Classification System," in American Federation of Information Processing Societies. *Proceedings of the Spring Joint Computer Conference.* Vol. 21. Palo Alto, Calif.: National Press, 1962, pp. 279–289.

100. M. E. Maron, and Kuhns, J. L., "On Relevance, Probabilistic Indexing and Information Retrieval," *Journal of the Association of Computing Machinery, 7*(1960):216–244.

SELECTED BIBLIOGRAPHY

User Studies

Bates, Marcia J. *User Success in Generating Headings for Catalog Searches* (unpublished doctoral dissertation, University of California, Berkeley, 1972.)

Buckland, Michael K. *Book Availability and the Library User*. Elmsford, N.Y.: Pergamon Press, 1975.

Childers, Thomas A. *Telephone Information Service in Public Libraries; A Comparison of Performance and the Descriptive Statistics Collected by the State of New Jersey* (unpublished doctoral dissertation, Rutgers University 1970.)

Evans, Charles. *Middle Class Attitudes and Public Library Use*. Littleton, Colo.: Libraries Unlimited, 1970.

Ford, Geoffrey, ed. *User Studes: An Introductory Guide and Selected Bibliography*. Sheffield: Centre for Research on User Studies, Occasional Paper, No. 1, 1977.

Franklin, Hardy R. *The Relationship between Adult Communication Practices and Public Library Use in a Northern Urban Black Ghetto* (unpublished doctoral dissertation, Rutgers University, 1971.)

Friedlander, Janet. *Physicians' Use of a Medical Library* (unpublished doctoral dissertation, Case Western Reserve University, 1970.)

Harris, Ira W. *The Influence of Accessibility on Academic Library Use* (unpublished doctoral dissertation, Rutgers University, 1970.)

Monat, William R. *The Public Library and Its Community: A Study of the Impact of Library Services in Five Pennsylvania Cities*. University Park: Pennsylvania State University, Pennsylvania Institute of Public Administration, 1976.

Slote, Stanley J. *The Productive Value of Past Use Patterns of Adult Fiction in Public Libraries for Identifying Core Collections* (unpublished doctoral dissertation, Rutgers University, 1970.)

Zweizig, Douglas. *Predicting Amount of Library Use: An Empirical Study of the Role of the Public Library in the Life of the Adult Public* (unpublished doctoral dissertation, Syracuse University, 1973.)

Library and Community Surveys

Arthur D. Little, Inc. *The Urban Central Library: Development Alternative for San Francisco*. San Francisco, Calif.: Arthur D. Little, Inc., 1970.

Bundy, Mary Lee. *Metropolitan Public Library Users: A Report of Adult Library Use in the Maryland Baltimore–Washington Metropolitan Area*. College Park, Md.: University of Maryland, School of Library and Information Services, 1968.

Chicago Public Library Survey. *Library Response to Urban Change; A Study of the Chicago Public Library*. Lowell Martin, Survey Director. Chicago, Ill.: American Library Association, 1969.

Ellis, Jack B. *Survey of Users of the Metropolitan Toronto Central Library: Report and Analysis*. Toronto, Canada: Metropolitan Toronto Library Board, 1971.

Martin, Lowell A. *Baltimore Reaches Out: Library Service to the Disadvantaged*. Deiches Fund Studies of Public Library Service, No. 3. Baltimore: Enoch Pratt Free Library, 1967.

Nelson Associates, Inc. *Public Library Systems in the United States: A Survey of Multijurisdictional Systems*. Chicago, Ill.: American Library Association, 1969.

Comparative and
International Librarianship

Asheim, Lester. *Librarianship in the Developing Countries*. Urbana: University of Illinois Press, 1966.

Bixler, Paul. *The Mexican Library*. Metuchen, N.J.: Scarecrow Press, 1969.

Danton, J. Periam. *United States Influence on Norwegian Librarianship 1890–1940*. Berkeley: University of California Press, 1957.

Gardner, Frank M. *Public Library Legislation: A Comparative Study*. Documentation, Libraries and Archives: Studies and Research, No. 2. Paris, France: UNESCO, 1971.

Hintz, Carl. *Internationalism and Scholarship; A Comparative Study of the Research Literature Used by American, British, French, and German Botanists* (unpublished doctoral dissertation, University of Chicago, 1952.)

Horrocks, Norman. *The Impact of the Carnegie Corporation of New York on Library Development in Australia: A Study of Foundation Influence* (unpublished doctoral dissertation, University of Pittsburgh, 1971.)

Khurshid, Anis. *Standards for Library Education in Burma, Ceylon, India, and Pakistan* (unpublished doctoral dissertation, University of Pittsburgh, 1969.)

Krzys, Richard A. *History of Education for Librarianship in Columbia*. Metuchen, N.J.: Scarecrow Press, 1969.

Linder, LeRoy H. *Rise of Current Complete National Bibliography in England, France, Germany, and the U.S., 1564–1939* (unpublished doctoral dissertation, University of Chicago, 1958.)

Ruggles, Melville J., and Swank, R. C., eds. *Soviet Libraries and Librarianship*. Chicago, Ill.: American Library Association, 1962.

PART III

Descriptive Statistics

CHAPTER 7

Measurement and Statistical Methods: An Introduction

ANALYSIS OF QUANTIFIED DATA

The term *statistic* or *statistics* is used in at least three distinct but related ways in the English language. "Statistics" as a plural noun is often used by laypersons to refer to a collection of numerical facts, or data. Thus, the practicing librarian might refer to a listing of circulation figures or library card registration information as statistics. Also in this sense, a traffic fatality is sometimes labeled a statistic.

In a second sense of the word, to the investigator conducting scientific research, the term *statistics* is a singular noun referring to a body of methods and techniques for analyzing numerical data, a shortened form of "statistical methodology." It is mostly in this latter sense that we use the term *statistics* in this text.

The word *statistic* is also used in yet a third sense, when referring to a numerical characteristic of a *sample*. The term *parameter* is used to specify the corresponding characteristic of the *population* from which the sample was drawn. Consider, for example, the population consisting of several hundred faculty members of library schools with programs accredited by the American Library Association. The average (mean) number of years of tenure held by members of this population is a parameter—a number characteristic of the population. In practice, an investigator interested in learning the value of this number might attempt to survey all members of the population. Alternatively, the investigator might select a random sample to survey, perhaps using the list published annually in the *Journal of Education For Librarianship* as a frame. The resulting average would be a statistic—calculated on the basis of the sample. A statistic is an estimate of the true value of a population parameter. Although only approximate, it is normally much less expensive to gather data and compute a sample statistic than to collect data and compute the actual population parameter. Thus, frequently, the true value of a parameter is never known. Procedures for inferring the range within which a population parameter is likely to fall, on the basis of a statistic computed from a random sample drawn from the population, comprise an important part of inferential statistical methodology.

Statistical techniques may have many purposes. *Descriptive statistics* consist of methods and procedures for summarizing, simplifying, reducing, and presenting *raw data,* to communicate the essence of the data to another. The purpose of such methods is essentially reportorial, as with the presentation of summary data to an administrator. The aims of *inferential statistics* are somewhat more ambitious. Inferential methods and techniques are used to make predictions, to test hypotheses, and to infer characteristics of a population from the characteristics of a sample. In general, techniques of inferential statistics proceed well beyond a mere description of a set of data; in some sense they also attempt to shed some light on the *meaning* of the data.

Library practitioners are familiar with many kinds of numerical data in a library, such as data pertaining to *quantitative* characteristics of library card holders or the circulation of library materials. Examples of such data include the number of male and female registered borrowers, the number of nonfiction and fiction books circulated during the past month, the number of children participating in the library's summer reading program, the distribution of publication dates associated with circulated materials, and the nonfiction preferences (by class) of various patron groups. Even though these and other data exist in every library, librarians have often been reluctant to subject them to rigorous quantitative analysis and to utilize statistical methodology as a facet of scientific method. In the next section we discuss some of the ways in which statistical methodology may be utilized by librarians. These topics will be expanded further in the chapters that follow.

APPLICATIONS OF STATISTICAL METHODOLOGY TO LIBRARIANSHIP

In the process of conducting research, librarians compile and collect many different types of numerical data. Although some of these data originate from the recorded observations of daily, routine library operations, others are generated in the form of responses to various questionnaires, tests, and other instruments that have been devised to obtain information regarding library phenomena. Knowledge of the techniques of quantitative analysis can aid librarians in making correct interpretations of these data.

The use of statistics can allow librarians to obtain the maximum amount of information from their research efforts. Using statistical methodology the librarian can test hypotheses; compute means and other measures of central tendency; assess the relationship between one variable and another; make predictions; determine the reliability and validity of instruments and measurements; generalize conclusions from sample data to populations; present research data in graphical and tabular formats; calculate the variability of research data; determine the significance of the difference between the performance of two groups; and much more. We shall explore techniques designed to accomplish some of these tasks in the following chapters.

As an introductory example of how statistical analysis might be utilized in library work, consider a group of school librarians who dutifully collect and record circulation data each day of the school year. At the end of the school year they will have perhaps 170 numbers, ranging from a minimum of 35 circulations in a day to a maximum of 210 circulations. Now suppose that these librarians are asked by their principals or school boards to report these data. How will they accomplish this task? The librarians could, of course, type 170 numbers on two or three sheets of paper and submit these sheets in response to the request. But *raw data* of this kind will probably be of little use to a busy administrator, who would not ordinarily have the time required to analyze the data. Ideally, our librarians should present their principals not with 170 numbers, but with tables, graphs, or even one or two single numbers computed from the circulation figures, *which in some sense represent the essence of the set of raw data collected.* Simplification and summarization of raw data for preparation of reports such as this are major purposes of methods of statistical analysis. As we remarked earlier, analytical methods of this kind fall in the domain of descriptive statistics.

Let us consider a second example of how a librarian might utilize techniques of statistical analysis. Suppose that two modules of instruction have been developed for teaching library skills to college freshmen; both contain the same information but one is a print module and the other is a videotape module. Which of these approaches to the instruction of basic library skills is most effective? To attempt to answer this question, the librarian might select two samples of college freshmen to whom the modules are presented. A standard test of library skills could then be administered to both groups to determine the effect of the instruction on each. The average score associated with each group could then be calculated, using a common technique of descriptive statistics (see Chapter 9). Suppose for the sake of discussion that these averages are 57 and 63 for the print and video modules, respectively. Which module was more effective?

Actually, the question posed in the preceding paragraph is not a very good one. There is, obviously, some evidence that the video module is the more effective of the two methods. *But should the evidence be judged sufficient,* that is, used as a basis for subsequent action? This is the crucial question and it is one that cannot be answered by descriptive statistics alone. Techniques for drawing inferences and predictions of this sort from raw data are part of inferential statistics.

A final commonly encountered example of the use of inferential statistics in librarianship arises from the occasional need for ascertaining certain characteristics of a population that is too large to examine in toto (e.g., the set of issues of all periodicals received by a library). Suppose that we wish to evaluate the potential use of the Ohio College Library Center (OCLC) serials control subsystem. As part of this project, we may need to estimate the proportion of periodicals in our collection which include an International Standard Serial Number (ISSN) printed in each issue, because for such periodicals retrieval of a catalog record is rapid as compared with the time required to retrieve a record when the ISSN is not known. In even a moderately sized library, examining a recent issue of every serial title for this characteristic would be a lengthy task. The proportion of serials with an ISSN can be *estimated,* by drawing a random sample from the population of serial titles and examining each serial in the sample for the characteristic in question, much as political polls estimate the proportion of voters favoring a candidate in an election. This procedure, although normally necessitating the examination of only a small fraction of the total population, obviously produces an *estimate,* that is, a number which is almost always somewhat in error. Thus, the relevant question to be posed is, "What is the size of the possible error to be expected from a given sample size?" Or, looking at the problem from another perspective, "What is the size of the sample that should be drawn to keep the expected error of our estimate within manageable or tolerable limits?" This issue contains elements of both descriptive statistics and inferential statistics, and is explored in Chapter 10.

STATISTICAL SYMBOLS

By convention, common symbols are frequently used by research workers in many different areas to refer to the same statistical concepts. We will attempt to follow these standard conventions as closely as possible in this text. Special signs and symbols that are used throughout the remainder of this text are listed in Appendix B. Readers will want to refer to this listing occasionally to refresh their memories about the usage of particular symbols.

MEASUREMENT AND SCALING

Before quantitative data can be analyzed statistically, they must first be gathered. Conceptually, there are essentially two different classes of quantitative data, based on how the data have been collected. Data that are the result of counting something can take on only a finite (usually relatively small) number of distinct values. Such data are termed *discrete*. Library examples of discrete data include the number of male or female borrowers, circulation data, records of reference inquiries, and acquisitions data.

A second type of data is obtained as a result of measurement. Essentially, measurement entails the transformation of the physical characteristics of research subjects into numbers. Measurement involves the application of a *scale* to the phenomenon of interest. A scale is characterized by the use of an arbitrary unit of measurement, against which the phenomenon in question is compared. Thus, data obtained by measurement are by their nature approximate, whereas data obtained by counting are theoretically exact. Measurement data can normally take on any value, from an infinite number of possibilities, between given limits on a scale. Such data are referred to as *continuous*. Examples of continuous data are readings obtained from a gas gauge or thermometer, and the heights and weights of persons. Perhaps an assessment of the relevance of a piece of library material to a patron should also be viewed as continuous; however, experiments in information retrieval have frequently assumed such judgments to be binary (relevant or nonrelevant). An index or measuring instrument is evaluated on the basis of its relevance, validity, and reliability.

In a fundamental paper published in *Science,* S. S. Stevens provided the first explication of a theory of scales for the measurement of operational variables.[1] Stevens identified and discussed properties of four types of scales: nominal, ordinal, interval, and ratio. The characteristics of these scales, distinguished by the empirical operations that are possible with each, are listed in Table 7.1, adopted from a table published in Stevens' paper. Theoretically, only certain statistics are permissible with each scale type.*

In the *nominal* scale, one may only determine whether two items are, or are not, equal with respect to an unordered set of categories. Examples of nominal scales are classifications of persons by sex, religion, political preference, national origin, and grade level. In none of these cases can it

---

* This is based on whether mathematical transformations leave the scale form invariant. For a useful treatment of this subject, see Coombs, "Theory and Methods of Social Measurement."[2]

Table 7.1. *Classification of Scales*

Scale	Empirical operations possible	Permissible statistics	Examples
Nominal	Determination of equality	Number of cases Mode Contingency correlation Chi-square	Classification of persons by sex, occupation, or grade level
Ordinal	The above plus determination of greater than	The above plus median Percentiles Rank-order correlation	Intelligence Grades of eggs or students Relevance of documents to queries Utility Position title within a library
Interval	All of the above plus determination of equality of intervals	All of the above plus mean Standard deviation Product-moment correlation	Temperature in Centigrade Most psychological scales
Ratio	All of the above plus determination of equality of ratios (existence of a true zero point)	All of the above	Temperature in Kelvin Length Weight Time Density Income of librarian Daily circulation totals

be stated that one category is greater than (superior to) a second category; only that the two categories are distinct and different.

In an *ordinal scale,* categories possess an inherent order, and a determination of greater than (or less than) is possible, in addition to a determination of equality. Many library data are ordinal. Theoretically, the median, percentiles, and rank-order correlation are permissible for use with data arising from ordinal scales, whereas statistics such as mean and standard deviation are not.

Interval scales are based upon the metric concept; thus, an investigator may say that the distance between adjacent interval scale categories are equal. Using the Farenheit scale, for example, we can be certain that 26°F is as much higher than 21°F as 88°F is above 83°F. In some research projects, ordinal scales are erroneously treated as though they were interval scales. Suppose, for example, that an investigator established a scale of relevance: "very relevant," "relevant," "marginally relevant," and "not relevant." If the investigator were willing to say that differences between each scale value were equal, that is, that the difference between "very relevant" and "relevant" were equal to the differences between "relevant" and "marginally relevant," and between "marginally relevant" and "not relevant," then numerical values could be assigned to these categories (e.g., 4, 3, 2, and 1). These numbers could then be treated as interval data, and statistics such as the mean and standard deviation could be utilized. Unless one agreed with the assertion that the differences between the relevance categories were equal, however, a scale of relevance should be treated as an ordinal scale, for which means and standard deviations would not be permissible statistical operations.

Most scales found in the physical sciences are *ratio scales,* such as scales measuring length and time. A ratio scale is an interval scale in which an absolute zero point exists—a point at which zero indicates a total absence of that which is being measured. This condition should be distinguished from a scale in which an *arbitrary* zero point has been specified. A good example of the difference between these can be found in the Centigrade and Farenheit temperature scales, which are interval scales and for which the zero point is arbitrary, and the absolute (or Kelvin temperature scale), in which zero degrees represents cessation of all molecular and atomic activity. Absolute zero is thus the temperature below which it is impossible to achieve, and represents the complete absence of motion. The distinction between an arbitrary zero point and a true zero point is important because most scales in the social sciences, although they possess zero points, are not ratio scales or even interval scales. Examples of ordinal scales with zero points are academic grades of students, IQ, and Graduate Record Examination scores. These are often treated as interval scales for purposes of statistical analysis, although strictly speaking this is not permissible.

Data obtained by counting can often be regarded as arising from a ratio scale, and thus such data can be analyzed with ratio scale methods. Because a true zero point exists in a ratio scale, such statements can be made as: "scale reading X is three times as high as scale reading Y." Clearly, such statements cannot be made with regard to the ordinal scale of IQ or the interval scale of temperature measured in Farenheit, for example. It is not true that a person with an IQ of 140 is twice as intelligent as a person with an IQ of 70, or that a temperature of 90°F measures three times as much heat as a temperature of 30°F. In both cases, the zero point on the scale has been arbitrarily assigned and does not reflect a complete absence of that which is being measured. Examples of data obtained from ratio scales in library and information science include salaries of librarians, daily circulation totals, and the number of relevant citations retrieved in a literature search.

An examination of Table 7.1 clearly reveals that a determination of appropriate statistical procedures for a given application is based in part on the origin of the data to be analyzed—whether the data arise from a nominal, ordinal, interval, or ratio scale. Investigators in library and information science have occasionally ignored this caveat, however, and have utilized whatever statistical procedure strikes their fancy, regardless of the origin of the data. It may be hoped that as research in librarianship becomes more sophisticated, this situation will improve.

SUMMARY OF REMAINING STATISTICAL CHAPTERS

Basic techniques of descriptive statistics are presented in Chapters 8 and 9. Chapter 8, "Graphical Representation of Data," treats pictorial approaches to the simplification, summarization, and representation of raw data, whereas Chapter 9, "Central Tendency and Variability," deals with numerical methods of accomplishing the same goal. Chapter 10, "The Normal Distribution," examines properties of commonly occurring frequency distributions and applies these properties to the problem of inferring characteristics of a population from characteristics of a sample. Chapter 11, "Linear Regression and Correlation," examines a mathematical model expressing a linear relationship between two variables and shows how the model can be used both to describe paired data and to make predictions based upon this description. Chapter 12, "Statistical Significance and Hypothesis Testing," examines several elementary procedures for analyzing raw data for the purpose of testing hypotheses regarding the data.

APPENDIX: PROBLEMS FOR SOLUTION

Identify each of the following data as arising from nominal, ordinal, interval, or ratio scales. Explain your reasoning.

Problems
1. A child's preferences for a sample of 10 picture books
2. Graduate Record Examination scores for library school students
3. Number of interlibrary loan requests processed during a fixed period of time
4. The academic ranks of a group of college professors
5. The number of titles retrieved by an OCLC author/title search key

6. Perceived usefulness of a given document to a research scientist
7. Number of "heads" obtained in ten tosses of a coin
8. Efficacy of various media for delivery of a unit of information
9. Costs associated with a set of serial publications
10. Categories of books in a public library (e.g., fiction, biography, etc.)

Answers

1. Ordinal
2. Ordinal
3. Ratio
4. Ordinal
5. Ratio
6. Ordinal
7. Ratio
8. Ordinal
9. Ratio
10. Nominal

REFERENCES

1. S. S. Stevens, "On the Theory of Scales of Measurement." *Science, 103*(1946):677–680.
2. Clyde H. Coombs, "Theory and Methods of Social Measurement," in Leon Festinger and Daniel Katz, eds., *Research Methods in the Behavioral Sciences*. New York: Holt, Rinehart and Winston, 1966, pp. 471–535.

CHAPTER 8

Graphical Representation of Data

INTRODUCTION

Certain paintings or photographs can convey a wealth of information to an observer, including qualitative feelings of mood and emotion as well as much quantitative detail concerning the scene. For complete communication of this sort to take place, however, the observer must possess a good deal of personal knowledge to which the scene can be related. In cases in which a scene contains few elements of familiarity to the observer—little communication can take place.

The purpose of the present chapter is to provide the reader with the competencies necessary to extract as much meaning as possible from the examination of a pictorial, or graphical representation of data. Communication is, of course, a two-way street. The student should not only learn how to *read* graphs and tables by careful study of the present chapter, but also how to construct them so that they will accurately capture the essence of a set of data. It is not an exaggeration to say that a well-constructed graph or table can easily convey more information than 10,000 observations in the form of raw data. We shall begin our study of the graphical representation of data by focusing on the concept of a frequency distribution.

FREQUENCY DISTRIBUTIONS

The *frequency distribution* is a means of imposing a degree of structure and order on numerical research data. Before data are organized, they are called *raw data*. In frequency distributions, raw numerical data are often ordered and arranged in an *array* according to their numerical values. Normally, the arrangement is from the least to the greatest observation (i.e., in ascending numerical order); however, the data can also be placed in descending order of magnitude. An *observation* is a recording of a single

Table 8.1. *Number of Days that 50 Selected Books Have Circulated*

18	26	15	13	24	21	5	17	10	20
31	4	7	9	14	8	10	20	13	11
22	19	13	16	9	12	35	13	29	21
12	6	9	12	11	6	9	28	16	17
38	19	27	15	12	16	6	31	26	21

research datum. If the data are quantitative rather than qualitative, then observations are numbers.

The following examples of the imposition of order on data illustrate the fundamentals of constructing arrays and frequency distributions. Suppose that the circulation periods in days of a group of 10 books are as follows: 13, 23, 15, 5, 7, 21, 10, 18, 19, and 12. In ascending order of magnitude the array would be: 5, 7, 10, 12, 13, 15, 18, 19, 21, and 23. In descending order of magnitude the array would be: 23, 21, 19, 18, 15, 13, 12, 10, 7, and 5. The *range* of a distribution is the difference between the two most extreme circulation periods (more generally, observations or scores). The shortest period of circulation for the 10 books in our example was 5 days and the longest period was 23 days. The range of the data is therefore 23 − 5 = 18 days.

Let us now turn our attention to another group of raw data. Table 8.1 provides the circulation time periods of a group of 50 books. An examination of the table will reveal many facts about the distribution. For example, the highest circulation period associated with any book is 38 days, the lowest circulation period is 4 days, and the range is therefore 34. The values of the three lowest ranking circulation periods are 4, 5, and 6; the values of the three highest ranking circulation periods are 31, 35, and 38. We could continue indefinitely making similar observations, but it is apparent that the raw data contained in Table 8.1 could be analyzed more easily if they were placed in numerical order. In Table 8.2, the raw data from Table 8.1 have been arranged into an array.

Notice that the data in Table 8.2 have been subdivided and grouped into 12 convenient class intervals (3–5, 6–8, 9–11, etc.) so that a visual analysis can be more easily accomplished. Each class interval contains three days. As we shall see later in this section, the array provides an efficient structure for recording numerical data so that simple statistical computations can be made. No breaks appear in the distribution, even though some of the values (circulation days) are actually not represented. This method of compressing distributions by clustering observations into intervals is

Table 8.2. *Array of Circulation Periods of 50 Selected Books*

Class intervals (days)	Circulation periods
36–38	38
33–35	35
30–32	31,31
27–29	27,28,29
24–26	24,26,26
21–23	21,21,21,22
18–20	18,19,19,20,20
15–17	15,15,16,16,16,17,17
12–14	12,12,12,12,13,13,13,13,14
9–11	9,9,9,9,10,10,11,11
6–8	6,6,6,7,8
3–5	4,5

called *grouping;* data organized in this manner are referred to as *grouped data.* By grouping data into classes, categories, or intervals, we can determine exactly how many individual observations fall within a class frequency. When data are tabulated by classes and class *frequencies* are indicated as in Table 8.3, the result is called a *frequency distribution.*

By scanning the array in Table 8.2, we can easily determine that the 10 highest ranking books according to length of circulation had the following values: 38, 35, 31, 28, 27, 29, 24, 26, 21, and 22. Similarly, the 10 lowest ranking books circulated for 4, 5, 6, 7, 8, 9, 10, 11, 12, and 13 days, respectively. We can also determine from Table 8.2 such facts as (*a*) 24 books (almost one-half of the total number) circulated for 14 or fewer days; (*b*) only 4 books circulated for more than 30 days; and (*c*) no books had a circulation period consisting of the following numbers of days: 3, 23, 25, 30, 33, 34, 36, and 37.

Representation of raw data in a frequency distribution eradicates some of the original detail of the research observations. For example, the fact that the class interval 6–8 contains the exact observations 6, 6, 6, 7, and 8 cannot be determined from Table 8.3, which indicates only that there were five observations in this interval. Ordinarily, data summarized in the form of a frequency distribution such as Table 8.3 are seldom or never referred to again in their original form. As we shall see, subsequent statistical calculations are often performed upon a frequency distribution rather than upon the raw data which were the basis of the distribution. Because representation of data in a frequency distribution invariably results in

Table 8.3. *Frequency Distribution*
Showing Circulation Periods
of 50 Selected Books

Days	Frequency (f)
36–38	1
33–35	1
30–32	2
27–29	3
24–26	3
21–23	4
18–20	5
15–17	7
12–14	9
9–11	8
6–8	5
3–5	2
	50 ($N = 50$)

some loss of information, calculations performed on grouped data are not as accurate as calculations performed upon the raw data would be. On the other hand, the advantages of grouping data into frequency distributions include obtaining a clearer picture of the relationships between the data, as well as facilitating subsequent quantitative analysis. A research worker is usually more than willing to make this tradeoff between accuracy and clarity of communication.

To construct a frequency distribution for a set of raw data, it is first necessary to determine the set of class intervals to be used. The raw data can then be tallied according to these categories, and the tallies can be totaled to obtain frequencies. Table 8.4 contains the monthly salaries of 40 professional librarians employed in the Jessup University Library. For these data, we will establish class intervals (in this case, intervals of salaries), make tallies, and determine frequencies for each interval.

Normally, 15 score intervals will allow a sufficient compression of raw data into a frequency distribution. More than 20 or fewer than 10 intervals are usually considered to be undesirable, by common convention. Too few intervals result in too much compression of the data and too great a loss of information. Conversely, if there are too many intervals, the advantages resulting from the data compression are lost.

To determine the interval width or number of appropriate points to be

Table 8.4. *Monthly Salaries of 40 Librarians at Jessup University*

750	680	816	792	660
935	965	920	880	845
855	820	1055	1070	1083
780	1040	575	833	610
1025	705	875	952	940
1128	896	1140	710	738
625	1160	640	1290	952
1230	870	1245	862	760

included in an interval, the range of the data can be divided by 15—the desired number of intervals—in order to determine the appropriate interval width. It is often useful to select an odd number rather than an even number for the interval width; in this case the midpoint of the interval is a whole number and thus can be easily determined and used in later statistical computations.

Let us return to Table 8.4 and construct a frequency distribution for these data. As the minimum monthly salary listed in Table 8.4 is $575 and the maximum is $1290, the range is $1290 − $575 = $715. Because $715/15 = $47.67, or approximately $50, we can divide the salary range into 15 class intervals, each having a width of $50. Figure 8.1 summarizes the distribution, tallies, and frequencies for these raw salary data and demonstrates how raw data can be ordered to facilitate their communication.

Monthly Salaries in Dollars	Tallies	Frequency
1250-1299	/	1
1200-1249	//	2
1150-1199	/	1
1100-1149	//	2
1050-1099	///	3
1000-1049	//	2
950-999	///	3
900-949	///	3
850-899	//////	6
800-849	////	4
750-799	////	4
700-749	///	3
650-699	//	2
600-649	///	3
550-599	/	1
		N = 40

Figure 8.1. *Tallies for distribution of salaries at Jessup University.*

GRAPHS

Data can be represented pictorially, or graphically, in a variety of ways. Several commonly used procedures will be discussed here. The general purpose of tables, graphs, and figures in the text of a research report is to communicate the essence of a research result or set of observations more clearly than the raw data themselves could possibly do. Frequently, a table or graph can greatly contribute to the reader's understanding of a research report. Report writers should make maximum use of graphical and tabular techniques for displaying data. Graphs, tables, figures, and charts should be placed near the textual part of the report where they are discussed or where the displayed data are first mentioned.

A common method of representing data graphically is to construct a *bar graph,* or *histogram.* A histogram consists of a set of rectangles with a common horizontal base. The size and position of each rectangle is determined by its class frequency, measured on the vertical, or *Y*-axis, and by the limits of its class interval, measured on the horizontal, or *X*-axis. Figure 8.2 represents a histogram of the book circulation data summarized in Table 8.3. Evident from an examination of Figure 8.2 is the fact that histograms allow the graphical representation of data in terms of fre-

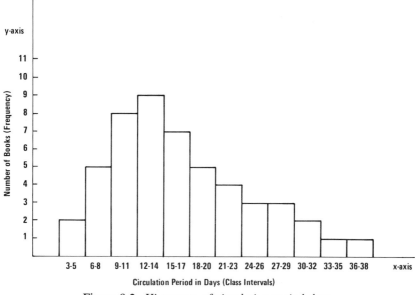

Figure 8.2. *Histogram of circulation period data.*

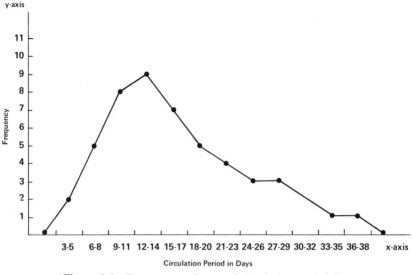

Figure 8.3. *Frequency polygon of circulation period data.*

quency classes and that the number of observations in each class is clearly indicated.

At times, research workers might desire to graph data in a *line graph,* or *frequency polygon.* A frequency polygon is constructed as follows: (*a*) Place a dot in the midpoint of the top of each rectangle (or of what would be a rectangle if a histogram were actually constructed); this value corresponds to the *midpoint* of the interval; (*b*) connect the dots with a straight line; and (*c*) extend the lines from both the lowest and highest class intervals to the horizontal base or zero line. Frequency polygons can have an infinite variety of forms. Figure 8.3 consists of a frequency polygon representing the same data that are displayed in Figure 8.2 and in Table 8.3. Notice that class intervals have been added at both the beginning and end of the distribution (intervals 0–2 and 39–41, respectively), each having a frequency of zero.

SMOOTHING FREQUENCY POLYGONS

If the data with which a frequency polygon is constructed were obtained from a sample, a process called *smoothing* will often produce a truer picture of population characteristics than simply graphing the irregular peaks and valleys which often result from sample data. A smoothed frequency for each interval can be computed by: (*a*) adding the frequency of a given interval to the frequencies of the two adjacent intervals (i.e., the intervals immediately to the left and the right), and then (*b*) obtaining an average frequency by dividing the sum of the three frequencies by 3. To smooth the first interval of the book circulation distribution in Figure 8.2, add the frequency for the 3–5 interval to the frequency of the 6–8 interval to the frequency of the 0–2 interval.

Frequency of interval to be smoothed = 2
Frequency of interval to the right   = 5
Frequency of interval to the left   = 0
                                                                    7

Thus, the smoothed frequency for the interval 3–5 is 7/3 = 2.3. Smoothed frequencies for the remaining 12 intervals are computed in a similar fashion, and a theoretical population frequency polygon can be approximated with the resulting smoothed frequency polygon for the sample.

Perhaps this point can be illustrated by examining an irregularly shaped frequency polygon. Figure 8.4 is a frequency polygon representing a sample drawn from a population. A number of jagged peaks and valleys ap-

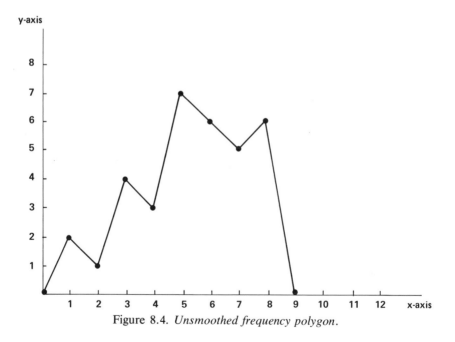

Figure 8.4. *Unsmoothed frequency polygon.*

pear in the polygon. The 10 frequency classes displayed in Figure 8.4 can be smoothed as shown in the following chart.

Frequency class	Computations
0	$\dfrac{0 + 0 + 2}{3} = \dfrac{2}{3} = .7$
1	$\dfrac{0 + 2 + 1}{3} = \dfrac{3}{3} = 1.0$
2	$\dfrac{2 + 1 + 4}{3} = \dfrac{7}{3} = 2.3$
3	$\dfrac{1 + 4 + 3}{3} = \dfrac{8}{3} = 2.7$
4	$\dfrac{4 + 3 + 7}{3} = \dfrac{14}{3} = 4.7$
5	$\dfrac{3 + 7 + 6}{3} = \dfrac{16}{3} = 5.3$
6	$\dfrac{7 + 6 + 5}{3} = \dfrac{18}{3} = 6.0$
7	$\dfrac{6 + 5 + 6}{3} = \dfrac{17}{3} = 5.7$
8	$\dfrac{5 + 6 + 0}{3} = \dfrac{11}{3} = 3.7$
9	$\dfrac{6 + 0 + 0}{3} = \dfrac{6}{3} = 2.0 -$

Note that the line of the frequency polygon begins and ends on the base line (i.e., at zero); this is a commonly followed convention. Figure 8.5 contains the smoothed version of the frequency polygon displayed in Figure 8.4.

CUMULATIVE FREQUENCY DISTRIBUTIONS

Cumulative frequency distributions provide a display of the total frequencies associated with each class interval up to and including a given interval. Table 8.5 contains cumulative frequencies for the data displayed in Table 8.3. These cumulative frequencies can also be represented as percentages of the total frequency. For example, the cumulative frequency for the interval 15–17 is $7 + 9 + 8 + 5 + 2 = 31$. Because the total frequency is 50, the cumulative percentage associated with this interval is $31/50 = .62 = 62.0\%$.

To determine cumulative frequencies, begin counting the number of

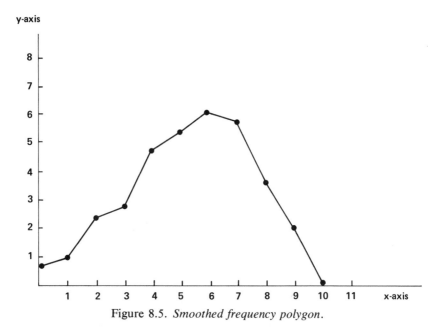

Figure 8.5. *Smoothed frequency polygon.*

cases (frequencies) in the lowest interval and then add each frequency to this number to obtain a partial sum at each step. Continue in this way, moving up the cumulative frequency column, until the highest score or score interval has been reached. The highest score interval should always

Table 8.5. *Cumulative Frequency
Distribution Showing Circulation
Periods of 50 Selected Books*

Days (X)	Frequency (f)	Cumulative frequency (cf)	Cumulative percentage (cp)
36–38	1	50	100
33–35	1	49	98
30–32	2	48	96
27–29	3	46	92
24–26	3	43	86
21–23	4	40	80
18–20	5	36	72
15–17	7	31	62
12–14	9	24	48
9–11	8	15	30
6–8	5	7	14
3–5	2	2	4

have a cumulative frequency corresponding to the total number (N) of actual scores or observations displayed. (In Table 8.5, $N = 50$; the cumulative frequency at the highest interval, 36–38, is also 50). Cumulative frequencies can be of value because they show what percentage of the cases fall below each score or score interval. To determine cumulative percentages, begin with the lowest cumulative frequency and compute the percent of the total observations (N) represented by the value in each increasing score interval ($2/50 = 4.0\%$; $7/50 = 14.0\%$, etc.). The total cumulative frequency represents 100% of the cases ($50/50 = 100.0\%$).

Graphical displays of cumulative frequency and percentage distributions are called the *cumulative frequency polygon* and the *percentage ogive*, respectively; both are illustrated in Figure 8.6. The vertical scale at the left of the figure indicates cumulative frequencies; the percentage cumulative frequency is indicated on the vertical scale to the right. Construction of the scale to determine cumulative percentages can be accomplished by placing the value 100.0% to correspond to the point representing the maximum cumulative frequency, and by dividing the remaining portions of the scale into increments representing percentages which fall between zero and 100%.

The primary advantage of a percentage ogive is that it allows the easy reading of percentiles. In Figure 8.6, the dashed lines and the dotted lines

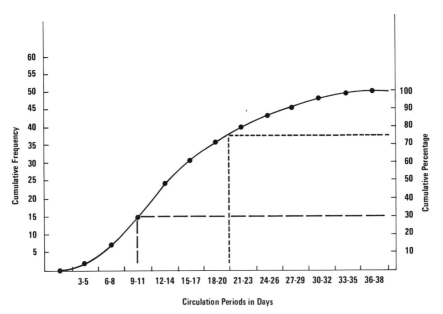

Figure 8.6. *Cumulative frequency polygon and percentage ogive.*

Table 8.6. *Bivariate Data for Two Variables, X and Y.*

Variable X	2	4	6	8	10	12	14	16	18	20	22
Variable Y	10	15	20	25	30	35	40	45	50	55	60

indicate that the thirtieth and seventy-fifth percentiles are approximately 10 and 20.5, respectively. This indicates that 30% of all the books circulated for not more than ten days, whereas 75% circulated for 20 or fewer days. Computation of percentiles such as these will be discussed in more detail in the next chapter.

BIVARIATE GRAPHS

When observations have been made of two variables and quantitative measures from each variable have been obtained, the data can be graphically represented in a *bivariate graph,* or *scatter diagram.* Values for the two variables are plotted in a bivariate graph in much the same fashion as coordinates are determined for a point on a map (read from left to right, then up). One variable is measured on the horizontal axis, or X-axis, and the other variable is measured on the vertical axis, or Y-axis. An example will help explain the construction of a bivariate graph. Listed in Table 8.6

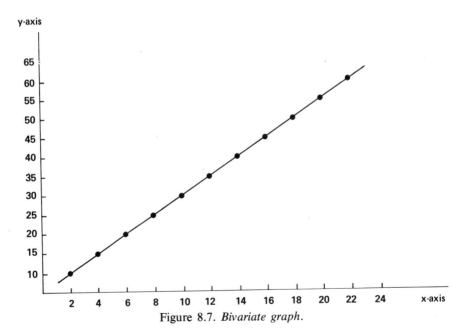

Figure 8.7. *Bivariate graph.*

are observations obtained for two variables, X and Y. Coordinates for these data have been plotted on the bivariate graph provided in Figure 8.7.

From an analysis of the values for X and Y, as well as from an examination of the bivariate graph which comprises these plotted data (Figure 8.7), one can see that the relationship between the two variables is of a perfect, positive nature. In other words, with each increase in the values for X there is a similar change in the values for Y. Furthermore, these changes are in the same direction; in our example, as X increases, so does Y; and conversely. Variables related in this way are said to be *positively correlated*. On the other hand, when Y tends to decrease when X increases, and conversely, then the relationship between the two variables is said to be negative. The variables in such a relationship are said to be *negatively correlated*.

Variables in the social and behavioral sciences are rarely found to change in identical amounts (i.e., unit for unit) as in Figure 8.7. There are few perfect linear relationships between two variables. Almost always, plotted points for variables will be dispersed over a bivariate graph in such a manner that a single straight line cannot be drawn to connect all of them. Plots of variables on a bivariate graph, however, will usually form some pattern that will permit determination of the existence of a positive or negative correlation—or no correlation at all.

In Figure 8.8 a straight line has been superimposed on a bivariate graph through the middle area of a cluster of plotted points. The closer the points are to the straight line, the more easily the relationship between the

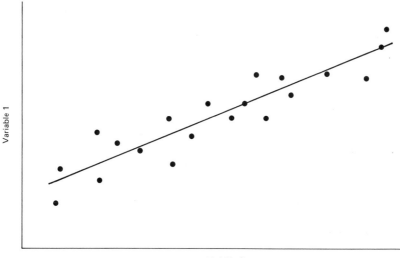

Figure 8.8. *Strong positive correlation between two variables.*

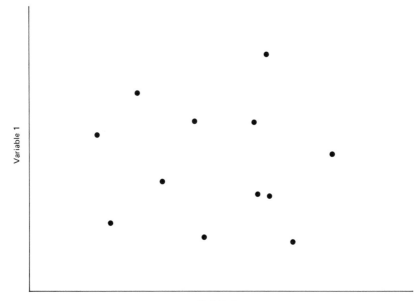

Variable 2

Figure 8.9. *No correlation between two variables.*

two variables can be recognized, and the higher is the correlation between them. Sometimes, scattergrams will be so irregular that no correlation at all is discernable (see Figure 8.9). We can then state that no apparent relationship exists between variables X and Y. These and related topics will be discussed in much greater detail in Chapter 11.

PIE CHART

A circular graph or *pie chart* can also be an effective means of presenting research data graphically in a written report. As an illustration of how to construct a pie chart, let us utilize the data provided in Table 8.7, which were generated by a survey conducted to determine the use being made of a public library by citizens classified into broad occupational groups.

To construct a pie chart for these data, we first determine how many of a circle's 360 degrees will be required to represent each of the occupational categories. This involves a change of occupational group *percentages* to *degrees* (°) of a circle. The total use of the library by all occupational groups equals one hundred percent; each percent corresponds to $360/100 = 3.6°$. To determine the portion of the circle to be occupied by each occupational category, multiply each of the percentages for occupa-

Table 8.7. *Public Library Use by*
Occupation

Occupation of library user	Percentage of total use
Student	25.0
Housewife	18.5
Retired	10.3
Salaried	30.2
Self-employed	16.0
	100.0%

tional groups in Table 8.7 by 3.6. For example, student use comprised 25.0% of the total; this is equivalent to (25.0) (3.6°) = 90.0°.

Once the number of degrees to be allowed for each occupational category has been determined, the circle can then be divided into areas as follows:

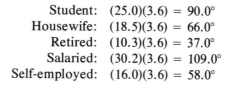

Student: $(25.0)(3.6) = 90.0°$
Housewife: $(18.5)(3.6) = 66.0°$
Retired: $(10.3)(3.6) = 37.0°$
Salaried: $(30.2)(3.6) = 109.0°$
Self-employed: $(16.0)(3.6) = 58.0°$

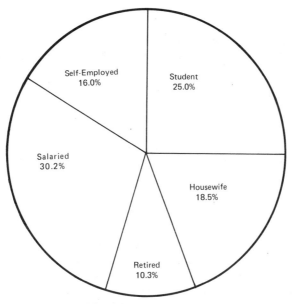

Figure 8.10. *Pie chart.*

The next step in constructing a pie chart is to place a protractor at the circle's center and measure the number of degrees determined to be the equivalent of the area for each occupational category. Figure 8.10 is a pie chart that graphically represents the percentage of library usage by various occupational groups, based upon the data contained in Table 8.7.

APPENDIX: PROBLEMS FOR SOLUTION

1. During the conduct of a research study involving a group of 40 library technicians, the following scores on a library aptitude test were obtained:

37	44	38	32	48	44	43	51	36	30
33	38	43	46	40	37	41	49	42	34
40	44	50	47	44	39	45	48	41	37
34	43	47	45	46	47	49	46	43	45

(*a*) Construct a frequency distribution beginning with the interval 30–31. (*b*) Construct a histogram based upon the frequency distribution; (*c*) construct a frequency polygon for the data; (*d*) construct a cumulative frequency distribution and a cumulative percentage distribution.

2. Construct a histogram, a frequency polygon, and a cumulative frequency polygon for the data reported in Figure 8.1.

3. For each of the following sets of maximum and minimum values of a set of data, determine the range of the data and a set of appropriate class intervals for the construction of a frequency distribution: (*a*) Maximum = \$7800, minimum = \$3300; (*b*) maximum = 32, minimum = 6; (*c*) maximum = 227, minimum = 84.

Answers

Range = \$4500. Because \$4500/15 = \$300, appropriate class intervals would be 3200–3499, 3500–3799, and so on.

4. Determine smoothed frequencies for the frequency polygon in Figure 8.11 and construct a frequency polygon for the smoothed data.

5. Record the date of publication of each volume in your personal library (or in a sample of size 100 or more if your library is too large to examine in toto). Construct a frequency distribution representing these data. Would you expect the results of this exercise to be different for a

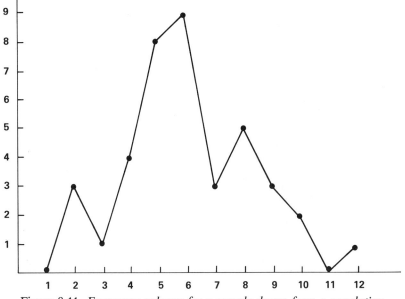

Figure 8.11. *Frequency polygon for a sample drawn from a population.*

student with strong interests in the humanities than for a student with strong interests in the sciences? Why or why not?

6. Two versions of a classification test were given to a group of 10 students enrolled in an advanced course dealing with the organization of information. The maximum possible score on both tests was 10. The data are summarized below.

Student	Score on Test 1	Score on Test 2
A	5.5	7.0
B	6.3	9.2
C	7.5	8.5
D	8.4	9.5
E	8.0	8.8
F	4.7	6.5
G	9.5	10.0
H	8.0	9.0
I	5.8	7.2
J	8.7	9.8

(*a*) Construct a bivariate graph representing the data; (*b*) describe the relationship between students' scores on the two tests; (*c*) if a student's score on Test 1 was 8.5, predict her score on the second test; (*d*) would you say that the two tests could be reasonably used interchangeably? Under what conditions?

Answers

(*b*) Strong positive relationship, or correlation, between the two sets of scores. (*c*) 9.5.

7. The acquisitions department of a university library reported the purchase of the following numbers of titles in several foreign languages during a 3-year period. Construct a pie chart in which these data are graphically displayed

Language	Number of titles
French	8236
German	12869
Spanish	10295
Italian	5148
Russian	6177
Japanese	3603
Chinese	2573
Other	2581

Answer

The relevant percentages are: French, 16%; German, 25%; Spanish, 20%; Italian, 10%; Russian, 12%; Japanese, 7%; Chinese, 5%; Other, 5%.

8. Earlier in this chapter the assertion was made that in samples, especially relatively small samples, there exist statistical fluctuations which probably are not characteristic of the population being sampled. For this reason, data are sometimes smoothed to better represent the characteristics of a population from the measured characteristics of a sample. Think of an example of a library population on which to test this assertion by first selecting a sample and constructing a frequency polygon to represent the data and then examining the entire population and constructing a frequency polygon for the population as a whole. Conduct the test. Is the smoothed version of the frequency polygon closer to that associated with the population than the unsmoothed polygon?

CHAPTER 9

Central Tendency and Variability

INTRODUCTION

Descriptive statistics is a generic term referring to a set of methods, procedures, and techniques of representing, summarizing, or otherwise communicating to an audience the essential characteristics of a set of raw data. The previous chapter dealt with one aspect of descriptive statistics, that of graphical representation.

The present chapter approaches the problem of describing a mass of raw data from two different perspectives, both involving the calculation of a single number which represents a particular characteristic of the data in question. These characteristics are *central tendency* and *variability*. Very generally, central tendency refers to the "average" value of a frequency distribution—a value that in some sense reflects the size of the "typical" or "most expected" datum. These concepts will be defined more exactly later. Variability refers to the extent to which the members of a population deviate, vary, or are dispersed, from the average value. We have already discussed one measure of variability, the *range*.

In the remainder of this chapter, several statistical or numerical measures of central tendency and variability of a set of raw data are introduced, and appropriate conditions for their use are discussed.

CENTRAL TENDENCY

Measures or indicators of central tendency are numbers, calculated from raw research data, which indicate the center, average, or typical value of the data. Data collected in research efforts are often measured in discrete units, such as the number of time periods required by subjects of an experiment to complete a library task. These observations could also consist of values of quantifiable variables such as subjects' ages, number of years of formal education or of library experience. However, unless these values are related to some statistical standard—some average—they have little significance to one who attempts to analyze or to extract meaning from them. Computing and reporting an average measurement is thus a useful method for gaining an understanding of the significance or meaning of a particular observation as well as for simply describing a group of observations.

By definition, measures of central tendency reveal an average score. In addition to an indication of where the typical respondent or subject falls within a group, measures of central tendency allow:

1. A comparison between an individual's score and the average score
2. A comparison between the average score of two or more groups
3. A comparison between the average accomplishment of a single person on two or more separate occasions
4. A comparison between the average accomplishment of a single group on two or more separate occasions

Let us be more precise about the meaning of *average*. The term is in common use and will be used in this text in three distinct senses. The most commonly used measures of central tendency or average are the mean, the median, and the mode. The term *mean* refers to the concept that many readers studied in junior high school and know as the "average"—the sum of a group of quantified observations divided by the number of observations.* The *median* is the middle score—the score that divides a distribution of ordered or ranked scores into two equal groups. The *mode* is the score that appears most often in a frequency distribution.

MEAN

Table 9.1 consists of a distribution of scores on a cataloging test obtained by 20 library science students. The data are arranged from the lowest to the highest. Also indicated in Table 9.1 are frequencies (*f*) for each score. Let us compute the mean of the distribution. The mean of 20 scores can be computed by adding all scores, then dividing the obtained sum by the total number (*n*) of scores. We use the symbol X to refer to an individual score. To express the procedure for computing the mean of a set of scores as a formula, it is common practice to use the capital Greek letter sigma (Σ) for the phrase "find the sum of." Thus, the mean of a frequency distribution is given by the formula $\bar{x} = (\Sigma x)/n$, where the symbol $\bar{x}$ refers to the mean of a sample. In an English sentence the formula

---

* More exactly, this is the definition of the *arithmetic mean*. There are other kinds of means not discussed in this book. We will continue to refer to the arithmetic mean as simply the mean.

Table 9.1. *Scores of 20 Students on a Cataloging Test*

Unordered scores	Ordered scores	Number of scores
94, 85, 96, 88	96	1
	95	0
89, 90, 90, 93	94	1
	93	2
88, 87, 91, 89	92	1
	91	3
92, 89, 93, 87	90	2
	89	4
89, 91, 84, 91	88	2
	87	2
	86	0
	85	1
	84	1

reads: "To compute the mean of a sample, find the sum of the individual scores and divide by the number of scores."

The symbol $\bar{x}$ (read "ex-bar") is used to distinguish the mean of a sample from the mean of a population. By convention, the Greek letter mu (μ) is used to refer to the latter concept. The symbols $\bar{x}$ and μ reflect the difference between a sample *statistic*—a number descriptive of a sample—and the corresponding population *parameter*. In the next chapter, we shall see how sample statistics can be employed to make inferences regarding the true value of population parameters.

The question of whether a particular set of data represents a sample or a population depends on how the investigator has defined the population in which he or she is interested. For example, the members of our cataloging class could be regarded either as a sample (e.g., of the set of all library science students in the United States) or as a population.

Let us return to the data displayed in Table 9.1 and treat our class as a population. The mean of a population is computed in exactly the same way as the mean of a sample. Then

$$\mu = (\Sigma x)/n = 1796/20 = 89.8.$$

Thus, the mean score of our population is 89.8.

COMPUTATION OF THE MEAN FROM GROUPED DATA

Research workers will frequently want to compute the mean of a distribution not from the raw data themselves, but from a frequency distribu-

Table 9.2. *Time Required by 55 Library Assistants to
Complete Shelving Tasks*

Number of minutes	Frequency (f)
120–129	1
110–119	1
100–109	3
90–99	5
80–89	9
70–79	14
60–69	10
50–59	5
40–49	6
30–39	0
20–29	1

tion in which the data have been grouped into intervals. Consider Table 9.2, which summarizes the values of 55 data items grouped into class intervals. Assume that the data were gathered as part of a study designed to measure the relative efficiency of student assistants in a large university library. During the course of a 2-month research project, 55 student assistants were each given a selected group of books to be shelved. Unobtrusive observations were made by research assistants, and a record was kept of the number of minutes required by each student to complete the assigned task. Data were then grouped according to time periods required to complete the assigned task. Grouping of time periods was by 10-minute intervals, where each observation was rounded to the nearest minute for purposes of classification. Thus, a time of 119.6 minutes was classified into the interval 120–129, whereas a time of 119.4 minutes was classified into the interval 110–119. The *real limits* of the interval 120–129 are therefore 119.5–129.5; the real limits of the interval 110–119 are 109.5–119.5, etc. A value of exactly 119.5 could be classified into either of the two intervals, depending upon the convention decided upon in advance by the investigator.

The mean of a set of data grouped into a frequency distribution can be computed approximately by assuming that the data in each interval are equally distributed throughout the interval. Figure 9.1 illustrates this assumption with the interval 90–99 (real limits 89.5–99.5). Intuitively, a consequence of this assumption is that the mean of the values in a given interval is simply the midpoint of the interval. Thus, the sum of these values is merely the product of the frequency f associated with that interval and the midpoint of that interval (M). These principles are illustrated

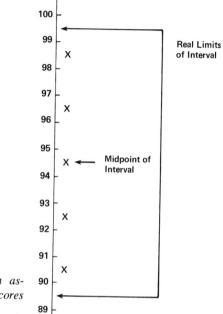

Figure 9.1. *The interval 90–99 with assumed equal distribution of the five scores displayed.*

by the assumed data displayed in Figure 9.1. The mean of the data is

$$\frac{98.5 + 96.5 + 94.5 + 92.5 + 90.5}{5} = \frac{472.5}{5} = 94.5,$$

which is just the midpoint of the interval. Thus, the sum of the five assumed values could have been computed in an alternate way, by multiplying the midpoint of the interval, 94.5, by the frequency of the interval, 5, as 94.5(5) = 472.5. These observations lead to a formula for computing the mean of a set of grouped data. Let M stand for the midpoint of an interval and let f stand for the frequency associated with that interval. Let n equal the total frequency. Then the mean of the distribution is given by the formula $\bar{x} = [\Sigma(fM)]/n$. In English, the formula says to multiply the frequency of each interval by the midpoint of the interval, to add the resulting products, and to divide by the total frequency. Note that $n = \Sigma f$. This procedure is illustrated in Table 9.3, which shows the computation of the mean of the grouped data in Table 9.2.

MEDIAN

A second kind of "average," or measure of the central tendency of a distribution, is the median. The median is simply the middle value when

Table 9.3. *Computation of the Mean with Grouped Data*

Number of minutes	Frequency (f)	Midpoint of interval (M)	fM
120–129	1	124.5	124.5
110–119	1	114.5	114.5
100–109	3	104.5	313.5
90–99	5	94.5	472.5
80–89	9	84.5	760.5
70–79	14	74.5	1043.0
60–69	10	64.5	645.0
50–59	5	54.5	272.5
40–49	6	44.5	267.0
30–39	0	34.5	0
20–29	1	24.5	24.5
	$n = \Sigma f = 55$		$\Sigma fM = 4037.5$

$$\bar{x} = (\Sigma fM)/n = 4037.5/55 = 73.4$$

the data have been arranged in ascending or descending order—the value that divides the distribution into two equal parts. Suppose, for example, that the nine librarians in a public library earn the following annual salaries: $8200, $8620, $8800, $9600, $9650, $10,450, $11,150, $12,600, and $13,450. Arranging these values in ascending or descending order, it is clear that the middle value of the distribution, in this case the fifth datum, is $9650. This is the median salary in the library.

In general, if an ordered distribution has n values where n is an odd number, the median is the $(n + 1)/2$th score. (In our example, the median is the $(9 + 1)/2 = $ fifth datum.) If n is an even number, there are two central values, corresponding to the $n/2$th and the $(n + 2)/2$th values in an ordered distribution. In this case, the median is generally taken to be the mean of these two central values.

Example 1

Find the median of the following distribution of $n = 12$ scores: 68, 80, 93, 88, 72, 80, 85, 85, 82, 78, 83, and 85.

Answer

Arranging the scores in numerical order, we obtain: 68, 72, 78, 80, 80, 82, 83, 85, 85, 85, 88, and 93. The middle values are the $12/2 = $ sixth and the $14/2 = $ seventh values, 82 and 83, respectively. The median of the distribution is therefore $(82 + 83)/2 = 82.5$.

The computation of the median from grouped data will be discussed in a later section of this chapter.

MODE

The mode of a distribution is simply the most common value in the distribution—the value associated with the highest frequency. The mode of a distribution of grouped data is just the midpoint of the most frequent interval. The mode of a distribution is the most typical value in the distribution; it is the value most likely to be associated with a randomly selected member of the population. The mode of the distribution in Example 1 is 85.

A distribution may or may not have a unique mode; a distribution with two modes is called *bimodal*. When a distribution is found to be bimodal, it frequently is the case that the population generating the distribution is more usefully regarded as two (or more) populations. For example, consider the population of persons found in the children's room of a public library during a given Saturday. These persons will be mainly children ranging in age from, say 2 or 3 years to perhaps 14 years, and in many cases, their parents. In a sense, then, there are actually two distinct populations involved in this situation. Regarding the group as a single population, an investigator might find that a variable such as age is distributed bimodally, reflecting what might more naturally be regarded as two populations. Reporting the mean or median of such a distribution as *the* measure of central tendency can be very misleading. Problem 12 provides an example of this situation.

COMPARISON OF MEAN, MEDIAN, AND MODE

Although the mean, the median, and the mode are all measures of central tendency, they are not always equally descriptive or useful in describing particular sets of data. In a physical sense, the mean is the center of gravity of the distribution. Imagine a weightless ruler on which weights, the amounts corresponding to frequencies, are placed at ruler positions corresponding to data values. (This is essentially a physical model of a histogram.) The mean is the point on the ruler at which the ruler will exactly balance. Figure 9.2 illustrates this concept with the data in Table 9.3. Note that the point of balance is indicated as being about 73.4, the approximate mean of the distribution. As the model depicted in Figure 9.2 suggests, the mean is very sensitive to extreme values. Even one datum can substantially affect the value of the mean if that value is in fact extreme as compared with the remaining data.

Conversely, the mode is not at all affected by extreme values. The most common frequency in a distribution remains the most frequent interval regardless of whether or not there happens to be one or more extreme values.

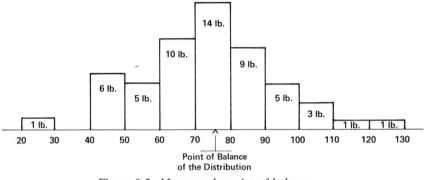

Figure 9.2. *Mean as the point of balance.*

The median of a distribution is affected by the addition of extreme values, but only insofar as the middle value of the distribution is pushed one direction or another by a slight amount. Ordinarily this effect would be minimal.

A distribution is *symmetric* if its left half is a mirror-image of its right half. Figures 9.3 and 9.4 display symmetric frequency distributions. Figure 9.3 is the important *normal distribution,* which will be treated in detail in Chapter 10. A special property of symmetric distributions is that in such distributions all three measures of central tendency—the mean, the median, and the mode—are equal. This statement is not true in a distribution that has more than one mode. The reader should be able to visualize a distribution that illustrates this situation.

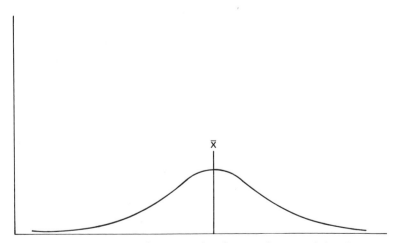

Figure 9.3. *A symmetric frequency distribution: the normal distribution.*

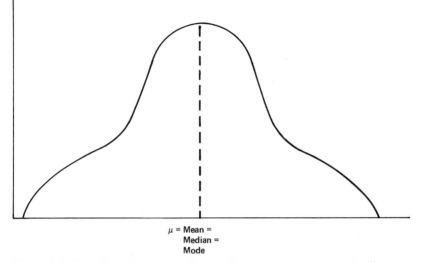

μ = Mean =
Median =
Mode

Figure 9.4. *Equality of mean, median, and mode in a symmetric distribution.*

Although the frequency distributions displayed in Figures 9.3 and 9.4 are symmetrical, frequency distributions of research data are often asymmetrical, or *skewed*. When a frequency curve has been constructed from a smoothed frequency polygon and the mode of the distribution is relatively near the upper end of the range, the distribution is said to be skewed to the left, or *negatively skewed*. On the other hand, if the mode is near the lower end of the range, the distribution is said to be skewed to the right, or *positively skewed*. The *tail* of the distribution shown in Figure 9.5 is pointed toward the left; therefore, the distribution is negatively skewed. In Figure 9.6, the mode is located at the lower end of the range, and the tail of the distribution points toward the right. Consequently, the distribution in Figure 9.6 is positively skewed. Note the relative position of the mean, median, and mode in the skewed distributions illustrated in Figures 9.5 and 9.6. These relationships are generally true in skewed distributions. That is, in a positively skewed distribution the mean will be greater than the median, which in turn will be greater than the mode. These considerations mean that a researcher's choice of a measure of central tendency will have a considerable effect on the reported "average" if the distribution is heavily skewed.

For example, consider the personal incomes of citizens of the United States. This distribution is heavily positively skewed, with the great majority of the population falling within the range $5000–$20,000. There are relatively few individuals, however, who earn hundreds of thousands or

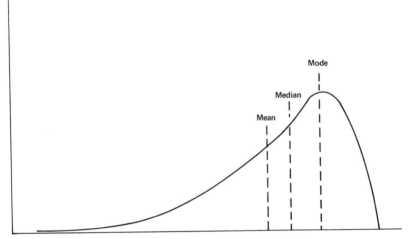

Figure 9.5. *A negatively skewed distribution.*

even millions of dollars annually. An incumbant politician wishing to make the "average" income of his or her constituency appear as high as possible might therefore deliberately report the mean income, rather than the median or the mode income.

Example 2

Consider the following costs associated with eight serial publications: $3200, $220, $140, $110, $40, $40, $35, $25. Which measure of central tendency most accurately reports the "average" cost of the eight publications?

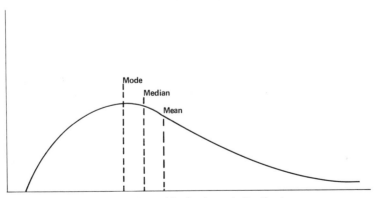

Figure 9.6. *A positively skewed distribution.*

Answer

The mean cost of a serial is $476.25, the mode is $40, and the median is $75. Thus, we have three average costs from which to choose. If the most frequently appearing value of $40 is reported as the average cost, all the higher costs are not taken into consideration. On the other hand, the mean of $476.25 is greater than seven of the eight costs and is in that sense misleading. With this positively skewed distribution it should be apparent that the median is in some ways the most appropriate measure of central tendency; thus the best average cost to report is perhaps $75. This example illustrates that when distributions contain very high or very low scores, the most appropriate measure of central tendency may be the median. In some cases, the mode of a distribution might be the most useful measure of central tendency; however, the mode is often relatively unstable. For this reason, the mode is normally used as a quick reference for determining an approximate value of the average.

COMPUTATION OF THE MEDIAN AND OTHER PERCENTILES WITH GROUPED DATA

The median of a distribution is the middle term when the data have been arranged in numerical order—that is, the datum which divides the distribution into two equal parts. If raw data have been grouped into intervals, however, the middle datum cannot be ascertained directly. For grouped data, the median is usually defined to be the $n/2$th data point.*

Table 9.4 illustrates this fact with a set of examination grades for a class of 30 students in an introductory information science course. In this example, the median is the $30/2 = 15$th datum. From the column labeled *cumulative frequency* in Table 9.4, it is apparent that the 15th datum falls somewhere in the interval 80–84.

Let us be more exact about this. Not only can we say that the fifteenth datum falls in the interval 80–84, but we can also see that it must be the sixth score of the nine in that interval. We can assume, based on these figures, that the median is 6/9 of the way through the interval, or a distance of $6/9(5) = 3 1/3$ units from the lower limit of the interval, 79.5. This is the common assumption upon which the process of *interpolation* is based. The median is thus computed to be 3.33 + 79.5, or 82.83. Rounded to the nearest score, we can say that the median grade on the examination was 83. Just as the computation of the mean and mode from grouped data is only approximate, so is the computation of the median from grouped data an approximation.

* This definition of the median for grouped data is the most commonly provided definition and for that reason has been adopted in this text.

Table 9.4. *Distribution of Examination Scores*

Exam scores	Frequency	Cumulative frequency
95–99	3	30
90–94	4	27
85–89	5	23
80–84	9	18[a]
75–79	4	9
70–74	2	5
65–69	1	3
60–64	0	2
55–59	0	2
50–54	1	2
45–49	0	1
40–44	1	1

[a] Median falls in this interval.

Once it has been determined that the median is in the ith interval, a formula that can be used to compute the median Md from grouped data is

$$Md = (c/f_i)\,(W) + L,$$

where

c = the number of cases needed,
f_i = the number of cases in the ith interval
W = the width of the ith interval
L = the lower limit of the ith interval.

Example 3

Find the median of the frequency distribution shown in the chart.

Interval	Frequency	Cumulative frequency
180–189	1	67
170–179	2	66
160–169	6	64
150–159	10	58
140–149	18	48
130–139	14	30
120–129	8	16
110–119	5	8
100–109	2	3
90–99	1	1

Answer

There are 67 scores in all. For grouped data, the median is defined to be the $n/2$th score, or the 33.5th score. This datum falls within the interval 140–149; it is the 3.5th score of the 18 scores within that interval. Thus

$$Md = 3.5/18 \,(10) + 139.5 = 1.94 + 139.5 = 141.44.$$

The median is the fiftieth percentile—the point above and below which 50% of the cases fall. The same interpolation procedure that we used to compute the median can be used to compute other percentiles as well. For example, the eightieth percentile is defined to be the point below which 80% of the cases in a distribution fall. In Example 3 above, the eightieth percentile is associated with the $(.80)(67) = 53.6$th datum. Similarly, the ninety-fifth percentile is associated with the $(.95)(67) = 63.7$th score.

Example 4

Compute the eightieth and ninety-fifth percentiles of the distribution displayed in Example 3.

Answer

The eightieth percentile is at the 53.6th datum, and therefore is in the interval 150–159. Then the 80th percentile $= (5.6/10)(10) + 149.5 = 155.1$. Similarly, the 95th percentile $= (5.7/6)(10) + 159.5 = 169.0$.

The terms *quartile* and *decile* are sometimes used to refer to particular percentiles. Specifically, the twenty-fifth, fiftieth, and seventy-fifth percentiles are also known as the first, second, and third quartiles, respectively, or more simply, Q_1, Q_2, and Q_3. The three quartiles of a distribution divide the distribution into four equal parts. Similarly, the nine deciles of a distribution divide the distribution into 10 equal parts. Note that the second quartile, the fifth decile, and the fiftieth percentile are all synonyms for the median of a distribution.

Example 5

Compute the quartiles of the distribution in Example 3.

Answer

Q_1 is the $(.25)(67) = 16.75$th data point and falls in the interval 130–139. Then

$$Q_1 = (.75/14)(10) + 129.5 = 130.$$

Q_2 was computed in Example 10.3 and found to equal 141.4. Q_3 is the 75th percentile and is associated with the $(.75)(67) = 50.25$th datum, falling in the interval 150–159.

$$Q_3 = (2.25/10) \ (10) + 149.5 = 151.75.$$

VARIABILITY

As Problem 5 suggests, a measure of central tendency does not suffice to characterize a frequency distribution completely. In that example, two frequency distributions with identical means were displayed. The distributions differed with respect to the extent of the data values' deviation from the mean; in one distribution the deviation was rather considerable, whereas in the other it was relatively slight. Thus, the mean, median, and mode, as measures of central tendency, do not in themselves always provide an adequate description of distributions of collected research data. Two frequency distributions containing numerical observations might have the same mean or median but be shaped quite differently. To describe a set of observations, researchers frequently need to know more than the typical or average observation; at times they must also determine how observations are spread out *around* a measure of central tendency.

For example, consider the following observations for the hypothetical per capita operating expenditures, in dollars, of several public library systems within two counties. The two populations are:

Raintree County	3.70	4.80	4.30	2.50	3.80	5.80	5.20	(μ = $4.30)
Freemont County		6.40	4.60	.50	1.90	8.10		(μ = $4.30)

The means of both populations is $4.30; however, it is evident that in Raintree County there is more uniform financial support for the operation of public libraries than there is in Freemont County. We can state that the *variability,* or the tendency of observations to be dispersed, is less in Raintree County because operating expenditures for the library systems in this county are not as dispersed around the average expenditure as is the case for the library systems in Freemont County. This is illustrated in Figure 9.7. In evaluating the systems in the two counties, we could safely conclude that the collections, services, and library staffs are probably quite different, reflecting the considerable difference in variability of expenditures which is evidenced by the data.

Another example will demonstrate why an indicator of dispersion is needed for a set of observations. Two assistants in a library acquisitions department were given a series of exercises to determine their abilities to search library holdings and "on-order" files prior to ordering new mate-

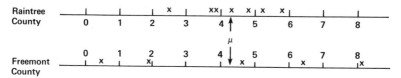

Figure 9.7. *Difference in variability between two distributions.*

rials from jobbers. In this particular study, the technical services department of the library attempted to discover how to eliminate unnecessary duplication of materials and to ascertain why searchers sometimes failed to recognize orders for works which were already in the collection and for which a duplicate copy was not needed. The 40 scores (20 scores each) of the two library assistants on the exercise were as follows:

Library Assistant A	90	60	70	80	50	80	70	80	50	90
	40	70	80	60	70	30	100	70	50	80
Library Assistant B	60	80	60	70	60	70	70	70	70	70
	70	50	70	80	80	80	60	60	80	60

From these data, we construct the frequency distribution shown in Table 9.5. Evident from an examination of the frequency distribution is the fact that, although the mean score for both library assistants is 68.5, the performance of Library Assistant A is quite different than that of Library Assistant B. B is much more consistent than A, who at times shows flashes of high efficiency and at other times performs very poorly. Some

Table 9.5. *Scores of Two Library Assistants on Searching Exercises*

Scores	Library assistant A frequency	Library assistant B frequency
100	1	0
90	2	0
80	5	5
70	5	8
60	2	6
50	3	1
40	1	0
30	1	0
20	0	0
10	0	0
	$\bar{x} = 68.5$	$\bar{x} = 68.5$

administrators will prefer an erratic worker such as A, but perhaps most will prefer a steady worker such as B. This much is certain: Library assistants A and B do not perform in the same way although their mean scores are equal. Clearly, the mean alone does not adequately describe the searching abilities and accuracy of these two persons. We also need a method for determining the extent to which the scores are spread out around that measure of central tendency.

The three most widely used measures of variability are the range, the mean deviation, and the standard deviation. We have already identified the *range* as the difference between the highest observation and the lowest observation. Compared with other measures of variability, the range is not very reliable, particularly if we are dealing with many observations from a large sample or population. The range takes only the two most extreme scores into account, and reveals nothing of the character of the distribution between these points.

As an example of the inadequacy of the range as a measure of variability, let us examine Table 9.6, which consists of a record of library visits by 42 registered borrowers at the Aspex Public Library. In the distribution displayed in Table 9.6, the bulk of the frequencies representing number of library visits are between the two class intervals 1–3 and 16–18. A wide gap containing no frequencies exists between class intervals 19–21 and 25–27, which bound the interval containing the highest numbers of visits and the next highest ones. In these data the greatest number of visits was 30 and the fewest was 1. Because one person visited the library 30 times

Table 9.6. *Use of Library during a 3-Month Period by 42 Registered Borrowers*

Number of library visits	Frequency
28–30	1
25–27	0
22–24	0
19–21	0
16–18	5
13–15	7
10–12	8
7–9	10
4–6	7
1–3	4

during the 3-month period, the range is $30 - 1 = 29$, whereas the other registered borrowers fall within a range of $18 - 1 = 17$ visits. This example illustrates that the range is limited insofar as it is a valid indicator of dispersion or variability. Its use is justified, however, when a hasty measure of variability is required.

MEAN DEVIATION

Clearly, a measure of variability is desired that considers the deviation of every value from the mean, and not simply the extreme values. One such measure is the *mean deviation*. The mean deviation is simply the mean *distance* of the data points to the mean of the distribution—the mean difference between the distribution mean and each datum, where each difference is expressed as a positive number. Symbolically, mean deviation (MD) can be expressed as $MD = [\Sigma|X - \mu|]/n$, where $|X - \mu|$ is read "the absolute value of $(X - \mu)$." To compute the value of $|X - \mu|$, express the difference between X and μ as a positive number. Thus,

$$|3 - 1| = 2 \quad \text{and} \quad |3 - 9| = 6.$$

Mean deviation expresses what the deviation from the mean of a distribution is likely to be (in either direction) for a randomly selected datum.

Consider again the hypothetical data provided earlier in the chapter for per capita operating expenditures, in dollars, for public libraries within two counties. These data are reproduced in Table 9.7, together with the deviations $(X - \bar{x})$ and the computation of the mean deviation for the two

Table 9.7 *Computation of Mean Deviation for Two Sets of Data*

Raintree County ($\bar{x} = \$4.30$)		Freemont County ($\bar{x} = \$4.30$)	
X	$X - \bar{x}$	X	$X - \bar{x}$
$3.70	.60	6.40	2.10
4.80	.50	4.60	.30
4.30	.00	.50	3.80
2.50	1.80	1.90	2.40
3.80	.50	8.10	3.80
5.80	1.50		12.40
5.20	.90		
	5.80		
$MD = 5.80/7 = \$.83$		$MD = 12.40/5 = \$2.48$	

sets of data. Note that the expected deviation from the mean of $4.30 in public libraries in Freemont County is almost three times the expected deviation from the same mean in Raintree County. These figures capture very concisely the difference in variability in the two populations.

VARIANCE AND STANDARD DEVIATION

Because of the difficulty in working with *absolute values* in advanced statistical topics, the mean deviation is not in common use as a measure of variability. We discussed the concept here chiefly as a means of introducing the related but much more commonly used *standard deviation*. The standard deviation will be referred to and used frequently throughout the remainder of the statistical chapters of the text. Before defining the standard deviation, we introduced the closely related measure of variability, the variance.

The *variance* σ^2 (the small Greek letter sigma, squared) of a distribution associated with a population is just the mean of the *squared deviations* from the mean. Symbolically, $\sigma^2 = [(X_1 - \mu)^2 + (X_2 - \mu)^2 + \cdots + (X_N - \mu)^2]/N$, where $X_1, X_2, \ldots, X_N$ are the values of the distribution and μ is their mean. This formula can be expressed more compactly as $\sigma^2 = [\Sigma(X - \mu)^2]/N$. Note the relationship between the formulas for variance and mean deviation; in the computation of the variance, the deviations are squared before they are summed.

In Table 9.8 the computation of the variance of a set of 10 raw data

Table 9.8. *Computation of the Variance*
for a Population

X	$X - \mu$	$(X - \mu)^2$
0	-4	16
0	-4	16
2	-2	4
3	-1	1
4	0	0
4	0	0
4	0	0
6	2	4
8	4	16
9	5	25
40		82

$\mu = (\Sigma X)/n = 40/10 = 4.0$

Variance $= \sigma^2 = [\Sigma(X - \mu)^2]/n = 82/10 = 8.2$

points representing a population is illustrated. The ten numbers are 0, 0, 2, 3, 4, 4, 4, 6, 8 and 9. The mean μ of the distribution is 4.0. From Table 9.8, one can see that the variance σ^2 of this distribution—the mean squared deviation—is 8.2.

The *standard deviation* of a population is closely related to the variance of the population; it simply is the square root of the variance. Thus the standard deviation of the distribution displayed in Table 9.8 is given by

$$\sigma = \sqrt{8.2} = 2.86.*$$

The variance and standard deviation of a distribution are important concepts, not only as general indicators of the dispersion, or variability, of a distribution, but also in understanding advanced statistical methods and techniques. Standard deviation is essential in any discussion of the normal distribution, for example, and is therefore an essential concept in sampling theory and in understanding results of standardized tests such as the Graduate Record Examination (see Chapter 10). Standard deviation is also an essential concept in correlation and regression (see Chapter 11) and in some kinds of hypothesis testing (see Chapter 12). We defer until these chapters any further discussion of the meaning and uses of standard deviation. The remainder of this chapter is devoted to details related to the computation of the standard deviation in certain of its applications.

STANDARD DEVIATION AND VARIANCE— SHORT FORMS

Two alternative formulas for the variance and standard deviation involve fewer computations than the definitions provided above. These are

$$\sigma^2 = \frac{\Sigma X^2 - n\mu^2}{n}$$

and

$$\sigma = \left[\frac{\Sigma X^2 - n\mu^2}{n} \right]^{1/2}$$

In Table 9.9 the computation of σ^2 and σ is illustrated, using the data contained in Table 9.8 and the short forms of the formulas for variance and standard deviation.

Just as the mean was calculated from grouped data, so can the variance and standard deviation be determined. Table 9.10 illustrates the computa-

---

* This value can be computed using a table of square roots, or much more efficiently and easily using a calculator with the square root function. See Chapter 13 for a discussion of the use of computers and calculators in statistical computations.

Table 9.9. *Short Form for Computation of Variance and Standard Deviation*

X	X^2
0	0
0	0
2	4
3	9
4	16
4	16
4	16
6	36
8	64
9	81
$\Sigma X = 40$	$\Sigma X^2 = 242$

$$\mu = (\Sigma X)/10 = 40/10 = 4.0$$

$$\sigma^2 = \frac{\Sigma X^2 - n\mu^2}{n}$$

$$= \frac{242 - (10) \cdot (4)^2}{10}$$

$$= \frac{242 - 160}{10}$$

$$= 8.2, \quad \text{and} \quad \sigma = \sqrt{8.2} = 2.86.$$

tion of the standard deviation for a set of grouped data, using a modification of the computational formula applied in Table 9.9. Note that even with the simplified version of the formula the calculations are somewhat lengthy. Therefore, use of a calculator is highly recommended. If a calculator with a memory is used, one can work through the necessary computations in Table 9.10 in just a few minutes.

SAMPLE STATISTIC VERSUS POPULATION PARAMETER

Earlier in this chapter a distinction was drawn between the mean of a sample, which we denoted by $\bar{x}$, and the mean of a population, represented by the Greek letter μ. The distinction reflects the difference between *knowing* a population parameter μ and *estimating* μ by computing a statistic $\bar{x}$ on the basis of a sample drawn from the population.

With respect to the mean, the computational formulas for μ and $\bar{x}$ are the same; in each case the mean is obtained by dividing the sum of the

Table 9.10. *Computation of Standard Deviation with Grouped Data*

Age interval	Midpoint of interval (M)	f	M^2	fM^2	fM
0–4	2	22	4	88	44
5–9	7	38	49	1862	266
10–14	12	8	144	1152	96
15–19	17	0	289	0	0
20–24	22	3	484	1452	66
25–29	27	8	729	5832	216
30–34	32	3	1024	3072	96
35–39	37	2	1369	2738	74
40–44	42	0	1764	0	0
45–49	47	1	2209	2209	47
50–54	52	2	2704	5408	104
55–59	57	0	3249	0	0
60–64	62	0	3844	0	0
65–69	67	1	4489	4489	67
		$n = 88$		$\Sigma fM^2 = 28302$	$\Sigma fM = 1076$

$$\mu = \frac{\Sigma fM}{n} = \frac{1076}{88} = 12.2 \text{ years}$$

$$\sigma^2 = \frac{\Sigma fM^2 - n\mu^2}{n} = \frac{28{,}302 - (88)(12.2)^2}{88}$$

$$= \frac{15204.1}{88} = 172.77$$

Then $\sigma = \sqrt{172.77} = 13.14$ years

observations by the total number of observations. In the case of variance and standard deviation, however, another situation prevails. Not only are different symbols employed for the standard deviation (and variance) of a population and a sample—σ and s, respectively—but the computational formulas are also different. When applied to a random sample, the formula for the standard deviation of a population *does not* accurately estimate the value of the standard deviation. It can be proved that when the standard deviation is estimated from a random sample drawn from a population, the formula

$$s = \left[\frac{\Sigma(X - \bar{x})^2}{n - 1} \right]^{1/2}$$

should be used. This formula is identical to the original definition of standard deviation, except for the denominator, which is $(n - 1)$ instead of n.

If the sample size is large, this correction has little effect. The number $n - 1$ is said to be the *number of degrees of freedom in s.*

The short version of this formula is

$$s = \left[\frac{\Sigma X^2 - n\bar{x}^2}{n - 1} \right]^{\frac{1}{2}}.$$

With grouped data, the short form for the standard deviation of a sample is given by

$$s = \left[\frac{\Sigma fM^2 - n \left(\frac{\Sigma fM}{n} \right)^2}{n - 1} \right]^{\frac{1}{2}}$$

APPENDIX: PROBLEMS FOR SOLUTION

1. The distribution provided in the chart contains the numbers of questions answered during a 45-day period by a public library's telephone reference service. Provide answers for the following questions: (a) On how many days did the reference service answer 29 or fewer questions? (b) On how many days were 30 or more questions answered? (c) What is the mean of the distribution? (d) What is the median of the distribution? (e) What is the mode of the distribution? (f) What is the percentage of days on which fewer than 39 but more than 26 questions were answered?

Number of questions (X)	Number of days (f)
45–47	1
42–44	2
39–41	4
36–38	5
33–35	5
30–32	6
27–29	8
24–26	5
21–23	3
18–20	2
15–17	2
12–14	1
9–11	1

Answers

(a) 22; (b) 23; (c) 29.8; (d) 30.0; (e) 28; and (f) 53.3%.

2. Book circulation figures for a 16-day period for one bookmobile station, or stop, are provided below. Determine the mean, median, and mode of the distribution.

23,	23,	40,	15,	20,	27,	19,	20
32,	28,	26,	29,	36,	17,	31,	20

Answers

Mean = 25.4; median = 24.5; mode = 20.0.

3. Which of the measures of central tendency determined in Problem 2 best reflects the typical daily book circulation record? Explain your answer.

4. The data below were recorded in a cataloging production study conducted in a technical services department of a college library. The data consist of the number of filmstrips classified during an experiment. Group and arrange the data into a frequency distribution, making the first interval 10–12; then compute the mean, median, and mode of the distribution.

16,	21,	27,	29,	10,	47,	32,	37
23,	26,	13,	22,	38,	33,	17,	41
29,	25,	34,	29,	24,	25,	19,	42
43,	14,	28,	31,	45,	24,	33,	30
27,	35,	30,	16,	34,	29,	20,	25

5. Survey research was conducted in a certain state among school librarians and media specialists to determine opinions about the direction and guidance provided by a state school library extension agency. In Figure 9.8, two frequency distributions of attitude scores are shown—one

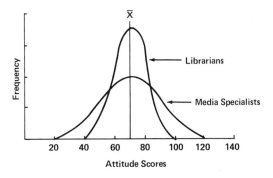

Figure 9.8. *Attitude scores for two populations of librarians.*

for librarians and the other for media specialists. Study the distributions, and answer these questions: (*a*) What is the value of the mean for the two distributions? (*b*) Which group is more dispersed around its mean? (*c*) Which group has the greatest number of extremely high scores? (*d*) Which group's scores are more homogeneous?

Answers

(*a*) 70; (*b*) media specialists; (*c*) media specialists; and (*d*) librarians

6. The following per capita operating expenditures in dollars were reported by 30 libraries, all of which are part of the Oakdale–Pinewood Regional Library System. Construct a frequency distribution for these data and determine the mean, median, and mode of the per capita operating expenses.

1.41	2.51	2.53	3.46	4.00	2.65
1.60	2.05	2.40	2.35	3.36	3.20
3.00	3.10	3.53	1.73	4.31	2.65
2.85	1.85	2.80	2.60	1.89	4.57
3.62	2.95	2.65	3.75	3.88	3.18

7. Invent a distribution of 10 numbers between 1 and 10, and compute the mean, median, and mode of the distribution. Now add an eleventh value, the number 65. How did the addition of this extreme value affect (*a*) the mean; (*b*) the median; and (*c*) the mode?

8. The data in the following frequency table summarize the holdings of some of the principal college libraries in the United States in 1876.* To the nearest hundred, find: (*a*) the mode; (*b*) the median; and (*c*) the mean of the data. (*d*) Is the distribution reasonably symmetric or is it positively or negatively skewed? (*e*) Can you see how the general shape of the distribution might have been predicted without the benefit of examining any data at all?

* Source: Table 1, Statistics of Some of the Principal College Libraries, 1876. In "Academic Libraries in 1876," by Edward G. Holley. *College and Research Libraries*, 37 (January 1976): 15–47.

Number of volumes	Number of college libraries
210000–215000	1 (Harvard College)
.	.
.	.
.	.
95000–99999	1 (Yale College)
.	.
.	.
.	.
45000–49999	1
40000–44999	1
35000–39999	1
30000–34999	3
25000–29999	6
20000–24999	7
15000–19999	9
10000–14999	25
5000–9999	15
0–4999	1

Answers

(a) 12,500; (b) 14,000; (c) 20,300; (d) positively skewed.

9. Why are the mean, median, and mode, when computed from grouped data, only approximately the values which would have been obtained if these measures had been computed from raw data? Invent an example to illustrate your answer.

10. Invent a symmetric frequency distribution and verify that the mean, the median, and the mode are equal in this distribution. What is the relationship between Q_1 and Q_3 in the distribution?

11. Do you think the following library phenomena would be characterized by positively skewed, negatively skewed, or symmetric frequency distributions? Why? (a) Incomes of the population of librarians in a college library; (b) number of volumes held by members of the population of U.S. academic libraries; and (c) annual budgets of U.S. academic libraries.

Answers

All are positively skewed distributions. See "The Analysis of Library Statistics," by Allan D. Pratt (*Library Quarterly, 45*(1975):275–286.) for a discussion of the latter two distributions.

12. The chart below provides the ages of the occupants of the children's room of a selected public library on a particular Saturday.

Age	Frequency
65–69	1
60–64	0
55–59	0
50–54	2
45–49	1
40–44	0
35–39	2
30–34	3
25–29	8
20–24	3
15–19	0
10–14	8
5–9	38
0–4	22

(*a*) Construct a histogram and frequency polygon for the distribution; (*b*) compute the mean, median, and mode of the distribution and discuss the results; (*c*) compute Q_1, Q_3, and the 90th percentile of the distribution.

Answers

(*b*) μ = 12.2 years; modes = 7 years and 27 years; median = 7.4 years; (*c*) Q_1 = 4.5; Q_3 = 13.3; 90th percentile = 29.8.

13. Read and discuss the following article: Piternick, George. "ARL Statistics—Handle With Care," *College and Research Libraries, 38* (September 1977):419–423.

14. Compute the standard deviation of the following distributions of per capita operating expenditures for two populations of public libraries within two counties, first using the definition of standard deviation, then using the short form.

Raintree County	3.70	4.80	4.30	2.50	3.80	5.80	5.20
Freemont County	6.40	4.60	.50	1.90	8.10		

Answers

Raintree County: $\sigma^2 = 1.02$, $\sigma = 1.01$; Freemont County: $\sigma^2 = 7.83$, $\sigma = 2.80$

15. Assume that the data provided in Problem 14 describe two *random samples* of libraries drawn from two populations and compute s^2 and s for the two samples.

Answers

$s_R^2 = 1.19$; $s_R = 1.09$; $s_F^2 = 9.79$; $s_F^2 = 3.13$.

16. Through algebraic manipulation of the formula expressing the definition of variance, try to derive the short form of the formula. That is, show that $[\Sigma(X - \mu)^2]/N = [\Sigma X^2 - N\mu^2]/N$.

17. Which of the following distributions would be characterized by the greatest mean? Standard deviation? Why? (*a*) Number of library books read during a 1-week period in a random sample of 20 high school students; (*b*) number of library books read during a 1-week period by a sample of 20 students selected randomly during personal visits to the high school library.

18. Gather data and test your hypotheses of Problem 4.

19. The grouped data represent the lengths (number of pages) of books in a random sample of 40 books drawn from the personal collection of one of the authors. (*a*) Compute the mean, median, and mode of the distribution. (*b*) What is the shape of the distribution? (*c*) Sketch a graph of the distribution. (*d*) Compute the standard deviation of the distribution. (*e*) Is there evidence in the data that two populations are involved rather than one? If so, how might the two populations be defined?

Number of pages	f
1041–1080	1
.	
.	
761–820	0
721–760	1
.	
. .	
541–580	0

(continues)

(continued)

Number of pages	f
501–540	3
461–500	1
421–460	1
381–420	3
341–380	1
301–340	0
261–300	5
221–260	3
181–220	5
141–180	7
101–140	6
61–100	2
21–60	1

Answers

(a) $\bar{x} = 275.5$, mode $= 160.5$, $Md = 212.5$; (b) heavily positively skewed; (d) $s = 198.4$ pages; (e) yes, there is a population of paperbound books and a second population of (much longer, on the average) hardbound books.

20. The following distribution represents the ages of a population of students in a graduate library school.

Ages	f	cf
60–64	1	50
55–59	2	49
50–54	6	47
45–49	2	41
40–44	7	39
35–39	5	32
30–34	6	27
25–29	9	21
20–24	12	12

(a) Compute the mean, median, and mode of the distribution; (b) compute Q_1, Q_3, the 30th percentile, and the 95th percentile of the distribution; (c) compute the range, the variance, and the standard deviation of the distribution.

Answers

(a) $\mu = 35.2$, $Md = 32.8$, mode $= 22$. (b) $Q_1 = 24.8$, $Q_3 = 43.4$, 30th percentile $= 26.2$, 95th percentile $= 55.8$. (c) range $= 44$, $\sigma^2 = 134.76$, $\sigma = 11.6$ years.

21. What is the largest possible value for σ? The smallest possible value? Characterize, as completely as you can, a distribution that has a standard deviation with the smallest possible value of σ.

The the distribution of the frequency

The distribution of the frequency with which values occur on the basis of chance alone. It is depicted by a smoothed curve called a normal curve. It approximates the distribution of many random variables.

The Normal Distribution

INTRODUCTION

The family of curves known as *normal distributions* is probably the most useful theoretical frequency distribution discussed in this text. Normal distributions are important, first because they describe many empirical frequency distributions in a wide variety of situations ranging from the heights of men to the weights of white rats, variations in manufactured products, and IQ.

Perhaps more importantly, normal distributions are basic to sampling theory and, as such, are applicable to all empirical populations from which random samples of sufficient size are to be drawn. Polls, community surveys, and other sampling situations arise frequently in librarianship, and for this reason understanding the normal curve is important.

The general shape of a normal curve is shown in Figure 10.1. Normal curves are symmetric, bell-shaped, and continuous curves. As one moves away from the mean of a normal distribution in either direction, the curve approaches the x-axis more and more closely, but never touches it. A normal distribution is completely characterized by two parameters, its mean and its standard deviation. Figure 10.2 displays two normal distributions with the same mean, but different standard deviations, whereas Figure 10.3 displays two normal distributions with different means but equal standard deviations.

AREAS UNDER THE NORMAL CURVE

The percentage of a normally distributed population falling between any two values is equal to the relative proportion of the area under the curve and between those points. Figure 10.4 summarizes the percentages of a normally distributed population falling between the mean and one standard deviation from the mean, between one standard deviation and two

249

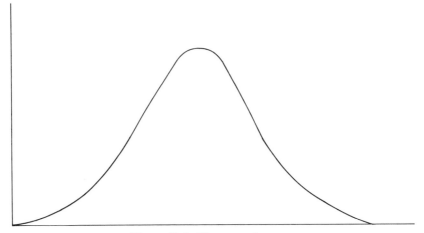

Figure 10.1. *The normal curve.*

standard deviations from the mean, between two and three standard deviations from the mean, and beyond three standard deviations from the
mean. Note that the total area under the curve is equal to 100%. *These
percentages are descriptive of every normal distribution regardless of the*

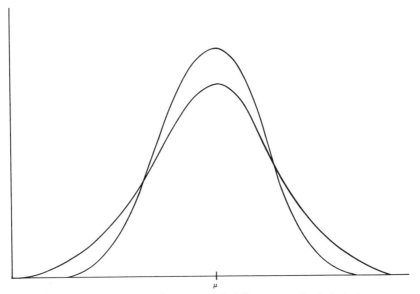

Figure 10.2. *Two normal curves with different standard deviations.*

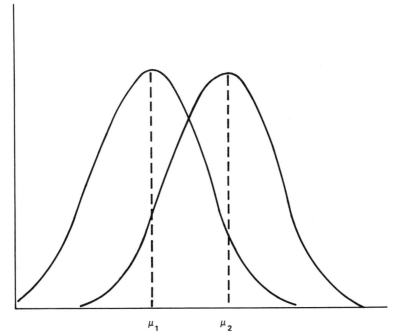

Figure 10.3. *Two normal curves with different means.*

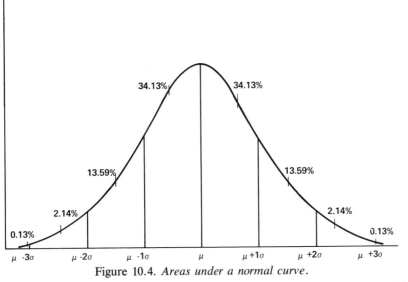

Figure 10.4. *Areas under a normal curve.*

value of its mean and standard deviation. Thus, for example, about 34% of a normally distributed population lies between the mean of the population and one standard deviation above the mean, whereas about 14% of the population lies between one standard deviation below the mean and two standard deviations below the mean. These percentages can be used to compute certain percentiles in a normal distribution.

Example 1

Compute the percentile associated with one standard deviation above the mean in a normal distribution.

Answer

Fifty percent of the population lies below the mean and another 34.13% lies between the mean and one standard deviation above the mean. Therefore, one standard deviation above the mean is associated with the 84.13th percentile.

Example 2

A student achieves a score on a cataloging test which is two standard deviations below the mean of the population of all those who took the test. If the test scores are distributed normally, what percentile is associated with the student's score?

Answer

The percentage of the population scoring less than three standard deviations below the mean is .13% and the percentage of the population between two and three standard deviations below the mean is 2.14%. Thus, the percentile associated with the score in question is .13% + 2.14% = 2.27%.

Example 3

What proportion of a normally distributed population falls within +1 and −2 standard deviations from the mean?

Answer

Adding the areas in question, we obtain 13.59% + 34.13% + 34.13% = 81.85%.

Example 4

Express the fourteenth percentile of a normal distribution in terms of standard deviations from the mean of the distribution.

Answer

This problem can be answered only approximately from Figure 10.4. By successively adding areas under the normal curve, it can be seen that 15.86% of the population is below -1σ. Thus, the fourteenth percentile is just to the left of this point, or about -1.1σ. A more exact method for solving this problem will be discussed later in this section.

Example 5

The distribution of IQ scores in a population is distributed normally with a mean of 100 and a standard deviation of 15. Convert IQ scores of 70 and 145 to percentiles.

Answer

A score of 70 is exactly two standard deviations below the mean. Thus, (as in Example 2) this score is at the 2.27th percentile. A score of 145 is three standard deviations above the mean. Only .13% of the population is above this point. Thus, an IQ of 145 is at the 99.87th percentile.

Figure 10.4 can be used to solve problems involving an exact number of standard deviations from the mean but can provide only approximate results for other problems. Fortunately, the normal distribution has been extensively tabulated. Appendix C reports areas between the mean and a given score under the normal curve which has a mean equal to 0 and a standard deviation equal to 1. (See Figure 10.5.) For this distribution, some-

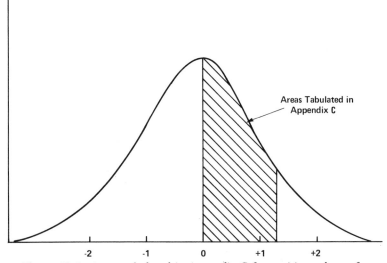

Figure 10.5. *Areas tabulated in Appendix C for positive values of* z.

times referred to as the *standard normal distribution,* individual scores are exactly equal to standard deviations from the mean; therefore, areas corresponding to scores can be obtained directly. For normal distributions with a mean μ and a standard deviation σ other than 0 and 1 respectively, a score X must be converted to a Z-*score* before consulting the table. This is done as follows: $z = (X - \mu)/\sigma$. Note that z is just the *number* of standard deviations σ of the score X from the mean μ in the distribution in question. The table provides values of z up to $z = 3.69$. Values of z beyond this point are not provided because the areas associated with such values are equal to .5000, to the nearest ten-thousandth.

Example 6

What percentile is associated with a score that is 1.4 standard deviations above the mean in a normal distribution?

Answer

The mean of the standard normal distribution tabulated in Appendix C is zero. Then the area between the mean and 1.40 standard deviations above the mean is .4192 (see Appendix C). This score corresponds to the .50 + .4192 = 91.92th percentile.

Example 7

What percentile is associated with an IQ of 120?

Answer

$$z = (X - \mu)/\sigma = (120 - 100)/15 = 20/15 = 1.33.$$

From Appendix C, the area in question is .50 + .4082, corresponding to the 90.82th percentile.

Example 8

Mensa, an organization for individuals with exceptional IQ's, advertises that it will accept memberships from persons falling within the top 2% of the population in intelligence, as determined by standardized tests. To what IQ score does the ninety-eighth percentile correspond?

Answer

Because Appendix C lists only areas from the mean to positive values of z, we look up .4800 in the area portion of the table. An area of .4800 corresponds to about 2.05 standard deviations above the mean. Because

$$Z = (X - \mu)/\sigma,$$

we have

$$2.05 = (X - 100)/15,$$

and

$$X = 15(2.05) + 100$$
$$= 30.75 + 100 = 130.75.$$

Example 9

Suppose that the heights of population of women are normally distributed with a mean of 64.3 inches and a standard deviation of 2.4 inches. What proportion of women in this population are less than 5 feet tall?

Answer

We first convert 5 feet = 60 inches to a z-score.

$$z = (X - \mu)/\sigma = (60 - 64.3)/2.4 = -4.3/2.4 = -1.79$$

From Appendix C, 46.33% of the population falls between 1.79 standard deviations below the mean and the mean. Thus, 50.00% − 46.33% = 3.67% of the population fall below a height of 5 feet.

Example 10

Find the proportion of a normally distributed population which lies between +2 and −2 standard deviations from the mean.

Answer

Adding the relevant areas, the proportion in question is (from Figure 10.4):   13.59% + 34.13% + 34.13% + 13.59% = 95.44%   or, to the nearest percent, 95%. Thus, approximately 95% of the population lies between ±2 standard deviations from the mean. This is a useful result and will be referred to later as we work with normal distributions. Appendix C shows that 95% of a population is more exactly contained within ±1.96 standard deviations from the mean.

Data commonly gathered by library researchers are often *not* distributed normally. As we have already seen, frequency distributions for variables such as "number of volumes held in academic libraries" and "number of pages in books" are not normal distributions and in fact are rather heavily skewed. On the other hand, other library data such as test scores, attitude scores, and so on, *are* distributed normally. As compared with other disciplines, research in librarianship is in its infancy; thus, our statement that many kinds of library data tend not to be distributed normally may not be a useful generalization for the future. But at least for the present it describes what we know to be true with respect to library statistics.

THE DISTRIBUTION OF SAMPLE MEANS

The normal distribution is extremely important in sampling theory because it describes a wide variety of situations in which random samples are drawn from populations *regardless of the identity* of the frequency distribution describing the parent population. Thus, even though a population may be heavily skewed, the distribution of means of random samples drawn from the population will tend to be normal as the sample size increases.

This situation is depicted in Figure 10.6, in which a portion of a negatively skewed distribution is shown. Imagine that ten random samples of size n are drawn from the population and their means $\bar{x}_i$ are computed and recorded. Figure 10.6 illustrates the location of the population mean μ as well as the means $\bar{x}_i$ of 10 hypothetical random samples of size n drawn from the population. Note that even though the population is skewed, the sample means are rather symmetrically distributed about the population mean μ. Furthermore, most of the sample means are relatively near the population mean. Finally, the mean $\bar{\bar{x}}$ of the sample means,

$$\bar{\bar{x}}_i = \frac{\Sigma \bar{x}_i}{10},$$

is very near the mean of the population.

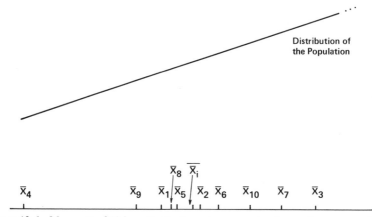

Figure 10.6. *Means $\bar{x}_i$ of 10 hypothetical random samples drawn from a population.*

The observed relationships are characteristic of a wide variety of sampling situations. We turn now to a more precise statement of these ideas.

THE CENTRAL LIMIT THEOREM

The Central Limit Theorem states that, for any distribution (not necessarily normal) with mean μ and variance σ^2, the distribution of the *means* of random samples drawn from the population is approximately normal. Thus, if a population is skewed, samples drawn from the population will also be skewed. The distribution of the means of these samples will not be skewed, however, but will be approximately normal. The distribution of sample means becomes closer and closer to being normal as the sample size n increases.

If the distribution of sample means is normal, then what are its mean and standard deviation? The Central Limit Theorem states that the mean of the distribution of sample means is μ (the population mean) and the standard deviation of the distribution is $\sigma/\sqrt{n}$. Note that as n increases, the standard deviation of the distribution of sample means decreases. Figure 10.6 illustrates this; the 10 sample means shown are much less dispersed around μ than is the parent population from which the samples are drawn.

The student still may be wondering about the meaning of the concept "the distribution of sample means." From what does the variation arise in a population of *means?* The answer is that because the means in question are associated with samples drawn at random from a population, *the act of sampling itself* can be expected to result in a good deal of fluctuation of the means $\bar{x}_i$ from the true population mean μ. This can easily be demonstrated in practice by selecting some random samples of size n from a class of students (or some other population such as the staff of a library) and computing the mean of the ages or weights associated with each sample.

The standard deviation $\sigma/\sqrt{n}$ of the distribution of sample means is sometimes referred to as the *standard error of the mean* (SE_μ).

Example 11

A population of books has mean $\mu = 260$ pages and standard deviation $\sigma = 180$ pages. Find the mean and standard deviation of the distribution of the means of random samples of size 16 drawn from the population. Also compute for samples of size 49; 100.

Answer

The mean of all three sampling distributions is 260. The standard errors are, respectively,

$$1SE_\mu = \sigma/\sqrt{n} = 180/\sqrt{16} = 45,$$
$$1SE_\mu = \sigma/\sqrt{n} = 180/\sqrt{49} = 25.7,$$
$$1SE_\mu = 180/\sqrt{100} = 18.$$

We turn now to a discussion of how the Central Limit Theorem can be used to infer characteristics of a population from characteristics of a random sample drawn from the population.

When is n "large enough" so that the sampling distribution of a population will be distributed approximately normally? Unfortunately, this depends on the population; the more the parent population is skewed, the larger n must be. See Snedecor and Cochran[1] for a discussion of this problem.

CONFIDENCE INTERVALS ON μ WHEN σ IS KNOWN

Very often we wish to *estimate* a mean of a population from the characteristics of a sample. In this case, because the whole population has not been examined, the mean of the population can be known only approximately. *A confidence interval on μ* is a range of numbers, within which the true mean μ of the population can be expected with a stated probability to fall. *A 95% confidence interval on μ* is a range of numbers within which the true mean can be expected to fall in 95 out of 100 cases. That is, if the experiment "select a random sample of size n" is conducted 100 times, and a different 95% confidence interval is constructed on the basis of each of the sample means, then the true mean μ will fall within approximately 95 of the 100 confidence intervals.

Now let us turn to the calculation of a 95% confidence interval on μ.

We have already observed (see Example 10) that 95% of the members of a normal distribution will fall within $+1.96$ and -1.96 standard deviations from the mean of the population. Thus, in a sampling distribution, 95% of the sample means fall within $\pm 1.96SE_\mu$ of the true population mean; 95 out of 100 samples will have a mean within $\pm 1.96SE_\mu$ of the population mean (see Figure 10.7).

This reasoning can be reversed. If 95 out of 100 samples have a mean within $1.96SE_\mu$ of the population mean μ, then μ will be within 1.96 standard deviations of a given sample mean 95 out of 100 times. That is, the true population mean will fall within the range $\bar{x} \pm 1.96SE_\mu$ in 95 out of 100 samples. The interval

$$(x - 1.96SE\mu \quad x + 1.96SE\mu)$$

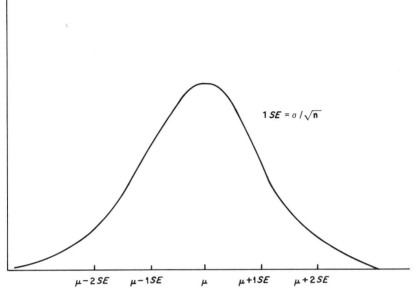

Figure 10.7. *Sampling distribution for a population with mean μ and variance σ^2.*

is called a 95% confidence interval on μ. We can be "95% confident" that $\bar{x} - 1.96SE_\mu \leq \mu \leq \bar{x} + 1.96SE_\mu$ for a given random sample with mean $\bar{x}$.

Example 12

Suppose that a random sample of size 100 has been drawn from a population of school media specialists in the Midwest. The mean salary of individuals in the sample is computed to be $12,300. From a previous study, the value of σ was calculated to be about $1800. What can be concluded about the mean salary of the *population* of school media specialists from which the sample was drawn?

Answer

By the Central Limit Theorem, the standard error of the sampling distribution is

$$1SE_\mu = \sigma/\sqrt{n} = 1800/\sqrt{100} = \$180.$$

Our sample mean was $12,300. Thus, a 95% confidence interval on the true (unknown) mean μ is $12,300 $\pm$ 1.96(180), or ($11,947.20,

$12,652.80). That is, we can be 95% confident that the true mean salary μ of the school media specialists in the population is given by the inequality $11,947.20 $\leq \mu \leq$ $12,652.80. Our best single-number estimate of the population mean μ is $12,300. Note that on the basis of a relatively small sample, a fairly tight estimate of the true mean μ can be made. This example illustrates the *power* of sampling. Imagine the difficulty and cost involved in calculating the mean of the population of school media specialists in, say, the entire Midwest—every last individual would have to be surveyed. A random sample of only 100 members of the population provides an estimate which is probably adequate for most purposes. Thus, through the collection of a relatively small sample, we can infer characteristics of the population from which the sample was drawn, with a fairly high degree of accuracy.

Example 13

Construct a 99% confidence interval for the data of Example 12.

Answer

We want 99% of the population to fall between $z \, SE_\mu$ from the mean; that is, 1/2 of 1% of the population to fall on either side of the interval. Therefore, we determine the value of z corresponding to an area of .495 in the area portion of Appendix C. That value is approximately 2.58. Then a 99% confidence interval on μ is given by

$$\bar{x} - 2.58 SE_\mu \leq \mu \leq \bar{x} + 2.58 SE_\mu$$

For the data of Example 12, $2.58 SE_\mu = $464.40, and a 99% confidence interval is, therefore, $11,835.60 $\leq \mu \leq$ $12,764.40.

Example 13 demonstrates that as a higher degree of confidence in the interval is required, the interval width necessarily increases. Intuitively, this result is as it should be. The level of confidence required is specified by the investigator in a particular research situation. Two commonly selected levels of confidence are 95% and 99%.

Example 14

Suppose a random sample of 400 school media specialists had been selected, and a mean salary of $12,300 computed. Compute 95% and 99% confidence intervals on μ.

Answer

$$1 SE_\mu = $1,800/\sqrt{400} = $90.$$

A 95% confidence interval on μ is given by $12,300 ± 1.96 ($90), or

$12,123.60 \le \mu \le$ $12,476.40. A 99% confidence interval is given by $12,300 $\pm$2.58 ($90) or $12,067.80 $\le \mu \le$ $12,532.20. Note how increasing the sample size increases the precision of the estimate.

DETERMINATION OF MINIMUM SAMPLE SIZE

The preceding examples involve the computation of confidence intervals for a *given* sample size. A closely related problem concerns the determination of a minimum sample size for a stated level of precision—that is, for a confidence interval of a given width. Instead of using the sample mean, standard deviation, desired confidence level (e.g., 95%), and sample size and computing a confidence interval based upon these data, this section discusses the computation of a minimum sample size from a desired confidence level, maximum desired width of the confidence interval, and the standard deviation of the population.

For example, suppose that, prior to the drawing of a sample during a research project, investigators decide that they want their estimate of a mean to be accurate to within $\pm$10 units, at a confidence level of 95%. That is, the investigators want a 95% confidence interval to be at least as accurate as $\mu \pm 10$. Because the precision of an estimate improves as sample size increases, our investigator will be able to achieve the desired accuracy for a given sample size. The problem is, what is the size of the sample which would result in the desired level of accuracy at the 95% level of confidence? Our reasoning is similar to that of the previous section. We want

$$1.96SE_{\mu} = 10, \quad \text{or} \quad 1SE_{\mu} = 10/1.96 = 5.10.$$

But we also know that $1SE_{\mu} = \sigma/\sqrt{n}$. Suppose that the value of the standard deviation of the population is known to be 30. Then

$$1SE_{\mu} = 5.10 = \sigma/\sqrt{n} = 30/\sqrt{n}.$$

Hence,

$$\sqrt{n} = 30/5.10, \text{ and } n = 34.6.$$

With a sample size of 35 or larger, the desired precision can be achieved. This is true regardless of the size of the original population.

THE *t*-DISTRIBUTION

The results of the preceding sections were based upon the assumption that the standard deviation of the population is known, at least approximately, whereas the mean is not known, and is to be estimated. For example, the standard deviation might be known from a previous investigation and the assumption made that its value is unchanged for purposes of the present study. Usually, neither the mean nor the standard deviation of the population is known, and both must be estimated in the sampling process. In these cases, the "t-distribution," not the normal distribution, is used to construct a confidence interval on μ.

As we discussed in Chapter 9, the standard deviation of a population estimated on the basis of a sample is given by

$$s = \left[\frac{\Sigma(X - \bar{x})^2}{n - 1} \right]^{1/2}$$

where n is the size of a random sample drawn from the population. The sample mean and standard deviation can then be used to construct a confidence interval on the mean as before, but using tables of the t-distribution rather than the normal distribution. A table of the t-distribution is provided in Appendix D.

Before, with the population standard deviation known (see previous sections), a confidence interval on the mean was given by the expression $\mu = \bar{x} \pm z \, (\sigma/\sqrt{n})$. In particular, for 99% and 95% confidence intervals, z was 2.58 and 1.96, respectively. An analagous procedure is followed when the standard deviation σ is not known. In this case, a confidence interval on μ is given by $\mu = \bar{x} \pm t \, (s/\sqrt{n})$, where the standard deviation s is computed from sample data, n is the sample size, and t is a number obtained from a table providing values of the t-distribution for various probabilities (see Appendix D). Thus, the procedure is identical to that of the previous section, except that t is used instead of z.

To use Appendix D, values of t are obtained by looking up the number of degrees of freedom $(n - 1)$ where n is the sample size, and the desired level of confidence. For example, with a sample of size 16, the values of t associated with 95% and 99% confidence intervals are 2.131 and 2.947, respectively. In these examples, α, the desired probability of error, is .05 and .01, respectively. (See Chapter 12.)

Example 15

Compute a 95% confidence interval on the mean μ of a population based on the following random sample of size 8: 8, 18, 16, 10, 12, 13, 13, 14.

Answer

$$\bar{x} = 104/8 = 13.0$$
$$s^2 = \frac{\Sigma(X - \bar{x})^2}{n - 1} = \frac{70}{7} = 10.$$

Therefore,

$$s = \sqrt{10} = 3.162.$$

From Appendix D, $t = 2.365$ on 7 df (degrees of freedom). The standard error of the mean is estimated by $s/\sqrt{n} = 1.118$. Then a 95% confidence interval on μ is given by 13.0 ± 2.365 (1.118) or $10.356 \leq \mu \leq 15.644$.

As a sample increases in size, the t-distribution approaches the normal distribution. An examination of Appendix D for $p = .05$ reveals that even for a sample of size 12 (11 df) $t = 2.201$, which is only about 12% larger than the value of z for the same probability in a normal distribution ($z = 1.96$ for a 95% confidence interval). Thus, for large samples, the t-distribution approximates the normal distribution, and even for moderately small samples the difference between values of t and values of z for the same probability is not substantial.

ESTIMATING THE VALUE OF A PROPORTION

We have discussed in some detail the concept of *the standard error of the mean*. Estimates of other parameters of a population have standard errors as well. See Arkin and Colton[2] for a listing of many of these.

One particularly useful standard error formula deals with estimating the value of the proportion of a population having, or not having, a particular characteristic. What proportions of a population are Democratic? Smokers? TV addicts? Golfers? Males? If p is the proportion in question, then the standard error of the estimate of p is given by

$$SE_p = \left[\frac{p(1 - p)}{n} \right]^{1/2}$$

where n is the sample size. Using this formula for SE_p, confidence intervals on p are computed as in the previous sections.

Example 16

A random sample of 100 members of a community reveals that 92% "never use the public library." Construct a 95% confidence interval on the population parameter p.

Answer

$$SE_p = \left[\frac{(.92)(.08)}{100} \right]^{1/2} = .0271$$

Then

$$p = .92 \pm 1.96(.0271), \qquad \text{or} \qquad 86.7\% \leq p \leq 97.3\%.$$

Example 17

As part of a special library's consideration of whether to implement the Ohio College Library Center's serial control subsystem, a sample of 140 serial titles was selected at random from the serial holdings of the library. The latest issue of each title was examined for the presence of either CODEN or ISSN. One or the other (or both) was found on only 26 titles. Construct a 95% confidence interval on this estimate.

Answer

Our estimate of p is $26/140 = .186$.

$$1SE_p = \left[\frac{(.186)(.814)}{140} \right]^{\frac{1}{2}} = .0329.$$

A 95% confidence interval on p is, therefore, given by $.186 \pm 1.96(.0329)$, or $12.2\% \leq p \leq 25.0\%$

APPENDIX: PROBLEMS FOR SOLUTION

1. Compute percentiles corresponding to the following z-scores in a normal distribution: (*a*) $z = -1.60$; (*b*) $z = -.36$; (*c*) $z = 0$; (*d*) $z = 1.42$; (*e*) $z = 2.28$.

Answers

(*a*) 5.48%; (*b*) 35.94%; (*c*) 50.00%; (*d*) 92.22%; (*e*) 98.87%.

2. Compute z-scores corresponding to the following percentiles in a normal distribution: (*a*) 10th; (*b*) 40th; (*c*) 75th; (*d*) 90th; (*e*) 99th.

Answers

(*a*) $z = -1.28$; (*b*) $z = -.25$; (*c*) $z = .67$; (*d*) $z = 1.28$; (*e*) $z = 2.33$.

3. John and Mary have IQ's of 90 and 105, respectively. If IQ's are distributed normally in the population with a mean of 100 and a standard deviation of 15, convert John and Mary's IQ scores to percentiles of the population.

Answer

John's IQ is at the 25.14th percentile and Mary's is at the 62.93th percentile.

4. Consider a population with a mean μ and a standard deviation σ. How is the standard error of the mean affected if: (*a*) The value of σ increases; (*b*) the sample size n increases; (*c*) the value of μ increases?

5. Consider a given confidence interval constructed on the estimated mean of a population. Discuss two ways to *narrow* (make tighter, smaller) this interval.

Answers

Decrease the level of confidence required; increase the sample size.

6. Provide a complete example illustrating Problem 5.

7. A public library wishes to select a random sample of a set of library card holders for the purpose of collecting data about library use. In a sample of 200 patrons, the mean number of books circulated in a given year was 8.6, with a standard deviation of 6.6. Compute a 95% confidence interval on this estimate of the mean.

Answer

$7.7 \le \mu \le 9.5$. Note that although the t-distribution is required to construct the confidence interval, the large sample size makes it equivalent to the normal distribution (i.e., $t = z = 1.96$).

8. A cataloging class selected a random sample of 20 catalog cards from the shelf list of the university library and decided that the classification number assigned to 5 of these 20 books corresponding to these cards was "at best, questionable; at worst, incorrect." Construct a 95% confidence interval on this estimate.

Answer

$SE_p = .097$ and $.06 \le p \le .44$. A larger sample should really be drawn to make the estimate more precise.

9. The mean number of years of education beyond high school in a sample of 15 public library users was found to be 2.2 with a standard deviation of 2.4, also computed from the sample. Construct a 95% confidence interval on this estimate.

Answer

$$.87 \le \mu \le 3.53.$$

10. Solve Problem 9, assuming that the standard deviation associated with the population was known to be 2.4 prior to the sampling.

Answer

$$.99 \leq \mu \leq 3.41.$$

11. Suppose σ is known to be 3.8 for a certain population, and it is desired to construct a 95% confidence interval on the mean of the population to within ± 1.0 of the sample mean. What is the minimum sample size required to achieve the desired accuracy?

Answer

$$n \geq 56.$$

12. Following the first presidential debates of 1976 between Gerald Ford and Jimmy Carter, the Associated Press conducted a poll of 1065 randomly selected viewers. The results of the poll found that 34.4% of those polled felt that Ford had won the debate and 31.8% felt that Carter had won. Construct a 95% confidence interval on each of these estimates. Can one conclude that in the population as a whole viewers preferred Ford over Carter?

Answer

$$SE_f = \left[\frac{(.344)(.656)}{1065} \right]^{1/2} = .0146$$

$$SE_c = \left[\frac{(.318)(.682)}{1065} \right]^{1/2} = .0143$$

A 95% confidence interval on the percentage of viewers preferring Ford is, therefore, $.344 \pm 1.96\,(.0146)$, or $31.5\% \leq f \leq 37.3\%$. In a similar way, a 95% confidence interval on the percentage of viewers preferring Carter is $29.0\% \leq c \leq 34.6\%$. These two confidence intervals overlap considerably; hence, one cannot conclude at a confidence level of 95% that the viewers in the population as a whole preferred Ford over Carter.

REFERENCES

1. George W. Snedecor and Cochran, William G., *Statistical Methods*, 6th ed. Ames: Iowa State University Press, 1968, pp. 51–56.
2. Herbert Arkin and Colton, Raymond R., *Statistical Methods*, 5th ed. New York: Barnes & Noble, 1970, pp. 149–150.

PART IV

Inferential Statistics

CHAPTER 11

Linear Regression and Correlation

INTRODUCTION TO REGRESSION AND CORRELATION

In its statistical sense, the term *regression* is used to describe a relationship between two or more variables. A typical relationship might involve a situation in which values of one variable tend to increase whenever values of the second variable increase. A *direct* relationship of this sort holds between age and blood pressure, between size of holdings of a library and annual circulation, between the length of documents and the number of articles (*a, an,* or *the*) contained in documents, between the age and weight of persons. An *inverse* relationship between two variables occurs when values of one variable tend to increase when values of the second variable decrease, and conversely.

A *regression curve* is a model of a mathematical relationship between two variables. In this text we will be concerned primarily with relationships of a particularly simple kind—*linear* relationships. A *regression line* is a straight line or linear relationship between two variables. If such a relationship is known to exist and is stated mathematically, we shall see that it is then possible to *predict* values of one variable from knowledge of the second.

As in much social science research, it will rarely be the case that a linear relationship is found to be perfect. That is, usually, an observed relationship is only approximately linear. The *correlation coefficient* is a statistical measure, a number, that expresses the strength of the relationship between two variables. Computation of the correlation coefficient will tell us *how well* our data are described by a linear model.

This chapter will begin to make explicit and precise the notions of correlation and regression, and will provide illustrations and problems from librarianship that are related to these concepts.

Bivariate Graphs

In previous chapters, our concern was centered about the analysis and description of frequency distributions characteristic of a single variable, such as age, salary, or number of volumes held. In Chapter 8, pictorial (graphical) representations of frequency data were constructed in the form of histograms and frequency polygons. A frequency polygon of a distribution of Grade Point Averages (GPA's) earned by a sample of college freshmen is presented in Figure 11.1. The variable of interest, cumulative GPA, is measured on the horizontal axis, or *X-axis*, whereas the frequency of each GPA interval is measured on the vertical axis, or *Y-axis*. This graphical method of representing frequency distributions of single variables is, as we have seen, quite typical.

In this chapter, we return to the graphical representation of data, but from a broader perspective. The concepts of regression and correlation, with which we are concerned here, deal with *pairs* of variables rather than a single variable. There are several reasons for analyzing a research situation in this way. We may, for example, wish to predict values of one variable (e.g., GPA) and search for a rational means for so doing. Or perhaps we are led to suspect a relationship between two variables from purely theoretical considerations. Perhaps we even have grounds to hypothesize a causal relationship between the two variables.

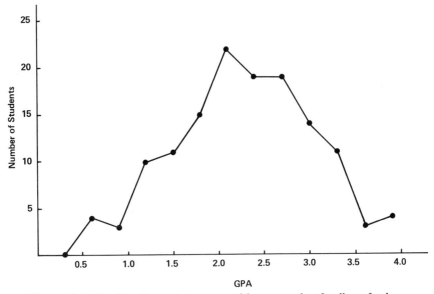

Figure 11.1. *Grade point averages earned by a sample of college freshmen.*

A crude but rather revealing initial indication of the extent of the relationship between two variables can be obtained by plotting both variables on the same graph, called a *bivariate graph,* or *scatter diagram.* Both variables are represented on a bivariate graph, one being measured on the *X*-axis, the other on the *Y*-axis. Each observation, or datum, is plotted as a single point on the graph. The location of each plotted point depends on its measured values for each of the two variables of interest corresponding to dimensions on the graph.

The relationship between IQ and GPA in a small sample of individuals is illustrated in Figure 11.2. Each point on the bivariate graph corresponds to a single person, and simultaneously displays both that person's IQ and GPA. To read these values from the graph (or to plot new points) we must construct imaginary perpendicular lines from each point to each axis (or from each axis). This is done for four individuals in Figure 11.2. Two individuals evidently possessed a measured IQ of 80, earning GPA's of 2.3 and 1.5. A third individual, with an IQ of 100, earned a GPA of 2.5. A fourth individual, with an IQ of 94, also earned a GPA of 2.5.

As revealed in Figure 11.2, there appears to be, at least in the small sample examined, a definite tendency for IQ and GPA to be related; as IQ increases, GPA tends to increase. In fact, we may be led to suspect that this relationship is in fact *causal* in nature.

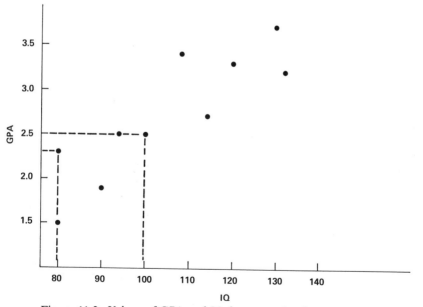

Figure 11.2. *Values of GPA and IQ for a sample of 10 individuals.*

We should add that, as in virtually all social science research, there are exceptions to the general statement expressed in the previous paragraph. There are no doubt other variables that have an effect on GPA, such as motivation, previous educational background, and possibly many other environmental and hereditary factors. These may be characterized as intervening variables.

A researcher who wishes to plot bivariate data on a scattergram must decide which variable is to be represented on which axis. Usually, the research hypothesis will imply the desirability of predicting values of one variable from prior knowledge of values of the second variable. The *dependent variable* is the variable that the researcher wishes to estimate or predict, and is customarily represented on the Y-axis. The *independent variable* is then represented on the X-axis. This convention was followed in Figure 11.2, in which the dependent variable, GPA, is represented on the Y-axis.

The Regression Line

We can be somewhat stronger in our statement concerning the relationship that evidently exists between GPA and IQ. Not only do these variables tend to increase together, but the relationship actually seems to be approximately *linear*. That is, the individual points lie roughly on a straight line, with the exceptions or deviations already noted. Figure 11.3 depicts a sketch of the line that seems to best fit the presented data. This line is called the regression line of y on x.

Algebraically, the equation of any straight line is of the general form $y = a + bx$. Quantities y and x are the dependent and independent variables respectively, whereas a and b are *constants*, or *parameters*, that characterize the particular line in question. These numbers completely determine the position of a given line. Number a is the *y-intercept*, or the value of y for which $x = 0$. (If $x = 0$ at the y-axis of the graph as is sometimes, but not always, the case, then the y-intercept is the point at which the line crosses the y-axis. The y-intercept is about 16 in Figure 11.4.) Number b is the *slope* of the line—the relative change produced in the value of y by a change in the value of x. Symbolically, $b = \Delta y/\Delta x$, where Δ (the Greek letter delta) stands for the phrase "the change in." *Parallel lines have the same slope.* The reader should verify this assertion by constructing some examples.

In English, the mathematical model $y = a + bx$ says that the value of the dependent variable which corresponds to any particular value of the independent variable can be predicted by multiplying the value of the

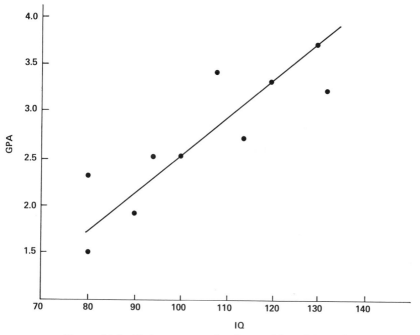

Figure 11.3. *Fitting a regression line to IQ and GPA data.*

independent variable *x* by a constant *b,* called the slope of the line, and adding a second constant *a,* called the *y*-intercept of the line.

We emphasize that the slope of the regression line reflects an "average" relationship between variables *x* and *y*. If *b* = 3, then *y* tends to increase by *about* three units for every unit increase in *x;* if *b* = −2, then *y* tends to decrease by about two units for every unit increase in *x*. Because in most cases the points on a scatter diagram will not all lie exactly on a line, however, there may be deviations from the line—perhaps substantial deviations.

Example 1

Figure 11.4 is a scatter diagram for which a regression line has been sketched. By inspection, the *y*-intercept *a* is about 16. The slope of the regression line can be calculated by constructing any triangle that illustrates the relative changes in *x* and *y* between any two points on the line, and by calculating the quantities Δx and Δy and the ratio $b = \Delta y/\Delta x$. We will now do this for two triangles in Figure 11.4, obtaining the same value for *b* in both cases.

In the larger triangle illustrated in Figure 11.4,

$$b \approx \Delta y / \Delta x = -10/12 = -5/6.$$

In the smaller triangle,

$$b \approx \Delta y / \Delta x = -5/6 = -5/6.$$

Thus, $b = -5/6$, and the equation of the regression line in Figure 11.4 is

$$y = 16 + (-5/6)x,$$

or more simply,

$$y = 16 - \tfrac{5}{6}x.$$

Because of the crude method employed in the computation of a and b (i.e., inspection of the graph), these values can only be regarded as approximate. A more refined procedure for calculating a and b will be discussed later in the chapter.

NONLINEAR RELATIONSHIPS

Conceptually, a linear relationship between two variables is the most simple relationship possible between two variables. Other kinds of relationships are possible and frequently exist. For example, in Chapter 5 we noted that the relationship between the age (n) of a book collection and its

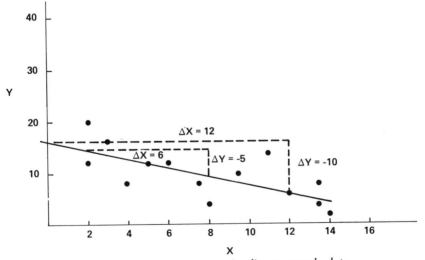

Figure 11.4. *Fitting a regression line to sample data.*

size (y) is *exponential,* not linear. The equation for this relationship is $y = Ae^{rn}$, where r is a parameter representing the rate of growth of the collection and A is the size of the collection at age $n = 0$. The graph that corresponds to an exponential relationship is *curvilinear,* or *nonlinear.* Many other nonlinear relationships are found to exist in research data. Sketches of commonly encountered curvilinear relationships in librarianship are depicted in Figure 11.5.

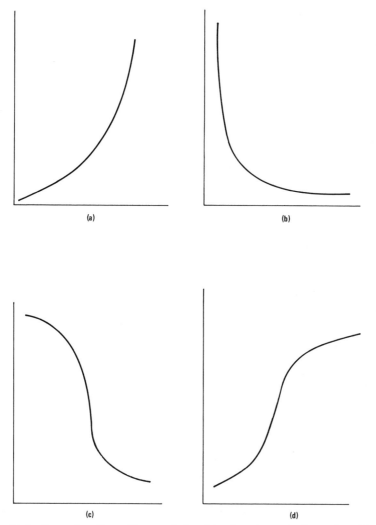

(a)

(b)

(c)

(d)

Figure 11.5. *Examples of curvilinear relationships found to exist for various library phenomena.*

Curve (*a*) of Figure 11.5 is the graph of an exponential distribution, and has been found to describe the growth of libraries (dependent variable) as a function of time (independent variable). Curve (*b*) is the graph of a hyperbolic distribution and is a graphical statement of Zipf's law as well as a form of Bradford's Law of Scattering of the scientific literature.[1] Curve (*c*) is a typical graph describing the effectiveness of information retrieval systems in terms of *recall* and *precision*.[2] Curve (*d*) depicts a logistic curve. Derek deSolla Price has hypothesized that this kind of curvilinear relationship is descriptive of the future growth of science and the scientific literature.[3]

Regression analysis can be applied to these and other examples of non-linear relationships,[4] but further treatment of this topic is beyond the scope of this text.

EXAMPLES OF REGRESSION LINES FOR SAMPLE DATA

Figure 11.6 illustrates several different sets of data to which regression lines have been fitted. Graph (*a*) is an example of a perfect direct relationship between two variables. The slope of the regression line in graph (*a*) is positive—the line rises from left to right because as *x* increases, so does *y*. Therefore, this relationship is a *direct* one. Because all of the points fall on the regression line, the relationship is also *perfect*.

An inverse relationship between two variables is illustrated in graph (*b*); the slope of the regression line is negative. Although the relationship is not perfect, it is clearly relatively strong in that all the data points fall near the regession line.

Graph (*c*) also illustrates a negative relationship between the two variables depicted; but evidently the relationship is relatively weak in comparison with that exhibited in (*b*).

Finally, graph (*d*) exhibits values of a pair of variables that are unrelated.

The term *correlation* refers to the strength of the linear relationship between two variables. Thus, a perfect positive correlation is exhibited by the regression line in graph (*a*), a strong negative correlation in graph (*b*), and a mild negative correlation in graph (*c*). The variables in graph (*d*) are uncorrelated.

The *correlation coefficient* is a number, calculated from bivariate data, which provides a numerical measure of the extent of correlation between two variables. Correlation coefficient will be given a precise mathematical definition somewhat later. However, we should briefly summarize the

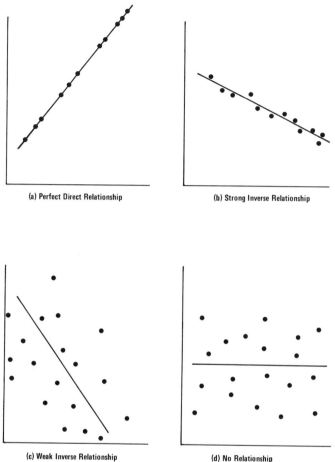

Figure 11.6. *Four examples of linear relationships.*

range of values of the correlation coefficient r and interpret some typical values before proceeding further.

The value of the correlation coefficient r ranges from $+1$ to -1. A perfect direct relationship such as that displayed in graph (a), Figure 11.6, is characterized by a value of r equal to $+1$, whereas a perfect inverse relationship is characterized by a value of r equal to -1. Totally unrelated variables are uncorrelated, and $r = 0$. A strong relationship is one in which r is near $+1$ or -1, whereas in a weak relationship, r is near 0. We will return to the concept of correlation coefficient later in this chapter.

REGRESSION AND PREDICTION

If the relationship between two variables is linear, and if the correlation between the variables is reasonably strong, then fairly accurate predictions can be made of values of the dependent variable for given values of the independent variable. For example, referring again to Figure 11.4, we found the equation of the regression line to be $y = 16 - \frac{5}{8}x$. For particular values of x, estimates of y can be obtained by substituting those values of x into the regression equation. We use the symbol $\hat{y}$ to refer to an *estimate* of y based on a known value of x. If $x = 18$, then our estimate $\hat{y}$ is the number 1, since $\hat{y} = 16 - \frac{5}{8}(18) = 1$. Similarly, if $x = 8$, then $\hat{y} = 9\frac{1}{3}$.

Example 2

Suppose that the relationship between IQ (measured on the x-axis) and GPA is roughly linear and can be expressed in terms of the regression equation $y = .04x - 1.5$, for a particular group of college freshmen.* Estimate the GPA that will be achieved by a member of this population if he or she has an IQ of 80; 100; 130.

Answer

Approximate values for these estimates could be read directly from Figure 11.3. More accurately, if $x = 80$, then $\hat{y} = .04(80) - 1.5 = 1.7$; if $x = 100$, $\hat{y} = 2.5$; if $x = 130$, $\hat{y} = 3.7$.

ADVANCED TOPICS

Two basic approaches may be taken in the task of correlation analysis, depending on the type of data to be analyzed. The *Pearson product-moment* correlation coefficient is utilized when the independent and dependent variables are interval or ratio variables (see Chapter 7). *Nonparametric* correlation methods are used when the data in question are ordinal—ranks or categories. To illustrate the latter problem, suppose that the academic libraries within a particular geographic area were ranked according to (*a*) holdings, and (*b*) number of professional librarians employed. These ranks are ordinal data, and the relationship between these two sets of rankings would be assessed with nonparametric correlation methods such as Spearman's rank order procedure. Although the comments we have made thus far in this chapter apply equally to each approach to correlation, the computational formulas in general differ for the

---

* See Figure 11.3. Note that the y-intercept cannot be read directly from this graph because x is not equal to zero on the y-axis.

two approaches. The reader who wishes to pursue the question of non-parametric correlation methods is referred to another text (e.g., Snedecor and Cochran, *Statistical Methods,* 1967). In the following sections, the Pearson product-moment approach to correlation will be discussed in some detail.

COMPUTATIONAL FORMULAS

In previous sections we have discussed the phenomenon of a linear relationship between two variables. Such a relationship can be described mathematically by sketching onto the bivariate graph the line that appears to be the "best fit" to the data points and then observing the value of the y-intercept and estimating the slope of the line. Having done this, the equation of the regression line is given by the formula $y = a + bx$. The strength of the relationship between x and y is measured by the correlation coefficient r, which ranges in value from -1 to $+1$.

We have previously seen that rough-and-ready estimates of the values of a, b, and r can be obtained from a bivariate graph. To compute the exact values of these quantities from raw data points, however, computational formulas are required. We provide such formulas in the next sections, with very little accompanying discussion. A later section will introduce the reader to a more detailed analysis of the derivations of these formulas.

FORMULA 1. THE SLOPE OF THE REGRESSION LINE

The slope b of the regression line can be computed from raw data points, based on the assumption of linearity, by the formula

$$b = \frac{(1/n)\Sigma xy - \bar{x}\bar{y}}{(1/n)\Sigma x^2 - \bar{x}^2},$$

where n is the number of data points and x and y are values of the independent and dependent variables, respectively.

FORMULA 2. THE y-INTERCEPT OF THE REGRESSION LINE

The y-intercept a is given by the equation $a = \bar{y} - b\bar{x}$, based on the assumption of linearity. Thus, if the means $\bar{x}$ and $\bar{y}$ are known and if b has been calculated, then the value of a can easily be computed.

Example 3

The four points $(0, -3)$, $(1, -1)$, $(3, 3)$, and $(7, 11)$ are all on the line $y = 2x - 3$. Note that b, the slope of the line, is 2 and a, the y-intercept of the line, is -3. The student should verify that these points lie on the line by substituting the values of x and y into the equation $y = 2x - 3$, for each of the four points.

If the expression for a and b given in Formulas 1 and 2 are adequate, we would expect to deduce the equation $y = 2x - 3$ by treating the four points as data points. Applying Formula 1 to the data, we obtain the following chart:

x	y	xy	x^2
0	-3	0	0
1	-1	-1	1
3	3	9	9
7	11	77	49
11	10	85	59

Therefore, $\bar{x} = 2.75$, $\bar{y} = 2.5$, $\Sigma xy = 85$, and $\Sigma x^2 = 59$. Thus,

$$b = \frac{21.25 - 6.875}{14.75 - 7.56} = 2.$$

Applying Formula 2, $a = 2.5 - 2(2.75) = -3$, and the equation of the best fit to the four points is, as it ought to be, $y = 2x - 3$.

Example 4

The 10 data points plotted in Figure 11.3 are displayed in the chart. Find the formula of the regression line based upon these data and Formulas 1 and 2.

x (IQ)	y (GPA)	xy	x^2
80	1.5	120	6400
80	2.3	184	6400
90	1.9	171	8100
94	2.5	235	8836
100	2.5	250	10000
108	3.4	367.2	11664
114	2.7	307.8	12996
120	3.3	396	14400
130	3.7	481	16900
132	3.2	422.4	17424
1048	27.0	2934.4	113120

Thus, $\bar{x} = 104.8$, $\bar{y} = 2.7$, $\Sigma xy = 2934.4$,   and $\Sigma x^2 = 113,120$.
Then

$$b = \frac{293.44 - 282.96}{11,312 - 10,983.04} = .032,$$

and

$$a = 2.7 - (.032)(104.8) = -.65.$$

The equation of the regression line is $y = .032x - .65$.

For small amounts of data, Formulas 1 and 2 can be applied manually to research data. If large data analyses are to be done, however, the student should consider using a packaged statistical program for the analysis (see Chapter 13). The same observation holds for the application of Formula 3.

FORMULA 3. THE CORRELATION COEFFICIENT

The correlation coefficient r is given by the computational formula

$$r = \frac{(1/n)\Sigma xy - \bar{x}\bar{y}}{\{[(1/n)\Sigma x^2 - \bar{x}^2][(1/n)\Sigma y^2 - \bar{y}^2]\}^{1/2}}$$

Note that the denominator of the above expression is just the product of parameters σ_x and σ_y (see Chapter 9). Although this formula and the development which follows are expressed in terms of σ_x and σ_y, analogous expressions exist for sample standard deviations $s_{x\cdot}$.

Example 5

The correlation between x and y with respect to the data in Example 3 above is computed as shown in the chart.

x	y	xy	x^2	y^2
0	−3	0	0	9
1	−1	−1	1	1
3	3	9	9	9
7	11	77	49	121
11	10	85	59	140

Thus, $\bar{x} = 2.75$, $\bar{y} = 2.5$.

$$\sigma_{xy} = (1/n)\Sigma xy - \bar{x}\bar{y} = \tfrac{1}{4}(85) - (2.75)(2.5) = 14.375.$$
$$\sigma_x = \sqrt{\tfrac{1}{4}(59) - (2.75)^2} = \sqrt{14.75 - 7.5625} = 2.681.$$
$$\sigma_y = \sqrt{\tfrac{1}{4}(140) - (2.5)^2} = \sqrt{35 - 6.25} = 5.362.$$

Then

$$r = \frac{14.375}{(2.681)(5.362)} = 1.00.$$

This is exactly what we should have expected, because the four data points are known to lie exactly on the regression line.

Example 6

Compute the correlation coefficient r between IQ and GPA from the data provided in Example 4.

x(IQ)	y(GPA)	xy	x^2	y^2
80	1.5	120	6400	2.25
80	2.3	184	6400	5.29
90	1.9	171	8100	3.61
94	2.5	235	8836	6.25
100	2.5	250	10000	6.25
108	3.4	367.2	11664	11.56
114	2.7	307.8	12996	7.29
120	3.3	396	14400	10.89
130	3.7	481	16900	13.69
132	3.2	422.4	17424	10.24
1048	27.0	2934.4	113120	77.32

$\sigma_y = .665$, $\sigma_x = 18.137$, $\bar{x} = 104.8$, $\bar{y} = 2.7$. Therefore

$$r = \frac{293.44 - (2.7)(104.8)}{(.665)(18.137)} = .869.$$

The reader will have noted that the computational formulas for the regression coefficient b and the correlation coefficient r are similar; that in fact much of the computation is repetitious. The relationship between σ_x, σ_y, r, and b is given by Formulas (4).

FORMULAS 4.   RELATIONSHIP BETWEEN
S_x, S_y, r, AND b

$$r = b(\sigma_x/\sigma_y), \quad \text{or} \quad b = r(\sigma_y/\sigma_x).$$

Thus, if b, σ_x, and σ_y are known, r can be simply computed by substitution into the first of Formulas (4). Similarly, if σ_x, σ_y, and r are known, then b can be easily calculated.

Example 7

From the data provided in Example (5), above, compute the regression coefficient b. Note that this result should agree with the result of Example 3.

Answer

$$b = r(\sigma_y/\sigma_x) = 1.00 \ (5.36/2.68) = 2.00.$$

Example 8

From the data provided in Example (6), compute b. This result should agree with the result of Example 4.

Answer

$$b = r(\sigma_y/\sigma_x) = .869 \ (.665/18.137) = .032.$$

Example 9

Consider a set of empirical data for which the regression line of y on x is given by the equation $y = 13.1x - 42.7$. Find the correlation coefficient r between x and y if $\sigma_x = 1.5$ and $\sigma_y = 21.1$.

Answer

$$r = b(\sigma_x/\sigma_y) = 13.1(1.5/21.1) = .931.$$

DERIVATION OF THE FORMULAS—
A CLOSER LOOK

The concept of the regression line implies finding a line which in some sense is a "best fit" to the points on a bivariate graph. In this section we examine a particular definition of "best fit" and the theoretical formulas for a and b which are implied by this definition.

A definition of best fit which is closely related to the concept of standard deviation is the *least-square* criterion. According to this definition, the least-squares best linear fit to bivariate data is provided by *that line which minimizes the sum of the squares of the vertical deviations $(\hat{y} - y)$ from the line*. Figure 11.7 illustrates a line which is fitted to bivariate data with each deviation $(\hat{y} - y)$ indicated.

The least-squares criterion says that the best fit to bivariate data is given by that line for which the number

$$S^2 = \Sigma(\hat{y} - y)^2 = \Sigma(a + bx - y)^2 \tag{1}$$

is a minimum. It can be shown[6] that S^2 achieves its minimum value when the coefficients a and b are selected such that

$$b = \sigma_{xy}/\sigma_x^2 \quad \text{and} \quad a = \bar{y} - b\bar{x}. \tag{2}$$

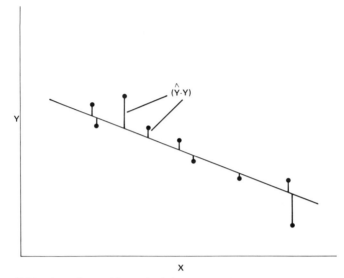

Figure 11.7 *Bivariate data with vertical deviations* $(\hat{y} - y)$ *from a fitted regression line.*

Quantity σ_x^2 in Equation (2) is the variance of x: $\sigma_x^2 = (1/n)\Sigma(x - \bar{x})^2$. Quantity σ_{xy} is called the *covariance* of x and y, and is given by the formula

$$\sigma_{xy} = (1/n)\Sigma(x - \bar{x})(y - \bar{y}). \tag{3}$$

Note the analogy between the variance and the covariance.

A somewhat simpler form, computationally, for b can be derived from Equation (2) by observing that

$$
\begin{aligned}
\sigma_{xy} &= (1/n)\Sigma(x - \bar{x})(y - \bar{y}) \\
&= (1/n)\Sigma(xy - \bar{x}y - \bar{y}x + \bar{x}\bar{y}) \\
&= (1/n)\Sigma xy - 1/n\Sigma\bar{x}y - 1/n\Sigma\bar{y}x + 1/n\Sigma\bar{x}\bar{y} \\
&= (1/n)\Sigma xy - \bar{x}\bar{y} - \bar{x}\bar{y} + \bar{x}\bar{y} \\
&= (1/n)\Sigma xy - \bar{x}\bar{y}.
\end{aligned}
$$

Also, as we showed in Chapter 9,

$$\sigma_x^2 = (1/n)\Sigma x^2 - \bar{x}^2.$$

Substituting these quantities into Equation (2) and simplifying, we obtain

$$b = \frac{(1/n)\Sigma xy - \bar{x}\bar{y}}{(1/n)\Sigma x^2 - \bar{x}^2}.$$

This expression is Formula (1), above. It is used to calculate the least-squares estimate of b from raw data points. Coefficient a can then be calculated by substituting the estimate for b into the equation $a = \bar{y} - b\bar{x}$.

We now return to the least-squares criterion for "best fit." The least-squares criterion states that the regression line which best fits bivariate data is that line for which S^2, the sum of the squared vertical deviations from the predicted regression line, is minimized. It can be shown[6] that when the values for a and b implied by the least-squares criterion are substituted into Equation (1) and simplified, Equation (1) becomes

$$S^2 = \sigma_y^2\{1 - [\sigma_{xy}^2/(\sigma_x^2\sigma_y^2)]\}. \tag{4}$$

Thus the total squared error S^2 is expressed as a product of σ_y^2—the variance of variable y—and the quantity $(1 - r^2)$, where

$$r = \sigma_{xy}/(\sigma_x\sigma_y). \tag{5}$$

Quantity r is called the *correlation coefficient*. If computational formulas for σ_{xy}, σ_x, and σ_y are substituted into Equation (5), the computational Formula (3) for calculating the value of r from raw data is obtained.

From Equations (4) and (5) we see that

$$S^2 = \sigma_y^2(1 - r^2). \tag{6}$$

From Equation (6), we can see that $S^2 = 0$ if and only if $\sigma_y^2 = 0$ or $(1 - r^2) = 0$. Assuming that $\sigma_y^2 \neq 0$ (as would normally be the case), we observe that quantity $(1 - r^2)$ equals zero if and only if $r = +1$ or $r = -1$. But if $S^2 = 0$, there are no deviations from the regression line, and the relationship is a perfect linear relationship. Thus, *in a perfect linear relationship, the correlation coefficient r is either $+1$ or -1.* And, as we will show subsequently, a positive value of r corresponds to a positive value of b; and a negative value of r corresponds to a negative value of b. Thus, if $r = +1$, the relationship between x and y is a perfect positive or direct relationship; if $r = -1$, the relationship is a perfect inverse relationship.

Consider again Equation (6) if $r = 0$. In this case the total squared error S^2 is just equal to the variance of y: $S^2 = \sigma_y^2$. If $r = 0$, fitting the points to a regression line does not reduce the original variance in variable y—there is evidently no relationship between x and y. Thus, *the correlation coefficient r between two variables is equal to zero if and only if there is no relationship between the variables.*

Values of r between $+1$ and -1 measure the strength of the linear relationship between x and y. For example, if $r = .7$, then the variance σ_y^2 is reduced by about half by fitting the data to the least-squares regression line: $S^2 = \sigma_y^2[1 - (.7)^2] = .51\ \sigma_y^2$. Thus, there is a fairly strong positive relationship between x and y, and the regression model succeeds in explaining half of the variance of y.

If $r = -.9$, then σ_y^2 is reduced by approximately 80%: $S^2 = \sigma_y^2[1 - (-.9)^2] = .19\ \sigma_y^2$. Evidently there is very little deviation from the regression line in this example.

A simpler computational formula for b or r can be deduced if the other is known and if σ_x and σ_y are also known. Equation (2) for b was

$$b = \sigma_{xy}/\sigma_x^2. \tag{7}$$

Equation (5) expressed r as a function of σ_{xy}

$$r = \sigma_{xy}/(\sigma_x \sigma_y). \tag{8}$$

From Equations (7) and (8) we deduce that

$$b = \frac{\sigma_{xy}}{\sigma_x^2} = \frac{\sigma_{xy}\sigma_y}{\sigma_x^2 \sigma_y} = r\,\frac{\sigma_y}{\sigma_x}.$$

Thus, we have derived Formulas (4) from the previous section:

$$b = r\,\frac{\sigma_y}{\sigma_x}, \tag{9}$$

and

$$r = b\,\frac{\sigma_x}{\sigma_y}. \tag{10}$$

Hence, if the standard deviations σ_x, σ_y, and r are known, the regression coefficient b can be computed simply by Equation (9); if σ_x, σ_y, and b are known, r can be computed by Equation (10).

REGRESSION, CORRELATION, AND SAMPLING ERROR

Even with sophisticated procedures for calculating the regression coefficients a and b, and the correlation coefficient r, another potential source of error exists. This arises from the fact that, in general, the data points of a scattergram are a result of sampling from a population. As with any other sample, then, a certain amount of sampling error can be expected. This fact implies the existence of a theoretical or "true" regression line, which will almost certainly deviate somewhat from our calculated line. By increasing the size of the sample, our calculated regression line will approach the true regression line. In a similar way, our estimate of the correlation coefficient r will only approximate the true value of the correlation coefficient. Figure 11.8 illustrates a regression line that has been

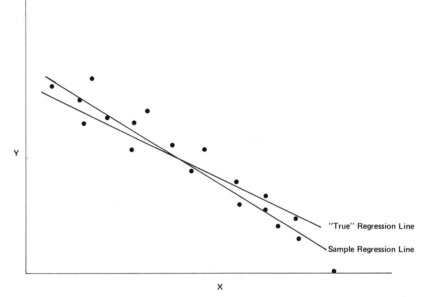

Figure 11.8. *Regression line calculated from sample data and true regression line.*

sketched in on the basis of the sample data displayed. The theoretical true regression line has been sketched on the same graph.

MULTIPLE REGRESSION

Frequently the fluctuations in the value of a dependent variable are not the sole result of the fluctuations in a single independent variable. Consideration of relationships among several independent variables x_1, x_2, x_3, . . . and a dependent variable y are treated in the subject of *multiple regression*. For example, a linear relationship between x_1, x_2, and y can be expressed as $y = a + bx_1 + cx_2$. Formulas for the calculation of numbers a, b, and c as well as for R, the coefficient of multiple correlation, can be derived. It is also possible to separate out the effect of each of the independent variables on the dependent variable. The relative measure of the association between the dependent variable and a particular independent variable, eliminating the effects of other independent variables, is known as a *coefficient of partial correlation*.

It is beyond the scope of the present chapter to discuss further the concepts of multiple regression. The reader is invited to refer to other texts for computational formulas and detailed and comprehensive treatments of this topic.*

EXAMPLES FROM LIBRARY RESEARCH

Example A

During the course of a simulation study of the use of copying machines in a large university library,[10] it became necessary to estimate the frequency distribution of the time spent at copying machines by the typical machine user. It was hypothesized that the relationship between "time spent" and "number of pages copied" would be roughly linear. By direct observation, data were collected and were plotted on a bivariate graph. On inspection, the resulting scattergram revealed a fairly strong positive relationship between the two variables. The technique of regression analysis was used to obtain the regression equation between time spent in minutes (t) and number of pages copied (p): $t = .87 + .42p$.

Note that in this example, the values $a = .87$ and $b = .42$ can be given physical interpretations. Quantity a is the set-up and clean-up time—the time required by users to extract the necessary change from pocket or purse, to find and prepare the desired pages to copy, and generally become organized, both before the copying begins and after it is completed. Quantity b is the mean time required for a typical user to copy a typical page.

The above regression equation was later used in the simulation model to convert values for "number of pages copied" to predicted values of "total time used." Thus, for example, the mean amount of time spent by two users with 7 and 70 pages to copy can be calculated to be 3.81 and 30.27 minutes, respectively.

Example B

Research in automatic indexing (computer selection of keywords from machine-readable text) is based on the assumption that the frequency by which substantive, content-bearing words occur in documents can be taken as an indicator of the semantic content of the document. Another factor which may, as an intervening variable, influence the number of occurrences of a content-bearing word in a document is the *length* of the document. That is, one might suspect that a long document "about" the topic of Oedipus complex might be expected to contain more occurrences

---

* See Snedecor and Cohran, *Statistical Methods,* 1967; Anderson and Bancroft, *Statistical Theory in Research,* 1952; and Lapin, *Statistics for Modern Business Decisions,* 1973.

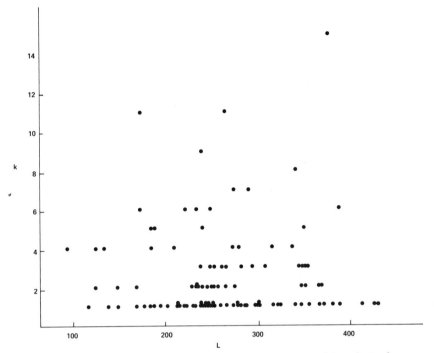

Figure 11.9. *Number k of specialty words in documents of length L, for seven selected specialty words.*

of the words "Oedipus complex" than a relatively short document, also about the subject. In a test of the hypothesis that the frequency of occurrence of a content-bearing word in a document is positively related to document length, a random sample of seven substantive words in the psychoanalytic literature was selected.

All documents (in this case, *abstracts* of documents) in which the words occurred in the data base under study were examined, and a bivariate graph of all data points, 121 points in all, was constructed. (See Figure 11.9.) The graph conveyed the visual impression that there was no relationship whatever between document length and frequency of occurrence of the seven content-bearing words in the sample. Subsequent calculation of the correlation coefficient verified this visual impression; r was calculated to be $+.04$, and the initial hypothesis was therefore rejected.[11]

Example C

In his analysis of circulation data at the M.I.T. Science Library, Philip Morse was led to hypothesize that the circulation of books could be described by a Markov process.[12] According to the Markov model, all the books of the class which circulate m times in a given year should circulate an average of $N(m)$ times in the following year, *where* N(m) *depends solely on* m. Circulation histories of approximately 300 books were collected and mean values of $N(m)$ for each m-class were computed. For example, it was found that for the class of books for which $m = 3$, $N(m) = 1.79$; a book that circulated three times in a given year circulated an average of 1.79 times in the following year.

The points $(m, N(m))$ were plotted on a bivariate graph, which revealed a strong association between $N(m)$ and m. The technique of least squares was used to compute regression coefficients a and b. The equation relating m and $N(m)$ was found by Morse to be $N(m) = .37 + .48m$. The expected circulation of a book in a given year from the M.I.T. Science Library is therefore .37 circulation plus approximately one-half of the previous year's circulation, independent of the age of the book. Thus, book circulation tends to decrease as book age increases. But if a book happens to gain or lose popularity suddenly, its circulation *the following year* can be well predicted from its most recent annual circulation record. Morse comments: "This behavior corresponds more realistically to the ups and downs of book popularity than do other models, based explicitly on book age."[13] Morse goes on to discuss the model and its implications in considerably more detail.

APPENDIX: PROBLEMS FOR SOLUTION

1. Consider the bivariate graph (Figure 11.10).

(a) By inspection, identify the extent of the correlation between variables P and Q. Is the correlation positive or negative? Is the relationship direct or inverse?

(b) Mentally sketch the regression line which seems to you to most closely represent the relationship. Find the y-intercept and the approximate slope of this line.

(c) Find the equation of the line.

(d) What is your predicted value for Q when P equals 10? 30? 100?

Answer

(a) Strong positive correlation, r is near $+1$; the relationship is direct. (b) $a = 1$, $b = \frac{1}{5}$, (c) $y = 1 + \frac{1}{5}x$; (d) 3, 7, 21.

2. Consider the relationship between the variables y (weight in pounds) and x (weight in kilograms). (a) Is this relationship linear? Why? (b) Find

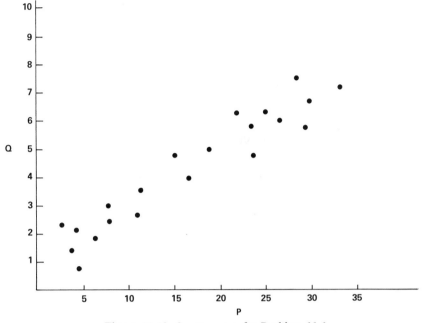

Figure 11.10. *Scattergram for Problem 11.1.*

the equation of the regression line. (*c*) What do you think the correlation coefficient *r* would be between *x* and *y* for a set of sample data?

Answer

  (*a*) Yes; (*b*) $y = 2.2x$; (*c*) $r = +1$.

3. Consider the relationship between the *utility* of scientific literature to scientists (*y*) and the *age* of the literature as measured by time elapsed since publication (*x*). (*a*) Sketch a graph of what you think this relationship might be. (*b*) Explain why the relationship is not linear. (*c*) Explain what the graph might look like for literature in the humanities.

Answer

  (*a*) The general shape of the graph looks much like Figure 11.5b. The relationship is described by a negative exponential distribution. (For a full discussion of this operations research model, see Brookes, "The Growth, Utility, and Obsolescence of Scientific Periodical Literature," 1970.[5])

4. Identify an empirical relationship between two variables and try to decide whether or not it is likely to be a linear relationship. Sketch a graph that reflects your hypothesis.

5. What can you say about a linear relationship in which (*a*) the regression line is perfectly horizontal; (*b*) the regression line rises from left to right; (*c*) the regression line is perfectly vertical; and (*d*) the regression line falls from left to right?

Answer

(*a*) No relationship; $r = 0$; (*b*) direct relationship; $0 < r < +1$; (*c*) no relationship; r is not defined; and (*d*) inverse relationship; $-1 < r < 0$.

6. Consider the regression equations given in (*a*)–(*c*). For each, sketch a graph of the relationship and compute a predicted value $\hat{y}$ when x equals 0; 12; 20. (*a*) $y = 7 + .7x$; (*b*) $y = 4x - 4$; and (*c*) $y = 122 - 4.5x$.

Answer

(*a*) 7; 15.4; 21; (*b*) -4; 44; 76; and (*c*) 122; 68; 32.

7. What is the slope of a line for which (*a*) y decreases two units for every increase in x by three units; (*b*) y increases by $\frac{1}{2}$ unit whenever x increases by two units; and (*c*) for every change in x, y changes identically?

Answer

(*a*) $b = -\frac{2}{3}$; (*b*) $b = +\frac{1}{4}$; and (*c*) $b = +1$.

8. Write an equation for a simple linear relationship between x and y. Then: (*a*) Find four points that lie on the line; (*b*) calculate s_x, s_y, and s_{xy}; (*c*) compute r; and (*d*) compute a and b.

Answer

(*c*) $r = +1$ or $r = -1$.

9. Define a research situation in librarianship which you hypothesize could be attacked by regression analysis. Try to state explicitly how you might collect and analyze data to test your hypothesis.

10. Define a research situation in librarianship which you hypothesize would require multiple regression for its complete analysis. Explain your reasoning.

11. The following data represent number of materials borrowed from the library by each member of a class of 12 elementary school students from Shaw School during a 1-week period. Variable *A* provides the age of each student, whereas variable *N* gives the number of materials checked out of the library.

(*a*) Plot the data points on a scattergram. Does there appear to be a correlation between *A* and *N*? Characterize the strength of the evident relationship.

(*b*) Calculate σ_A, σ_N, and σ_{AN}.

(*c*) Find the equation of the regression line of *N* on *A*.

(*d*) Calculate the correlation coefficient *r*.

(*e*) Based on the data provided, evaluate the null hypothesis: "There is no relationship between library use and age of students in Shaw School."

A	N
6	0
11	3
7	2
8	4
8	6
10	11
11	10
10	8
6	0
6	0
7	3
8	10

Answer

(*a*) Except for one aberrant point, there appears to be a fairly strong positive correlation between *A* and *N* in the data provided. (*b*) $\sigma_A = 1.74$ years; $\sigma_N = 3.96$ books; $\sigma_{AN} = 4.81$. (*c*) $N = 1.59A - 8.37$. (*d*) $r = +.70$. (*e*) Tentatively reject the null hypothesis.

12. The following data represent actual reference and circulation data from 34 urban and suburban public libraries for 1973.*

---

* Source: *The Bowker Annual of Library and Book Trade Information*, 20th Edition. New York: R. R. Bowker, 1975, pp. 223–224. Three libraries with reference figures exceeding 3 million have been omitted from the table. See also "Circulation, Reference, and the Evaluation of Public Library Service," by Stephen P. Harter and Mary Alice S. Fields. *RQ* 18 (Winter, 1978): 147–152.

(a) Plot the data points on a scattergram. Does there appear to be a correlation between reference and circulation statistics?

(b) Calculate σ_C, σ_R, and σ_{CR}.

(c) Find the equation of the regression line of R on C.

(d) Calculate r. Does the result support your answer to (a)?

Circulation (in millions)	Reference (in millions)	Circulation (in millions)	Reference (in millions)
1.7	.1	4.4	.8
3.9	.6	2.4	.3
2.9	1.2	3.6	.8
2.8	.3	5.5	1.9
2.1	.1	3.7	1.3
2.7	1.2	2.8	.3
1.7	.2	3.4	.5
1.5	.2	2.3	.6
1.4	.4	4.5	.6
1.5	.1	3.4	.4
1.9	.3	3.7	1.3
1.6	.4	5.3	.7
1.6	.1	2.2	.8
1.9	.2	2.6	.1
1.3	.1	3.7	.5
9.1	1.9	4.3	1.0
5.4	.7	5.2	.6

Answers

(b) $\sigma_C = 1.62$; $\sigma_R = 0.48$; (c) $R = .22C - .08$; and (d) $r = +.73$.

13. Find the reduction in the total squared error $S^2 = (\hat{y} - y)^2$ if (a) $r = 0$; (b) $r = .3$; (c) $r = .6$; (d) $r = 1.0$; and (e) $r = -.6$.

Answers

(a) 0%; (b) 9%; (c) 36%; (d) 100%; and (e) 36%.

REFERENCES

1. Ferdinand F. Leimkuhler, "A Literature Search and File Organization Model," *American Documentation, 19*(April 1968):131–136.
2. Gerard Salton, "System Testing," in Gerard Salton, *Dynamic Information and Library Processing.* Englewood Cliffs, N.J.: Prentice-Hall, 1975.
3. Derek J. deSolla Price, *Little Science, Big Science.* New York: Columbia University Press, 1963, pp. 20–32.

4. R. L. Anderson and Bancroft, T. A., "Curvilinear Regression: Orthogonal Polynomials," in R. L. Anderson and T. A. Bancroft, *Statistical Theory in Research*. New York: McGraw-Hill, 1952.

5. B. C. Brookes, "The Growth, Utility, and Obsolescence of Scientific Periodical Literature," *Journal of Documentation, 26*(December 1970):283–294.

6. School Mathematics Project, *Further Mathematics: V. Statistics and Probability*. London and New York: Cambridge University Press, 1971, pp. 92–93.

7. George W. Snedecor and Cochran, William G., *Statistical Methods*. Ames: Iowa State University Press, 1967, pp. 381–418.

8. R. L. Anderson and Bancroft, T. A., *Statistical Theory in Research*. New York: McGraw-Hill, 1952.

9. Lawrence L. Lapin, *Statistics for Modern Business Decisions*. New York: Harcourt Brace Jovanovich, 1973.

10. Stephen P. Harter, *A Prototype Model of a Network of Copying Machines,* (unpublished paper, 1972).

11. Stephen P. Harter, "A Probabilistic Approach to Automatic Keyword Indexing. Part I. On the Distribution of Specialty Words in a Technical Literature," *Journal of the American Society for Information Science, 26*(July–August 1975):197–206.

12. Philip Morse, *Library Effectiveness: A Systems Approach*. Cambridge, Mass.: M.I.T. Press, 1969.

13. Morse, *Library Effectiveness,* p. 93.

14. George W. Snedecor and Cochran, William G., *Statistical Methods*. Ames: Iowa State University Press, 1967, pp. 193–195.

CHAPTER 12

Statistical Significance and Hypothesis Testing

INTRODUCTION

STATISTICAL HYPOTHESES

The concepts of hypothesis testing have been alluded to previously, in Chapter 2. We return to these concepts in the present chapter, with an explicit examination of several simple types of tests. Before turning to these tests, however, we should briefly review several important ideas. A *statistical hypothesis* is essentially a mathematical (statistical, or probabilistic) model of a real-world problem. Examples of statistical hypotheses are: "Men and women are equally likely to be administrators in Warren County schools"; "This coin is fair, that is, when tossed, is equally likely to come up heads as tails"; and "Drugs A and B are equally effective in the treatment of the common cold."

If an hypothesis states that there is no difference between two or more classes with respect to some characteristic, then the hypothesis is termed a *null hypothesis*. Often, an investigator believes that a real difference does in fact exist between two classes. Stating such an hypothesis as a null hypothesis, the investigator then hopes that collected data will permit the rejection of the null hypothesis. A statistical test of a null hypothesis consists essentially of a calculation of the likelihood, or *probability,* that a set of observed data could have resulted (by chance) from a "no difference" relationship between two classes.

CONCEPTS OF PROBABILITY

Because the scope of this text does not permit the discussion of probability theory at length, suffice it to state that the following are properties of probabilities:

1. A probability p is a number between 0 and 1 which is associated with the occurrence of an *event*.

297

2. To assign an event the probability 1 means that the event is *certain* to occur.
3. To assign an event the probability 0 means that the event is certain not to occur.
4. If a probability *p* is associated with an event where $0 \leq p \leq 1$, and if a large number of cases are examined, then the *proportion* of time the event in question occurs will approach the number *p*. Thus, for example, if a six-sided die is tossed many times, the proportion of "threes" obtained will approach the probability *p* of tossing a 3. Intuitively, $p = \frac{1}{6}$ for a fair die. On the average, then, one out of six rolls of the die should turn up a 3.

Property (4) is a *relative frequency* approach to a definition of probability. Other definitions are possible, but we shall not make them here. For our purposes, it is sufficient to have an intuitive comprehension of the meaning of probability in the long-range sense provided by property (4).

HYPOTHESIS TESTING

Consider an experiment in which a coin has been tossed five times resulting in five heads and no tails. There is clearly some evidence that the coin might be biased, yet it is just as clear that the observed result might well be due entirely to chance. A statistical test of the null hypothesis, "the coin is fair" (i.e., the probability of tossing a head on any given trial is one out of two) would assess the probability that the observed result could have been obtained by chance, given that the coin is fair. That is, such a test would provide a numerical answer to the question, "Just how unlikely is it to toss a coin five times and obtain the observed distribution of heads and tails?" In terms of property (4) above, the probability *p* associated with this event in a fair coin can be approximated by conducting the experiment (tossing a fair coin five times) many times and observing the proportion of times the event (five heads, no tails) occurs. Indeed, the probability *p* in question could be calculated, approximately (though not very efficiently) in this way.

Having computed the probability associated with the occurrence of the event in question, the investigator is then in a position to judge the statistical *significance* of the fact that the observed event did in fact occur. His assessment clearly concerns the *size* of the probability in question. If the probability associated with the event is relatively large, then the occurrence of the event is evidently not significant; if the probability of the event is very near zero, then the fact that it happened is relatively rare, or unusual—that is, worth noting. Such an event may, therefore, be judged significant. The point at which a probability is judged to be significant is set by the individual investigator. A level of significance of .05 is not uncommon in social science research.*

Let us be more specific concerning the steps involved in hypothesis testing. The basic approach we will follow is:

1. A probability α (e.g., .01, or .05) is selected by the investigator. This number is the *level of significance* of the test.
2. The probability p of obtaining the observed data, *assuming that the null hypothesis is true,* is calculated.
3. If the computed probability p exceeds the chosen level of significance α, then, evidently the data are not significant and the null hypothesis cannot be rejected. On the other hand, if p is smaller than α, then the data evidently are significant and the null hypothesis can be rejected.

Note that we have not yet explained how to calculate the probabilities associated with a particular event. This detail will be different for each of the statistical tests of significance discussed; thus, it will be explained individually for each test. Before turning to a discussion of these tests, we should briefly discuss the concept of *error* in statistical hypothesis testing.

TYPE I AND TYPE II ERRORS

Let us assume that an investigator has stated an hypothesis and proceeds to test the statistical significance of some empirical data. What are the possible results of such a test? There are four possibilities, summarized in the chart below.

True state of nature	Hypothesis is false	Hypothesis is true
Action of investigator		
Reject hypothesis	C	E
Cannot reject hypothesis	E	C

* The reader will note that the concept of "level of significance" in hypothesis testing is closely related to the concept of "degree of confidence" in the construction of confidence intervals (see Chapter 9). A 95% confidence interval on the mean of a population, constructed on the basis of a random sample, will contain the population mean in 95 out of 100 samples. The probability that a confidence interval constructed from a particular sample *does not contain* the population mean is just .05.

The investigator may act correctly or act in error, each in two ways. He may fail to reject a false hypothesis or reject a true hypothesis, and thus err. Or, he may correctly reject a false hypothesis, or fail to reject a true hypothesis. Because all statistical hypothesis testing is probabilistic in nature, the investigator can never be certain that his or her action (accept or reject) was correct. There will always be a chance that an error was made.

We have already discussed one type of error, the act of rejecting a true hypothesis. The probability of this happening is just the probability that the observed result could have occurred by chance, given the truth of the null hypothesis. This is the level of significance discussed earlier and its size is under control (i.e., can be set) by the investigator. The probability of falsely rejecting a true hypothesis is sometimes referred to as a Type I error or an α-error. At the .05 level of significance, a Type I error will occur five out of every 100 experiments.

The second type of error, a Type II error, or β-error, is often more difficult to assess. A Type II error takes place when an hypothesis is not rejected when it should have been. The problem in assessing the probability of Type II error is that if the hypothesis is false, there are usually many alternatives that could be true.

Generally, by decreasing the probability of a Type I error (for example, by decreasing α from .05 to .01) the probability of a Type II error is increased. Only by increasing the sample size can both types of error be reduced. The investigator's decision as to which type of error he or she would prefer to make depends on the nature of the problem under investigation. If dire consequences are associated with rejecting a true hypothesis, then α should be relatively very low. For example, suppose a new chemical additive is being tested for its effect on the human nervous system. It could be disasterous to reject the hypothesis, "This additive has a dangerous side effect," when it is in fact true. On the other hand, it may do not particular harm, comparatively speaking, to accept this hypothesis when it is false. In this case, then, the probability of falsely rejecting the hypothesis should be made as small as possible, and the level of significance selected should be very small, perhaps as small as .001 or even smaller.

We turn now to a study of a particularly useful test of hypotheses, the chi-square test.

THE CHI-SQUARE TEST

In much of our previous statistical work, we have dealt with sample statistics as estimates of population parameters. Tests of hypotheses arising from such problems are termed *parametric* tests. In this section we examine an important *nonparametric* test, the chi-square test. The chi-square test is normally applicable in situations in which determination of population parameters such as the mean and standard deviation is not an issue. Rather, the data in question fall naturally into discrete categories and are summarized in what is called a *contingency table*. Individual entries in the table are called *cells*.

Consider the hypothetical example of data displayed in a contingency table in Table 12.1. Political preferences for a population of 110 men and 200 women are displayed in Table 12.1. A careful study of the table will reveal that there appears to be somewhat of a sex difference indicated in political preference. To see this, observe that there are approximately twice as many women in all as men (200 to 110). Thus, *assuming no sex difference in political preference,* there should be roughly twice as many female Republicans as male Republicans; twice as many female Democrats as male Democrats; twice as many female Independents as male Independents; and twice as many females in the category "Other" as there are males in the same category.

The reader will note that this is not quite the case in the observed data. In actual fact, there are not nearly twice as many female Democrats or female Republicans as the number of males in these categories. On the other hand, the number of women Independents and "Other" appears to exceed what we would normally expect if political preference is independent of sex. Thus, the data appear to suggest that women in this particular population are somewhat more "independently minded" than are men.

Let us look more closely at the argument developed in the preceding paragraph and attempt to refine it. The proportion of women in the population is exactly 200/310, or 64.5%. If political preference is, in fact, independent of sex in this population, we would expect approximately 64.5% of all Democrats to be women, 64.5% of all Republicans to be women, and so on. More specifically, of the 156 Democrats, we would expect

Table 12.1. *Political Preferences of 310 Persons*

Political preference	Men	Women	Total
Democrat	62	94	156
Republican	35	42	77
Independent	7	33	40
Other	6	31	37
	110	200	310

(.645)(156) = 100.6 persons to be women and the remainder (55.4) to be men. Of the 37 "Other," we would expect approximately 23.9 to be women and 13.1 to be men. In a similar fashion, *expected values* for all cells in a contingency table can be computed, based on the assumption that sex has no effect on political preference, the null hypothesis.

The observed data displayed in Table 12.1 have been combined in Table 12.2 with the computed expected values (in parentheses) for each cell, based on the hypothesis that sex has no effect on political preference. Readers should verify the values of some of these figures to test their understanding. The extent to which the observed data deviate from expected frequencies, given the hypothesis that sex has no effect on political preference, is made explicit by Table 12.2. But we still do not know whether the differences between observed and expected categories are *significant,* or whether, in fact, they can be attributed to chance, random fluctuations.

It is obvious that the observed cell frequencies differ somewhat from the expected frequencies. But are the differences significant? Can we formally reject the null hypothesis that "sex has no effect on political preference" and conclude that women in our population tend to be more independently minded than men? The means by which these questions can be answered are provided by the chi-square test.

To conduct the chi-square test on contingency table data, the statistic

$$\chi^2 = \Sigma \frac{(O - E)^2}{E}$$

is computed, where E and O refer to expected and observed frequencies, respectively, and the summation is made over all the cells of the table. Clearly, the number χ^2 (chi-square) is a measure of the closeness of the expected and observed frequencies. The larger the value of χ^2, the greater the difference between the two categories; a perfect match between ob-

Table 12.2. *Observed and Expected Values for Political Preference*

Political Preference	Men		Women		Total
	Observed	Expected	Observed	Expected	
Democratic	62	(55.4)	94	(100.6)	156
Republican	35	(27.3)	42	(49.7)	77
Independent	7	(14.2)	33	(25.8)	40
Other	6	(13.1)	31	(23.9)	37
	110		200		310

served and expected values for all cells would result in a value of χ^2 equal to zero. Next, the number of *degrees of freedom* (*df*) in the contingency table in question must be computed. The *sum* of each row and each column should be equal for expected and observed frequencies. This places a linear constraint on the data. Thus, all but one cell in each row and column may vary freely, and the total number of degrees of freedom is $df = (R - 1)(C - 1)$, where R and C are the number of rows and columns in the tables, respectively.

When the value of χ^2 has been computed and the number of degrees of freedom has been determined, the *statistical significance* of the result is obtained from Appendix E. Using Appendix E, one can infer the likelihood that the observed deviation χ^2 could have resulted purely by chance, for the given number of degrees of freedom. The numbers p in the table provide the probability that a value of χ^2 would be obtained *by chance,* as large or larger than the values listed in the table. For example, for $df = 1$, an obtained value of χ^2 greater than 3.84 would occur with probability less than .05. Also for $df = 1$, a value of χ^2 greater than 6.63 is associated with a chance probability which is less than .01.

Example 1

Test the data in Table 12.1 for the null hypothesis that sex has no effect on political preference. Reject the hypothesis if $p \le .05$.

Answer

$$
\begin{aligned}
\chi^2 &= \frac{(62 - 55.4)^2}{55.4} + \frac{(35 - 27.3)^2}{27.3} + \frac{(7 - 14.2)^2}{14.2} \\
&+ \frac{(6 - 13.1)^2}{13.1} + \frac{(94 - 100.6)^2}{100.6} \\
&+ \frac{(42 - 49.7)^2}{49.7} + \frac{(33 - 25.8)^2}{25.8} \\
&+ \frac{(31 - 23.9)^2}{23.9} \\
&= .79 + 2.17 + 3.65 + 3.85 + .43 + 1.19 + 2.01 + 2.11 \\
&= 16.2 \\
df &= (4 - 1)(2 - 1) = 3.
\end{aligned}
$$

Consulting Appendix E, we see that at the .05 level at 3 *df* a value of χ^2 is significant if it is larger than 7.81. Because $16.2 \gg 7.81$, the result is highly significant. Thus, we can reject the null hypothesis and conclude that sex evidently does have a statistically significant effect on political preference.

Example 2

The following data summarize circulation data for a college library over a 1-week period. Test the hypothesis that no significant statistical difference exists between the fiction and nonfiction circulation patterns of undergraduate and graduate students using this library.

	Pieces of fiction circulated	Pieces of nonfiction circulated	Total
Undergraduate	370	830	1200
Graduate	180	520	700
	550	1350	1900

Answer

Because undergraduates constitute 1200/1900 = 63.2% of the circulation totals, we would expect 63.2% of the 550 fiction books to be associated with undergraduates (347.6). The remaining expected values are provided in the chart following.

	Fiction circulated		Nonfiction circulated		
	Observed	Expected[a]	Observed	Expected[a]	Total
Undergraduate	370	(347.6)	830	(853.2)	1200
Graduate	180	(202.4)	520	(496.8)	700
	550		1350		1900

[a] The expected values do not sum exactly to 1200 and 700 because of round-off errors.

Thus,

$$\chi^2 = \frac{(370 - 347.6)^2}{347.6} + \frac{(830 - 853.2)^2}{853.2} + \frac{(180 - 202.4)^2}{202.4}$$
$$+ \frac{(520 - 496.8)^2}{496.8} = 1.44 + .63 + 2.48 + 1.08 = 5.63.$$

The number of degrees of freedom is $(2 - 1)(2 - 1) = 1$. Consulting Appendix E, we can see that our result is significant at the .05 level but not at the .01 level. Depending upon the level of significance that had been selected by the investigator, the result may lead either to the rejection of

Table 12.3. *Holding of Library Cards, by Sex, in Two Communities*

	Community A				Community B		
	Men	Women	Total		Men	Women	Total
Card holders	80	100	180	Card holders	800	1,000	1,800
No card	920	900	1820	No card	9,200	9,000	18,200
	1000	1000	2000		10,000	10,000	20,000

the null hypothesis or to a failure to reject it. At the commonly selected level of .05, the null hypothesis would be rejected.

EFFECT OF SAMPLE SIZE

When the *numbers* of items falling into the cells of a contingency table are not known, the chi-square test cannot be used, even if the proportions involved are known. This is illustrated by Table 12.3 in which data are provided that represent the number of men and women holding public library cards in two hypothetical communities.

A careful examination of Table 12.3 will reveal that the proportions characterizing the two communities are identical. Specifically, exactly 8% of the men and 10% of the women in both communities hold library cards. However, a chi-square test to determine whether the differences are significant reveals an interesting fact. The data descriptive of Community A are not statistically significant (even at the .10 level), whereas the data descriptive of Community B are highly significant. Thus, the null hypothesis that no sex difference exists with respect to the holding of library cards is rejected in the second case but cannot be rejected in the first. Readers should verify these assertions by making their own calculations.

The previous example illustrates that sample size is important in the chi-square test. Thus, occasionally a truly significant difference cannot be demonstrated by the test because the sample size is too small. Conversely, a trivial difference (but a true difference) might result in a rejection of the null hypothesis of no difference because of a very large sample size.

YATES' CORRECTION FOR CONTINUITY

The chi-square test is based on the normal approximation to the Poisson and binomial probability distributions. Because the former distribution is continuous and the latter two (frequency) distributions are discrete, a slight bias results. This may be corrected by using the so-called *Yates'* *correction for continuity.* Using this correction rule, the value of χ^2 should be calculated by the formula*

$$\chi^2 = \Sigma \frac{(|O - E| - \frac{1}{2})^2}{E}$$

It is usually not worthwhile to use the Yates' correction for continuity except in 2 × 2 tables in which the expected cell frequencies are less than 5.0 for any one cell. [1,2]

SUMMARY OF PROPERTIES OF THE CHI-SQUARE TEST

1. Entries in cells are frequencies, not proportions, resulting from a random sample.
2. The sum of expected frequencies should equal the sum of the observed frequencies for each column and each row.
3. The number of degrees of freedom in an $R \times C$ contingency table is $(R - 1)(C - 1)$.
4. Yates' correction for continuity should be used if cell values are small, especially in 2 × 2 contingency tables.
5. A value of χ^2 reveals a significant difference at level p (e.g., $p = .05$) if χ^2 exceeds the tabular value for $(R - 1)(C - 1)$ *df,* at the stated probability p. If this occurs, the null hypothesis can be rejected at the level of p.

TESTING "GOODNESS OF FIT"

The chi-square test can be usefully employed to test an hypothesis regarding the fit of a theoretical frequency distribution such as the normal distribution or the Poisson distribution to empirical data. Such a test should be employed as part of an investigation involving an operations research model, for example (see Chapter 5). In such a test, the "goodness," or closeness, of the fit of the theoretical distribution to empirical data is tested. The test is conducted in much the same way as the chi-square test is used to conduct a test on the independence of contingency table data, namely, by calculating expected frequencies and computing the value of $\chi^2 = \Sigma(O - E)^2/E$. In general, the number of degrees of freedom in this test is $(N - 1)$, where N is the number of frequency classes, with one additional degree of freedom subtracted for each parameter es-

---

* $|O - E|$ is read "the absolute value of the difference between O and E" and simply means the difference between these values *with the signs ignored.*

timated from the data. That is, if two parameters are estimated from the data, then $(N - 3)$ is the number of degrees of freedom. An example should clarify the procedure.

Example 3

The queuing model discussed in Chapter 5 is predicated upon the assumption that arrivals to the queuing system occur at random; more precisely, that the empirical data are described by a Poisson distribution. The following data were gathered by counting the number of arrivals to a circulation desk in each of sixty 1-minute intervals. Thus, there were four 1-minute intervals in which no one appeared, there were twelve intervals in which exactly one person appeared, and so on. Test the hypothesis that the data are described by a Poisson distribution.

k	f (number of intervals in which k arrivals occurred)
0	4
1	12
2	12
3	14
4	6
5	6
6	4
7	1
8	0
9	1

Answer

We compute the mean of the distribution to be $172/60 = 2.9$, rounded to the nearest tenth. The theoretical formula for a Poisson distribution is $P(k) = (e^{-\lambda}\lambda^k)/k!$, where λ is the mean of the distribution (see Chapter 5). Thus, *if* our empirical data are indeed described by the Poisson distribution, the formula for that distribution is $P(k) = [e^{-2.9}(2.9)^k]/k!$. This formula is used to compute *expected* values $E(k)$, assuming that the distribution is in fact Poisson. Referring to Table 5.2, $e^{-2.9} = .055$. Then

$$P(0) = [(.055)(1)]/1 = .055.$$

This is the *probability* that a given 1-minute interval will contain exactly zero arrivals, assuming Poisson arrivals with a mean number of 2.9 arrivals per minute. Therefore, in 60 such intervals, we would expect

$$E(0) = 60P(0)$$
$$= 60(.055) = 3.3 \text{ intervals to contain exactly zero arrivals.}$$

Similarly, $P(1) = [(.055)(2.9)]/1 = .160$ and $E(1) = 60(.16) = 9.6$. In a similar fashion, the remaining expected values can be calculated, and the following chart obtained.

k	Observed $O(k)$	Expected $E(k)$
0	4	3.3
1	12	9.6
2	12	13.9
3	14	13.4
4	6	9.7
5	6	5.6
6	4	2.7
7	1	1.1
8	0	.4
9	1	.1
10 or more	0	.2

To conduct the test, frequency classes are grouped in such a way that no frequency class has an expected value smaller than 5.0. The following chart is obtained by this process.

k	$O(k)$	$E(k)$
0 or 1	16	12.9
2	12	13.9
3	14	13.4
4	6	9.7
5 or more	12	10.1

There are five frequency classes in the coalesced table, and one parameter (the mean, 2.9) was estimated from the empirical data. Thus, the chi-square test is conducted on $(5 - 1) - 1 = 3 \, df$.

The value of χ^2 is

$$\frac{(16 - 12.9)^2}{12.9} + \frac{(12 - 13.9)^2}{13.9} + \frac{(14 - 13.4)^2}{13.4}$$
$$+ \frac{(6 - 9.7)^2}{9.7} + \frac{(12 - 10.1)^2}{10.1}$$
$$= .74 + .26 + .03 + 1.41 + .36$$
$$= 2.8.$$

Consulting Appendix E on $3df$, we see that the hypothesis that the data are described by a Poisson distribution function cannot be rejected. Thus, our test supports the hypothesis that the data can be described by a Poisson distribution.

THE SIGN TEST

Another useful, nonparametric, statistical method that is simple to conduct is the *sign test*. The sign test is appropriate to use whenever data are *binary*, that is, can be classed as belonging to one of only two categories (labeled for convenience as 1 or 0; + or −, etc.).

The archtypical example of the use of the sign test is an experimental situation in which the members of a group have been subjected to a type of treatment and a record is maintained of whether each member improves (+) or fails to improve (−) as a result of the treatment. The *extent of change* is not measured (or, if known, is not utilized) in the sign test; only the fact of improvement or unimprovement is utilized.

Example 4

Suppose that "In a recent test, 8 out of 10 bartenders tested preferred Smaltz beer over brand X." Is the preference statistically significant?

Answer

The data can be represented symbolically as shown in the chart that follows.

	Beer preference	
Bartender	Smaltz beer	Brand X
1	x	
2	x	
3	x	
4	x	
5	x	
6	x	
7		x
8		x
9	x	
10	x	

Note that the problem is conceptually equivalent to tossing a coin 10 times and observing 8 heads and asking, "Is this a fair coin," or more accurately, "Is there sufficient evidence to condemn this coin as biased?" We are interested in learning whether or not there is a statistically significant difference between preferences for Smaltz beer among bartenders or whether the observed difference could reasonably be attributed to chance. In terms of coin tossing, we are interested in the probability of tossing 8 out of 10 heads, or better, *given that the coin is fair.* In other words, we wish to determine whether there is a statistically significant difference between the number of heads and tails obtained in the tossing.

The mathematics of coin tossing is described by the binomial distribution, which permits one to compute such probabilities exactly. Many excellent texts treat the binomial distribution; one of the best is Feller's classic text on probability theory.[4] This subject cannot be treated here Because the normal distribution provides a good approximation to the binomial distribution, however, and because the chi-square test is based upon the normal distribution,[*] we are able to discuss how the calculation of binomial probabilities can be approximated using the chi-square test. Refer also to Problem 3 at the end of the chapter, in which the test of Jack's accident proneness can be expressed in terms of coin tossing as "What is the probability of tossing seven or more heads (or seven or more tails) out of nine tosses?"

To conduct the sign test on the data of Example 4 using the chi-square approximation, we observe that the expected number of heads resulting from ten tosses of a fair coin in 5; thus, χ^2 can be computed as

$$\chi^2 = \frac{(|8 - 5| - .5)^2}{5} + \frac{(|2 - 5| - .5)^2}{5} = 2.5.$$

Because the probability of obtaining a value of χ^2 equal to 2.71 or greater is .10, we cannot reject the chance hypothesis even at the .10 level. The reported experiment did not obtain statistically significant results.

Example 5

An expert in curriculum development devised a module of instruction to be presented on video tape, and decided to conduct a small test so that the model could be compared with a traditional print module covering the same material. The test was designed to determine student preferences. (Note that this is not the same as testing the *effectiveness* of the module.) Sixteen students were selected at random, and were given both modules.

---

[*] See, for example, *Further Mathematics,* vol. 5, 1971, for an elementary discussion of this relationship. The normal distribution can also be used to perform the sign test.

Eight students took the video tape module first, followed by the print module; the remaining students were treated in the reverse order. Students were then polled as to their preference. The results were: 12 of the 16 students chose the print module. At the .05 level of significance, can an hypothesis of equal preference be rejected?

Answer

$$\chi^2 = \frac{(|12 - 8| - .5)^2}{8} + \frac{(|4 - 8| - .5)^2}{8}$$
$$= 3.06.$$

The hypothesis cannot be rejected. There is no statistically significant difference between the choice of one instructional module over the other in this example.

SOME PARAMETRIC TESTS

We turn now to an examination of a few simple tests of hypothesis which involve sample and population *parameters,* the mean and standard deviation. First, consider a research situation in which an investigator desires to test the statistical significance of a sample mean, when the population parameters are known.

TESTING THE SIGNIFICANCE OF A SAMPLE MEAN

Consider a situation in which both the mean score for a test and standard deviation of a population are known; that is, neither parameter needs to be estimated from sample data. Further suppose that the mean of a sample is known and that it is desired to test the null hypothesis that the sample has been drawn from the population. Does the sample mean differ enough from the population mean to be judged statistically significant?

We already possess the knowledge to conduct such a test, using properties of the sampling distribution of the mean (see Chapter 10).

Example 6

Each section of the Graduate Record Examination (GRE) is a standardized test in which the mean score earned by members of the total population of persons taking the test is 500 and the standard deviation is 100. Suppose that 121 applicants for a graduate program of studies in a given year earned a mean score of 540 on the mathematics portion of the GRE.

Test the null hypothesis that the 121 students constitute a random sample from the population.

Answer

We have previously discussed the important Central Limit Theorem. (The reader may wish to review these pages before proceeding.) This fundamental result states that whatever the distribution of a population with mean μ and standard deviation σ, the statistic $z = (\bar{x} - \mu)/(\sigma/\sqrt{n})$ is distributed approximately normally with mean equal to 0 and standard deviation equal to 1. The denominator of the expression is the standard deviation of the sampling distribution and is called the standard error of the mean. Thus, the statistical significance of a result such as that given in Example 6 can be evaluated using Appendix C. We have $z = (540 - 500)/(100/\sqrt{121} = 4.4$. Hence, our sample mean is more than four standard deviations from the population mean. Consulting Appendix C, we conclude that the null hypothesis can be rejected.*

Now let us consider a situation in which the population parameters are not known.

TESTING THE SIGNIFICANCE OF A DIFFERENCE BETWEEN THE MEANS OF PAIRED SAMPLES

One approach to comparing the speed of the OCLC system in retrieving catalog records, as opposed to manual systems, is to apply the sign test (see Problem 9). Suppose that, instead of recording whether the OCLC system is faster or slower than the manual system, the actual times involved are recorded. The data would then consist of 14 pairs of numbers, such as those recorded in Table 12.4. The rightmost column of Table 12.4 records the difference (d) between the two systems, where d is the time taken for the manual search minus the time required for the OCLC search.

As is the case in Problem 9, we wish to test the null hypothesis that there is no difference in the retrieval time required to use the OCLC system and manual systems. Because we make use of the actual times involved, however, our test here will be much more sensitive than the sign test used to solve Problem 9. We compute the mean difference $\bar{d}$ between the OCLC performance and manual system performance as $\bar{d} = 22.4/14 = 1.6$. Thus, there is a difference between the methods. But is the difference statistically significant? To test the null hypothesis that there is no difference between usage times for the two methods, we assume that the devia-

---

* This procedure is exactly equivalent to constructing a confidence interval about the mean μ and observing whether or not the sample mean falls within the interval. If it falls outside the interval, we can conclude that it is unlikely the sample was drawn from the population.

Table 12.4. *Required Time in Minutes to Retrieve Cataloging Information*

Item number	OCLC	Manual systems	d
1	.6	2.1	1.5
2	1.2	1.3	.1
3	.8	7.2	6.4
4	2.8	1.3	-1.5
5	1.3	4.0	2.7
6	1.2	5.1	3.9
7	4.8	3.4	-1.4
8	1.4	3.2	1.8
9	1.7	2.8	1.1
10	2.1	4.3	2.2
11	2.4	3.3	0.9
12	1.0	2.4	1.4
13	.6	2.1	1.5
14	.3	2.1	1.8

tions d_i are normally and independently distributed with mean equal to zero. In general, we can then estimate the standard deviation of the population of difference (σ_d) by calculating

$$s_d = \left[\frac{\Sigma(d - \bar{d})^2}{n - 1} \right]^{1/2}.$$

In our example, $s_d = \sqrt{4.047} = 2.01$. The standard error of the mean difference, SE_d, is therefore $SE_d = s_d/\sqrt{n} = 2.01/\sqrt{14} = .537$.

We are now able to test the null hypothesis that no difference exists between the two methods; that is, the true mean difference μ_d is equal to zero. Because σ_d was estimated from the data, the *t-test** will be applied, with $n - 1$ df. In our example

$$t = (\bar{d} - \mu_d)/SE_d = (1.6 - 0)/.537 = 2.98.$$

To test the null hypothesis, compare the value of t obtained to the tabular values listed in Appendix D. If the value of t exceeds the tabular value for the predetermined probability p, the null hypothesis can be rejected. Consulting Appendix D, we see that on 13 df the computed value of t is significant at a probability (α-value) between .05 and .01. Thus, at the .05 level of significance, we can safely reject the hypothesis that the two methods are equivalent.

---

* The reader may wish to review Chapter 10, in which the *t*-distribution is introduced.

Test of Significance of the Correlation Coefficient

The significance of a computed correlation coefficient may be computed using the t-test. To conduct a test on the null hypothesis that the true population correlation coefficient is equal to zero, compute the statistic

$$t = r \left[\frac{n - 2}{1 - r^2} \right]^{1/2}.$$

The value of t can then be compared with the appropriate value in the t-table, on $(n - 2)df$.

Example 7

Suppose a correlation coefficient of $r = +.60$ is computed on the basis of (*a*) a sample of size 10 and (*b*) a sample of size 20. Test the null hypothesis that $\rho = 0$ in each of the two cases.

Answer

If $n = 10$, then

$$t = r \left[\frac{n - 2}{1 - r^2} \right]^{1/2}$$

$$= \frac{.60 \sqrt{8}}{(1 - .36)^{1/2}} = 2.12.$$

From Appendix D, the null hypothesis cannot be rejected at the .05 level on 8 *df*.

If $n = 20$, then $t = 3.18$. Consulting Appendix D on 18 *df*, we see that the null hypothesis can be rejected at the .01 level.

Our final example of statistical hypothesis testing also involves the comparison of the means of two samples.

Testing the Significance of a Difference between the Means of Two Independent Samples

Suppose now that we have two samples that are not paired (as in the previous test), indeed, are not even (necessarily) equal in size. As before, we wish to test the significance of the observed difference between the means of the two samples.

Example 8

The mean and the standard deviation of the salaries of the 121 female teachers and the 49 male teachers in Coolidge College are summarized in our chart.

Males' salaries	Females' salaries
$\bar{x}_m = \$11{,}200$	$\bar{x}_f = \$9800$
$s_m = \$1240$	$s_f = \$920$
$n_m = 49$	$n_f = 121$

Ignoring other factors, can a case be made for sex discrimination?

Answer

The null hypothesis is that the observed difference between salaries of male and female faculty members is not statistically significant, that is, it could well have arisen by chance alone. To test the hypothesis, we first compute $SE_{\mu_1-\mu_2}$, the standard error of the difference between the two means. We assume that the two samples are independent. It can be shown[6] that

$$SE_{\mu_1-\mu_2} = \sqrt{SE_{\mu_1}^2 + SE_{\mu_2}^2}$$

From previous work, we know that

$$SE_{\mu} = \sigma/\sqrt{n}, \quad \text{or} \quad SE_{\mu}^2 = \sigma^2/n.$$

Hence,

$$SE_{\mu_1-\mu_2} = \left[\frac{\sigma_1^2}{n_1} + \frac{\sigma_2^2}{n_2} \right]^{1/2},$$

where

$\sigma_1 = $ estimate of σ based on the first sample
$\sigma_2 = $ estimate of σ based on the second sample
$n_1 = $ number of items in the first sample
$n_2 = $ number of items in the second sample

Once the standard error of the difference $SE_{\mu_1-\mu_2}$ has been calculated, the remainder of the test is identical to the previous test, where we use $SE_{\mu_1-\mu_2}$ and $\bar{x}_1 - \bar{x}_2$ instead of SE_d and $\bar{d}$, respectively. Thus, we calculate the statistic

$$t = \frac{\bar{x}_1 - \bar{x}_2 - 0}{SE_{\mu_1-\mu_2}}$$

Because the two samples are assumed to be independent and two means have been estimated from the data, the number of degrees of freedom used in this test is $n_1 + n_2 - 2$.

Returning to our example of the salaries of teachers in Coolidge College, we calculate

$$SE_{m-w} = \left[\frac{(1240)^2}{49} + \frac{(920)^2}{121} \right]^{1/2} = \$195.89,$$

or slightly less than \$200. The observed difference between salaries of males and females is \$11,200 − \$9800 = \$1400. This is more than 7 *SE* above the mean. More exactly,

$$\begin{aligned} t &= \frac{\bar{m} - \bar{f} - 0}{SE_{m-f}} \\ &= \frac{11,200 - 9800}{195.89} \\ &= 7.15. \end{aligned}$$

On 168 *df,* this result is highly significant even at the .001 level.* Thus, we can reject the null hypothesis and conclude that (unless there are other undiscovered independent variables) there does, indeed, appear to be a sex bias with respect to the faculty salaries at Coolidge College.

ANALYSIS OF VARIANCE   *we can test the differences between several samples*

The two parametric tests that we examined provide a method for testing the significance of the difference between two sample means. Many research situations exist in which the differences between *several* samples, not merely two, must be tested. For example, suppose that scores on an achievement test are available for each student enrolled in five sections of a college mathematics class. Mean scores for the five sections were 59, 63, 81, 49, and 66. Now we can test the hypothesis that each of the sections can be viewed as a random sample from the same population; that the observed differences in the five sections can reasonably be attributed to chance (sampling error). The set of methods for conducting such a test is called *analysis of variance.* Except for this brief introduction, however, the topic is not discussed in this text. The student should consult another text for further discussion of analysis of variance.[7-9]

SUMMARY

A null *hypothesis* is essentially a statement of "no difference." A *statistical test* of a null hypothesis consists of stating a *level of significance* α, which is commonly .05 or .01 in social science research. Then for each

---

* Note that either Appendix C or Appendix D (on ∞ degrees of freedom) can be used to check this result. See Chapter 10 for a review of the relationship between the normal distribution and the *t*-distribution for a large number of degrees of freedom.

test, the *probability* is computed that the observed result could have occurred by chance, that is, assuming the null hypothesis. If the computed probability is less than the selected level of significance, then, evidently the observed difference is intolerably unlikely and the null hypothesis can safely be *rejected*.

A wide variety of additional tests of statistical hypotheses is available to the researcher. It is beyond the scope of this text to present a discussion of all such tests; a detailed treatment of this topic would require a complete volume in itself. Rather, we have attempted to introduce students to some of the basic principles of hypothesis testing. In their study of the principles presented, we hope that students have understood the essentials of some of the simpler tests.

APPENDIX: PROBLEMS FOR SOLUTION

1. Identify a research question in librarianship which can be tested using the chi-square test. State a positive hypothesis and restate it as a null hypothesis. Explain how data could be collected to test the hypothesis.

2. All professional employees of a college were classed by sex (male or female) and by position (administrative or faculty). The resulting data have been arranged in the 2 × 2 contingency table shown below. From these data, test the null hypothesis that there is no significant difference between the job levels of male and female employees at the college.

Classification of College Employees

	Male	Female
Faculty	28	82
Administrator	10	6

Answer

Males constitute $38/126 = 30\%$ of the population, whereas females constitute 70%. Thus, we expect 30%, or 33, of the 110 teachers to be male and 30%, or 4.8, of the 16 administrators to be male, and $\chi^2 = .76 + .32 + 5.63 + 2.41 = 9.12$. Consulting Appendix E on 1 *df*, we see that the distribution of college employees according to sex and job level would have occurred by chance with probability less than .01; therefore, the null hypothesis can be rejected.

3. By the time two children had reached age 10, they had experienced a total of nine serious accidents; Jack had experienced seven and Jill had experienced only two. At the .05 level of significance, was Jack accident-prone as compared with Jill? That is, is there a statistically significant difference at the .05 level of probability between the number of accident experiences by the two children?

Answer

The null hypothesis is that Jack and Jill are equally likely to experience a serious accident. Thus, out of a total of 9 accidents, we would expect each child to have experienced 4.5 accidents. Because expected frequencies are less than 5.0, we use the Yates' correction for continuity, for

$$\chi^2 = \frac{(|7 - 4.5| - .5)^2}{4.5} + \frac{(|2 - 4.5| - .5)^2}{4.5} = 1.78.$$

With 1 *df*, the obtained value for χ^2 is associated with a probability only slightly less than .20. Thus, we cannot reject the null hypothesis, and have no statistically significant evidence of Jack's accident-proneness.

4. Faculty members of a library school were polled as to their preference for a new name for their school. Specifically, each member was asked whether the name should include the word *media*. The faculty were also classed according to their primary areas of specialization, either "print" or "nonprint." The resulting data are given below. Test the hypothesis that preference for the word *media* in the name of the school was not affected by the faculty members' areas of specialization.

Faculty Members' Preferences for the Term "Media"

	Include *media* in name	Do not include *media* in name
Print specialization	0	7
Nonprint specialization	4	1

Answer

This is a contingency table in which expected frequencies are small; hence, again we use Yates' correction for continuity. We find that $\chi^2 = 5.18$. The null hypothesis can, therefore, be rejected.

5. A public library maintained statistics for 1 month (rounded to the nearest 10) on the circulation of four categories of fiction. The data were categorized according to two groups of borrowers, adult and young adult, and are summarized below. Test the null hypothesis that the relative popularity of the four fiction categories is the same for the two user groups.

Circulation of Types of Fiction among
Adults and Young Adults

	Young adult	Adult
Western	0	40
Gothic	100	500
Mystery	30	640
Science fiction	10	80

Answer

Circulations to young adult readers comprise exactly 10% of the total number of books borrowed. Expected circulations to young adults in the four fiction categories are, therefore, 4, 60, 67, and 9, respectively. Chi-square is computed to be in excess of 55, on 3 *df*. The hypothesis can thus be strongly rejected at the .01 confidence level because a statistically significant difference exists among the choice of types of fiction according to the two age groups.

6. The following data represent library use data collected by the Detroit Public Library as reported in *Newsletter on Library Research.*[3] Assuming that the data represent a random sample of adults, can one conclude that adult users of the Detroit Public Library are more likely to be one sex or the other?

	Users	Nonusers
Female	97	172
Male	86	120

Answer

Since $\chi^2 = 1.57$, the hypothesis of independence cannot be rejected. Use of the Detroit Public Library does not appear to be related to sex.

7. The following empirical data represent the number of arrivals occurring in forty 1-minute intervals to a bank of copying machines in an aca-

demic library. Test the goodness-of-fit of the Poisson distribution to the data.

k	Number of intervals with k arrivals
0	19
1	12
2	7
3	1
4	1

Answer

The mean of the distribution is .8, rounded to the nearest tenth. The Poisson distribution is a good fit to these data and, therefore, the hypothesis of Poisson arrivals cannot be rejected.

8. The following set of data summarizes the results of a test of the effectiveness of a new drug. Use the sign test to determine whether there is a significant difference between the rate of improvement among the 20 patients who were given the drug, at the .05 level.

Patient observation number	Improvement (+)/ No improvement (−)
1	+
2	−
3	+
4	+
5	+
6	−
7	+
8	−
9	+
10	+
11	+
12	−
13	+
14	+
15	+
16	+
17	+
18	−
19	−
20	+

Answer

Since $\chi^2 = 2.45$, the null hypothesis that the drug has no effect cannot be rejected.

9. A college library wishes to test the relative speed of the OCLC on-line cataloging system as compared with the use of the National Union Catalog and other manual tools in terms of retrieving cataloging information. (*Note:* There are other parameters of interest in addition to speed, notably cost.) A random sample of 20 titles was drawn and the time periods required for both methods were recorded. *For the 14 titles which were found by both methods,* the OCLC system proved to be faster in 12 cases. (*a*) Test the significance of the data at the .05 level. (*b*) Why should one be cautious in interpreting the results of (*a*)? (*c*) How might this experiment have been improved?

Answer

(*a*) $\chi^2 = 5.78$; at the .025 level there is a significant difference between the time periods required by the two methods used to obtain cataloging information.

10. A (possibly biased) coin has probability p of obtaining heads and probability $q = 1 - p$ of obtaining tails. It can be shown, for example, in Feller (p. 268)[4], that the mean number of heads (the expected number of heads to be obtained) in n tosses is np and the standard deviation is $\sqrt{npq}$. That is, the theoretical mean and standard deviation of the binomial distribution are np and $\sqrt{npq}$, respectively. Use these facts together with the fact that the normal distribution approximates the binomial to find a formula for computing the probability that r or more heads will be obtained from n tosses of a fair coin.

Answer

The normal deviate z is given by the formula $z = (x - \mu)/\sigma$. In our case $\mu = np$ and $\sigma = \sqrt{npq}$, where $p = q = \frac{1}{2}$. Also, because we are approximating the discrete binomial distribution with the continuous normal distribution, we must use the correction for continuity. Hence, the probability that r or more heads will be obtained is approximated by the area to the right of z in the standardized normal curve, where $z = (r - .5n - .5)/.5\sqrt{n}$.

11. Use the formula established in Problem 10 to compute the probability of obtaining 8 or more heads in 10 tosses of a fair coin.

Answer

$$z = (|8 - 5| - .5)/.5\sqrt{10} = 1.58.$$

From Appendix C, we obtain a probability of .0571.

12. Using the chi-square approximation, compute the approximate probability of obtaining (*a*) nine or more heads or tails in ten tosses of a fair coin; (*b*) ten heads or tails in ten tosses of a fair coin.

Answer

(*a*) $\chi^2 = 4.9$; the probability is, therefore, approximately .03; (*b*) $\chi^2 = 8.1$; the probability is, therefore, less than .005.

13. The exact binomial probability of tossing five heads in five tosses of a fair coin is $(\frac{1}{2})^5 = \frac{1}{32} = .03125$. The probability of obtaining five heads or tails is, therefore, $2(.03125) = .0625$. Solve this problem in two other ways, (*a*) using the normal approximation; (*b*) using the chi-square approximation.

Answer

(*a*) $z = 1.79$, hence, the approximate probability equals $.0367 + .0367$, or .0734; (*b*) $\chi^2 = 3.2$; the probability is, therefore, between .05 and .10.

14. One hundred and forty-four graduating seniors of Kostly College took the Graduate Record Examination (GRE) and earned a mean score of 470 on the verbal portion of the examination. Did this group of students score exceptionally poorly on the exam?

Answer

$$z = 3.6; p = .0002.$$

15. Over a period of several years, the mean number of public library books circulating per capita in a community was 5.6, with a standard deviation of 18.9. In a random sample of 64 high school graduates, the mean number of books circulated was 7.2. Is there statistical evidence that more books tend to circulate to high school graduates than to non-graduates from this public library?

Answer

Since $z = .68$, p is approximately .25.

16. An automobile manufacturer wishes to test the effect of a new antipollution device on gasoline consumption. Eight automobiles were selected and tested under identical conditions, once with and once without the new device. A summary of the results is provided below. Test the null hypothesis that there is no significant difference in gasoline consumption between automobiles with or without the antipollution device.

Gasoline Consumption in Miles per Gallon (Mpg) of 8 Automobiles

Automobile number	Mpg with device	Mpg without device
1	14.7	16.1
2	8.3	8.6
3	28.4	32.1
4	12.0	13.6
5	9.3	12.3
6	16.2	16.8
7	18.0	20.1
8	11.2	12.1

Answer

$$t = 4.05. \text{ On 7 } df, .001 > p > .01.$$

17. An experiment involving the use of the card catalog was conducted on the members of an eighth-grade class. At the beginning of the school year, all students were given an initial test on the use of the card catalog. A random sample of the class was then given a unit of instruction in the use of the card catalog, whereas the remaining students did not receive instruction. The students were retested at the end of the school year. The improvements in test scores were then computed; the results are summarized below. Test the null hypothesis that the unit of instruction (the treatment) had no effect on students' performance at the card catalog.

Improvement in Test Scores

Students having no instruction	Students having instruction
$\bar{x}_N = 6.2$	$\bar{x}_I = 4.6$
$s_N = 14.6$	$s_I = 8.4$
$n_N = 12$	$n_I = 14$

Answer

$$t = 1.76. \text{ On } 24 \, df, \, .05 < p < .10.$$

REFERENCES

1. R. L. Anderson and Bancroft, T. A., *Statistical Theory in Research.* New York: McGraw-Hill, 1952.
2. Herbert Arkin and Colton, Raymond R., *Statistical Methods,* 5th ed. New York: Barnes & Noble, 1970.
3. *Newsletter on Library Research* (June 16, 1976), p. 12.
4. William Feller, *An Introduction to Probability Theory and Its Applications,* vol. 1, 3rd ed. New York: Wiley, 1968.
5. The School Mathematics Project, *Further Mathematics, Vol. 5, Statistics and Probability.* London and New York: Cambridge University Press, 1971, pp. 51–76.
6. George W. Snedecor and Cochran, William G., *Statistical Methods,* 6th ed. Ames: Iowa State University Press, 1967, pp. 20–29.
7. Lawrence L. Lapin, *Statistics for Modern Business Decisions.* New York: Harcourt Brace Jovanovich, 1973, pp. 353–365.
8. Clinton I. Chase, *Elementary Statistical Procedures,* 2nd ed. New York: McGraw-Hill, 1976, pp. 177–191.
9. George W. Snedecor and Cochran, William G., *Statistical Methods,* 6th ed. Ames: Iowa State University Press, 1967, pp. 20–29.

PART V

Aids to Research

CHAPTER 13

The Computer and Calculator as Aids to Research

INTRODUCTION

Before the development of the electronic computer, statistical computations were accomplished manually or, if research workers were lucky enough to have access to one, by means of a desk calculator. Prior to the early 1960s, analysis of data collected in large-scale, ambitious research projects might take weeks or even months to accomplish. Today, the speed of the computer allows the same analysis to be performed in minutes or even seconds. Therefore, projects can now be undertaken which might not have been considered two decades ago because of the enormity of the associated data analysis problem.

As an aid to understanding automatic computational procedures, the general hardware configuration of a typical computer system will be briefly introduced in this chapter, as will the concept of programming. Several commonly encountered environments and approaches to the performance of statistical computations will then be described. These are (a) the use of a statistical software package through a large computation center (e.g., a computation center associated with a university); (b) the use of programmable minicomputers and microcomputers; and (c) the use of pre-programmed calculators.

In each of these three approaches to statistical analysis, many of the needed routines are already programmed for the user; that is, the formulas and procedures for conducting a test of hypothesis or a regression analysis or even the construction of a scattergram are contained in the computer system's collection of programs (*software*). Thus, all the research worker or analyst needs to know is how to communicate the data to the computer properly and how to select a relevant technique of statistical analysis. Obviously, the investigator also must know how to interpret the results after data analysis has been performed by automatic computational devices.

Contrary to what some might think, the sophisticated capabilities of computer hardware and preprogrammed statistical software packages do not decrease the investigators' responsibilities. Although the drudgery associated with computation has been effectively removed from data analysis by the computer, the analyst is left with the creative managerial decisions relating to the choice of statistical technique and the interpretation of results.

For data analysis associated with small projects (such as the problems in this text), it may frequently be more efficient for researchers to perform their computations manually rather than to use a computer. In such cases, the use of an inexpensive calculator, ideally with memory functions and the square-root function, is strongly recommended. Presently, such calculators may be purchased for as little as $5.–$10. This price is obviously within the range of virtually every individual who aspires to conduct a quantitative analysis of research data.

COMPUTER SYSTEM HARDWARE

Our purpose in this chapter is to provide a brief introduction to how data processing equipment can be used effectively in the analysis of research data. Additional research will have to be undertaken by readers for applications and data processing environments which affect them. With respect to this purpose, we can regard the principal functional hardware components of a computer system as: (a) input/output media; (b) internal storage; (c) external (auxiliary) storage media; and (d) central processing unit (CPU). The relationship between these functional components is illustrated in Figure 13.1 and in the ensuing discussion.

Input media are the means by which data and programs are entered into internal memory for later processing. Some commonly used input media are listed in Figure 13.1. In large computing centers (e.g., as may be found in county systems or in a university) the most common method of inputing data and programs is still the punched card, although data are often stored on other storage media and later entered into the system in that way. In particular, the concepts of time sharing and on-line processing have made the use of terminal keyboards, cathode-ray tube displays, and printers more common as input–output media. The high-speed printer is the most common output device in large computing systems. For applications that require direct access to data, disk and drum storage is typically used, whereas magnetic tape is by far the cheapest medium for applications that do not require direct access.

Other kinds of input–output and storage devices are employed with minicomputers, microcomputers, and programmable calculators. Infor-

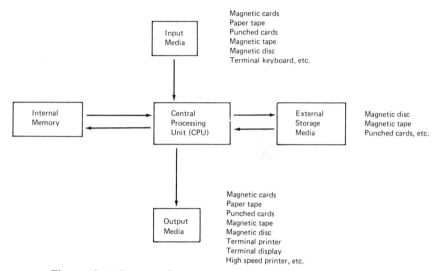

Figure 13.1. *Functional components of computer system hardware.*

mation may be input by means of a keyboard and switches that are built into the unit. Output may be presented in the form of displays or in printed form. Some programmable calculators, such as the Hewlett–Packard HP-41C and the Texas Instruments TI58, utilize magnetic cards as well as a keyboard for the storage, input, and output of data. Some machines can also be attached to a special optional thermal printer to provide hard copy printout. Others contain built-in thermal printers for the display of results.

For additional discussion of input, output, or storage media in computing systems, the reader should consult one of the many texts written to explicate these devices (e.g., Doyle, *Information Retrieval and Processing*, 1975).[1]

The central processing unit performs two essential functions, *control* and *arithmetic processing*. As Figure 13.1 indicates, the CPU controls— gives precise direction to—the input of data and programs, intermediate processing, and the output of results. To perform this function, the CPU stores and retrieves data and program instructions from the internal memory, brings in data from external storage media, performs arithmetic calculations, and produces specific outputs when appropriate. Thus, the control of the total system is maintained by the CPU, which can be regarded as analogous to the human brain. The reader should be able to comprehend how the analogy can be extended to include the concepts of input, output, and even auxiliary storage. The analogy collapses, however, when the concept of control is examined more closely. In the final analysis, the control that is exercised by the CPU is based upon a set of specific and explicit instructions—one or more computer programs—which are supplied by humans. Ultimate control in this sense rests not with the CPU but with the programmer who supplies the instructions, that is, the *software*. We turn now to a discussion of computer system software from the perspective of statistical analysis.

COMPUTER SOFTWARE

A computer program is an ordered set of procedures designed to accomplish one or more well-defined tasks. A program, or set of programs, is referred to as *software* to distinguish it from the machinery, or hardware, utilized in the computer system. Several types of software ought to be distinguished: original programs, operating systems, and program packages.

Original programs are written by an individual, or group of individuals, for a particular application. Such programs are prepared when an application demands an original approach to an old or new problem, or when existing programs are deemed to be inefficient or excessively expensive—or simply unavailable. Students taking beginning courses in computer programming learn to write simple, original programs. Today, most original programs are written in so-called higher level computer languages such as FORTRAN, COBOL, or PL/1. Special computer programs called *compilers* then translate these programs into a set of machine language instructions—instructions that are understandable to the computer.

In large data processing systems, a series of integrated programs supervise such functions as the scheduling of individual programs; operation of compilers; use of program packages; and the operation of input, output, and storage devices. These programs are known collectively as an *operating system*. To provide communication with an operating system, a special language sometimes known as a *job control language* is required. A few commands in this language are necessary regardless of the particular nature of the statistical analysis that will be conducted.

Unless the intended application is fairly esoteric, however, a research worker interested in utilizing the computer for statistical analysis would not need to learn to write original programs in languages such as FORTRAN. Programs for performing all of the standard analyses have already been written and are generally available. To use one of these programs, investigators need only record their data in machine-readable form (e.g., on punched cards or magnetic tape) and to instruct the operating system associated with the computer system being used in (*a*) a description (format) of the data; (*b*) the input device to be utilized; and (*c*) the statistical analyses that will be called upon. Prewritten programs to analyze statistical data can be found in several forms:

1. In a large computer center, in the form of statistical packages such as Statistical Package for the Social Sciences (SPSS) or the Biomedical Statistical Packages (BMD and BMDP)
2. With a minicomputer, such as those made by Wang, in the form of special statistical packages written specifically for that machine
3. With programmable calculators, in the form of software directly accessible through keystroking or stored on magnetic cards and indirectly accessible through keystroking

Each of these alternatives will be introduced in subsequent sections of this chapter. However, the reader should be aware that detailed instructions for performing particular statistical analyses with a specific computer system will not be provided here. These should be obtained directly from the source in question—the university computation center user's guide, the documentation provided with a minicomputer, the programmable calculator's owner's manual, and so on.

STATISTICAL PACKAGE FOR THE
SOCIAL SCIENCES (SPSS)

In this section, SPSS is examined as a prototype package for the statistical analysis of quantified research data. In their introduction to the SPSS manual, the developers of SPSS indicated a number of reasons for working on a new software package: (*a*) because of the tremendous variety among already existing computer programs, learning transfer was almost nil and debugging of errors was very difficult; (*b*) data formats among the programs varied considerably, which meant a number of editing, recoding, and other housekeeping chores; and (*c*) documentation associated with existing programs was poor or nonexistant.[2] The development of SPSS is based upon efforts to solve these problems and the authors of SPSS have progressed considerably toward their solution.

Although SPSS contains prewritten programs for statistical analysis, users must indicate to the system which of these they wish to employ, characteristics of the data on which the analyses are to be conducted, and the data themselves. Punched cards for communicating this information to SPSS are called *control cards*. More than 75 different types of control cards may be used with SPSS. The SPSS conventions used to construct

Table 13.1. *SPSS Program to*
Conduct Correlation
and Regression Analysis

File name	SCATLIB
Variable list	VAR1, VAR2
Input medium	CARD
N of cases	30
Input format	Freefield
Scattergram	VAR2 with VAR1
Options	7
Statistics	All
Read input data (data)	
Finish	

the control cards constitute a language, with its own syntax and vocabulary (keywords). These language rules must be followed by the analyst who runs an SPSS program.

To illustrate the ease with which an SPSS program can be written, consider the program listed in Table 13.1. This program performs a correlation and regression analysis on a set of bivariate data. Each line in the program is a separate SPSS statement, or instruction, and accomplishes a particular function. The correct order of the statements is important to maintain as well. The function of each statement of the program is illustrated in Table 13.2.

The preceding SPSS program illustrates that a fairly sophisticated set of analyses can be utilized in a short—10 statements—and easily written set of instructions. This is generally true with SPSS. Unfortunately, this ease of access and use implies at least two kinds of misuse of SPSS programs.[3]

The first type of misuse involves a tendency to allow consideration of previous and potential hypotheses, theories, concepts, and ideas (in short *thought*) to be supplanted by "fishing expeditions" on the data. Because potential relationships among variables can be tested so easily with SPSS and other statistical software packages, one is tempted to consider wholesale examinations of possible relationships, whether or not pertinent theory suggests that the relationships might exist. In the long run, library and other social science research will suffer from this practice, unless it is resisted.[4]

The second type of misuse arises from a lack of understanding of invoked statistical procedures. In SPSS and other packages, one may use a given statistical procedure without having the slightest understanding either of the procedure or the information (or analysis) produced. The

Table 13.2. *Explanation of Statements in an SPSS Program*

SPSS statement		Explanation
File name	SCATLIB	Identifies the user-provided name of the data file. In this case the name of the file is SCATLIB. (Required if reference to the file is to be made at a later time.)
Variable list	VAR1, VAR2	Names variables to be referred to in the program. Variable names invented by the user, in this case VAR1 and VAR2. (Required.)
Input medium	Card	Specifies input medium, in this case, punched card. (Required.)
N of cases	30	Specifies number of cases in data file, in this case, 30. (Conditionally required.)
Input format	Freefield	Specifies the format of the data on the input medium. In this case, no format is specified. (Conditionally required.)
Scattergram	VAR2 with VAR1	A procedure card, specifying the particular statistical procedure to be followed. In this case the procedure card requires that a scattergram be plotted with (VAR1, VAR2). (At least one procedure card is required.)
Options	All	Specifies the statistics (associated with the procedure) that are desired. In this case regression and correlation coefficients are computed, as well as other statistics, and a *t*-test for significance is conducted.
Read input data		Instructs system to read input data. (Required.)
(data)		*(user-supplied data cards)*
Finish		Signals end of program. (Required.)

SPSS manual attempts to avoid this type of misuse by including a useful prose description of each statistical procedure and examples of its potential use.

In 1975, SPSS was available for use in nearly 600 computer installations. Thus, this statistical package is accessible to most investigators. Other statistical software packages also exist and are generally available.[5-7]

SPSS was discussed in this chapter as a prototype, and as the package which is perhaps most widely available. Another common package is the BMD (Biomedical Computer Programs) software package. Although the programs in BMD were developed especially for data analysis in medical research, they are also applicable to and used extensively in many other disciplines. Examples of the use of SPSS as a library research tool are provided and discussed in a useful booklet published by the School of

Library and Information Sciences of Brigham Young University as an Occasional Research Paper.[8]

PREPROGRAMMED ELECTRONIC CALCULATORS

Most research scholars are aware of the phenomenal effect the electronic calculator has had on the act of calculation. Without a doubt, these little machines are revolutionizing the teaching of arithmetic in our schools. In addition, the revolution has affected students' performance of simple calculations, as well as more complex calculations by scientists, engineers, businesspersons, and other professionals.

At the heart of the technology on which the development of the electronic calculator is based is the integrated circuit—a tiny chip of silicon, smaller than a fingertip, which contains the power of thousands of transistors. These chips are quite inexpensive to mass-produce, which explains the remarkably low prices of modern calculators, microcomputers, and minicomputers.

Two basic types of electronic calculators are available, and can greatly facilitate statistical computations. Inexpensive and moderately priced *preprogrammed* calculators cannot be programmed by the user. They are capable of performing a fixed set of computations which range from the basic four functions $(+, -, \times, \div)$ to dozens of sophisticated engineering and business applications. However, such a calculator cannot be made to perform an operation that is not already a part of its repertoire. Several other, *programmable* calculators can be purchased at greater cost. When used in conjunction with input/output devices, these calculators are actually small computer systems of considerable power. In the paragraphs that follow, we will discuss the use of: (*a*) inexpensive (approximately $10) preprogrammed calculators with a few basic functions and capabilities; (*b*) moderately expensive (approximately $20 and up) preprogrammed calculators with many basic functions, including a selection of statistical functions; and (*c*) expensive ($90 and up) programmable calculators and computers with many basic preprogrammed functions as well as the capability of programmability.

INEXPENSIVE PREPROGRAMMED CALCULATORS

For students who believe that they have limited future uses for statistical computation, we recommend a unit with *at least* the following capabilities: (*a*) the four functions, $+, -, \times, \div$; (*b*) the square root function, $\sqrt{}$; and (*c*) a memory with the capability of **M+**, **M−**, **MR**, **MS**, and **MC**.

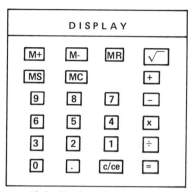

Figure 13.2. *Keyboard of an inexpensive calculator.*

The square root function is recommended because it is required for standard deviation and standard error computations. Without this function, the student would have to consult and know how to use a table of squares and square roots.

The memory capabilities we recommend will facilitate all computations requiring the summation of a large number of quantities, which themselves must be computed. Examples are the computation of standard deviations, correlation and regression coefficients, and computation of the mean from grouped data.

The minimal basic keyboard containing the recommended functions is illustrated in Figure 13.2. To perform a simple computation such as dividing 1287 by 9, the user strikes the following keys:

and the quotient (143) is displayed on the display panel. To compute the square root of this result, the user would simply press the square root key ($\sqrt{\ }$), and the result, 11.96 to the nearest hundredth, will be displayed.

The five memory keys have the following functions:

MS stores the number currently displayed on the display panel in a special memory location where it can be retrieved or modified at a later time. If there is already a number in the memory, depressing MS will store the new number there, replacing (and thus destroying) the previous number.

M+, M− adds (subtracts) the number on the display to (from) the number currently stored in the memory. If the memory contains the number 0, depressing M+ has precisely the same effect as depressing MS.

MC cancels the memory. Regardless of the current contents of the memory, depressing **MC** will replace that number with the number 0.

MR displays the current contents of the memory.

The reader should be able to understand that depressing the **MR** key, followed by the **M−** key, serves exactly the same function as depressing the **MC** key. Some calculator manufacturers omit the **MC** key for this reason.

The capability of squaring numbers is also required in many statistical procedures. Although some calculators have an X^2 key, most do not. In the case of most calculators, however, users can square a displayed number by depressing × and =. Try it before you purchase your calculator. Thus, the value 121.67 can be squared as follows:

$$\boxed{1}\ \boxed{2}\ \boxed{1}\ \boxed{.}\ \boxed{6}\ \boxed{7}\ \boxed{\times}\ \boxed{=}\ ,$$

rather than as

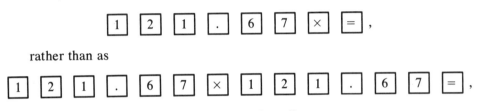

$$\boxed{1}\ \boxed{2}\ \boxed{1}\ \boxed{.}\ \boxed{6}\ \boxed{7}\ \boxed{\times}\ \boxed{1}\ \boxed{2}\ \boxed{1}\ \boxed{.}\ \boxed{6}\ \boxed{7}\ \boxed{=}\ ,$$

obviously a considerable savings in keying effort.

Consider the following example that illustrates the computation of the mean of a set of grouped data. The data used are those originally displayed in Table 9.2. (See Table 13.3.) Recall that the computation of the mean is accomplished by multiplying the midpoint of each interval by the

Table 13.3. *Time Required by 55
Library Assistants to
Complete Shelving Tasks*

Number of minutes	Frequency (*f*)
120–129	1
110–119	1
100–109	3
90–99	5
80–89	9
70–79	14
60–69	10
50–59	5
40–49	6
30–39	0
20–29	1

frequency associated with that interval and then recording each product. To obtain the mean, these products are then summed and divided by the total frequency. This operation is expressed symbolically as $\bar{x} = (\Sigma Xf)/N$, where X is the midpoint of an interval, f is its frequency, and $N = \Sigma f$ is the total frequency. Using our basic calculator, this problem can be solved without writing a single number on paper. We can accomplish it by using the keyboard to compute the intermediate products and then by using the M+ key to sum these products in the memory as we proceed. The sequence

produces the first product, 124.5. This product can then be stored in the memory of the calculator by depressing **MS.** Now the second product can be computed as

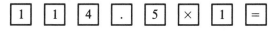

This product can be added to the first simply by depressing **M+.** Now the memory should contain a partial sum, the sum of the first two products, 239.0. (Depress **MR** to check this.) The third product can be computed as

 .

As illustrated earlier, this product, 313.5, can be added to the first two by depressing **M+.** Continuing in this way, the entire sum can be computed. The last product will be computed as

$$\boxed{2}\ \boxed{4}\ \boxed{.}\ \boxed{5}\ \boxed{\times}\ \boxed{1}\ \boxed{=} ,$$

and the product, 24.5, added to the previous sum by depressing **M+.** The memory now should contain the grand total (ΣXf). This sum can be displayed by depressing **MR.** To compute the mean, then, divide this number by the total frequency, N. Thus, the sequence

$$\boxed{\text{MR}}\ \boxed{\div}\ \boxed{5}\ \boxed{5}\ \boxed{=}$$

produces the final mean, $\bar{x}$. A set of procedures similar to this can easily be deduced to compute standard deviations, the correlation coefficient, etc., all of which require little or no recording of intermediate results on paper.

Some calculators have statistical operations such as the computation of the standard deviation as preprogrammed routines. These are considerably more expensive than the basic machine previously discussed. In the following section of this chapter, capabilities of some of the more sophisticated preprogrammed calculators currently available on the market will be summarized.

Moderately Expensive Preprogrammed Calculators

This short section lists some of the currently marketed, preprogrammed calculators that perform limited statistical computations. This is a fast-growing field, and eventually many more capabilities will probably be available. Costs may also be expected to decline. For these reasons, we anticipate that this material may be somewhat outdated by the time it is published. Nevertheless, we hope that it may serve to give the reader a flavor of the minimum capabilities currently available in preprogrammed calculators.

In Table 13.4, statistical features, functions, and prices of four preprogrammed calculators are summarized. Of course, each calculator listed offers many mathematical, business, and other functions in addition to those indicated; we have concentrated on the statistical computations which come as preprogrammed routines. To obtain a listing of current capabilities of Hewlett-Packard, Texas Instrument, Casio, or other manufacturers' preprogrammed calculators, the reader is advised to obtain up-to-date product literature from an authorized dealer.

Table 13.4. *Statistical Functions Performed by Four Moderately Expensive Preprogrammed Calculators*

Functions	Casio FX-68 ($29.95)	HP-32E ($70)	TI Business Analyst-II ($45)	TI-55 ($40)
Summation	×	×	×	×
Mean	×	×	×	×
Standard deviation	×	×	×	×
Linear regression		×	×	×
Linear estimate		×		
Correlation coefficient		×	×	×
Normal distribution		×		
Factorial	×	×		×
Variance				×
Programmability				×

Programmable Calculators and Computers with Magnetic Card or Tape Input

Presently, a number of programmable calculators, microcomputers, and minicomputers are available that offer preprogrammed statistical routines stored on magnetic cards or tape. When a particular application is desired, the user must select and input the appropriate program from the instrument's software library. The data can then be entered, after which the program will perform the desired calculation.

The Wang minicomputer includes a set of statistical software packages, as do several of the Hewlett-Packard and Texas Instrument programmable calculators. Virtually all of the statistical routines treated in this book are available with these machines, as well as other, more advanced, statistical procedures. Tables 13.5 and 13.6 list some of the advanced statistical routines available on magnetic card for the TI-58C and the HP-41C, respectively.

Because tremendous and rapid changes are taking place in the development of both hardware and software, any statement more precise than that already given in this section will soon be obsolete. Readers are advised to inquire about the most recent developments in hardware and

Table 13.5. *Advanced Statistical Routines Available on Magnetic Card for the TI-58C*

Random number generator
Data entry programs
Means and moments
Histogram construction
Theoretical histogram
Data transforms
t-statistic evaluation
Contingency table analysis
Two-way analysis of variance
Rank sum
Multiple linear regression
One-way analysis of variance
Normal distribution
Binomial distribution
Chi-square distribution
t-distribution
F-distribution

Table 13.6. *Advanced Statistical*
Routines Available on
Magnetic Card for
the HP-41C

Basic statistics for two variables
Moments, skewness and kurtosis
Analysis of variance (one-way)
Analysis of variance (two-way, no replications)
Analysis of covariance (one-way)
Curve-fitting
Multiple linear regression
Polynomial regression
t-statistics
Chi-square evaluation
Contingency table
Spearman's rank correlation coefficient
Normal and inverse normal distribution
Chi-square distribution

software available in their institutions, or within their budgets. Prices of programmable calculators, microcomputers, and minicomputers will assuredly continue to drop, as was the case with preprogrammed pocket calculators. Just as certainly, more and more statistical software will continue to become available for these machines, at continually reduced prices. We are currently approaching the potential that likely will be realized by 1984: that the prices of hardware and software will be such that budding research workers will easily be able to afford their own computing systems, complete with a full set of statistical routines; and more, that the increased power and convenience of use of these systems will be such that the researcher cannot afford *not* to own and use one. In our opinion, the future of personalized, individualized, statistical computing systems is indeed bright.

CONCLUSIONS

As in many other applications of data processing technology to librarianship, electronic computers and calculators have become increasingly important in the conduct of scientific research. Regardless of the required level of statistical computation—from the simple calculation of a mean or standard deviation to the analysis of covariance—from the needs of the seasoned medical researcher to the novice taking a first course in statistics—an applicable computer or calculator is available. Although the beginning student may be satisfied with a four-function calculator, the advanced student may prefer to invest in a preprogrammed calculator that includes a variety of built-in statistical functions and applications. For relatively short computations, one or the other of these approaches is normally most efficient.

The research scholar who needs to perform large-scale statistical analyses is advised to investigate a statistical software package such as SPSS. With this approach, keypunching can be performed by clerical staff. The data can then be carefully proofread to ensure accuracy. The staff of the local computation center will be able to offer expert advice on various problems involved in the utilization of particular statistical software packages.

Regardless of the category of statistical problem that happens to fit a specific need, the investigator can save time and energy by using some form of computer or calculator in performing data analysis. The electronic revolution has facilitated the removal of much of the drudgery of computation from the research task, thus freeing investigators to devote more time to the conceptualization of the research problem. We urge the library researcher to take advantage of this potential.

REFERENCES

1. Lauren B. Doyle, *Information Retrieval and Processing*. Los Angeles, Calif.: Melville, 1975.
2. Norman H. Nie, Bent. Dale H., and Hull, C. Hadlai, *SPSS: Statistical Package for the Social Sciences*. New York: McGraw-Hill, 1970, p. viii.
3. Nie, Norman H., Hull, C. Hadlai, Jenkins, Jean G., Steinbrenner, Karin, and Bent, Dale H., *SPSS: Statistical Package for the Social Sciences*. 2nd ed. New York: McGraw-Hill, 1975.
4. Charles Davis, "Research Record," *Journal of Education for Librarianship, 17* (Winter 1977), pp. 182–183.
5. D. T. Muxworthy, "A Review of Some Statistical Packages," *Bulletin of the Institute of Mathematics and its Applications,* (May–June 1974):171–174.
6. F. Yates, "The Use of Computers for Statistical Analysis: A Review of Aims and Accomplishments," *Bulletin of the International Statistics Institute, 44*(1971):39–52.
7. James W. Frane, "The BMD and BMDP Series of Statistical Computer Programs," *Communications of the ACM, 19*(October 1976):570–576.
8. Maurice P. Marchant, Smith, Nathan M., and Stirling, Keith H., *SPSS as a Library Research Tool*. Provo, Utah: School of Library and Information Sciences, Brigham Young University, 1977.

CHAPTER 14

Writing the Research Proposal

INTRODUCTION

Among the basic proficiencies required of the modern research scholar is the ability to write technical reports that contain lucid expository prose. In the scientific community, written records about the planning and conduct of inquiries describe both proposed and completed research. Although research proposals and reports have some areas of commonality, each of these written documents will be approached separately; research proposals provide a profile of an *anticipated* project, and research reports furnish detailed descriptions of *accomplished* investigations. Inadequate attention has been concentrated upon the values and techniques of research proposal and report writing in library science literature, even though the significance of disciplined inquiry is more recognized today than in any period of librarianship's history. Our attention in this chapter is directed to the purpose, structure, and use of research proposals. In addition, some of the appropriate guides and sources of information useful for the preparation of effective proposals in librarianship will be discussed. In the final chapter of this book, our attention will be focused upon the preparation of reports about *completed* research.

PLANNING AN INVESTIGATION

A general model for the conduct of a scientific inquiry was presented in Chapter 1. Readers who plan to undertake a research project in the near future would probably benefit by reviewing that section. Indeed, the making of plans for the conduct of research and the writing of pertinent proposals are very closely related. A *research proposal* is a document that describes the essential features of a study to be conducted in the future, as well as the strategy whereby the inquiry may be logically and successfully accomplished. This planning document often contains the following elements: an outline of the research problem, a statement of the significance of the problem, a review of related studies, a discussion of the procedures and methods for data collection and analysis, and a note about the study's limitations. Therefore, the proposal is a communication vehicle that can describe a set of planned research activities (i.e., the purpose, scope, plan, and methodology of an anticipated inquiry); it is also a tool that affords investigators an opportunity to arrange ideas and to determine expected steps in the pursuit of research questions or in the testing of hypotheses. Although research workers in a given project may not have a reasonable probability of solving a selected problem, the proposal should clearly demonstrate the writer's appreciation for such a solution, as well as assure readers that the selected investigative approach is at least equal to alternative methods. For this reason, writers of proposals must ensure that their plans can be clearly understood and the explanations will be properly appreciated. Therefore, emphasis ought to be placed upon exactness—that is, a high degree of precise writing which reflects the empirical nature of the anticipated study. Among the important preliminary matters that should be considered by the writer is the question of *who* will read the proposal and why; the composition of the targeted audience ought to determine the nature of the written research plan and the manner in which the selected methodology will be described. In the *MLA Style Sheet,* William R. Parker noted: "The effectivenss of all writing, including scholarly writing, depends in part on making certain assumptions and not making others about the interest and previous knowledge of the reader."[1]

The scope of a proposal will often depend upon specifications or expectations of actual or would-be sponsors of the research project being characterized. Proposals written for agencies, or prepared under the auspices of institutions, might devote attention to such matters as requirements for research project staff members, estimates of financial costs for the project, and other related research needs. In the academic community, some graduate schools have developed their own guidelines for the preparation of research proposals. These instructions are often used by students to tailor research programs and plans to certain academic specifications. George R. Allen noted: "The proposal is an important step in the thesis or dissertation process. It should not be viewed as constricting or restrictive or as a needless waste of time."[2] A proposal prepared by a candidate for an advanced degree from a library school is usually reviewed and approved or disapproved by a designated faculty research committee. Once accepted, the document is often respected as a contract between a student and the academic institution. Although it is possible to conduct an inquiry, even one of exceptional merit, without benefit of a formally prepared proposal, inexperienced investigators who intend to initiate a meaningful study are generally advised to first prepare a detailed, written plan for their research. We should note here that when all components of a planned study are presented in the form of a brief summary comprised of only one or two pages, the term *prospectus* is sometimes used to describe such a document and to differentiate it from a more detailed proposal.

VALUE OF RESEARCH PROPOSALS

When adequately prepared, written research plans can aid investigators in clarifying for themselves the exact nature of inquiries and appropriate procedures for the successful completion of projects. Proposals can help researchers prepare for all the critical steps relevant to a disciplined study. These documents also serve as announcements of research intentions. In addition, proposals form the bases for intelligent discussions about the strengths and weaknesses of forthcoming projects. Besides letting an advisory committee or potential sponsor know that the writer is clearly aware of what he or she plans to accomplish by means of research, the research proposal can pinpoint conceptual and theoretical errors, as well as weaknesses in selected designs and methods. Well-formulated plans for careful studies can prevent misinterpretations about research intentions and techniques. As Robert Travers has recognized: "Without such a research plan it is difficult for the critic to provide a comprehensive review of the proposed study."[3]

With a suitable proposal in hand, evaluators and consumers of research can better decide what progress might be expected in all phases of a study. In the academic community, the proposal is often used to gauge whether a student is ready to proceed along a specified course of action that could result in a thesis or dissertation which will contribute to librarianship's store of knowledge. In *Thesis Writing: A Guide to Scholarly Style*, Ralph Albaugh wrote: "Because a thesis is supposed to contribute to the sum total of human knowledge, the student, in his prospectus, should be able to defend his thesis on the ground that it is worthy of investigation, no matter how slight the eventual contribution may be."[4] Proposals often have practical utility for students who attempt to convince faculty advisors that a thesis or dissertation project will be a serious inquiry, rather than an unimaginative compendium of facts or figures. According to David Cook, " . . . the importance of a proposal rests on the simple premise that without a carefully worked-out proposal there is no assurance that the student will know what he is doing."[5] All of the preliminary steps required prior to the initiation of a research project are necessary for the conduct of a careful study; these series of procedures often help to guarantee a more efficient and thorough investigation. When investigators fail to take the necessary planning steps, the outcome of the research can be wasted motion or even invalid results.

As pointed out previously, proposals also convey research intentions to potential sponsors or to agencies that offer grants for the support of investigative projects. Thus, proposals are sometimes used to gauge the degree of research expertise and intellectual maturity of persons who apply for financial support. In the final analysis, the proposal presents an integrated approach to inquiry; it can also serve as an index of the writer's skill to communicate the purpose and significance of an investigative project. When an anticipated study has been soundly conceptualized and logically described, the proposal often serves as a strong indicator of the degree of success that is likely to be realized in a project.

GENERALIZABLE COMPONENTS OF PROPOSALS

In this section, the most desirable components of an effective investigative plan are identified and characterized. First, the proposal should serve as a scenario of developments in a study—from the statement of the primary problem to the ultimate production of a written research report. To determine the proposal's length and scope of coverage, writers often use as guidelines such factors as the nature of the intended audience and the purpose of the research. Complete proposals are comprised of the following components: a title, a discussion of the research problem, a review of the literature, an explanation of the process and procedures to be utilized, a description of data analysis techniques to be employed, and a statement about limitations of the research. Writers of some proposals will direct attention to additional topics to fulfill requirements of sponsoring agencies or institutions. From the standpoint of the research act itself, however, we shall limit our attention to generalizable components, approaching each in the order of its usual location in the research proposal.

SUGGESTED MODEL FOR THE PREPARATION OF PROPOSALS

Title

The title of the research proposal should accurately reflect the contents and scope of the suggested inquiry. An explicit title should be selected rather than a vague one. For example, "Libraries and Reading" is too vague; however, "The Effects of Library Summer Reading Programs on Student Achievement" is more explicit and reflects the nature of the inquiry specifically and precisely. When the scope of the research is revealed by the title, readers can more readily determine the true nature of the planned study. But extremely long, elaborate, and intricate proposal titles should be avoided whenever possible.

The Research Problem

A statement of the research problem is necessary so that the intent of the investigator can be set forth and justified by an explanation of existing knowledge gaps which might be filled. The general subject area of the inquiry is first identified here, and the related germane research problem is discussed. The research worker's credibility can often be established by a discussion of the problem's history. Therefore, complete proposals often contain an explanation of how the problem developed, what approaches have been attempted in the past to solve the problem, and other closely related topics. In effect, the historical overview can demonstrate that the investigator has a complete perspective of the research task. An explanation might also be offered here of why a solution to a specific problem is needed, together with a brief projection of the anticipated benefits of the study and its significance—that is, the reason(s) the inquiry will be worth the required time and effort. The nature of the specific research problem should be described, including the identification of specific hypotheses, research questions, or concepts that will be dealt with. Anticipated results may also be briefly characterized, particularly if these are not reflected in stated hypotheses. Independent and dependent variables are also usually identified in this section of the proposal. Assumptions that underlie the problem but which will not be subjected to tests are often identified here as well. Much of the information contained in this section of the proposal can also be used subsequently in the research report.

Literature Review

Another component of thorough proposals is a well-organized review of relevant research and theory. By associating the proposed study with extant library or information science theory, the proposal writer attempts to establish a relationship between a specific research problem and the greater topic or area into which the inquiry falls. Discussions about related research should be appropriate for the nature and scope of the planned study. Cited studies ought to be examined critically, rather than merely mentioned or tersely characterized. Sources of important, related findings should also be noted. In summarizing the literature, closely related studies should be grouped and discussed collectively rather than individually. Writers ought to clearly explain the relationship of the proposed inquiry to previously conducted investigations, as well as to a body of relevant theory. As is the case with "The Research Problem" section of the model presented here, much of the information contained in the literature review can be incorporated into the final research report prepared upon completion of the study.

Procedures of the Study

This section of the research proposal usually includes a rather detailed discussion of the selected methodology, including a full review of the data-gathering process and an adequate explanation of how hypotheses will be tested. A thorough methodological section usually contains rather detailed information about technical aspects of the study and the research design, as well as the appropriateness of selected methods to the solution of the problem, described in sufficient detail so that readers can determine whether selected methods are free of weaknesses, insofar as the anticipated project is concerned. For example, if the research involves the collection of data from selected samples, both the population and the sample(s) are identified and described fully. Operational definitions for all variables ought to be provided. Furthermore, a description of the operational environment of the research project might also be offered. If the study will utilize an experimental model, explanations regarding the selection of control groups are also made. When appropriate, explanations of the preparation and pretesting of measuring instruments are also offered. If selected research methods are very complex, descriptions of procedures can often be improved by an explanation of how controls and precautions will be exercised to help ensure that data-gathering methods will be applied correctly, particularly when the investigator plans to make generalizations from samples to populations. Care must be taken to ensure that the methods selected to attack the problem are suitable and fit the practical situation in which the research will be conducted. The research approach outlined in the proposal should follow logically from an analysis of possible alternative methodologies. An effective proposal will demonstrate that the advocated methods are not inferior to other investigative procedures that could be used.

Data Analysis

An explanation of techniques to be used for data analysis is an important part of most research proposals. The proposal should contain a clear outline of methods that will be employed to collect, describe, and analyze data, as well as a description of safeguards that will be applied to help ensure the correct application of investigative techniques. Quality of the proposal can be enhanced if tentative plans for graphical or tabular presentations of data are also outlined (e.g., in tables and figures), when appropriate for a given study. When hypotheses will be tested in the course of an investigation, the anticipated use of statistical procedures should be indicated and briefly explained. Likewise, expected usage of computers or other devices for the computation and analysis of data should be explained here.

Limitations of the Study

In the final section of many proposals, limitations of anticipated inquiries are recognized and succinctly stated. Here, statements about relevant parameters and constraints imposed by the method(s) and by the research setting are also frequently included. A discussion of the possible effects of research limitations on findings should also be offered, especially in cases where constraints or handicaps appear to pose serious threats to the conduct of a meaningful and successful inquiry. Competent researchers also often include information here about technical needs of a proposed study, as well as the availability and accessibility of information sources, the competencies of research associates and assistants who will help carry out the project, and any unique requirements necessary for the satisfactory completion of the research.

INADEQUACIES OF PROPOSALS

Research proposals are usually evaluated by critics on the basis of the following criteria: (a) clarity of the project description; (b) degree to which the proposed research appears to have been planned and organized; (c) appropriateness of methodologies selected to solve the research problem; and (d) significance and purpose of the suggested project. When proposals are prepared in support of a research grant request—or when an inquiry is to be sponsored by a library or some other institution or agency— evaluations of these documents generally also consider the researchers' backgrounds, experience, and records of scholarly productivity. Agencies which provide grants for the pursuit of research often require that proposals objectively demonstrate clear needs for investigative projects. Furthermore, would-be sponsors of research will likely expect good reasons for the grant applicant's belief that the proposed project's outcome will be of definite benefit. Proposals are often judged on the basis of such factors as the degree of institutional commitment and the quality of resources available to carry out a project—if the research is to be conducted within or by institutions (e.g., libraries, schools, state library agencies, or library schools). Normally, funding agencies are particularly interested in the appropriateness of the project design, the suitability of plans to monitor the methodology and to evaluate the outcome, and the reasonableness of a project's budget. When research funds are being sought, researchers should first determine the sources of funds and priorities of pertinent granting agencies. Knowledge of the kinds of projects funded in the past by agencies will also be helpful to persons who seek financial assistance.

Gerald Smith has outlined some of the inadequacies of research proposals that were submitted together with requests for federal grants.[6] As research coordinator of the U.S. Office of Education, Smith had an opportunity to examine many library science proposals. In his reflections upon these documents, Smith identified some of the most common inadequacies of proposals, including: (*a*) the choice of projects or research problems that were not of universal significance, that were unclear or inappropriate, that lacked a theoretical framework, or that were too practice-oriented; (*b*) insufficient reviews of related research; (*c*) incomplete or unclear statements of research objectives; (*d*) failure to provide thorough explanations of investigative procedures and methodologies; and (*e*) inability of the proposal writer to communicate research intentions effectively.

Criteria used for the funding of research projects by the National Science Foundation (NSF) provide useful guidelines for writers of many types of proposals for scientific research. The National Science Foundation is a federal agency which was established in 1950 to promote and advance scientific progress. In fulfilling its mission, the National Science Foundation sponsors scientific research, encourages and supports improvements in science and education, and fosters scientific information exchange. Research projects in the mathematical, physical, environmental, biological, social, behavioral, and engineering sciences are supported by the agency; however, excluded from National Science Foundation financial support are projects in the arts and humanities, business areas, social work, and clinical medicine. In 1974, the National Science Board (the National Science Foundation's policymaking body) approved the following criteria for the selection of projects to be funded.

NATIONAL SCIENCE FOUNDATION CRITERIA FOR THE SELECTION OF RESEARCH PROJECTS*

Category A

Criteria relating to competent performance of research—the technical adequacy of the performer and of his institutional base:

* The following 11 points are taken from the NSF *Guide to Programs* (1979).[7]

1. The scientist's training, past performance record, and estimated potential for future accomplishment;
2. The scientist's demonstrated awareness of previous and alternative approaches to his problem;
3. Probable adequacy of available or obtainable instrumentation and technical support.

Category B

Criteria relating to the internal structure of science itself:

4. Probability that the research will lead to important discoveries or valid, significant, and conceptual generalizations within its field of science or (in most favorable cases) extending to other fields as well;
5. Probability that the research will lead to significant improvements or innovations of investigative method—again with possible extension to other fields of science.

Category C

Criteria relating to utility or relevance:

6. Probability that the research can serve as the basis for new invention or improved technology;
7. Probable contribution of the research to technology assessment—that is, to estimating and predicting the direct and indirect, intended and unintended, effects of existing or proposed technologies;
8. Identification of an immediate programmatic context and user of the anticipated research results.

Category D

Criteria relating to future and long-term scientific potential of the United States:

9. Probable influence of the research upon the capabilities, interests, and careers of participating graduate students, postdoctoral associates, or other junior researchers;
10. Probability that the research will lead to radiation and diffusion, not only of technical results, but also of standards of workmanship and a tradition of excellence in the field;
11. Anticipated effect upon the institutional structure of U.S. science.[7]

COSTS AND BUDGETARY CONSIDERATIONS

Research grants are used to pay the direct costs of projects, to defray participant expenses, and to meet indirect cost allowances. Financial support for research in library and information science is becoming more competitive; thus, persons who prepare cost proposals ought to be thoroughly familiar with budgetary fundamentals. Budgets for research projects are plans in which expected operating costs have been adjusted to the estimated or fixed grant income or other funds that will be used for necessary expenses. The budget delineates how a research project is to be fiscally implemented, and provides evaluators of a proposal with a better overview of the planned inquiry. Because research projects differ in many respects, budgetary elements and justifications for items in the budget should coincide with the special needs of each study.

Grant applications submitted to such agencies as government organizations and philanthropic foundations contain analyses of anticipated costs. Proposal evaluators examine the costs listed to determine whether the budget is a reasonable and accurate reflection of anticipated costs and whether itemized expenses fall within allowable requirements for the preparation of cost proposals; these agencies generally expect a fairly high degree of budgetary detail. Standardized budget summary forms are often required as a part of the proposal packet; therefore, granting agencies sometimes provide detailed budget instructions and copies of printed forms to be completed and submitted by grant applicants.

As a general rule, private foundations and corporations do not require highly structured analyses of costs; however, these organizations expect reasonable budgetary summaries. Proposals to private or commercial agencies typically contain cost schedules based on formats selected by the proposal writers. Whatever the possible source of funding may be, the grant writer should conform to budgetary expectations of the agency to which a research proposal will be submitted. Budgets are often evaluated separately by contracting officers; therefore, cost summaries must often be submitted on special forms that are expected to be properly completed and signed by an authorized representative of the host institution.

The following are typical budgetary categories for research projects: (*a*) salaries and wages for personnel, for example, the principal investigator and all research associates; (*b*) staff benefits; (*c*) nonexpendable equipment and supplies; (*d*) travel; (*e*) automatic computation costs; (e.g., data processing and computer analyses of data); (*f*) postage and telephone costs; (*g*) printing and publication costs; (*h*) indirect costs; and (*i*) miscellaneous costs. The funds needed are grouped into appropriate budget categories. When budgetary subcategories are needed to clarify major cost areas, funding agencies sometimes require that additional information be submitted on supplementary budgetary sheets referenced to appropriate sections of the main cost proposal.

Expenses that will definitely be incurred in the course of an investigative project are called *direct costs;* these costs can be readily associated with various research activities. Included in direct costs are salaries, wages, and benefits for staff members; expendable and unexpendable equipment and supplies; transportation and travel; and postage, telephone, printing, and similar expenses.

Costs incurred by both the host institution and the activities of research projects in the pursuit of mutual objectives are called *indirect costs;* thus, such expenses cannot be readily assigned to a specific entity or activity. Indirect costs are necessary for the support of routine operations of the host institution and for the performance of overall institutional programs. Typically, indirect costs include "overhead" expenses—administrative operations, intangible services, and the maintenance of such necessary support services as libraries, information centers, and computer facilities. Funds associated with the normal operation, maintenance, and depreciation of facilities and the salaries of administrative or other support personnel of the host institution are often included in the category of indirect costs. The nature of the institution's organizational structure is taken into consideration when costs are ascribed to either the direct or indirect category. Indirect cost rates are usually well-established at institutions where research projects are routinely carried out. If the funding organization or agency allows for the reimbursement of indirect costs, the proposal writer should determine the percentage permitted and the section of the budget to which such costs can be applied.

Budgets for projects must be realistic reflections of the goals and objectives of the research that will be performed. Furthermore, each budgetary item ought to be justified adequately. The budget should be an outgrowth of research activities that are detailed in the narrative portion of the proposal. Requests for grants may be rejected when accompanying budgets are unrealistic or when listed costs fall outside allowable amounts specified by relevant guidelines. The content and format of a budget for a research project will depend upon the nature and complexity of the investigative activity, the cost of the study, and the special requirements of agencies to which the proposal will be submitted. Proposal guidelines usually note the items or activities that are eligible for funding; thus, an important initial consideration in relation to the preparation of a budget is that of identifying eligible and ineligible cost items. Requests made to granting agencies for funds should not be inflated. The practice of asking for more than is needed (padding the budget) is often viewed negatively by proposal evaluators, many of whom are keenly aware of typical costs for various kinds of investigative activities.

Proposed budgets must be line-itemized, fiscally realistic, and based upon the project's descriptive narrative. A high degree of specificity is urged in most budgets. Some proposal writers make a practice of checking each budget line item to determine whether it is explained sufficiently in the proposal narrative. Such checks help to ensure that evaluators of proposals will be adequately informed about the relationship of costs to the objectives of the project. Writers of proposals must also provide for such contingencies as cost-of-living increases and salary increases, as well as for any anticipated rate changes for utilities, rent, and insurance. Budget preparation within institutional settings (e.g., in libraries or at universities) will require close collaboration among proposal writers, project directors, the budget analysts within host institutions. These persons ought to be aware that the budget is a reasonable estimate, and that degrees of discretionary latitude are usually allowed when monies are expended for investigative projects.

The Budget

Personnel

Salaries

Staff salaries are usually major budgetary items. The personnel section should contain a list of needed staff members, the job-titles of all project personnel to be employed, full-time equivalencies, working hours per week, lengths of employment, and salaries. Salaries should be reasonable—that is, not too high or too low. Release-time salary costs for personnel should also be computed and listed, even though such costs might be "in-kind" donations of the host institution. Salaries budgeted for a project director ought to be based upon the scope and complexity of the proposed inquiry. Compensations suggested for research assistants and secretaries are usually adjusted to prevailing salaries for persons who perform similar duties within the geographic area or, when applicable, at the host institution. Part-time employees usually do not receive retirement and vacation pay or similar fringe benefits.

Fringe Benefits

Allotments may be requested for the employee's share of such benefits as Social Security (FICA) and retirement. When applicable, the computation of staff benefits should reflect routine accounting practices of host institutions. Indirect costs, including those for salaries and fringe benefits for all personnel associated with a project, should be computed and displayed in the budget. These costs include Social Security, retirement, insurance, Workman's Compensation, and unemployment compensation. When indirect cost reimbursements will be requested, the requests ought to be based upon approved rates for such costs. The appropriate rate is specified in the budget; the basis for the rate's compensation is also shown. Indirect cost rates can usually be obtained from the host institution's business office or from an officer designated to endorse research proposals prior to their submission to external funding sources.

Consultants

When consultant services are required, honoraria are typically adjusted to the host institution's established fee-rate. Project budgets should contain listings of the number of days of employment and the honorarium per day for each consultant needed. Many government agencies have established maximum rates for such payments; therefore, astute proposal writers ensure that fees for consultants fall within allowable compensation ranges. Contracts for consultant services usually outline the specific task(s) to be performed in a project. Normally, project funds are used to pay a consultant's travel and per diem costs; therefore, these expenditures are entered in the budget.

Non-Personnel

Facilities

If needed, expenses for facilities are also outlined in the budget. These costs are usually kept in line with the fair market-value within the relevant geographic area. Rental charges are typically based upon the number of required square feet of space, multiplied by the cost per square foot for each month of use.

Utilities and Services

Project costs for utilities and services will include such necessities as fuel, water, electricity, and telephones. These itemized costs are usually computed using the dollar amount required for each service per month as a base.

Equipment

Cost proposals also contain lists of needed major and minor equipment. Granting agencies often define and categorize equipment that will or will not be funded for various kinds of research projects. Applicable guidelines should be consulted to determine the kinds of equipment for which support may be requested. All needed equipment should be adequately justified in proposals. Anticipated cost requirements for the repair, maintenance, and servicing of equipment are also often included in the budget. When project equipment will be rented, required items are listed, along with the cost for each item per month, multiplied by the number of months of anticipated use. If proposal guidelines do not permit major equipment purchases, needed equipment can often be leased. Such costs should also be detailed.

Supplies and Materials

When project supplies are inadequate, research personnel cannot perform their jobs properly; therefore, such needed expendable items as typewriter ribbons, paper, and other office supplies are grouped into appropriate categories and listed in the budget. Moreover, necessary copying services ought to be itemized. Copies of materials are becoming indispensable in many kinds of research projects. Therefore, the method of reproduction is indicated, along with the anticipated number of units to be reproduced.

Travel

Both staff and non-staff travel requirements of a project are anticipated and entered in the budget. Travel costs are usually grouped into appropriate categories, for example, local, state, regional, and foreign. Transportation requirements of support and ancillary staff members (e.g., consultants, advisors, interviewers, evaluators, and so on) should not be overlooked in the travel section. Costs for travel are usually based upon the host institution's regular allowances for these expenses.

Evaluation Costs

Proposal writers should not overlook costs associated with evaluations of completed projects and expenses that will be incurred when research findings are disseminated in printed reports. When applicable, evaluation and dissemination methods and related costs are included in the budget. As a general rule, the larger the research grant is for a project, the more likely the funding agency will require a formal project evaluation, as well as a detailed report of the entire study. Funds necessary for these evaluations and reports must not be overlooked.

Miscellaneous Costs

Anticipated expenses that do not appear to be appropriate for any of the budget categories discussed in other sections of the cost proposal are placed in a category labeled "Miscellaneous Costs."

Table 14.1 shows a sample budget for a research project and is offered as a model for the preparation of cost proposals. It contains many elements that are commonly found in project budgets.

Table 14.1. *Project Budget*

Total $167,562.22	Requested $136,263.44	Donated $31,298.78
1. Personnel Sub-total	$100,537.00	$26,583.44
A. Salaries and wages		
Executive director at $1852/month (100%) × 12 months	22,224.00	
Project director at $1500/month (100%) × 12 months	18,000.00	
Five on-site interviewers at $497.50/month (50%) × 8 months		19,900.00
Two telephone interviewers at $412.50/month (50%) × 4 months		3300.00
Secretary at $810/month (100%) × 12 months	9720.00	
Two clerk/typists at $756/month (100%) × 12 months	18,144.00	
Salaries and wages	$68,088.00	$23,200.00
B. Fringe benefits		
FICA (6.13% × $68,088)	$4,174.00	
FICA (6.13% × $23,200)		$1,422.00
Workman's compensation (.2% × $68,088)	136.00	
Workman's compensation (.2% × $23,200)		46.00
Unemployment (.4% × $68,088)	272.00	
Unemployment (.4% × $23,200)		93.00
Retirement (7.10% × $68,088)	4,834.00	
Insurance (5 × $24.88/month × 12 months)	1,493.00	
Fringe benefits	$10,909.00	$1,561.00
C. Consultant and contract services		
Government document consultant 6 hours/week × $18.02/hour × 12 weeks		1297.44
Indexing consultant 18 hours/week × $30/hour × 26 weeks	14,040.00	
Volunteer indexer (university student) at $52.50/week × 10 weeks		525.00
Time and motion studies (services to be performed on a contract basis), $2500/month × 3 months	7500.00	
Consultants and contracts	$21,540.00	$1822.44
2. Non-Personnel Sub-total	$35,726.44	$4715.34
A. Space Costs		
Laboratory rent $600/month × 12 months	$7200.00	
Utilities for laboratory $150/month × 12 months	1800.00	
Testing space contributed by university library $25/week × 10 weeks		250.00
Briefing auditorium donated by the University Players theatre project at 100/week × 5 weeks		500.00
Space costs	$9000.00	$750.00

(*Continued*)

357

Table 14.1. (*Continued*)

Total $167,562.22	Requested $136,263.44	Donated $31,298.78
B. Rental/purchase of equipment		
Unabridged dictionary at $35.00	35.00	
Two subscriptions to abstracting services at		
$180/subscription/year	360.00	
Four telecopier machines at $75.50/month × 12 months	3624.00	
Loadmaster duplicator leased at $60.75/month × 12		
months	729.00	
Six large folding tables at $30 year	180.00	
Thirty folding chairs at $12 year	360.00	
Three electric typewriters provided by the university for		
1 year at $100/each/year		300.00
Rental/purchase of equipment	$5288.00	$300.00
C. Consumer Supplies		
Ten reams of telecopier paper at $4.12	$41.20	
Thirty reams of duplication paper at $3.75	112.50	
Office supplies (desk top) for 12 staff at $130.68/year	1568.16	
Two gross rubber cement at $72/each	144.00	
Consumer supplies	1865.86	
D. Travel		
Local		
Mileage for five interviewers, 350 miles/month at		
$.18/mile × 4 months	$1260.00	
Travel expenses for seven interviewers to attend work- shops on interview training, 50 miles/week at		
$.18/mile × 2 weeks	126.00	
Staff mileage/per diem for project director to attend regional meetings of project sponsor (200 miles/month		
at $.18 × 4)	144.00	
Per diem for project director	90.00	
Out-of-State		
Two consultants × 3 trips × $250/trip	1500.00	
Travel	$3120.00	
E. Other costs		
Postage (to be paid by university)		$820.00
Use of four telephones at $60/month × 12 months	$2880.00	
Fire insurance	225.00	
Printing and duplicating costs	960.00	
Indirect costs (10% of total direct costs:		
$123,875.86 × .10 and $28,453.44 × .10)	12,387.58	2845.34
Other costs	$16,452.58	$3665.34

SOURCES OF INFORMATION FOR LITERATURE SEARCHES

Literature searches are accomplished by examinations of both general and specialized bibliographical tools, indexes, abstracts, directories, catalogs of library holdings, and other appropriate reference guides. The search for relevant reports and related literature is limited only by the research worker's imagination, bibliographical expertise, persistence, and determination. Numerous useful bibliographical tools are contained in the collections of most medium-sized and large libraries, particularly in those located at universities or at other research institutions. Union catalogs (local, regional, state, and national) aid investigators in identifying valuable sources of information and provide bibliographical citations for many relevant publications. These tools help locate specific materials in library collections. When necessary, union catalogs serve as guides for obtaining needed publications on interlibrary loan.

Periodical indexes and abstracts are essential to the conduct of thorough literature searches. Indexes can be used to locate both recent and retrospective information in scholarly journals or in other periodicals. When citations are found for journal articles of possible use as sources of background information, the *Union List of Serials* can be consulted to locate libraries in which the desired journals are available, should the need arise to request copies of articles. Abstracts of research reports can also provide information in digest form, thereby saving valuable time and allowing the bypass of irrelevant materials. Reviews of books sometimes provide information and lead researchers to additional materials. Investigators should also be aware that many research libraries now provide searches of machine-readable bibliographic data bases on-line, using a computer terminal. Literature searches can often be made much more rapidly and effectively in this way than with manual techniques and printed tools. Many useful indexes such as ERIC and *Social Sciences Citation Index* are available in both machine-readable and printed forms. Research workers should check local libraries to determine which indexes or abstracts are available on-line.

Generally, the most appropriate place to begin a literature search is with references and bibliographies provided in books, articles, and research reports about the topic to be explored. Most substantial reports of completed studies contain numerous bibliographic references and lists of relevant publications. Many periodical indexes and other guides to published information are available, including sources that are discussed briefly in the section that follows.

BIBLIOGRAPHIES, INDEXES, AND ABSTRACTS

The most basic guide to current library science periodical and monographic literature is *Library Literature; An Author and Subject Index* (H. W. Wilson Co., 1934 to date. Bimonthly). More than 200 library science periodicals are indexed in this tool on a systematic basis. Among these periodicals are the following journals in which research reports are frequently published: *The Library Quarterly, Journal of the American Society for Information Science, Library Resources & Technical Services, Journal of Library History, School Media Quarterly, Journal of Academic Librarianship, Special Libraries, Journal of Library Automation, Journal of Documentation, College & Research Libraries, Information Processing and Management,* and *Drexel Library Quarterly.*

Additional indexes published by the H. W. Wilson Company are also useful in literature searches; among these are the following: *Education Index* (1929 to date. Monthly); *Social Science and Humanities Index* (1916 to date. Quarterly); *Applied Science and Technology Index* (1958 to date. Monthly); *The Readers' Guide to Periodical Literature* (1905 to date. Semimonthly); and *Business Periodicals Index* (1958 to date. Monthly). The great advantage of these indexes to researchers are author and subject entry arrangements in single alphabets—features that facilitate faster and more efficient literature searches.

Several machine-readable data bases contain substantial coverage of the library and information science literature, and are appropriate for on-line information searches. Among these are *Social Sciences Citation Index, Inspec,* ERIC, and *Library and Information Science Abstracts* (LISA). A detailed, useful discussion of this coverage has been provided by Donald T. Hawkins and Betty Miller.[8]

For a general list of bibliographical tools relating to library science, readers may wish to consult Theodore Besterman's *Bibliography, Library Science, and Reference Tools: A Bibliography of Bibliographies* (Rowan & Littlefield, 1971). In addition, Paul Wasserman's *Library Bibliographies and Indexes: A Subject Guide to Resource Materials . . .* (Gale Research Co., 1975) can also be of value in some literature searches. J. Periam Danton's *Index to Festschriften in Librarianship* (R. R. Bowker Co., 1970) should not be overlooked as a guide to some significant library science literature. For retrospective bibliographies of library science publications, research workers can make use of the following indexes: Margaret Burton and Marion E. Vosburg's *A Bibliography of Librarianship* (London: Library Association, 1934); Harry G. T. Cannons' *Bibliography of Library Economy* (American Library Association, 1927); Ann Harwell Jordan and Melbourne Jordan's *Cannons' Bibliography of Library Economy, 1876–*

1920; An Author Index with Citations (Scarecrow Press, 1976); *Five Years' Work in Librarianship,* 1928–1965 (London: Library Association, 1965); and *Library and Information Science Abstracts: Cumulative Index 1929–1973* (Learned Information, 1975).

Two useful bibliographic guides that are issued as serials are the following: *Information Hotline* and *Information: Reports and Bibliographies,* both published by Science Associates/International, Inc. Issues of these publications contain lists of dissertations, upcoming courses and conferences, lists of recent NSF grants and contracts pertaining to library and information science, and news about various developments in the information industry. For a comparison of English-language and foreign indexing tools of value to librarians and information scientists, readers may wish to consult Tom Edwards' article entitled "Comparative Analysis of the Major Abstracting and Indexing Services for Library Science" (*Unesco Bulletin for Libraries 30*:18–25, January 1976).

Persons who conduct literature searches should also be aware of special subject bibliographies published in journals or issued as separate works. Many of these lists have been prepared for various topics and problem areas within library and information science, and only a few relatively recent and useful ones are cited in the following representative group: *Cooperation between Types of Libraries, 1940–1968* (ALA, 1970), by Ralph H. Stenstrom; "Bibliography on Library Literature in Japan" (*Library Quarterly 41*:54–60, January 1971), by Adrian Jones; "Bibliography on Standards for Evaluating Libraries" (*College & Research Libraries 32*:127–144, March 1971), by Signe Ottersen; *Asian Libraries and Librarianship; an Annotated Bibliography of Selected Books and Periodicals, and a Draft Syllabus* (Scarecrow Press, 1973), by Godfrey R. Nunn; *Index to User Studies* (The Hague, Netherlands: International Federation for Documentation, 1974); *Instructional Materials for Teaching the Use of the Library: A Selected Bibliography* (San Jose, Calif.: Claremont House, 1975), by Shirley Hopkinson; *Programmed Instruction in Librarianship; A Classified Bibliography of Programmed Texts and Other Materials 1960–1974* (Graduate School of Library Science, University of Illinois, Occasional Papers, no. 124, 1976), by Henry M. Yaple; "Bibliography of Community Analyses for Libraries" (*Library Trends 24*:619–643, January 1976), by John B. Albright; *Communication Research in Library and Information Science: A Bibliography on Communication in the Sciences, Social Sciences, and Technology* (Libraries Unlimited, 1975), by Thomas J. Waldhart and Enid S. Waldhart.

Other special compilations cover various aspects of technical services, among which are the following useful bibliographies: *Management and Costs of Technical Processes: A Bibliographical Review, 1876–1969* (Scarecrow Press, 1970), by Richard M. Dougherty and Lawrence E. Leonard; *Library Acquisitions: A Classified Guide to the Literature and Reference Tools,* 2nd ed. (Libraries Unlimited, 1971), by Bohdan S. Wynar; *Library Technical Services; A Selected Annotated Bibliography* (Greenwood Press, 1977), compiled by Rose Mary Magrill and Constance Rinehart; *Serials Automation in the United States: A Bibliographic History* (Scarecrow Press, 1976), by G. M. Pitkin; and "Classification Literature" (*International Classification* 5:47–62, March 1976).

Two kinds of very specialized libraries were subjects of the following useful bibliographies: "Map Librarianship, Map Libraries, and Maps: A Bibliography 1921–1973" (SLA, *Geography and Map Division Bulletin*, no. 95:2–35+, March 1974), by A. E. Schorr; and "Church Libraries; A Bibliography on Sources of Information from 1876 to 1969" (*Catholic Library World* 41:377–379, February–March 1970).

Academic libraries were the object of the following subject bibliographies published in professional journals: "Academic Library Cooperation; A Selected Annotated Bibliography" (*Library Resources & Technical Services* 20:270–286, Summer 1976), by Diana M. Chang; and "Academic Library Instruction; A Bibliography, 1960–1970" (*Drexel Library Quarterly* 7:327–335, July–October 1971), by Allen Mirwis.

Additional examples of some useful special bibliographies in the field of library science are the following works: *Index to Research in School Librarianship 1960–1974* (U.S. Department of Health, Education and Welfare, National Institute of Education, 1976); *Reference Service: An Annotated Bibliographic Guide* (Libraries Unlimited, 1977), by Marjorie E. Murfin and Lubomyr R. Wynar; *Planning, Programming, Budgeting Systems and Management by Objectives,* 3rd ed. (Smoothie Publications, 1974), by John L. Noyce; and *Continuing Professional Education in Librarianship and Other Fields: A Classification and Annotated Bibliography, 1965–1974* (Garland Publishing, 1975), by Mary Ellen Michael.

Mention should also be made here of the Educational Resources Information Center (ERIC). Various bibliographic and abstracting services offered by this system are valuable to persons who need information about many kinds of research projects. Established in 1965 by the U.S. Department of Health, Education and Welfare (HEW), ERIC is a bibliographic/abstracting service that serves as an alternative to traditional methods for the dissemination of research reports. The ERIC dissemination system is based upon a model of outward diffusion from a central source, rather than upon the use of such conventional linkages as professional conventions, journals, commercial publishers, and additional systems with which many educators, librarians, and other interested persons have expressed dissatisfaction for one reason or another. ERIC is coordinated by the

National Institute of Education, an agency within HEW. Noncommercial educational materials are collected by 16 ERIC clearinghouses located over the nation. These materials are first abstracted, indexed, and microfilmed; then, they are entered into the ERIC data bank. Lengthy document abstracts are published monthly in *Resources in Education* (RIE), an indexing and abstracting guide to educational literature and research reports, including studies in librarianship. Microfiche editions of many of these documents are available from ERIC at very reasonable prices. (A list of ERIC microfiche holdings may be obtained from ERIC Documents Reproduction Services, Customer Services, P.O. Box 190, Arlington, VA 22210). Another ERIC publication that is often used by research scholars in librarianship is *Current Index to Journals in Education* (CIJE) (v. 1– , 1969 to date). This tool provides citations for articles published in approximately 780 major educational and education-related journals.

Research workers can make more effective use of ERIC tools by consulting the *Thesaurus of ERIC Descriptors,* 7th ed. (Macmillan Information, 1977), which serves as an aid to the identification of key words pertaining to the subject of a search. Automatic searches of the ERIC data bank can be performed by computers at any of the system's clearinghouses and at many libraries and information centers, particularly at large research libraries. The ERIC Clearinghouse on Information Resources is currently located at Syracuse University.

DISSERTATIONS AND THESES

Because dissertations and theses serve as sources of information about completed research, investigators can make use of such retrospective or current bibliographies as the following: *Library Science Dissertations, 1925–1960* (U.S. Office of Education, 1963), by Nathan M. Cohen and others; *Library Science Dissertations, 1925–1972: An Annotated Bibliography* (Libraries Unlimited, 1974), by Gail A. Schlachter and Dennis Thomison; *Guide to Theses and Dissertations: An Annotated Bibliography of Bibliographies* (Gale Research, 1975), by Michael Reynolds; *Doctoral Dissertations in Library Science: Titles Accepted by Accredited Library Schools, 1930–1972* (Xerox University Microfilms, 1973); *Master's Theses in Library Science: 1960–1969* (Whitston, 1975), by Shirley Magnotti; and *Library and Information Studies in the United Kingdom and Ireland, 1950–1974: An Index to Theses* (London, Eng.: Aslib, 1976), edited by Peter J. Taylor.

For lists of current, on-going doctoral dissertation projects in the United States, persons who conduct literature searches can consult lists of approved topics published periodically in the *Journal of Education for Librarianship*. This list is entitled "Doctoral Dissertation Topics Accepted in

Library and Information Science." It is a record of works in progress, rather than completed dissertations. Arrangement of the list is alphabetical by names of degree candidates. Each citation includes the tentative dissertation title, date the topic was approved, approving institution, and name of the degree candidate's major faculty advisor. Many of the approved studies listed in the *Journal of Education for Librarianship* are subsequently completed and submitted by students in fulfillment of degree requirements; however, some of the proposed dissertations apparently never reach fruition. Furthermore, users of the list should be aware that some of the studies are changed either in scope or title and that a few are abandoned altogether.

Three doctoral dissertations completed in the mid-1970s contain information about the contemporary climate of library science research and related matters. These dissertations are, *Library Education and Library Research: An Analysis of Institutional and Organizational Context* (Rutgers University, 1975), by Ruth M. Katz; *Research in Library Science as Reflected in Core Journals of the Profession: A Quantitative Analysis (1950– 1975)* (University of California, Berkeley, 1977), by Bluma C. Peritz; and *Characteristics Related to Productivity among Doctoral Graduates in Librarianship* (University of California, Berkeley, 1975), by Nancy D. Lane.

BIOGRAPHICAL DATA SOURCES

Information about many persons who have been active in the profession or who have made contributions in one way or another to librarianship can be obtained from a variety of current and retrospective biographical sources. For a listing of numerous active members of the library profession, the following directory is often useful: *A Biographical Directory of Librarians in the United States and Canada* (ALA, published periodically). The forerunner of this directory was *Who's Who in Library Service,* which can be consulted for information about many inactive or deceased librarians. Other sources of information about current library science scholars and practitioners are the issues of *The Library Quarterly,* each of which contains a biographical section about contributors. Biographical sketches of persons whose articles are published in each issue are included in the section. A relatively recent addition to the area of library science retrospective biography is the *Dictionary of American Library Biography* (Libraries Unlimited, 1977), Bohdan S. Wynar, general editor. This work contains biographical sketches of deceased librarians who made significant contributions to the development of librarianship or to the study of library science.

Other biographical guides to various persons currently in the profession are the *ALA Membership Directory* (1950 to date) and the annual directory issue of the *Journal of Education for Librarianship,* which lists library schools and their faculty members. Many specialized library associations and local, state, and regional library organizations also publish membership directories which can be used as a supplement to larger compilations of names. Frequently, these lists are included in the serial publications of organizations, or as special issues of these publications. Current biographical information for some librarians and information scientists and persons in other professions can often be found in reference publications of the R. R. Bowker Company, including the *Directory of American Scholars,* 4 vols. (1978); *American Men and Women of Science,* 13th ed. (1976); *American Library Directory,* 31st ed. (1978); and *Leaders in Education,* 5th ed. (1974). Biographical directories of writers can also be consulted for background information about the careers and work of persons who have written books. Among these works, *Contemporary Authors* (Gale Research, 1962 to date) serves as one of the most useful bio-bibliographical guides to current authors. When information about people cannot be located in readily available directories, *Biography Index* (Wilson, 1946 to present) should be consulted. This publication is a quarterly index to biographical materials in books and magazines.

DICTIONARIES AND ENCYCLOPEDIAS

Special dictionaries and encyclopedias should not be overlooked as aids to research workers and writers of proposals. Among the most pertinent dictionaries in the area of library and information science are the following works: *Elsevier's Dictionary of Library Science, Information and Documentation in Six Languages* (Elsevier Scientific, 1973) compiled by W. E. Clason; *A Glossary of Indexing Terms* (Clive Bingley, 1976), by Brian Buchannan; *The Librarians' Glossary of Terms Used in Librarianship,* 3rd rev. ed. (Seminar Press, 1971), by Leonard M. Harrod, and *A.L.A. Glossary of Library Terms, with a Selection of Terms in Related Fields* (American Library Association, 1943). *The Dictionary of Education,* 3rd ed. (McGraw-Hill, 1973), by Carter V. Good, is often of value when research topics or problems in the field pertain to educational issues and topics.

The most definitive library science encyclopedia is the *Encyclopedia of Library and Information Science* vol. 1– , (Dekker, 1968 to present. In process), edited by Allen Kent, Harold Lancour, and Jay E. Daily. This work contains fairly lengthy articles about various topics relevant to library science and librarianship. Articles are signed, and many of them are followed by bibliographies of selected publications pertaining to the topics covered. Another encyclopedia in the field is the *Encyclopedia of Librar-*

ianship, 3rd. ed. (Hafner, 1966), edited by Thomas Landau. When investigations interface with issues or problems in other disciplines, researchers in the field often turn to such encyclopedias as the following: *The Encyclopedia of Education,* 10 vols. (Macmillan, 1971); *Encyclopedia of Science and Technology,* 15 vols. (McGraw-Hill, 1971); *Encyclopedia of the Social Sciences,* 15 vols. (Macmillan, 1930–1935); and *International Encyclopedia of the Social Sciences,* 17 vols. (Macmillan and the Free Press, 1968). For an international reference guide to products, systems, and services of the information industry, readers sometimes turn to the *Encyclopedia of Information Systems and Services,* 3rd ed. (Gale Research, 1978). This publication contains more than 2000 entries on approximately 2500 organizations, and it focuses upon storage and retrieval systems, computer service companies, computer retrieval systems, and other related topics.

Directories and Guides

The basic compilation of libraries in the United States is the *American Library Directory,* 1979–1980, 32nd ed. (Bowker, 1979), edited by Jaques Cattel Press. *The ALA Handbook of Organization 1978–1979* (American Library Association, 1978) serves as a directory of the various offices and divisions of the largest professional organization within librarianship. Two useful directories of special libraries are available; they are: *Directory of Special Libraries and Information Centers,* 3 vols., 5th ed. (Gale Research, 1979); and *Subject Directory of Special Libraries,* 5 vols. (Gale Research, 1976), edited by Margaret L. Young and others. A guide to academic and other nonprofit research organizations that are permanent and carry on continuing research programs is the *Research Centers Directory,* 6th ed. (Gale Research, 1978). Because various agencies of the federal government have collected useful research materials, the following guide might be of use to some researchers: *Federal Library Resources: A User's Guide to Research Collections* (Science Associates/International, Inc., 1973), compiled by Mildred Benton.

For a comprehensive list of library associations and related organizations, readers can consult Josephine R. Fang and Alice H. Songe's *International Guide to Library, Archival, and Information Science Associations* (Bowker Co., 1976). An excellent directory of library science professional journals and other periodicals is *Library and Library-Related Publications: A Directory of Publishing Opportunities in Journals, Serials, and Annuals* (Libraries Unlimited, 1973), by Peter Hernon and others.

A number of special directories such as the following are often also beneficial to research workers: *Directory of Health Sciences Libraries in the United States* (American Medical Association, 1975), compiled and edited by Susan Crawford and Gary Dandurand; *Interlibrary Loan Policies Direc-*

tory (American Library Association, 1975), by Sarah K. Thomson; and *Directory of Academic Library Consortia,* 2nd ed. (Systems Development Corp., 1976), edited by Donald V. Black and Carlos A. Caudra.

Guides to resources in libraries are sometimes used for the location of subject collections of value to various research projects. The following such guides are only a few of the many aids to research within librarianship: *Subject Collections: A Guide to Special Book Collections and Subject Emphasis as Reported by University, College, Public, and Special Libraries and Museums in the United States and Canada* 5th ed., rev. and enlarged (Bowker Co., 1978), compiled by Lee Ash; *Guide to Reference Sources in the Computer Sciences* (Macmillan Information, 1973), by Ciel Carter; *Subject Collections in Children's Literature* (Bowker, 1969), edited by Carolyn Field; *British Library Resources: A Bibliographic Guide* (Mansell, 1973), by Robert B. Downs; and *Guide to the Research Collections of the New York Public Library* (American Library Association, 1975), compiled by Sam P. Williams.

In addition to the reference sources discussed in previous sections of this chapter, various other handbooks, manuals, yearbooks, and guides related to library science and librarianship may also be of use to researchers. Space does not permit a listing of additional possible resources; therefore, readers are advised to consult any number of guides to basic reference materials and services, depending upon the topic or problem area of a selected research project. We should also point out that, although most of the indexes, bibliographies, and other information sources discussed in the preceding bibliographic essay are especially relevant to library and information science, research workers should not overlook similar materials prepared for other disciplines, professions, or fields of study—especially those within the social and behavioral sciences.

SUMMARY

The first step in a scientific investigation is deciding on the specific topic to be explored—that is, that particular aspect of a problem which is to be closely examined. Before writing a proposal for a research project, an investigator must have acquired sufficient background knowledge about the topics to be explored and should, of course, be particularly interested in the targeted problems. In addition, selected research problems and subjects should be of potential interest and significance to other persons within librarianship. Research workers must take care to avoid the selection of topics or problems that are too unmanageable or too complicated to be properly treated and fully developed or explored. They should also ensure that selected investigative tasks can be adequately confronted and solved within a reasonable time frame—unless extensive and prolonged studies are anticipated.

Careful planning, including a thorough familiarization with theoretical implications of proposed studies, is essential to the conduct of meaningful inquiry. The planning stage of a research project in librarianship, as well as in other disciplines and fields of study, is very critical. Inexperienced investigators are forewarned that preparations for studies (including the writing of research and cost proposals) often require more time than the actual conduct of research itself. Planning should center around the selection of a research design that permits clear and precise interpretations of results. When methods are selected which maximize the potential to produce clear results associated with relevant variables, both internal and external validity of studies are enhanced.

Research planning is facilitated by an in-depth examination of all factors associated with the problem; by a clear understanding on the part of investigators of the fundamentals of scientific method; and by a complete review of relevant literature, including an analysis of the results of related, previously conducted studies. The importance of research proposals to the planning process cannot be overemphasized, particularly in regard to their usefulness to beginning research workers. Without carefully devised research plans, investigators usually are at a loss to conduct effective studies. Furthermore, without such written guidelines, there is no concrete assurance to investigators' peers in the community of scholars that researchers will know *what* they are doing and *why* they are doing it. Thus, considerable thought and preparation ought to be devoted to the writing of proposals.

Although proposals differ from one research project to another (particularly in respect to format), the typical plan for a study provides a statement of the problem; a review of the relevant literature—including recognition of associated research and theory; the identification of what data are needed and the sources of these data; a description of planned investigative methods and procedures; and an explanation of how the collected data will be analyzed, displayed, and reported. Good proposals are communication vehicles used to convey research intentions to the scientific community; they are also devices that investigators can employ to execute productive and meaningful inquiries.

REFERENCES

1. William R. Parker, *The MLA Style Sheet*. New York: Modern Language Association, 1951, p. 26.

2. George R. Allen, *The Graduate Students' Guide to Theses and Dissertations: A Practical Manual for Writing and Research.* San Francisco, Calif.: Jossey-Bass, 1973, p. 34.
3. Robert M. W. Travers, *An Introduction to Educational Research.* 3rd ed. New York: Macmillan, 1969, p. 83.
4. Ralph M. Albaugh, *Thesis Writing: A Guide to Scholarly Style.* Ames, Iowa: Littlefield, Adams, 1957, p. 106.
5. David R. Cook, *A Guide to Educational Research.* Boston: Allyn & Bacon, 1965, p. 185.
6. Gerald R. Smith, "Inadequacies of Research Proposals," *Library Trends, 13*(July 1964):69–70.
7. National Science Foundation, *Guide to Programs, Fiscal Year 1979.* Washington, D.C.: Government Printing Office, 1978, pp. vi–vii.
8. Donald T. Hawkins and Miller, Betty, "On-Line Data Base Coverage of the On-Line Information-Retrieval Literature," *On-Line Review, 1*(1977):59–64.

SELECTED BIBLIOGRAPHY

SOURCES OF ADDITIONAL INFORMATION

Ammon-Wexler, Jill and ap Carmel, Catherine. *How to Write a Winning Proposal.* Santa Cruz, Calif.: Mercury Communications, 1976.
Brogan, John A. *Clear Technical Writing.* New York: McGraw-Hill, 1973.
Brusaw, Charles T., and Alred, Gerald J. *Practical Writing; Composition for the Business and Technical World.* Boston, Mass.: Allyn & Bacon, 1973.
Brusaw, Charles T., Alred, Gerald J., and Oliu, Walter E. *Handbook of Technical Writing.* New York: St. Martins' Press, 1976.
Fear, David E., *Technical Communication.* Glenview, Ill.: Scott, Foresman, 1977.
Fear, David E. *Technical Writing.* New York: Random House, 1973.
Harris, John S., and Blake, Reed H. *Technical Writing for Social Scientists.* Chicago, Ill.: Nelson-Hall, 1976.
Jones, Walter P. *Writing Scientific Papers and Reports.* 7th ed. Dubuque, Iowa: W. C. Brown, 1976.
Mandel, Siegfried. *Writing for Science and Technology; A Practical Guide.* New York: Dell, 1970.
Orlich, Donald, and Orlich, Patricia R. *The Art of Writing Successful R&D Proposals.* Pleasantville, NY.: Redgrave, 1977.
Pauley, Steven E. *Technical Report Writing Today.* Boston, Mass.: Houghton Mifflin, 1973.

CHAPTER 15

Writing the Research Report

INTRODUCTION

The most insightful, systematic, and rigorous inquiries within librarianship will have minimal impact if research activities are not reported or reported poorly. Thus, reporting is an important facet of the research process, and scholars have a scientific obligation to effectively communicate news about completed investigations. *Research reports* are detailed and accurate accounts of the conduct of disciplined studies accomplished to solve problems or to reveal new knowledge. Most reports about inquiries within library and information science are prepared for the benefit of persons within the field; however, some accounts about research are directed to people in related fields—or even to the general public. The principal investigators of sponsored studies are often required to prepare detailed, written reports of research activities and conclusions. Whereas some findings of original investigations are reported verbally at conferences or at professional meetings, many research reports are published in one form or another. These written reports can be useful, provided that they are well-prepared, thorough, and disseminated in an appropriate publication vehicle.

Research reports must be complete, well-organized, and carefully written if their contents are to contribute to librarianship's store of knowledge. The production of an effective report depends upon a combination of factors, some of which are related to the abilities of research workers and others to the editorial capabilities and discriminatory powers of editors and publishers. These factors include the following components: the ability of investigators—their skills with analysis and synthesis and their expository powers—and the perceptiveness and evaluative powers of journal editors and referees. In turn, all of these factors contribute to the degree of success that the audience might achieve in comprehending the reports. Thus, in this chapter, we shall explore some of the fundamentals of effective report writing, insofar as research workers are concerned,

371

placing emphasis upon the following topics: (*a*) selection of an appropriate audience and publication vehicle; (*b*) major components of completed research reports; (*c*) fundamentals of style and grammar; and (*d*) preparation of manuscripts.

SELECTING REPORT VEHICLES AND AUDIENCES

Research reports can be prepared for a variety of audiences; however, most accounts of inquiries are geared to scholars or to research-minded readers. When the nature of a study is more practical than theoretical— that is, when an inquiry has implications for operations—the research report may be directed to practicing professionals in the field. A major factor in the selection of an audience is the chosen communication vehicle. For example, a research article written for a scholarly journal such as the *Library Quarterly* should differ appreciably from a similar article prepared for a professional journal of discussion. The *Library Quarterly* is a scholarly research journal published at the University of Chicago. Its audience is comprised primarily of scholars, students, and erudite specialists. In contrast, *Library Journal* is a popular, widely read professional periodical published by the R. R. Bowker Co., and it is directed toward all practicing librarians. Thus, research articles prepared for publication in these journals differ insofar as emphasis, detail, and style are concerned.

A variety of publication outlets are receptive to reports about library and information science inquiries. As already noted, investigators may be able to communicate scholarly research articles in *Library Quarterly*. Many articles contained in this journal are based upon substantive studies, a number of which are notable dissertations and theses prepared by recipients of advanced degrees at library schools. The *Journal of Education for Librarianship,* published by the American Association of Library Schools, systematically reports studies relating to all facets of library education. *College and Research Libraries,* issued by the American Library Association, features research reports—particularly those that pertain to academic library collections, services, and personnel. *Library Resources and Technical Services,* another ALA publication, is receptive to accounts of research about the processing and organization of library materials, data processing in libraries, and library resources. Original studies relating to library history are included in the *Journal of Library History* and *Library History.*

Among other periodicals that feature library science research reports from time to time are *Catholic Library World, Law Library Journal, Library Association Record* (British), *Aslib Proceedings* (British), *School Media Quarterly, Special Libraries, RQ* (ALA Reference Services Division), and *Wilson Library Bulletin.* Research relating to information science and computer science is often reported in the *Journal of Library Automation, Journal of the American Society for Information Science,* and *Journal of Documentation.* In addition to these, the following serial publications feature research reports about information processing and retrieval: *Journal of the Association for Computing Machinery, Information Processing and Management, Communications of the Association for Computing Machinery,* and *Journal of Chemical Documentation.* Publications of state and regional library associations are additional outlets for research reports, particularly studies of potential local appeal, relevance, and application. The following publications are examples of these journals: *Bay State Librarian, British Columbia Library Quarterly, California Librarian, Mountain Plains Library Quarterly, Ohio Library Association Bulletin, Pacific Northwest Library Association Quarterly, Southeastern Librarian,* and *Texas Library Journal.*

Library related research reports are also published occasionally in journals outside the field. If the research technique or subject of an inquiry is of potential interest to scholars in other fields, librarians might also investigate the possibility of getting reports about studies into print in the literature of other disciplines and professions. Research articles written by librarians have been accepted for publication by journals such as *Educational Broadcasting Review, Journal of Educational Research, Journal of Experimental Education, Phi Delta Kappan, AAUP Bulletin,* and *Public Opinion Quarterly.* Reports of research in the area of information science have occasionally been published in *Science* and *Nature.* As an aid to the location of additional publication vehicles, the *Directory of Scholarly and Research Publishing Opportunities*[1] contains a list of more than 10,000 scholarly and research journals in the United States. It also provides information about publishing requirements, including details concerning the preparation of manuscripts.

Fugitive mimeographed or near-print reports of mixed quality are acquired and indexed by various clearinghouses of the Educational Resources Information Center (ERIC). Designed to make possible the early identification and acquisition of reports of interest to the educational community, this service of the Office of Education, U.S. Department of Health, Education and Welfare provides citations and abstracts for research reports in the monthly *Resources in Education.* Reproductions and microform copies of reports upon which ERIC abstracts are based can be obtained at a modest cost through the Educational Document Reproduction Service. Through this service, research reports are made more accessible to larger audiences. Citations for all ERIC library and information science reports are also indexed in *Library Literature*. Thus, investigators can place elusive research reports in the bibliographic mainstream of the literature of the field. Research workers should not overlook the ERIC system as a means of communicating unpublished reports to larger audiences.

Occasionally, reports of library science research are issued as monographs. Some examples of these are the following: John P. Comaromi's *A Survey of the Use of the Dewey Decimal Classification in the United States and Canada*[2]; Lowell Martin's four surveys conducted under the auspices of the Diches Fund Studies of Public Library Services[3]; James Freeman's *Public Library Use in Denver*[4]; Stanley J. Slote's *Weeding Library Collections*[5]; Ray E. Held's *The Rise of the Public Library in California*[6]; and Ann Prentice's *The Public Library Trustee: Image and Performance on Funding.*[7] Furthermore, sponsored studies are often published as institutional or agency reports. Some examples are the following: Gerald M. Gee's *Urban Information Needs*[8]; *California Public Library Systems: A Comprehensive Review with Guidelines for the Next Decade*[9]; Ray L. Carpenter's *A Study of Public Library Patrons in North Carolina . . .*[10]; and *A Study of Minnesota Public Library Services: Costs and Implications.*[11]

The selection of a publication vehicle in which to communicate a research report should depend upon the topic of the study, the nature of the material presented, and the desired audience. If a research undertaking has wide theoretical implications for future studies, a scholarly journal might be selected so that an in-depth treatment can be given to the inquiry's conception, design, and implementation. If a study was conducted to solve an immediate, practical problem, however, the investigator might choose a journal directed toward practicing professionals. Research activities and their products are sometimes described in several reports designed for different audiences. For example, an author writing about a large-scale study that could be of interest and significance to many librarians or of possible applicability in many libraries might prepare each of the following reports, among others: (*a*) a lengthy article that contains a discussion of all aspects of a study and is designed for a scholarly journal; (*b*) a less extensive report which concentrates on the application of research findings to library practices; and (*c*) a general news release that presents only the conclusions of a study for the benefit of laypersons or practicing librarians. The scope, depth, and detail of these three types of research reports would differ, because each account is written for a specific audience.

Perhaps some examples of the communication of research reports by more than one outlet would be helpful to readers. For instance, preliminary results of the 1972–1974 Southeastern States Cooperative Library Survey were first presented at a conference of the Southeastern Library Association in 1974. A synopsis of the library personnel section of the survey was also distributed in pamphlet form at the conference.[12] Later, the *Southeastern Librarian* featured a preliminary report of the survey.[13] A final, detailed, and comprehensive report comprised of 535 pages was released in 1975 by Georgia Institute of Technology's Industrial Development Division.[14] Another example of the use of multiple outlets for reports is the 1970 survey of censorship attitudes among public librarians, conducted by Charles H. Busha. A report of the initial study undertaken among graduate students at Indiana University as a first pretest of the survey questionnaire was published in the *Journal of Education for Librarianship*.[15] Because the subsequent five-state survey served as a basis for a doctoral project at Indiana University, one report was a dissertation.[16] A lengthy article containing a summary of the survey research and its conclusions was then published in the *Library Quarterly*,[17] and a brief synopsis of major findings was also featured in the ALA *Newsletter on Intellectual Freedom*.[18] The dissertation that had served as a basis for all these articles was then revised and expanded and issued as a book in the series Research Studies in Library Science, published by Libraries Unlimited.[19] Each of these publications was different in regard to scope, detail, and emphasis; thus, the reports were designed for specific audiences and had unique purposes.

Writers of research reports should be aware that manuscripts submitted to scholarly journals are generally evaluated by referees who judge all prospective articles in terms of their value and suitability for publication. Although some journals engage the services of a regular group of referees, others distribute manuscripts to subject experts—that is, referees selected to perform a one-time, usually anonymous service. Refereed journals tend to be the more scholarly publications of a given field or profession. Editors often provide referees with evaluation guidelines. To investigate refereeing practices of journals, the Institute of Electrical and Electronics Engineers (IEEE) conducted a study of the acceptance and rejection of manuscripts.[20] The report of the IEEE study is worthy of attention; it noted that articles based upon research are typically evaluated by the investigator's peers, who are generally critical of the methodology employed, the interpretation of data, and the overall worthiness of the research report and its implications. Referees also make judgments on the clarity and style of submitted manuscripts. Ethics of the publishing field are based upon the assumption that manuscripts have not been previously published nor submitted concurrently to other journals. In a similar vein, manuscripts are considered to be privileged information by both editors and referees.

When an editorial staff has issued style manuals or procedures for the preparation and submission of manuscripts, the task of tailoring reports to publishers' requirements is made easier. For example, the American Psychological Association has issued the *Publication Manual,*[21] an editorial guide for contributors to psychological journals. In addition, the widely accepted *MLA Style Sheet,*[22] prepared by the Modern Language Association of America, is also a guide to the preparation of manuscripts. Numerous journals—particularly in the area of the humanities—have noted that "Manuscripts should be prepared in conformity with the *MLA Style Sheet.*" Once a vehicle has been selected, conscientious authors always consult whatever publications manuals are available from its editors. Furthermore, astute investigators become very familiar with characteristics of published articles in journals that are under consideration as possible research-report outlets. Many report writers follow the practice of submitting queries to prospective publishers, briefly outlining the nature and scope of their work and inquiring about the suitability of research articles for publication. Queries of this nature can often save time and unnecessary effort. Once an article has been tentatively accepted for publication, its chances of getting into print are increased appreciably if writers place emphasis upon the level of detail, explanation, clarity, and precision required by a journal's editorial staff. Recognition of readers' needs will also enhance both publication success and the quality of the research article.

ORGANIZATION OF REPORTS

Scholars in the field have complained from time to time that muddled explanations are offered by authors of research reports. Indeed, reporters have sometimes failed to clearly state hypotheses or research questions and to adequately explain how data were collected and analyzed. Although poor research reporting might reflect the shortcomings of some completed inquiries, deficiencies of reports could also be the result of investigators inadvertently omitting or glossing over research details on the assumption that readers will understand the described investigative methodology without benefit of detailed explanations. Drawing upon his experience as an editor of the *Library Quarterly,* Leon Carnovsky provided some basic guidelines to authors of research articles to be submitted to journals. Although these standards for the writing of articles might appear to be obvious, Carnovsky indicated that they were frequently ignored by writers. Thus, he suggested the following measures: (*a*) manuscripts must be typed (double spaced) with wide margins on sturdy paper; (*b*) footnotes should be accurate; (*c*) quotations ought to be exact; (*d*) a manual of style should be followed systematically so that documentation is uniform; (*e*) an appropriate journal ought to be selected in which to communicate the report; and (*f*) "respect" must be shown for the English language.[22] As indicated previously, an awareness of the needs and expectations of a periodical's audience can allow reports to be structured from the reader's point of view. Generally, this process entails placing emphasis upon or deemphasizing certain aspects of a study or providing more or less detail, depending upon readers' needs and interests. Regardless of the level of research awareness among readers, most audiences expect a well-organized and cohesive explanation of the essentials of completed research, including a statement of the study's purpose, a discussion of how the project relates to other completed inquiries, details about data collection and analysis, and a presentation and summary of research conclusions. Careful attention to aspects of a study that are likely to attract the most interest will further lead to more meaningful organization and presentation.

Once a suitable journal has been targeted as an outlet, the report writer structures the article for the selected publication. Competent reporters usually attempt to include the following information in reports: *who* conducted the research, *when* the study was carried out, *why* it was undertaken, *how* it was accomplished, *what* data were collected, *how* the data were analyzed, and *what* conclusions were drawn. When an investigator has carefully conducted a project, the task of providing a well-written research report is greatly facilitated. Reports can be variously organized, depending upon the nature and scope of an investigation; however, these narrative accounts are often structured according to the process by which the research was conceptualized and accomplished. From an examination of several published reports in scholarly journals, readers can, no doubt, recognize a general pattern; yet, the elements may differ somewhat from report to report, particularly in regard to the amount of detail presented. In their efforts to explain accomplished investigations, scientists often make use of the following generalized format for their research reports.

GENERAL INTRODUCTION: EXPLANATION OF THE THEORETICAL OR PRACTICAL CONTEXT OUT OF WHICH THE RESEARCH PROBLEM ORIGINATED

Here, in an introduction, the reader is told why the study was undertaken—that is, the significance of the research problem and the purpose of the overall project. Information about background elements and the rationale of the study is also provided so that the inquiry can be placed in its proper setting. Furthermore, the scope and limitations of the study are stated, and unusual or unfamiliar terms are defined.

REVIEW OF THE LITERATURE: CRITICAL SUMMARY OF DIFFERENT FACETS OF THE RESEARCH PROBLEM AS REPORTED IN EXISTING SOURCES

A literature review is included here, the length of the presentation depending upon the extent of relevant literature, the complexity of the inquiry being reported, and the needs of an audience. Frequently, a statement is included about contributions of the research to larger investigative problems. Furthermore, the reporter sometimes comments briefly in this section on the state of the art.

CONCEPTUAL FRAMEWORK OF THE STUDY: EXPLANATION OF THE HYPOTHESES OR THE RESEARCH QUESTIONS

Assumptions are carefully and precisely identified in this part of the report, and the general research problem is narrowed down and restated in terms of specific hypotheses or research questions. Hypotheses and questions are often discussed in terms of their relationship to objectives of the study. Operational definitions of concepts in the hypotheses or in the research problem are also provided. When a study was not designed to test hypotheses, the overall thesis of the inquiry is clearly outlined. In any event, theoretical and practical implications should be discussed thoroughly in this part of the report.

DATA COLLECTION: EXPLANATION OF PROCEDURES AND METHODS USED

The writer focuses attention in this section of the report on how the research problem was attacked and the sources of relevant data, including methods used to obtain them. An exact, detailed description of all steps taken to collect data is offered (e.g., selection of subjects; the location of the study; instruments of measurement used; and special problems pertaining to the study's design, such as sampling methods, control and experimental groups, and test effects). Adequate descriptions of procedures will facilitate better understanding of how the study was accomplished. When pertinent, methods used to validate and to pretest instruments are also described. In addition, limitations inherent in the study's methodology should be discussed in terms of actual or possible negative effects on results of the inquiry.

DATA ANALYSIS: EXPLANATION OF HOW THE COLLECTED INFORMATION WAS ANALYZED

Here, the reporter completes the explanation of how the research problem was addressed. Statistical methods used to test hypotheses are explained; if other data analysis techniques were employed, they are described. The audience's level of sophistication in regard to quantification techniques and statistical analysis should govern the extent to which technical details of data analysis are explained. If appropriate, data are also presented in this section of the report in visual formats such as tables, diagrams, figures, or other graphical devices. The use of visual aids should be based upon their potential value to improve the reader's comprehension of research data and implications of these data.

GENERAL CONCLUSIONS: EXPLANATION AND INTERPRETATION OF THE RESEARCH FINDINGS AND THE DECISIONS

Results of the completed study with respect to the hypotheses and to the validation of findings are described here. The reporter also focuses on the interpretation of findings in regard to the theoretical body of knowledge from which the research problem originated and to the stated objectives of the study. To stimulate greater reader comprehension of the results, research objectives might also be restated here. In the presentation of interpretations, arguments should be developed in logical, sequential steps. When necessary, original hypotheses are also clarified and reformed for the benefit of subsequent investigators in the targeted problem area. Implications of the completed inquiry to library practices should also be discussed so that readers are not left to guess about applications of research findings. Suggestions for additional related studies are also frequently offered in this section.

Although other frameworks for research reports can be used, our generalized scenario is acceptable to many scholars in the scientific community, and it has proved to be effective in logically presenting the results of most types of research. Writers must decide upon the most appropriate organization for their own reports, relying primarily upon expectations and needs of the desired audience. But whatever the selected organization may be, the approach to research reporting ought to be based upon a meaningful framework. Good organization aids in the development of logical explanations. A complete report of an inquiry typically provides both general information for practicing professionals and discussions about technical details of possible use to scholars and other investigators. Good research reports are prepared in sufficient detail to allow replications of the described study by other persons.

If aspects of investigations such as sample selection, data-gathering instruments, experimental designs, and statistical methods are not clearly explained with sufficient detail, persons who attempt to use the described methodology are left uninformed about important elements of the inquiry. In addition, ineffective reporting can lead to doubts concerning the validity and reliability of research data and conclusions. Thus, a solidly conducted research project can be rendered almost useless by poor reporting.

ADDITIONAL SUGGESTIONS FOR REPORTS

Summaries of research reports are also sometimes prepared by reporters. These summaries usually take the form of an *abstract,* which includes a statement of the research problem, a summary of methodology, and the results. Abstracts should contain only essential information about an inquiry; they ought to be stringent condensations of research reports. Thus, one or two short paragraphs are sufficient to note key elements of a study. The digested information in abstracts is used by persons who are too busy to read all relevant literature. Scholars are especially dependent upon these summaries to locate works of interest and to eliminate those that do not warrant their further attention. The abstract that follows contains succinct, yet adequate, information relating to the basic elements of an inquiry concerned with book selection methods of academic libraries.

Sample Abstract

Evans, G. Edward, "Book Selection and Book Collection Usage in Academic Libraries," *Library Quarterly 40*(**July 1970**):**297–308.**

A condensation of a 1969 University of Illinois doctoral dissertation, conducted to test the hypothesis that more titles matching needs of academic library users are selected by librarians than by faculty members or by means of blanket-order approval plans. Random samples of 500 current-imprint monographs from four unmatched libraries were chosen from collections acquired by each selection method. Circulation records were then examined to determine actual book usage during a 1-year period. The significance of circulation differences was tested with the chi-square statistic, and the hypothesis was supported. Results imply that librarians having greater contact with users will develop more useful collections.

In addition to abstracts, introductions are also provided in research reports, as indicated previously. The best introductions tend to be specific rather than long discourses. Sufficient information should be provided in introductions so that the significance of the research is made explicit. A project's value can usually be demonstrated by an explanation of how research questions are significant in terms of repercussions on associated theories. Unusual words or terms should also be defined in the introduction. This will aid reader comprehension of the subject matter and tends to be especially useful to persons who are unfamiliar with the topic of the inquiry. Although investigators have a scientific obligation to relate their work to similar studies conducted by other scholars, reporters should judiciously mention only the most closely related research projects and their results. Thus, cautious writers refrain from overzealous discussions of related studies and do not pad reports with tangental literature. On the other hand, research scholars should not fail to place their work within the body of pertinent theory and associated inquiries of other investigators in the field.

Scientists are obligated to clearly explain how evidence was gathered, evaluated, and used in regard to hypotheses or research questions. Vague descriptions are avoided; they can cause doubts about the investigator's ability and integrity. Research evidence might consist of test scores, information obtained from interviews, measurements produced by experimentation, questionnaire data, assorted facts verified by observation or obtained from authoritative sources, historical data, or a variety of other selected facts or figures. Whatever the evidence may be, no facet of the data-collection method should be slighted in scholarly research reports. Unnecessarily lengthy and overcomplicated discussions of statistical methods can be avoided by referring the reader to sources that contain more complete explanations about the employed techniques. Reporters should also be candid when weaknesses in the design and implementation of an inquiry are described. If weaknesses are not pointed out in research reports, critics are apt to quickly identify them. A failure to describe a study's faults could cause doubts to be raised about an inquiry. When results of a study are evaluated, careful scholars remain aware that findings, interpretations, conclusions, and implementations are not synonomous concepts. Research conclusions are based upon collected evidence and are developed from findings. Implications are estimates of the meaning and value of research findings. Effective reporters also avoid the use of various meanings for the same term. Carelessly written research reports lead to unclear communication; thus, attempts to achieve precision should always be made.

The task of report writers is to synthesize an entire research project. Good syntax in research reports is the product of careful attention to connecting ideas and elements so that the message is clearly stated. Subheadings are useful as guideposts to readers. These headings do not eliminate the need for transitional elements between sections, although subheads do set off various parts of reports. Titles selected for research reports should accurately reflect the nature and scope of a study. Ambiguous titles should be avoided; they only obfuscate the topic of the reported investigation. Bibliographies at the end of research reports serve as records of sources of information and as guide to additional knowledge. Works included in bibliographies of supplementary sources should be highly selective. Footnotes must be adequate both for the purpose of documentation and the needs of readers who may desire additional, relevant information. Some research workers—especially historians—rely heavily upon information recorded in both published and unpublished documents; thus, the extensive documentation necessary for certain investigations will entail numerous footnotes and a long bibliography. Credit should be given to sources of the following borrowed materials: (*a*) ideas that are not original on the part of the conductors of the study; (*b*) direct quotations obtained from written or printed records; (*c*) obscure information or facts, and (*d*) previously compiled quantitative data (i.e., statistical information recorded in reference sources such as census publications). Documentation allows credit for the work, ideas, and collected data of other scholars. A common tendency of beginning research workers and inexperienced writers is excessive documentation ("over-footnoting"). The amount of documentation provided in a report should be based upon both the nature of the problem and the employed methodology. Over-documentation can often be avoided when information obtained from several sources is skillfully synthesized.

Outlines can be used by report writers to organize pertinent information into a finished narrative. An *outline* is essentially a skeletal framework upon which a report is constructed from developmental materials. A complete outline assists the writer in recognizing logical relationships between narrative elements of reports. Outlines are also useful for the construction of cohesive paragraphs and sections that are effectively connected with transitional sentences. *Topical outlines* are cryptic lists of written elements of a document. On the other hand, *sentence outlines* contain complete statements about narrative elements. Thus, topical outlines are telescopic, whereas sentence outlines are groups of complete thoughts. Most writers prefer to work with topical outlines because of their ease of preparation and brevity. Although some writers despair of preparing outlines, scholars who attempt to write effective research reports can benefit from the system of logic that outlines tend to impose upon a mass of information. Therefore, the time and effort required to produce a good outline are worthwhile; these frameworks can conserve energy and assist writers in preparing reports that present research information in a logical manner.

Reporters should bear in mind that the publication of a report places an investigation in an open arena of scrutiny and evaluation. The peers of an investigator will judge a completed research undertaking primarily on the basis of the research report. Although poorly conducted studies cannot be disguised very easily by well-written reports, the best research efforts can be obscured by poor reporting. Careless mistakes in a report may cause discerning readers to question the quality of a completed project; thus, reporters must strive for accuracy. For example, when manuscripts are typed and visual aids are prepared for a report, the writer ought to be watchful for errors. In a similar vein, galley proofs of printed reports must be proofread thoroughly. Particular attention should be focused on the accuracy of quantitative data in graphical materials, as well as misspelled words and typographical errors.

GRAMMAR, PUNCTUATION, AND WORD USAGE

Writers who aspire to produce precise and clearly worded research reports pay particular attention to diction, syntax, and transition between narrative sections. Phrases or subordinate clauses are not used as though they are complete thoughts; thus, reports are comprised of complete sentences. All sentences must be carefully checked to verify that correct forms of verbs are used. Verbs should agree in number with the subjects of sentences, and pronouns should agree with their antecedents. Capitalization is used for the first letters of proper names; titles preceeding names; place names; and the first letters of all words in titles of publications, excluding words that are articles or conjunctions. Titles of books, films, plays, and poems should be italicized (underlined in manuscripts). If foreign words or phrases are used, they are also italicized. Italics can also be employed to place emphasis, but excessive italicization for this purpose is avoided. Abbreviations should also be avoided, but acronyms can be used sparingly if they are properly identified when they first appear in the text. Words, phrases, or clauses listed in a series should be separated with commas. Otherwise, sentence structure is used as a guide to the placing of commas. Superfluous commas should be avoided. All direct quotations and words used in a special sense are set off with quotation marks. Dashes should be used to set off parenthetical elements in the text and to indicate sudden breaks of thought. Parenthetical expressions may also be designated within parentheses. Brackets are used to indicate corrective elements supplied in direct quotations or to set off interpolations injected into borrowed material. When two or more words are used as one word, they are joined with a hyphen (or hyphens).

Colloquialisms, slang, unconventional words, dialectial phrases, and jargon should be avoided in formal reports. Standard English words are always preferable to unusual, obsolete, or unique terms. In the preparation of narratives about research activities, exact words are used; a specific rather than a vague term should be chosen. Trite cliches and hackneyed expressions are also avoided; good writers also refrain from wordiness and repetition. To promote unity and logical thought, sentences are not filled with too many ideas or details. Whenever possible, a simple sentence is used rather than a complex one. Dangling modifiers and misplaced clauses must also be avoided.

Research terminology is replete with words that are sometimes misspelled or incorrectly used. Because precision is a criterion of scientific inquiry, writers of reports usually attempt to prepare their accounts of investigations accordingly. Thus, words are chosen carefully so that no doubt will arise about meanings of terms or narrative sections. The following list contains problem words, many of which are often found in research reports in librarianship. The most commonly preferred spellings are indicated in the list. Some of the terms are frequently confused with similar sounding words; thus, their correct usage has been indicated. This list should be valuable to writers of research reports when uncertainty arises about word usage or correct spellings.

Some Problem Words Often Used in Research

abbreviation

abridgment

accede (to yield), confused with exceed (to surpass)

accept (to take), confused with except (to exclude)

accommodate

accreditation

acknowledgment

acquaint

acquisition

addendum; *pl.* addenda

affect (influence), confused with effect (result)

agendum; *pl.* agenda

allusion (indirect reference), confused with illusion (false image)

alumnus (masculine singular)

alumni (masculine plural, and plural for males and females together)

alumna (feminine singular)

alumnae (feminine plural)

amateur
ambiguity
analogy; *pl.* analogies
analysis; *pl.* analyses
annotation
anonymous
antithesis
antiquarian
appendix; *pl.* appendixes or appendices
apprenticeship
ascent (rise), confused with assent (consent)
atheneum
axis; *pl.* axes
basis; *pl.* bases
biased
bibliography (list), confused with biography (story of a life)
breach (gap), confused with breech (lower part)
caliber
calligraphy
canceled
candidate
cassette
catalog (British spelling is catalogue)
causal (cause), confused with casual (not planned; aimless)
channeled
citable
collation
colophon
commiserate
complement (to make complete), confused with compliment (praise)
comprehensive
concise
concordance
consummate
continuously
corollary
crisis; *pl.* crises
criterion; *pl.* criteria
cuneiform
curriculum; *pl.* curricula
cyclopedia
datum; *pl.* data
desideratum; *pl.* desiderata
device (contrivance), confused with devise (invent)

diagrammatic
discreet (prudent), confused with discrete (distinct)
doctoral
dossier
eleemosynary
elicit (to draw out), confused with illicit (illegal)
ellipsis
empirical
encyclopedia (British spelling is encyclopaedia)
enlightenment
entrepreneur
enumerative
epilogue
equilibrium; *pl.* equilibriums or equilibria
erratum; *pl.* errata
etiquette
etymology (word origin), confused with entomology (study of insects)
exhibitor
existence
extant (in existence), confused with extent (range)
extraneous
farther (distance), confused with further (moreover)
festschriften
formula; *pl.* formulas or formulae
fledgling
forbear (endurance), confused with forebear (ancestor)
foresee
forgettable
fulfill
gazeteer
genius; *pl.* geniuses
guarantee (verb), confused with guaranty (noun)
guttural
heterogeneous
homogeneity
hypotenuse
hypothesis; *pl.* hypotheses
idiosyncrasy
imprimatur
incunabulum; *pl.* incunabula
independence
index; *pl.* indexes or indices

indict (to accuse), confused with indite (to compose)

indigenous

inequity (unfairness), confused with iniquity (sin)

infer (deduce), confused with imply (indicate)

ingenious (skillful), confused with ingenuous (simple)

intelligentsia

interest

irrelevant

its (possessive pronoun), confused with it's (contraction of it is)

judgment

laboratory

liaison

license

likable

locus; *pl.* loci

maneuver

matrix; *pl.* matrices or matrixes

maximum; *pl.* maximums or maxima

medieval

medium; *pl.* media

memorandum; *pl.* memoranda

millieu

millennium

minutia; *pl.* minutiae

misspell

monolog

Newbery (award), confused with Newberry (library)

occurred

occurrence

omission

ordinance (law), confused with ordnance (military arms)

paradigm

paralleled

parameter

parenthesis; *pl.* parentheses

parsimony

perceived

perennial

perform

personal (individual), confused with personnel (staff)

perspective (view), confused with prospective (expected)

pharmacopoeia

phenomenon; *pl.* phenomena

Phoenician

phraseology

precedents (examples), confused with precedence (priority)

prerequisite (requirement), confused with perquisite (privilege)

principal (chief), confused with principle (proposition)

privilege

programmer

proponents

provenance

pseudonym

qualitative

quantitative

questionnaire

referable

registrar

reminiscence

renaissance

reparable

reprography

respectively (in reference to two or more, in the order mentioned), confused with respectfully (in a respectful manner)

retrieval

retrospective

rhetorical

rubricate

satellite

scurrilous

serendipity

soliloquy

sometime (formerly), confused with some time (some time ago) and with sometimes (at times)

sponsor

stationary (fixed), confused with stationery (paper)

statue (sculpture), confused with stature (height) and statute (law)

stenciled

stereotype

stratagem

stratum; *pl.* strata

substantiate

subtlety

surreptitious

syllogism
symbolization
synonymous
synopsis; *pl.* synopses
synthesis
tableau; *pl.* tableaus or tableaux
tactician
thesaurus; *pl.* thesauri
thesis; *pl.* theses
totaled
transferable

transferred
travelog
troop (soldiers), confused with troupe (actors)
vacillate
vellum
vicissitude
vilify
vying
willful

PREPARATION OF MANUSCRIPTS

Weaknesses in manuscripts are often caused by carelessness of writers. Observation of a few, simple guidelines and attention to editorial requirements of journals will strengthen reports. Because specific requirements for the preparation and submission of manuscripts vary somewhat from publisher to publisher, only the most commonly used and generally accepted procedures will be reviewed. Writers of reports that will be submitted for publication should consult with editors of journals concerning all unique requirements. Then, manuscripts should be typed with double or triple spacing, depending upon editorial requirements of specific publications. In any event, single-spaced manuscripts should never be submitted. Standard size sheets of paper which measure $8\frac{1}{2}$ by 11 inches should be used for manuscripts. A thorough cleaning of the type and a fresh typewriter ribbon will contribute to more legible copy. Usually, only one original copy of a manuscript is submitted to journals; however, a few editors require an original plus one copy. Usually a mimeograph, ditto, or photocopy of the original manuscript is not submitted, but a copy of the manuscript should be kept by the author for future reference should the need arise. Typed sheets of manuscripts must be neat and uniform. Margins at least 1-inch wide should be left on both sides of pages, as well as at the top and bottom. With the exception of paragraph indentions and long, direct quotations, a uniform left-hand margin should be maintained. The title of the report is centered at least $1\frac{1}{2}$ inches below the top of the first manuscript sheet; it should be typed in upper- and lowercase letters and should not be underlined. The author's name is centered below the title and is also typed in large and small letters. Some inexperienced writers tend to underline excessively, but only those words or phrases to be set in italics should be underlined.

Separate sheets for illustrative materials such as tables, graphs, figure captions, and drawings are often required for manuscripts. Notes are made in the typed text to indicate the exact location of such visual aids as they will appear in the printed article. Pages are numbered in Arabic numerals (i.e., 1, 2, 3, etc.), in consecutive order, and in a consistent position on typed sheets. If insertions or deletions are necessary in finished manuscripts, a few can be made; however, too many changes can produce an untidy typewritten document. The following system can be used to number inserted pages: 12a, 12b, etc. Deletions may result in condensations of sections of the manuscript; thus, some numbered pages might have to be corrected. For example, assume that page 6 was deleted from a manuscript. The writer could then renumber page 5 as page 5–6. Most authors place their names and addresses in the upper, right-hand corner of the manuscript's title page. In some cases, writers also place their last names in the upper, right-hand corner of all pages that follow the title page. This measure will aid typesetters in locating and identifying manuscript pages that might be temporarily misplaced during the printing process.

Authors of reports should carefully copyread typed manuscripts, verifying all quotations and footnotes with original sources. If minor corrections or insertions are necessary, they can be typed or written in ink above the line of the manuscript that contains the error or omission. Manuscripts or individual pages with excessive corrections or insertions should be retyped. Most authors prepare a cover letter to accompany their submitted manuscripts. These letters briefly outline the research worker's qualifications, background, and interest with reference to the subject of the completed inquiry. Manuscripts ought to be mailed to publishers in heavy envelopes or secure packages. A stiff cardboard filler for the manuscript is suggested when illustrative material such as photographs, drawings, or similar graphical works are to be included with mailed papers. Manuscripts should always be sent to publishers by first-class mail, and a self-addressed envelope with sufficient unattached postage should be included for possible return of a rejected article. Sheets of submitted materials should not be stapled or fastened with anything other than a paper clip; editors prefer to work with loose sheets as they perform editorial tasks and prepare instructions to printers.

SUMMARY

Reporting is the last major step in the conduct of a research project. Effective reports of completed research can communicate the procedures and results of studies both to scholars and practicing professionals in librarianship. Poorly prepared research reports can do a disservice to the most significant and rigorously conducted studies. On the other hand, good reports effectively record all important elements of an investigation and facilitate the replication of studies so that data and conclusions can be verified. Although the writer's task is made easier when research has been conducted with sound procedures, the reporter must carefully interpret the aims, methods, and results of inquiries, whatever the strengths or weaknesses of these studies may be.

Research reports will vary with respect to the proportion of the written record that is devoted to explanations of descriptive and quantitative evidence in contrast to the proportions devoted to explanations of the qualitative analysis and synthesis, and to the testing of hypotheses and the drawing of inferences. Investigators must select the appropriate vehicle(s) in which to publish their research reports; writers must also structure their reports so that essential elements of inquiries are recorded clearly and accurately. The utilization of an appropriate framework for the report will help to ensure logical narratives that enhance reader interest and comprehension. Complete accounts of scientific activities will relate reported studies to other significant inquiries. Effective reports must contain adequate explanations of the research hypothesis or question, research design, methodology used to implement the design, analysis of data, conclusions, and implications of completed projects. Attention to fundamentals of good expository writing will help research workers to improve the quality of reports. When the writer has adequately analyzed and synthesized the research process, the report is ready to be exhibited in an appropriate publication. In the arena of public scrutiny, critics will utilize the investigative account to determine the quality and value of the described research.

REFERENCES

1. Alvin Renetzky, *Directory of Scholarly and Research Publishing Opportunities: A Guide to Academic Publishing Opportunities in the Humanities, Social Sciences, and Science and Technology*. Orange, N.J.: Academic Media, 1971.
2. John P. Comaromi *et al., A Survey of the Use of the Dewey Decimal Classification in the United States and Canada*. Albany, N.Y.: Forest Press, 1975.
3. Lowell A. Martin, *Students and the Pratt Library: Challenge and Opportunity* (1963); *Space in Pratt Central* (1964); *Baltimore Reaches Out; Library Services to the Disadvantaged* (1967); and *Adults and the Pratt Library: A Question of the Quality of Life* (1974). Baltimore, Md.: Deiches Fund Studies of the Public Library, 1963–1974.
4. James Freeman, Byrden, John P., and Jaeckel, Eric F., *Public Library Use in Denver*. Denver, Colo.: Denver Urban Observatory, 1974.
5. Stanley J. Slote, *Weeding Library Collections,* Research Studies in Library Science, no. 14. Littleton, Colo.: Libraries Unlimited, 1975.
6. Ray E. Held, *The Rise of the Public Library in California*. Chicago, Ill.: American Library Association, 1972.

7. Ann Prentice, *The Public Library Trustee: Image and Performance on Funding.* Metuchen, N.J.: Scarecrow Press, 1973.

8. Gerald M. Gee, *Urban Information Needs: A Replication; A Report of the Syracuse/ Elmira Study.* Syracuse, N.Y.: Syracuse University Center for the Study of Information and Education, 1974.

9. Peat, Marwick, Mitchell and Co., *California Public Library Systems; A Comprehensive Review With Guidelines for the Next Decade.* Sacramento: California State Library, 1975.

10. Ray L. Carpenter, *A Study of Public Library Patrons in North Carolina: Socioeconomic, Media Use, Life Style Characteristics of North Carolina's Public Library Clientele.* Raleigh: North Carolina Division of the State Library, 1975.

11. Westat, Inc., *A Study of Minnesota Public Library Services: Costs and Implications; Final Report.* St. Paul: Minnesota State Department of Education, Office of Public Libraries, 1974.

12. Southeastern Library Association, *Librarians in the Southeast: Preliminary Findings of the Southeastern States Cooperative Library Survey.* Atlanta: Georgia Institute of Technology, Industrial Development Division, Engineering Experiment Station, 1974.

13. Mary Edna Anders, "Your Survey Moves Ahead," *Southeastern Librarian, 24*(Summer 1974):11–13.

14. Mary Edna Anders, *The Southeastern States Cooperative Library Survey, 1972–1974: Tables.* Atlanta: Georgia Institute of Technology, 1975.

15. Charles H. Busha, "Student Attitudes Toward Censorship and Authoritarianism," *Journal of Education for Librarianship, 20*(Fall 1970):110–136.

16. Charles H. Busha, *The Attitudes of Midwestern Public Librarians toward Intellectual Freedom and Censorship* (unpublished doctoral dissertation, Indiana University, 1971).

17. Charles H. Busha, "Intellectual Freedom and Censorship: The Climate of Opinion in Midwestern Public Libraries," *Library Quarterly, 42*(July 1972):283–301.

18. Charles H. Busha, "Censorship and the Midwestern Public Librarian," *Newsletter on Intellectual Freedom, 20*(September 1971):103–104.

19. Charles H. Busha, *Freedom versus Suppression and Censorship,* Research Studies in Library Science, no. 8. Littleton, Colo.: Libraries Unlimited, 1972.

20. Stephen Juhasz, "Acceptance and Rejection of Manuscripts," Special Issue: Record of the 1975 IEEE Conference on Scientific Journals, *IEEE Transactions on Professional Communication* PC-18, no. 3 (September 1975):177–184.

21. *Publication Manual of the American Psychological Association.* Washington, D.C.: American Psychological Association 1967, 1973 reprint.

22. *The MLA Style Sheet,* 2nd ed. New York: Publications Center, Modern Language Association of America, 1970.

SELECTED BIBLIOGRAPHY

GUIDES AND MANUALS FOR RESEARCH REPORT WRITING

Allen, George R., *The Graduate Student's Guide to Theses and Dissertations: A Practical Manual for Writing and Research.* San Francisco, Calif.: Jossey-Bass, 1973.

Campbell, William G., *Form and Style in Thesis Writing*. 4th ed. Boston, Mass.: Houghton Mifflin, 1974.

Cole, Arthur H., and Bigelow, Karl W., *A Manual of Thesis Writing for Graduates and Undergraduates*. New York: Wiley, 1960.

Flesch, R. *The Art of Readable Writing*. New York: Harper & Row, 1949.

Foster, John, Jr., *Science Writer's Guide*. New York: Columbia University Press, 1963.

Gunning, Robert. *The Technique of Clear Writing*. New York: McGraw-Hill, 1968.

Hook, Lucyle, and Gaver, Mary V., *The Research Paper*. 3rd ed. Englewood Cliffs, N.J.: Prentice-Hall, 1962.

Janis, J. Harold. *Writing and Communication in Business*. 3rd ed. New York: Macmillan, 1978.

Jordan, Lewis. *The New York Times Manual of Style and Usage: A Desk Book of Guidelines for Writers and Editors*. New York: Times Books, 1976.

Koefod, Paul E., *The Writing Requirements for Graduate Degrees*. Englewood Cliffs, N.J.: Prentice-Hall, 1964.

Machlup, Fritz, *The Production and Distribution of Knowledge in the United States*. Princeton, N.J.: Princeton University Press, 1962.

A Manual of Style. 12th ed. Chicago, Ill.: University of Chicago Press, 1969.

Menzel, Donald H., Jones, Howard Mumford, and Boyd, Lyle., *Writing a Technical Paper*. New York: McGraw-Hill, 1961.

Mills, Gordon H., and Water, John A., *Technical Writing*. 4th ed. New York: Holt, Rinehart and Winston, 1978.

Pauley, Steven E. *Technical Report Writing Today*. 2nd ed. Boston, Mass.: Houghton Mifflin, 1979.

Rathbone, Robert R., and Stone, James B., *A Writer's Guide for Engineers and Scientists*. Englewood Cliffs, N.J.: Prentice-Hall, 1962.

Reisman, S. J., ed. *A Style Manual for Technical Writers and Editors*. New York: Macmillan, 1962.

Rogers, Anna C., *Graphic Charts Handbook*. Washington, D.C.: Public Affairs Press, 1961.

Ross, Robert, *Research: An Introduction*. New York: Barnes & Noble, 1974.

Skillin, Marjorie E., and Gay, R. *Words into Type, A Guide in the Preparation of Manuscripts*. 3rd ed. New York: Appleton, 1974.

Spear, Mary E., *Practical Charting Techniques*. New York: McGraw-Hill, 1969.

Strunk, W., Jr., and White, E. B., *The Elements of Style*. New York: Macmillan, 1972.

Turabian, Kate L., *A Manual for Writers of Term Papers, Theses and Dissertations*. 4th ed. Chicago, Ill.: University of Chicago Press, 1973.

U.S. Government Printing Office. *Style Manual*. Rev. ed. Washington, D.C.: U.S. Government Printing Office, 1973.

Appendices

One-Thousand Random Digits

8175	0734	5956	3472	1688	4641	5675	8676	2680	0280
8306	3875	4739	0547	4934	5388	2056	2729	1824	1034
9896	0156	4581	9920	3443	0305	2271	4474	3269	6710
9308	4336	9855	4064	8542	3025	1574	0166	6863	0241
6388	8008	1210	5160	9657	1506	4774	7556	1007	8081
8065	1280	6410	6256	2576	2680	7910	0931	0140	3025
0442	3840	0881	1375	3577	1824	5681	6676	5227	1506
9536	7456	7616	9062	7949	3269	2737	5689	3215	2680
9352	5919	0034	1198	1866	6863	4911	3647	3362	1824
4599	0345	1156	3520	8195	1007	1179	3006	3030	3269
1508	1902	3633	3904	1580	0140	0904	0360	1809	6863
7406	1760	1986	2412	9640	3479	0720	2960	2724	1007
8488	9760	4419	1774	9296	2160	1840	7616	4201	0140
0461	2576	5275	4707	4156	6656	3856	0034	6484	4558
1252	3577	8256	1558	2723					
6750	7949	1615	2736	1472					
5625	1866	0822	8569	6678					
6406	8195	7568	4277	5956					
0368	1580	2746	2927	4739					
3542	9640	4051	6732	4581					
5457	9296	4106	3198	9855					
7788	4156	8592	2272	1210					
6529	2723	8224	6198	9245					
6278	1472	6341	4152	4700					
4132	6678	2082	2391	2099					
5891	3023	8687	1156	0422					
7038	1385	4639	3363	7808					
5334	9182	5203	3097	9648					
4515	3091	0712	5914	0839					
3852	5542	0694	9753	0392					
8379	7163	1210	8137	5366					
2076	9367	6345	4641	7939					
3097	7406	2590	5388	0277					
5914	8488	7081	0305	6729					
9753	0461	1405	3025	2794					
1210	1252	9740	1506	8064					

(*continued*)

Statistical Symbols Used in the Text

μ	Mean of a population. In queuing theory, μ refers to the mean rate of service provided by a service facility.
λ	Mean of a Poisson distribution. In queuing theory, λ refers to the mean arrival rate to a service facility.
ρ	Correlation coefficient associated with a population. In queuing theory, ρ also refers to the mean fraction of time a service facility will be busy.
X	An individual score in a distribution of scores.
Σ	Indicates "find the sum of," or "add."
n	The total number of scores in a distribution.
$\bar{x}$	Mean of a sample.
M	The midpoint of a class interval.
Md	Median of a distribution.
Q_1, Q_2, Q_3	Quartiles of a distribution (the twenty-fifth, fiftieth, and seventy-fifth percentiles, respectively).
σ	Standard deviation of a distribution.
σ^2	Variance of a distribution.
SE_μ	Standard error of the mean.
SE_p	Standard error of a proportion.
Δ	The amount of change observed in a quantity.
$\approx$	Approximately equal to.
r	Correlation coefficient computed on the basis of a sample.
$\hat{y}$	Predicted value of dependent variable, obtained by substitution into a regression equation.
α	Level of significance selected by an investigator for a statistical test of hypothesis. An α-error takes place when a true hypothesis is rejected.
β	A β-error takes place when a false hypothesis cannot be rejected.
χ	Identifies the χ^2 test of significance.

Cumulative Normal Frequency Distribution*

(Area under the standard normal curve from 0 to Z)

z	.00	.01	.02	.03	.04	.05	.06	.07	.08	.09
.0	.0000	.0040	.0080	.0120	.0160	.0199	.0239	.0279	.0319	.0359
.1	.0398	.0438	.0478	.0517	.0557	.0596	.0636	.0675	.0714	.0753
.2	.0793	.0832	.0871	.0910	.0948	.0987	.1026	.1064	.1103	.1141
.3	.1179	.1217	.1255	.1293	.1331	.1368	.1406	.1443	.1480	.1517
.4	.1554	.1591	.1628	.1664	.1700	.1736	.1772	.1808	.1844	.1879
.5	.1915	.1950	.1985	.2019	.2054	.2088	.2123	.2157	.2190	.2224
.6	.2257	.2291	.2324	.2357	.2389	.2422	.2454	.2486	.2517	.2549
.7	.2580	.2611	.2642	.2673	.2704	.2734	.2764	.2794	.2823	.2852
.8	.2881	.2910	.2939	.2967	.2995	.3023	.3051	.3078	.3106	.3133
.9	.3159	.3186	.3212	.3238	.3264	.3289	.3315	.3340	.3365	.3389
1.0	.3413	.3438	.3461	.3485	.3508	.3531	.3554	.3577	.3599	.3621
1.1	.3643	.3665	.3686	.3708	.3729	.3749	.3770	.3790	.3810	.3830
1.2	.3849	.3869	.3888	.3907	.3925	.3944	.3962	.3980	.3997	.4015
1.3	.4032	.4049	.4066	.4082	.4099	.4115	.4131	.4147	.4162	.4177
1.4	.4192	.4207	.4222	.4236	.4251	.4265	.4279	.4292	.4306	.4319
1.5	.4332	.4345	.4357	.4370	.4382	.4394	.4406	.4418	.4429	.4441
1.6	.4452	.4463	.4474	.4484	.4495	.4505	.4515	.4525	.4535	.4545
1.7	.4554	.4564	.4573	.4582	.4591	.4599	.4608	.4616	.4625	.4633
1.8	.4641	.4649	.4656	.4664	.4671	.4678	.4686	.4693	.4699	.4706
1.9	.4713	.4719	.4726	.4732	.4738	.4744	.4750	.4756	.4761	.4767
2.0	.4772	.4778	.4783	.4788	.4793	.4798	.4803	.4808	.4812	.4817
2.1	.4821	.4826	.4830	.4834	.4838	.4842	.4846	.4850	.4854	.4857
2.2	.4861	.4864	.4868	.4871	.4875	.4878	.4881	.4884	.4887	.4890
2.3	.4893	.4896	.4898	.4901	.4904	.4906	.4909	.4911	.4913	.4916
2.4	.4918	.4920	.4922	.4925	.4927	.4929	.4931	.4932	.4934	.4936
2.5	.4938	.4940	.4941	.4943	.4945	.4946	.4948	.4949	.4951	.4952
2.6	.4953	.4955	.4956	.4957	.4959	.4960	.4961	.4962	.4963	.4964
2.7	.4965	.4966	.4967	.4968	.4969	.4970	.4971	.4972	.4973	.4974
2.8	.4974	.4975	.4976	.4977	.4977	.4978	.4979	.4979	.4980	.4981
2.9	.4981	.4982	.4982	.4983	.4984	.4984	.4985	.4985	.4986	.4986
3.0	.4987	.4987	.4987	.4988	.4988	.4989	.4989	.4989	.4990	.4990

(Continued)

* Reprinted by permission from *Statistical Methods*, sixth edition by George W. Snedecor and William G. Cochran, © 1967 by Iowa State University Press, Ames, Iowa 50010.

Continued

z	.00	.01	.02	.03	.04	.05	.06	.07	.08	.09
3.1	.4990	.4991	.4991	.4991	.4992	.4992	.4992	.4992	.4993	.4993
3.2	.4993	.4993	.4994	.4994	.4994	.4994	.4994	.4995	.4995	.4995
3.3	.4995	.4995	.4995	.4996	.4996	.4996	.4996	.4996	.4996	.4997
3.4	.4997	.4997	.4997	.4997	.4997	.4997	.4997	.4997	.4997	.4998
3.5	.4998	.4998	.4999	.4999	.4999	.4999	.4999	.4999	.4999	.4999

Percentage Points of the *t*-Distribution*

Degrees of freedom	.5	.2	.1	.05	.01	.001
1	1.000	3.078	6.314	12.706	63.657	636.62
2	.816	1.886	2.920	4.303	9.925	31.598
3	.765	1.638	2.353	3.182	5.841	12.924
4	.741	1.533	2.132	2.776	4.604	8.610
5	.727	1.476	2.015	2.571	4.032	6.869
6	.718	1.440	1.943	2.447	3.707	5.959
7	.711	1.415	1.895	2.365	3.499	5.408
8	.706	1.397	1.860	2.306	3.355	5.041
9	.703	1.383	1.833	2.262	3.250	4.781
10	.700	1.372	1.812	2.228	3.169	4.587
11	.697	1.363	1.796	2.201	3.106	4.437
12	.695	1.356	1.782	2.179	3.055	4.318
13	.694	1.350	1.771	2.160	3.012	4.221
14	.692	1.345	1.761	2.145	2.977	4.140
15	.691	1.341	1.753	2.131	2.947	4.073
16	.690	1.337	1.746	2.120	2.921	4.015
17	.689	1.333	1.740	2.110	2.898	3.965
18	.688	1.330	1.734	2.101	2.878	3.922
19	.688	1.328	1.729	2.093	2.861	3.883
20	.687	1.325	1.725	2.086	2.845	3.850
21	.686	1.323	1.721	2.080	2.831	3.819
22	.686	1.321	1.717	2.074	2.819	3.792
23	.685	1.319	1.714	2.069	2.807	3.767
24	.685	1.318	1.711	2.064	2.797	3.745
25	.684	1.316	1.708	2.060	2.787	3.725
26	.684	1.315	1.706	2.056	2.779	3.707
27	.684	1.314	1.703	2.052	2.771	3.690
28	.683	1.313	1.701	2.048	2.763	3.674
29	.683	1.311	1.699	2.045	2.756	3.659

(*Continued*)

* Adopted from Table 12, "Percentage Points of the *t*-Distribution," p. 146, in *Biometrika Tables for Statisticians,* Vol. 1, by E. S. Pearson and H. O. Hartley. 3rd Ed. (Cambridge: Cambridge University Press, 1966).

Continued

Degrees of freedom	.5	.2	.1	.05	.01	.001
30	.683	1.310	1.697	2.042	2.750	3.646
40	.681	1.303	1.684	2.021	2.704	3.551
60	.679	1.296	1.671	2.000	2.660	3.460
120	.677	1.289	1.658	1.980	2.617	3.373
∞	.674	1.282	1.645	1.960	2.576	3.291

Percentage Points of the χ^2 Distribution*

Degrees of freedom	.25	.10	.05	.01	.001
1	1.32	2.71	3.84	6.63	10.83
2	2.77	4.61	5.99	9.21	13.82
3	4.11	6.25	7.81	11.34	16.27
4	5.39	7.78	9.49	13.28	18.47
5	6.63	9.24	11.07	15.09	20.52
6	7.84	10.64	12.59	16.81	22.46
7	9.04	12.02	14.07	18.48	24.32
8	10.22	13.36	15.51	20.09	26.13
9	11.39	14.68	16.92	21.67	27.88
10	12.55	15.99	18.31	23.21	29.59
11	13.70	17.28	19.68	24.73	31.26
12	14.85	18.55	21.03	26.22	32.91
13	15.98	19.81	22.36	27.69	34.53
14	17.12	21.06	23.68	29.14	36.12
15	18.25	22.31	25.00	30.58	37.70
16	19.37	23.54	26.30	32.00	39.25
17	20.49	24.77	27.59	33.41	40.79
18	21.60	25.99	28.87	34.81	42.41
19	22.72	27.20	30.14	36.19	43.82
20	23.83	28.41	31.41	37.57	45.32
21	24.93	29.62	32.67	38.93	46.80
22	26.04	30.81	33.92	40.29	48.27
23	27.14	32.01	35.17	41.64	49.73
24	28.24	33.20	36.42	42.98	51.18
25	29.34	34.38	37.65	44.31	52.62
26	30.43	35.56	38.89	45.64	54.05
27	31.53	36.74	40.11	46.96	55.48
28	32.62	37.92	41.34	48.28	56.89

(*Continued*)

* Adopted from Table 8, ''Percentage Points of the χ^2 Distribution,'' pp. 136–137. From *Biometrika Tables for Statisticians,* Vol. 1, by E. S. Pearson and H. O. Hartley. 3rd Ed. (Cambridge: Cambridge University Press, 1966).

Continued

Degrees of freedom	.25	.10	.05	.01	.001
29	33.71	39.09	42.56	49.59	58.30
30	34.80	40.26	43.77	50.89	59.70
40	45.62	51.81	55.76	63.69	73.40
50	56.33	63.17	67.50	76.15	86.66
60	66.98	74.40	79.08	88.38	99.61
70	77.58	85.53	90.53	100.43	112.32
80	88.13	96.58	101.88	112.33	124.84
90	98.65	107.57	113.15	124.12	137.21
100	109.14	118.50	124.34	135.81	149.45

Index

A

A

Abstracting services in library science, 361
Abstracting, automatic, 23, 179–180
Abstracts of research reports, 359, 380–381
Academic curricula, 3
Academic libraries, 6, 119
  consortia, 362, 367
  services in, 159–160
  surveys in, 165
Access
  to library materials, 22
  to public libraries, 157–158
Accuracy of histories, 99
Acquisition of library materials, 362
Administration of libraries, 146
Administrative judgments, 7
Adult education, 120, 155
Adult services, 162, 166
Aging, 155
Air Force Library Service, 120
Amateur historians, 109
Ambiguous questions, 63, 73
American Library Association (ALA), 57,
    80, 120, 157, 172, 173, 372
Analysis of data, 348–349, 379
  descriptive statistics, 189–247
  inferential statistics, 267–324
Analysis of variance, 49, 316
Annual reports of libraries, 109
Annuals, 106
Anonymity of respondents, 26
Anxiety of research subjects, 26
Applied research, 8
Appointments for interviews, 78
Architecture of libraries, 119
Archives, 101–102, 106
Arithmetic mean, 220

Arrays, 201
Art works, 107
Asking questions, 64–74
Association of Research Libraries, 120
Assumptions in research, 11, 13, 19, 58
Attitudes, 55, 81–82, 85
  and behavior, 66–67
  questions to measure, 66–68
  research on, 155
  scales, 12
  scores on, 9
Audience research, 155
Audiovisual materials, 11, 97
Audiovisual services, 120, 166
Authoritarianism, 85
Autobiographies, 109
Automatic abstracting, 23, 179–180
Automatic classification, 179–180
Automatic indexing, 23, 179–180, 288–289
Automation
  in libraries, 146
  in the United States, 362

B

Balking in queuing theory, 133
Bar graphs, 206
Barometers, 12
Basic research, 7
Best-selling books, 174
Bias, 73, 150
  in historical inquiry, 99–100
  protection against, 38
  in questionnaires, 59, 72
Bibliographic coupling, 179–180
Bibliographic expertise, 11
Bibliographies, 109

Bibliometrics, 179
Bimodal distributions, 224
Binomial distribution, 310
Biographies, 109, 119
  as history, 93
  of librarians, 362
Bivariate graphs, 212, 270–272
Black Americans, 174
Black librarians, 57, 97, 120
Book cards, 110
Book catalogs, 120, 146
Book collections, special, 367
Bookmobile services, 146, 166
Books as information sources, 11
Bradford's Law of Scattering, 179, 276
Brainstorming, 177
British library resources, 367
Browsing in libraries, 23, 50, 156
Budgets
  consultants, 355
  direct costs, 353
  facilities, 355
  fringe benefits, 354
  indirect costs, 353
  of libraries, 150–151, 362
  overhead expenses, 353
  per diem costs, 355
  preparation of, 351–358
  for proposals, 351–358
  salaries, 354
  sample budget, 357–358
  supplies for, 356
  travel costs, 356
  utilities and services, 355
Buffalo, State University of New York at,
    122, *see also* New York universities
Business and industrial libraries, 120

C
Calculators, electronic, 334
  inexpensive, use of, 334–338
  moderately expensive, characteristics of,
    338
  programmable, 339–340
California, University of
  Berkeley, Library, 119
  Los Angeles, 178
Cambridge University, 82
Carnegie Corporation of New York, 157

Cataloging of library materials, 120
Catalogs, 22, 106, 109
  book, 120, 146
  format of, 46–47
  records in, 22–23
  use of, 82, 86–87
Case studies, 19, 151–154
Case Western Reserve University, 83, 158
Categories in content analysis, 171–172
Causality, 13, 37, 43–44, 160, 271
  in historical studies, 99–101
  multiple causation, 100
Censorship, 85–86, 113, 155
Central limit theorem, 257
Central tendency, measures of, 219–232
  comparison of mean, median, and mode,
    225–226
  deciles, 231
  mean, 220–223
  median, 223–224, 229–232
  mode, 225
  percentiles, 229–231, 254–256
  quartiles, 231
  in a skewed distribution, 229–230
Charleston County (South Carolina) Li-
    brary, 163, *see also* South Carolina
    libraries
Checklists, 12
Chicago
  Public Library, 57, 164–165
  University of, 95, 122, 140, 372, *see also*
    Illinois, University of
  Library, 119, 120
Child development, 175–176
Children's literature, 80–81, 175–176, 367
Chi-square test, 46, 50, 300–303
  degrees of freedom in, 303
  effect of sample size on, 305
  summary of properties, 306
  testing goodness of fit, 306–308
  Yates' correction for continuity in, 305–
    306
Chronicles, 106
Chronologies, 99
Church libraries, 362
Circulation of materials, 22, 290
Circulation records, 110
Citation analysis, 179
City directories, 106
Classification literature, 362

Classification, automatic, 179–180
Clearinghouse on Information Resources, 363
Colloquialisms, 384
Colonial libraries, 95
Color as an instructional variable, 48–49
Columbia University, 112, *see also* New York universities
Communication
  agencies, 168
  barriers, 177
  behavior, 79
  media, 6, 22–23, 97, 156
  messages, 171
  patterns of library users, 166
  research, 171–176, 361
  in the sciences, 361
  systems, 155
  telefacsimile in, 163–164
Community
  agencies, 168
  analysis, 361
  leaders, 168
  needs, 168
  surveys, 53, 147, 167–169, 186
Comparative librarianship, 147, 169–171, 187
Compilers, 330
Compound interest, 128–132
Computer sciences, 367
Computers, 97, 155
  as aids to research, 327–341
  applications to library catalogs, 86
  statistical software, 330–331
  system hardware, 328–330
  use in simulation, 125–126
Conclusions of research, 379
Confidence intervals
  on μ when σ is known, 258–261
  on μ when σ is not known, 261–263
  on the value of a proportion, 263–264
Connecticut, *see* Yale University
Consensus opinions, 178
Consortia of libraries, 367
Constructs, 13
Consultants, 55, 109, 146, 355
Contemporary history, 120
Content analysis, 147, 171–176
  units in, 172
  weaknesses of, 174

Continuing education, 362
Continuous data, 195
Control in experimental research, 35–38
Control group, 35
Cooperation among libraries, 361–362
Corrections in manuscripts, 388
Correlation, 212–214
Correlation coefficient, 276, 285
  covariance and, 281, 284
  formulas for, 281–286
  nonparametric methods, 278
  partial correlation, 287
  Pearson product-moment, 278
  relation between regression coefficients and, 282
  scatter diagram and, 212–215, 270–272
  testing the significance of, 314
Costs of research projects, 351–358
Covariance, 281, 284
Cover letter for mail survey, 58
Cranfield II experiments, 47–48
Cross-cultural studies, 169
Culturally deprived citizens, 151
Cumulative frequency distribution, 209–212
Cumulative frequency polygon, 211
Curvilinear graphs, 275

D

Data analysis, 348–349, 379
  descriptive statistics, 189–247
  inferential statistics, 267–324
Data collection, 12, 378
  in case studies, 151–154
Data processing, 58
  equipment, 97, 328–330
  software, 327–336
Decentralization of libraries, 149
Deception in research, 26
Deciles, computation of, 231
Decision theory, 180
Deductive reasoning, 10, 13
Deeds, 106
Definitions, importance of in research, 22
Degrees of freedom
  in chi-square test, 303
  in standard deviation, 240
  in t-test, 313, 314

Delphi method, 176–178
Demographic characteristics, 156
Description, 5, 147–151
Descriptive community survey, 167
Descriptive research, 145, 149, 170
Descriptive statistics, 189–247
  central tendency, 219–232
  graphical representation of data, 201–218
  introduction to, 190–194
  measurement and scaling, 195–198
  normal distribution, 249–266
  variability, 232–247
Detroit, *see also* Michigan, University of
  Public Library, 319
Diaries, 106, 107
Diches Fund, 374
Direct costs, 353
Direct observation, 145
Directional questions, 71
Disadvantaged citizens, 151
Discrete data, 195
Discrimination in publishing, 80–81
Dissertations, 24, 95–96, 113, 119–120, 345, 362
Documentary research, 178–180
Documentation of sources, 382
Documents
  in historical inquiry, 108–110
  official, 108
  transmission of, 163

E
Economic data, 98
Economic institutions, 168
Economics, research in, 79–80
Education, *see also* Higher Education Act
  for librarianship, 113
  of research subjects, 9
Educational institutions, 168
Educational Resources Information Center
    (ERIC), 359, 362–363, 373–374
Electron microscopes, 12
Elementary school teachers, 87
Emotionalism, 8–9
Employment practices in libraries, 64–65
Encyclopedias, 174
Equipment for research, 355–356
Error, concept of in hypothesis testing,
    299–300
Estimating μ when σ is known, 258–261

Estimating μ when σ is not known, 261–263
Estimating the value of a proportion, 263–264
Ethics of research, 25–27, 58, 148
Ethnic groups, 162, 175–176
Euclidean geometry as a mathematical system, 126
Evaluation
  of documents, 107
  of an experiment, 42–43
  of libraries, 361
  of proposals, 352
  of research, 27–29, 160–164, 356
  studies, 147
Evidence in historical research, 106–107
Ex post facto study, 43–46
Experimental research, 7, 13, 35–51
  control in, 35–38
  error in, 42–43
  evaluation of, 42–43
  in evaluations, 161
  examples of in librarianship, 44–51
  ex post facto study, 43–46
  external validity of, 8, 43
  factorial designs in, 40
  field experiments, 37
  four-cell design, 38–40
  internal validity of, 38
  in a laboratory, 37
  pretest in, 37–40
  posttest in, 37–40
  quasi-experimental design, 43
  randomization, 37–38
  reproducibility of, 38
  sensitivity of, 42
  simulations, 161
  treatment in, 36
Explanations, 4
Exploratory community survey, 167
Exponential distribution, 136
Exponential growth, 128–132, 275
External criticism, 108
External surveys, 166
External validity of an experiment, 43
Eyewitness accounts, 114

F
Facilities for research, 355
Facsimile communication, 163

Factorial designs in experimental research, 40
Factual questions, 66
Faculty members and the library, 159–160
Faculty status for librarians, 146
Federal library agencies, 55
Fiction in libraries, 120, 174, 175
Field experiments, 37
Field methods, 54
Films, 9, 106, 166
Filmstrips, 175
Filter questions, 71
Fines for overdues, 23
Fixed-alternative responses, 74–76
Florida, University of, 165
Four-cell experimental design, 38–40
Frame for selection of sample, 60
Freedom to Read Statement, 172
Freedom of thought and expression, 25
Frequency distributions, 201–205
    construction of, 201–206
    skewed, 227–228
    smoothing, 207–209
    symmetric, 226–227
Frequency polygons, 206–207
Fringe benefits, 354

G
Gallup poll, 55, *see also* Polls
Geiger counters, 12
Generalizations, 10
Georgia
    Institute of Technology, 375
    University of, 164
German universities, 3
Goodness of fit, 306–308
Government agencies, 168
Government documents, 158–159, 162–163
Graduate Record Examination, 237
Graduate students and research, 16
Grammar, 383–387
Grants for research, 349
    preparation of proposals for, 351–358
Graphical materials, 349
Graphical representation of data, 201–218
    bivariate graphs, 212, 270–272
    cumulative frequency distribution, 209–212
    frequency distribution, 201–205
    frequency polygons, 206–207

histograms, 206
    interpolation in, 229
    pie chart, 214–215
    in regression analysis, 272–275
    skewed frequency distributions, 227–228
    smoothing frequency polygons, 207–209
Great Depression, 97, 119, 175
Greenville County (South Carolina) Library, 163, *see also* South Carolina libraries
Grouped data, 203

H
Hardware, computer, 328–330
Harris Poll, 55
Health, Education and Welfare, Department of, 362
Health-science libraries, 83–84, 366
Herzberg's motivation-hygiene theory, 86
Higher Education Act, 97
Histogram, 206
Historical dissertations, 95–96, 119–120
Historical documents, criticism of, 108
Historical evidence, 102–110
    accuracy of, 99
    searching for, 102–106
Historians, amateur, 109
Historical research, 19, 91–120, 147
    accuracy of, 99
    contemporary, 120
    deficiencies of, 111
    evaluation of sources in, 106–110
    evidence in, 106–107
    examples in librarianship, 111–113
    external criticism, 108
    information sources for, 117–118
    internal criticism in, 108
    in librarianship, 92–98
    narratives in, 110–111
    obtaining evidence in, 98–102
    oral history in, 103, 114
    primary sources for, 101
    quantification in, 98
    secondary sources for, 102
    selected bibliography, 117–120
Hoover Institution on War, Revolution and Peace Library, 120
Humanism, 113
Human beings as research subjects, 25–26
Hypotheses, 10, 13, 15, 24, 57, 58, 150, 378
    in case studies, 153

in historical studies, 98
statistical, 297
Hypothesis testing, 153, 172–173, 297–324
errors in, 299–300
nonparametric tests, 300–311
parametric tests, 311–317
steps in, 299

I

Illinois, *see also* Chicago
University of, 122
Image of librarians, 173
Income of research subjects, 9
Incunabula, 113
Indexes, 23, 178, 359
Indexing, automatic, 23, 179–180, 288–289
Indexing services in library science, 361
Indexing systems, relative performance of, 47–48
Indiana
State Library, 119
University, 375, *see also* Purdue University Libraries
Indirect costs, 353
Inductive reasoning, 10, 13
Inferential statistics, 267–324
analysis of variance, 49
chi-square test, 46, 50, 300–303
definition of, 192
regression and correlation, 212–214, 269–295
sign test, 309–311
t-test, 47, 261–263
Information explosion, 131
Information, use of, 155
Information agencies, 168
Information centers, 151, 366
Information science associations, 366
Innovations, 55
Institutionalization of research, 4
Instruments of research, 12
Intellectual curiosity, 24
Intellectual freedom, 85–86
Intellectual honesty, 27, 101
Intensity questions, 71
Interlibrary loan
policies, 366–367
services, 84, 163–164
Internal criticism of documents, 108

Internal surveys, 166
Internal validity of an experiment, 38
International librarianship, 170–171, 187
International Library Information Center, 170
International Standard Serial Number, 194
Interpolation, 229
Interpretation of findings, 15
Interval scale, 196
Interviewing, 77–79, 150
advantages of, 77–78
appointments for, 78
disadvantages of, 78
neutrality in, 78
use of tape recorders in, 106
Intuition, 10, 19
Inventive planning, 177

J

Japan, library services in, 120
Jargon, 73, 384
Job control language, 330
Jobs
applications for, 65
dissatisfaction in, 86
performance in, 69, 77
satisfaction in, 86
task index for, 83
Johns Hopkins University, 2
Journals as outlets for research reports, 372–376

K

Kentucky colleges and universities, 154
Knowledge, discovery of, 10
production of, 5
scientific, 7

L

Labor unions, 9, 80
Laboratory experiments, 37
Language as a variable, 9
Least-squares criterion, 283
Legal documents, 109
Legends, 106
Legislation about libraries, 108
Leicester University, 82
Letters, 109

Level of significance, 299
Librarians as historians, 99
    status of, 55
Libraries, *see also* specific libraries
    architecture of, 119
    in Asia, 361
    development of, 100–101
    founding of, 100–101
    health science, 83–84, 366
    influence of, 155
    in Louisiana, 119
    in New England, 119
    in Ohio, 120
    as organizations, 147
    as social institutions, 29
    in South Carolina, 120
Library
    associations, 55, 97, 111–112
    budgets, 150–151
    buildings, 165, 169
    clientele, 151–152
    collections, 11, 22, 169
    education, 113
    extension, 120
    facilities, 165
    history, 91–120
        definition of, 93
    instruction, 361–362
    job tasks, 83–84
    leadership, 111–112
    materials
        location of, 159
        suitability of, 154
    personnel, 165–166
    programs, 120
    projects, evaluation of, 161
    resources, 166
        in Great Britain, 367
        surveys, 165
    schools, 8, 24, 67, 151
        faculty in, 77
        instruction in, 69
    services, 120
        evaluation of, 154–160
    surveys, 53, 109, 147, 164–167, 186
    usage, 154–160
    users, 151–152, 166
        characteristics of, 156
Library Bill of Rights, 68, 172
Library of Congress, 173

Library science
    associations, 366
    literature, 17
    publications, 366
    research, 6, 362
        future of, 29
Library Services and Construction Act, 97,
    163
Likert scales, 75, 81
Limitations of studies, 349
Linear estimate of a dependent variable, 278
Literature reviews, 19–22, 347–348, 378
Literature search, 19–22, 58, 61, 97, 359–366
Literature, growth of, 179
Loan policies in libraries, 125
Local histories, 109
Los Angeles, *see also* California, University of
    Public Library, 119

M

Mail questionnaires, 63–64
    cover letter for, 58
    postage for, 58
Males in librarianship, 112
Management problems in librarianship, and
        operations research, 121
Manuscripts, 107
    preparation of, 387–388
Map libraries, 362
Markov process, 290
Maryland, *see* Johns Hopkins University
Mass media of communication, 156
Master's theses, 362
Materials for research, 356
Mathematical models
    concept of, 126–128
    exponential growth, 128–132
    queuing theory, 132–138
    testing the fit of, 138
Measurement and scaling, 6–7, 8, 12, 195–
        198
    interval scales, 196
    nominal scales, 195
    ordinal scales, 196
    ratio scales, 196–197
Mean, 220–223
    as center of gravity of a distribution,
        225–226
    computation from grouped data, 221–223

Mean deviation, 235–240
Media content, 171–176
Median, 223–224
    computation with grouped data, 229–232
Medical libraries, 83–84
Memoirs, 107
Mensa, 254
Messages in communications, 171
Methodology of research, 11, 17, 19, 348, 378–379
Michigan, *see also* Detroit
    University of, 96, 119
Microforms, 23, 97, 158
Mode, 225
Models, 13
    concept of, 123–126
    mathematical models, 126–138
    testing the fit of, 138
Modern Language Association, 376
Monte Carlo method, 125
Motion pictures, 174
Multiple causation, 100
Multiple regression, 287
Muniments, 107

N
Narratives in historical inquiry, 110–111
National Science Foundation, 350
National Science Foundation grants and contracts, 361
Nelson Associates, Inc., 186
Negative exponential distribution, 291
Networks in school libraries, 84
Neutrality in interviewing, 79
New Jersey school libraries, 84, 175
Newspapers, 171
New York Public Library, 119, 164, 367
New York universities, *see* Columbia University; State University of New York at Buffalo; Syracuse University
Nominal research, 167
Nominal scale, 195
Nonlinear relationships between two variables, 274–276
Nonparametric tests of hypotheses
    chi-square test, 300–303
    sign test, 309–311
Nonparametric correlation methods, 278

Normal distribution, 249–266
    use in sampling, 256–261
    and z-scores, 254–256
Novels, 171, 173, 174
Null hypotheses, 42, 297

O
Objectivity, 8, 150–151
    in content analysis, 174
    in historical inquiry, 111
Observations, 11–12, 24, 147–151
    controlled, 148
    as data, 201
    direct, 145
    obtrusive, 148
    participant, 148
    structured, 149
    unobtrusive, 148
    visual surveillance, 147
Occupations of research subjects, 9
OCLC, Inc., 194, 264, 312–313, 321
Official documents, 108
Ohio, *see* Case Western Reserve University
Open housing, 67
Open-ended questions, 71
Operating systems, 330
Operations research, 121–143, 290
    computer simulation, 125–126
    definition of, 122
    examples of in librarianship, 138–140
    systems analysis, 124–125
Opinions, 55
    consensus, 176–177
    questions to measure, 66–68
Opinion Survey of Midwestern Public Librarians, 85
Oral history, 103–114
Oral tests, 12
Ordinal scale, 196
Organization of library materials, 11
Outlines, 382–383
Overdue fines, 23
Overhead expenses, 353
Overseas library technical assistance, 97, 120

P
Paired sample means, testing the difference between, 312–313

Panels for Delphi studies, 176
Parameters, 191, 221
Parametric tests of hypotheses
  analysis of variance, 316
  testing the significance of
    the correlation coefficient, 314
    a difference between the means of
      paired samples, 312–313
    a difference between the means of two
      independent samples, 314–316
    a sample mean, 311–312
Partial correlation, 287
"Paul Revere's Ride", 87
Pearson product-moment correlation, 278
Pennsylvania, *see also* Pittsburgh University
  regional resource centers, 162
Percentage ogive, 211
Percentiles, computation of, 229–231, 254–
  256
Per diem costs, 355
Perfect linear relationship, 277, 285
Performance levels, 160–161
Performance measures, 162
Performance of libraries, 155
Personal privacy, 26–27
Photocopying, 166
Photographs, 106
  as historical evidence, 109
Physical inspection, 151
Pie chart, 214–215
Pittsburgh, University of, 170
Planning for research, 16
Planning library services, 169
Poetry in libraries, 87
Poisson process, 135–136
  testing goodness of fit for, 306–308
Political data, 98
Political institutions, 168
Politics and libraries, 157, 167
Polls, 55–56
Populations, 56–57, 59–61, 191
Population parameter
  confidence interval on when σ is known,
    258–260
  confidence interval on when σ is not
    known, 261–263
  and sample statistics, 238
Postage for mail surveys, 58
Posttest, 37–40

Pragmaticism of research, 8
Precision as a measure of retrieval effective-
  ness, 48, 276
Predicting the value of a dependent variable,
  278
Presidential elections, 56
Pretest, 37–40
Pretesting questionnaires, 58, 72, 76
Primary sources of information, 101
Prime display of books in a public library,
  49–50
Prisoners, rehabilitation of, 155
Privacy, 26–27, 67
Probability
  concepts of, 297–298
  model, 60
Problem words, 384–387
Professionalism
  in librarianship, 6, 80, 83–84
  and research, 25–27
Program objectives, 160–161
Programmed instruction, 361
Programming in libraries, 362
Project evaluation, 160–164
Projective questions, 69
Property taxes, 69, 73
Proportion, estimating the value of, 263–
  264
Proportional samples, 60–61
Proposals, 343–369
  evaluation of, 352
  titles for, 346
Prospectus, 345
Public knowledge of libraries, 55
Public Law 480, 97
Public librarians, 119
  in the Midwest, 85
Public libraries, 95, 157, 150–151
  architecture of, 119
  in California, 81
  directors of, 174–175
  in the Southeast, 119
  surveys of, 165
  users of, 81–82
Public Library Inquiry, 157
Public opinion polls, 55–56
Public relations materials, 109
Publication outlets, 371–376
Publics of libraries, 167

Publishers of books, 80–81
Publishing results of research, 371–376
Punctuation, 383–384
Purdue, *see also* Indiana
    University Libraries, 130, 139, 158
Pure research, 8

Q
Quality of library services, 82
Quantification in historical research, 98
Quartiles, computation of, 231
Quasi-experimental design, 43
Questionnaires, 12, 59, 61–64, 71–74, 166
    organization of, 73–74, 76
    pretesting of, 58, 72, 76
    response alternatives, 73–76
Questions in surveys, 59, 64–71
    ambiguous, 63, 73
    attitude, 66–68
    directional, 71
    factual, 66
    filter, 71
    fixed alternative, 74–76
    intensity, 71
    projective, 69
    structured, 70–71
    tricky, 72
    unstructured, 70–71
    writing of, 71–74
Queuing theory, 132–138
    balking in, 133
    predictive formulas for, 134–137
    reneging in, 133
    testing the fit of a queuing model, 138, 306

R
Racial discrimination, 23
Rand Corporation, 121, 176
Random number table, use of, 40–42
Random number generator, 125
Random samples, 60–61
Randomization, 37–38, 60
Range, 202
Ratio scale, 196–197
Reader services, 82
Reading, 157
Reading lists, 109
Reading speed, 9
Real limits of an interval, 222

Reasoning process, 10–11
Recall as a measure of retrieval effective-
    ness, 48, 276
Records in historical inquiry, 106–107
Reference librarians, 11
Reference questions, 57
Reference services, 22, 120, 154, 159–160,
    362
    evaluation of, 163–164
Regional resource centers, 162
Registers, 107
Registration forms, 110
Regression, nonlinear, 274–276
Regression and prediction, 278
Regression coefficients, 272–274
    effective of sampling error on, 286
    examples from library research, 288–290
    formulas for, 279, 283–286
    multiple regression, 287
    relationship between correlation coeffi-
        cient and, 282
Regression line, 272–274, 276
Relationships between variables, 13
Relevance assessments, 47
Reliability, 8
    of data, 97
    of observations, 149
Renaissance, Italian, 113
Reneging in queuing theory, 133
Replication of studies, 16, 97–98
Reporting research results, 371–389
Reproducibility of an experiment, 38
Reprography, 97
Research
    collections in the New York Public Li-
        brary, 367
    competencies, 17–18
    economists, 79–80
    journals, 372–376
    in librarianship, 7, 362
    libraries, 3–4, 119
    methods in librarianship
        experimental, 35–51
        historical, 91–120
        operations, 121–143
        other methodologies, 145–187
        survey, 53–90
    problems, 19, 347, 377–378
    proposals, 343–369
        costs and budgeting, 351–358

criteria for evaluation of, 350–351
grants for, 349
inadequacies of, 349–350
model for, 346–349
planning for, 16, 343–345
sources of information for literature
search in, 359–367
value of, 345–346
questions, 15–16, 57, 58
reports, 19, 343, 371–391
conclusions of, 379–380
corrections in, 388
grammar, punctuation, and word usage
in, 383–387
organization of, 376–380
preparation of, 387–388
publication of, 372–376
scholars, information needs of, 80
terminology, 7–15, 384–387
Reserve book services, 166
Resolution on Challenged Materials, 68, 172
Respondents in survey research, 60, 78–79
Response alternatives in questionnaires,
73–76
Review of literature, 378
Rolls, 107
Roper poll, 55, *see also* Polls
Rounds in Delphi studies, 176–178

S
Salaries of research workers, 354
Sample means
confidence intervals on, 258
distribution of, 256
testing the significance of, 311
Sample size, 61, 261
Sample statistic and population parameter,
238
Samples, 54, 58
proportional, 60–61
random, 60–61
selection of, 56, 59–61
stratification of, 60–61, 85
Sampling
and central limit theorem, 257
confidence intervals and, 258–264
determination of minimum sample size,
261
distribution of sample means, 256–261

frame for, 60
and regression, 286
standard error of the mean, 257
use of random number table with, 40–42
Scale numbers, assignment of, 12
Scaling, 195–198
zero point in, 197
Scaling questions, 74–76
Scatter diagram, 212–215, 270–272
Schedules, 107
School media centers, 82, 84–85, 87, 175–
176
collections in, 84–85
networks in, 84
research in, 165, 362
Science, 4
in librarianship, 4–5
Scientific inquiry, model of, 19–22
Scientific knowledge, 3, 7
Scientific method, 4–5, 15–23, 29
basic concepts of, 7–15
model of, 18–21
Scientific research, criteria for, 350–351
Scientists, 4
Search and screening procedures, 65
Searching for historical evidence, 102–105
Secondary sources of information, 102
Selection of library materials, 11, 23, 44–46,
172
Selection of respondents in surveys, 60–61
Selection policies, 11
Self-perception questions, 68–69
Semantic differential scale, 76–77
Sensitive areas of research, 26
Sensitivity of an experiment, 42
Sentence outlines, 382
Serendipity in research, 24
Serials, 22, 146
Sex discrimination, 23, 55
Sex roles in librarianship, 111–112
Shelving of materials, 11
Sign test, 309–311
Significance, statistical, 298–299
Simulation, 125–126, 288
Skepticism in research, 101
Skewed frequency distributions, 227–228
Slang, 73, 384
Slope of a regression line, 272, 279
Smoothing frequency polygons, 207–209
Social change, 155

Social data, 98
Social institutions, 168
Social libraries, 96
Social Science Research Council, 157
Social standards, 25
Software, computer, 327, 330
  BMD statistical package, 333
  compilers, 330
  misuse of, 332
  operating systems, 330
  SPSS, 331–334
South Carolina libraries, 120, *see also*
    Charleston County (South Carolina)
    Library; Greenville County (South
    Carolina) Library
Southeastern States Cooperative Library
    Survey, 165, 374
Special libraries, 6, 120, 146
  directory of, 366
Speeches, 106, 173
Sponsorship of research, 24
SPSS, 331–334
Standard deviation, 236–240
Standard error of the mean, 257
Standards of action questions, 69
State aid to libraries, 73
State-of-the-art reviews, 25
State library agencies, 55, 109, 120
State library consultants, 146
Statistical significance, 298–299
Statistics
  applications to librarianship, 192
  definition of, 191
  descriptive, 189–247
  inferential, 267–324
  of libraries, 147, 157
  and scaling, 196
  symbols used in, 194
Status surveys, 55, 164
Stimulus response, 9
Stratification in sampling, 60–61, 85
Structured observations, 149
Student assistants, 146
Subject collections, 367
Subjectivity, 8
Subjects of research
  anxiety of, 26
  education of, 9
  human beings as, 25–26

income of, 9
occupations of, 9
Summated rating scales, 74–76
Supplies for the conduct of research, 356
Survey research, 53–90
  concept of population in, 56–57
  examples in librarianship, 79–87
  external surveys, 166
  guidelines for, 58–59
  instruments in, 58–59
  interviews in, 77–79
  participants in, 60, 78–79
  principles of, 54–56
  questionnaires, 61–74
  sample selection in, 59–61
  scaling in, 74–76
  selected bibliography, 89–90
  selection of respondents for, 60–61
  semantic differential scale, 76–77
Symbols, statistical, 194
Symmetric frequency distributions, 226–227
Syracuse University, 363, *see also* New
    York universities
Systems analysis, 124–125

T
t-test, 47, 261–263, 312–316
Tape recorders, 103
  use in interviews, 106
Technical reports, 343, 371–389
Technical services, 57, 362
Technical terms, 73
Technological development, 7
Technological forecasting, 177
Telefacsimile communication, 97, 163
Terminology of research, 7–15
Testing hypotheses, 153, 172–173, 297–324
Texas, University of
  library, 119
  medical school, 83
Theft of library materials, 146
Theoretical knowledge, 3, 13, 15
Theoretical questions, 4
Theoretical research, 8
Theory, 13–15, 17, 153, 348
Theses, 24
Titles for proposals, 346
Topical outlines, 382
Trade books, 81

Transcriptions of taped recordings, 114
Travel costs, 356
Treatment in experimental research, 36
Tricky questions, 72
Truth, 5, 10
Typing of manuscripts, 387–388

U

Unconsciously transmitted evidence, 107
Unions, labor, 9, 80
Units in content analysis, 172
Union Theological Seminary Library, 119
United Nations Library, 120
Use of libraries, 22
User studies, 147, 154–160, 186
Users of libraries, 151–152, 156, 166
Utilities and services, 355
Utility of scientific literature, 291

V

Validity, 8
    checks, 149
    of experiments, 38, 43
Values, 177
Variability, 232–247
    mean deviation, 235–240
    range, 202
    standard deviation, 236–240
    variance, 236–240
Variables, 10, 57, 347
    independent and dependent, 22, 272
    linear relationship between, 272–276
    nonlinear relationships between, 274–276

predicting the value of a dependent variable, 278
    quantitative, 9
    relationships between, 13
Variance, 236–240
    analysis of, 49, 316
Visual surveillance, 147

W

Washington State University Library, 119
Weights for fixed responses, 74–75
Women in librarianship, 70, 97, 111–112
Word usage, 383–387
Works Progress Administration, 120
World War II, 169
Writing research reports, 371–389
    grammar in, 383–387
    problem words, 384–387
    publication outlets, 371–376
    topical outlines, 382
    typing of manuscripts, 387–388
    word usage, 383–387
Writing survey questions, 71–74

Y

Yale University, 86
y-intercept of a regression line, 272, 279
Yates' correction for continuity, 305–306

Z

z-scores, 254–256
Zipf's law, 276